Lord Ashcroft, KCMG, is an international businessman, author and philanthropist.

He has a life-long interest in bravery and gallantry medals. His collection of Victoria Crosses – the largest in the world – and George Crosses can be seen in the Lord Ashcroft Gallery, alongside other similar decorations owned by, or in the care of, the Imperial War Museum in London. He is also a Trustee of the Imperial War Museum Foundation Ltd, Vice Patron of the Intelligence Corps Museum, and a principal benefactor to the Bomber Command Memorial, donating £1 million to the cause.

Heroes of the Skies is Lord Ashcroft's eighth book, and the fourth in his widely acclaimed 'heroes' series, which tell the stories of the acts of bravery that have inspired him. The author's royalties from each of his books on gallantry have been donated to military charities.

Marshal of the Royal Air Force **Sir Michael Beetham**, GCB, CBE, DFC, AFC, is the President of the Bomber Command Association, which has been responsible for the Bomber Command Memorial that was unveiled in June 2012 in Green Park, central London.

After volunteering to join the RAF in 1941, aged eighteen, he served with distinction as a bomber pilot during the Second World War. He remained in the RAF on a permanent commission after the war and ended his forty-one years in the RAF as Air Chief Marshal, which meant he was head of the RAF during the Falklands War. Today he is the senior Marshal of the RAF.

Also by Michael Ashcroft and available from Headline

Victoria Cross Heroes
Special Forces Heroes
George Cross Heroes

www.lordashcroft.com
www.heroesoftheskies.com

Heroes of the Skies

MICHAEL ASHCROFT

FOREWORD BY
MARSHAL OF THE ROYAL AIR FORCE
SIR MICHAEL BEETHAM GCB, CBE, DFC, AFC

headline

The right of Michael Ashcroft to be identified as the Author of
the Work has been asserted by him in accordance with the
Copyright, Designs and Patents Act 1988.

First published in 2012 by
HEADLINE PUBLISHING GROUP

First published in paperback in 2013 by
HEADLINE PUBLISHING GROUP

1

Cataloguing in Publication Data is available from the British Library

Paperback ISBN 978 0 7553 6390 2

Typeset in GaramondThree by Avon DataSet Ltd, Bidford-on-Avon, Warwickshire

Picture research by Jane Sherwood
Plate design by Ben Cracknell Studios

Printed and bound in the UK by Clays Ltd, St Ives plc

Headline's policy is to use papers that are natural, renewable and recyclable
products and made from wood grown in sustainable forests. The logging and
manufacturing processes are expected to conform to the environmental
regulations of the country of origin.

HEADLINE PUBLISHING GROUP
An Hachette UK Company
338 Euston Road
London NW1 3BH

www.headline.co.uk
www.hachette.co.uk
www.lordashcroft.com
www.heroesoftheskies.com

CONTENTS

Acknowledgements VII

Foreword by Marshal of the Royal Air Force Sir Michael Beetham GCB, CBE, DFC, AFC XI

Author's royalties XV

Preface XVII

CHAPTER 1: Building the collection 1

CHAPTER 2: First World War VCs 15

CHAPTER 3: Second World War – Battle of Britain fighter pilots 45

CHAPTER 4: Second World War – other fighter pilots 141

CHAPTER 5: Second World War – bomber aircrew 221

CHAPTER 6: Second World War – special bombing missions 297

CHAPTER 7: Second World War – reconnaissance operations 335

CHAPTER 8: Second World War – escape and action on the ground 353

CHAPTER 9: Post-Second World War gallantry 381

Select Bibliography 421

Index 427

ACKNOWLEDGEMENTS

I am grateful to all those individuals whose brave deeds enabled me to write this book. Almost to a man, the living medal recipients were enormously helpful to me in preparing their write-ups. Five men who feature prominently in my book, Ted Maslen-Jones, Bill O'Brien, Jeff Niblett, Bill Scarratt and Shaun Wyatt, were generous with their time and provided face-to-face interviews. Jimmy Thiele, a New Zealander now living in Australia, was equally helpful and provided a telephone interview. And I am grateful to Hugh Cawdron, the author of *Based at Burn MkII*, for assisting me with my write-up on the late David Wilkerson.

I am greatly indebted to Angela Entwistle, my corporate communications director. Angela, along with her team in my London office, has worked with dedication and energy to get this project off the ground. Furthermore, she has played a key role in promoting this book.

My thanks go to Michael Naxton, my medals consultant, for his considerable help. Indeed, it was originally Michael's idea that my groups of medals for gallantry in the air should form the basis for a book. Michael, who is also the curator of the Ashcroft VC Collection, enabled me to benefit from his expertise and was kind enough to read, and correct, the proofs of this book.

Furthermore, two notable experts in the field of gallantry medals have kindly assisted me: David Erskine-Hill, of Dix Noonan Webb (DNW) auctioneers, and Richard Black, of The London Medal Company – though both under the pressure of time – gave me tips for my research as well as read, and corrected, the original manuscript. However, I am not absolving myself of blame for any errors in the book: if there are mistakes, then they are all my own.

My gratitude also extends to the diligent research of the various specialist auction houses whose cataloguers have delved into the lives of some of the medal recipients who appear in this book. I have relied heavily on their work for some of my write-ups. I do not know of all those who contributed to this 'cause' but the auction houses include Dix Noonan Webb (DNW), Spink, Bosleys, Glendinning's (now part of Bonhams), Sotheby's and Christie's. The individual cataloguers, whose work I have benefited from, are undoubtedly led by David Erskine-Hill, who has been prolific in this field. However, my thanks also go to John Hayward, Mark Quayle, Oliver Pepys, Richard Black (albeit in his capacity as a dealer) and others for their contributions.

I am grateful, too, for some splendid material on a number of the medal recipients in books, pamphlets, magazines, and on the internet, including the websites of individual squadrons. I have had access to some excellent obituaries of numerous airmen that have appeared in newspapers, particularly the *Daily Telegraph, The Times*, the *Independent* and the *Guardian*.

Yet again, I am grateful to Headline for publishing a book of mine on bravery and for bringing my passion for gallantry to a wider audience. This is my fourth book on courage in the past seven years for Headline and, as always, Emma Tait and Emily Furniss have been a delight to work with.

This book has been written in conjunction with a six-part Channel 5 television series, also entitled *Heroes of the Skies*. My thanks go to Ian Russell, of Cineflix, John Hay, of Channel 5, and others for their help in making this series, which I presented.

I have left my biggest thank you to the end. I owe an immense debt of gratitude to Marshal of the RAF Sir Michael Beetham GCB, CBE, DFC, AFC, a distinguished and decorated Second World War bomber pilot. Sir Michael, whom I got to know through our joint support for the new Bomber Command Memorial, has been kind enough to write the Foreword to this book. Now in his ninetieth year, Sir Michael has done great service in his role as President of the Bomber Command Association. I feel privileged that such a courageous airman and respected leader of men has done me the honour of endorsing my book.

FOREWORD
by Marshal of the Royal Air Force
Sir Michael Beetham GCB, CBE, DFC, AFC

The year 2012 is a significant one in the history of the RAF. First, it marks the centenary of the formation of the Royal Flying Corps, the forerunner of the RAF. Secondly, it has seen the dedication and unveiling by Her Majesty The Queen of the long-overdue Bomber Command Memorial in Green Park, central London. Now, thanks to the enthusiasm of Lord Ashcroft, 2012 sees the publication of a splendid new book that champions the gallantry of RAF and other aircrew over the past century.

Heroes of the Skies is Lord Ashcroft's fourth book on the subject of bravery and in his writing he displays a great passion for courage, in general, and gallantry medals, in particular. It has been known for some time that Lord Ashcroft has built up the world's largest collection of Victoria Crosses (VCs), which are on display in the gallery bearing his name at the Imperial War Museum. However, this book reveals that Lord Ashcroft has also amassed some quite remarkable groups of medals for gallantry in the air – well over eighty in total.

As *Heroes of the Skies* makes abundantly clear, behind every decoration is a wonderful story of one man's bravery, usually in the face of great adversity. Most, though not all, medals for gallantry in the air are the result of courage against a wartime enemy. Such bravery is invariably linked to qualities that Britain and the Commonwealth nations value so highly: loyalty, duty, sacrifice, service, patriotism and more.

When the Battle of Britain began in 1940, I was a schoolboy staying for the summer in Hilsea, just outside Portsmouth, where my father was in charge of an Army training battalion. I saw the German aircraft coming in to bomb the harbour and the Hurricanes and Spitfires cutting into them. It was spectacular and I said to my father: 'That's for me.' The following year, after turning eighteen, I volunteered to join the RAF, trained as a bomber pilot and, in 1943, joined 50 Squadron flying Lancasters. At the time the main focus of the bombing campaign was against the industrial cities of Germany, including the capital, Berlin. It was a gruelling campaign and I completed a tour of thirty operations during 1943/4.

As a result of my own wartime experiences, I am delighted to see that the bulk of Lord Ashcroft's collection of medals for gallantry in the air is made up of awards to Second World War airmen and, in particular, that it includes three VCs (from a total of nineteen) that were awarded to members of Bomber Command.

I got to know Lord Ashcroft through my role as President of the Bomber Command Association and as a result of his very considerable support, including a substantial donation, for the Bomber Command Memorial. It therefore comes as no surprise to me that he has decided that all his author's royalties from this book are to be donated to the Royal Air Force Benevolent Fund. Once again, this is a cause dear to my own heart, particularly as the charity has agreed to care for and maintain the Bomber Command Memorial in the future.

I commend Lord Ashcroft for his generosity, just as I commend his book to one and all. By writing *Heroes of the Skies*, Lord Ashcroft has done a great service to all our airmen who have risked and, in some cases given, their lives for their country, their sovereign, their comrades and for greater freedom. This is a book to be cherished and savoured.

AUTHOR'S ROYALTIES

Lord Ashcroft has decided that all his author's royalties from *Heroes of the Skies* will be donated to the Royal Air Force Benevolent Fund. Founded in 1919, the fund is the RAF's leading welfare charity, looking after serving and former members of the RAF as well as their partners and dependent children.

In June 2012, after the unveiling of the new Bomber Command Memorial in Green Park, central London, the fund became the custodian of the monument and will be responsible for its ongoing preservation.

PREFACE

It was Leonardo da Vinci, the Renaissance painter, sculptor and inventor, who said: 'When once you have tasted flight, you will forever walk the earth with your eyes turned skyward, for there you have been, and there you will always long to return.' Mark Twain, the American author and humourist, wrote: 'The air up there in the clouds is very pure and fine, bracing and delicious. And why shouldn't it be? – it is the same the angels breathe.' While Sir Walter Raleigh, the official historian of the RAF (rather than his namesake, the Elizabethan courtier), said: 'The engine is the heart of an aeroplane, but the pilot is its soul.'

All three men have one thing in common: they capture a wonderfully romantic image of flying. I have long been fascinated by a special human trait – bravery – that can also conjure up great images of derring-do. So when flying and courage combine – as they do repeatedly in this book – it makes for a heady mix.

This book is the result of my admiration for bravery and my desire to champion the courage of others. It is based on my collection of more than eighty groups of gallantry and service medals to airmen that span nearly a century, from the First World War to the present conflict in Afghanistan. It has also been written to mark the 100th anniversary of the Royal Flying

Corps, founded in 1912 and the forerunner to the RAF.

The write-ups in this book vary considerably in length. In some cases, there is an abundance of material on an individual in the form of his pilot's logbooks, diaries, letters, military records, lengthy citations and other sources. In other cases, there is little in existence that details his life, career or the details of his gallantry. In rare cases, it is not known today if a medal recipient is alive or dead. If anyone reading this book can fill in some of the gaps, I will endeavour to update individual entries for future editions of my book.

Heroes of the Skies is being published in conjunction with a six-part Channel 5 documentary series that I am presenting. The series examines some heroic pilots whose decorations are not part of my collection. There are write-ups on four such pilots in this book and, on each occasion, the individual's panel giving his details contains an asterisked footnote to indicate that his medals are not part of my collection. To avoid any confusion, however, the four pilots whose decorations I do not own are Douglas Bader, George Beurling, Francis 'Gabby' Gabreski and Robin Olds.

Each individual's write-up in the book has a panel preceding it that gives the medal recipient's name and the rank he held when first decorated, along with the highest rank (if different from the original one and listed in brackets) he held during his military career. The panel also has information on the service, or services – RAF, Army, Royal Navy and Royal Marines – in which the medal recipient served. Furthermore, it gives the name of the gallantry medal, or medals, with which he was decorated and the date, or dates, that these were formally announced in the *London Gazette*, the UK's official publication for such announcements. The decorations are listed chronologically rather than in seniority. The exception to this is the award of a second (or, in rare cases, a third or fourth) identical award (or Bar) when this decoration is listed immediately after the first, or subsequent, awards. I have included all decorations but not appointments to assorted Orders, such as the CBE, although I have tried always to refer to such awards in the write-up itself. In some cases, where two, or more, men were decorated for the same action, they are given a joint write-up.

A small number of the medal recipients who feature here also appeared in my book *Victoria Cross Heroes*. I make no apology for telling the astonishing stories of these brave men for a second time in *Heroes of the Skies*.

1

BUILDING THE COLLECTION

THE ORIGINS OF A PASSION

As a teenager, I was fascinated by flying and I read extensively about the Wright brothers and their first flight. I regard staging the first powered flight as one of modern mankind's greatest achievements. I would love to have been an eyewitness on 17 December 1903 when the American brothers, Orville and Wilbur, flew the *Wright Flyer* from a primitive air strip four miles south of Kitty Hawk, North Carolina. The aircraft, adapted from gliders which the brothers had trialled over the previous three years, made four brief, low-altitude flights that day, just three days after their first attempt at flight had ended in an immediate crash-landing and damage to their aircraft. Each of the four successful flights ended with a bumpy and unintended 'landing'. The last flight, with Wilbur at the controls (the brothers took it in turns to fly), saw the aircraft travel 852 feet and remain in the air for fifty-nine seconds. This was sufficient to enter the record books and in Washington, DC, the respected Smithsonian Institution later described the *Wright Flyer* as 'the first powered, heavier-than-air machine to achieve controlled, sustained flight with a pilot aboard. It flew forward without losing speed and landed at a point as high as that from which it started.'

My boyhood admiration for the Wright brothers stemmed more from their courage than their technical ability to design their aircraft. I have had a lifelong fascination with bravery and I am a great believer in another Mark Twain quote: 'Courage is the mastery of fear, not the absence of fear.' I have no doubt that the Wright brothers had a fear of flying but they conquered this fear. When I read about their exploits, I wondered what must have been going through their minds as they took off for a (short) journey into the unknown. By this time, they were achieving heights and speeds that, if something went wrong (and it often did during the early days of flight), the pilots were likely to be killed or seriously injured. I wondered how many advancements in life had started because someone was willing to risk his, or her, life in the interests of scientific or technical progress. I eventually credited the Wright brothers with beginning a process that led from early aircraft flying to the first human space flight, all in less than sixty years.

I marvelled, too, at just how rapidly flying developed from the first flight in late 1903 to the Great War of 1914–18, when air combat was very much a part of the conflict. I had an immense respect for the airmen of the First World War, including those who literally dropped their bombs by hand. I took a special interest in the fighter aces (a pilot credited with five, or more, aerial victories), who took to the skies time and again in single-engine biplanes with only a primitive machine-gun for protection. Inevitably, these early aircraft were relatively cumbersome and were easy targets from the ground and the air. As a result, these men had a short life expectancy, even if they were the most skilled and experienced of flyers. Yet sometimes they flew missions not just every day, but several times a day. Some of the technical advances during the war were intriguing, too: with machine guns mounted behind the propeller, one of the earliest problems was to devise a way of firing through the propeller without the bullets hitting the blades and bouncing back, thus endangering the pilots.

As a schoolboy, I have to admit that it was the infamous 'Red Baron' who caught my imagination more than any of the British aces of the day. Manfred von Richthofen, who served with the Imperial German Air Service during the First World War, is arguably the best-known pilot of all time. He was the 'ace of aces', being credited with eighty confirmed combat victories, a superior tally to any other pilot. Yet even the Red Baron, who flew a red Fokker triplane, could not survive the war: he was shot down and killed near Amiens, France, on 21 April 1918. I have always been able to recognise courage by the 'enemy': I am certainly not naive or jingoistic enough to suggest that only the British or Allied forces were capable of showing great bravery in war, whilst the enemy was cowardly. For me, the concept of bravery is not, and never will be, limited to just one side in a battle or conflict.

I also took an interest in some of the pioneering pilots of the inter-war years. After the war, the public became fascinated by flight and at fairs and shows, particularly in the US during the 1920s, pilots would be the star attractions showing off their skills and their aircraft to an admiring audience. Such were the advances in aviation technology that on 20/21 May 1927 Charles Lindbergh, the American aviator and explorer, was able to make the first non-stop transatlantic flight in a fixed-wing aircraft from New York's Long Island to an airfield on the outskirts of Paris. Once again, I tried to imagine what was going on in Lindbergh's mind as he flew his single-seat, single-engine monoplane, *Spirit of St Louis*, for 3,600 miles and nearly thirty-four hours non-stop. He had simply a magnetic compass, his airspeed indicator and luck to keep him going as he flew through snow and sleet in an epic journey that captured the imagination of the American public. It is little wonder that Lindbergh was known as 'Lucky Lindy', because his chances of survival when he set off must have been, at best, negligible. Lindbergh was also a US Army reserve officer, and the rewards for his exploits included the Medal of Honor, the nation's highest bravery decoration.

I also enjoyed reading about the exploits of some of the great women pilots. I could not learn enough about the life and times of Amelia Earhart, the American aviation pioneer. Earhart was the first woman to receive the US Distinguished Flying Cross (DFC): the decoration was awarded for becoming the first woman aviator to fly solo across the Atlantic Ocean. Earhart set many other flying records before, during an attempt to circumnavigate the globe in 1937, her aircraft disappeared over the central Pacific Ocean near Howland Island on 2 July 1937. Her body was never found but she was officially declared dead nearly two years later. I also took an interest in the exploits of Amy Johnson, the daring English aviatrix. Either flying alone or with her husband, Jim Mollison, Johnson set numerous long-distance flight records in the 1930s. She flew for the Air Transport Auxiliary during the Second World War only for her Airspeed Oxford aircraft to come down in adverse weather conditions and, when a rescue attempt failed, she drowned in the Thames Estuary on 5 January 1941.

So my early fascination with flying involved people getting into the air, then staying in the air over long distances, both of which involved substantial courage. However, once flying became more 'routine', my great interest turned almost exclusively to military aviation and the experiences of pilots in war situations. Yet I was also gripped by the exploits of test pilots, who carried out flights that involved a high degree of risk.

I was enthralled by the exploits of the airmen of the Second World War, just as I had been by their counterparts during the Great War. As a boy, I loved reading about the wartime adventures of our Spitfire and Hurricane pilots. I was engrossed by the exploits of fighter pilots during the Battle of Britain and I was fascinated by the 'Dambusters', the name given to 617 Squadron for its exploits during Operation Chastise. Pilots flew in dangerously low to drop 'bouncing bombs' to target German dams on 16/17 May 1943.

As readers of my three earlier books on gallantry will know, I developed an interest in bravery when I was about twelve years old. I was born the year after the end of the Second World War and the momentous events of the 1939–45 conflict inevitably filled many family conversations when I was a child. I was also inspired by the courage of my father, Captain Eric Ashcroft, who as a lieutenant had been wounded as he ran onto Sword Beach as part of the D-Day landings of 6 June 1944. Gradually, this interest in bravery, in general, developed into one for gallantry medals, in particular, and I bought my first Victoria Cross (VC), Britain and the Commonwealth's premier award for gallantry, in 1986. Although originally intended as a one-off, this purchase eventually led to me building up the world's largest collection of VCs, now totalling more than 170 such decorations. As the collection grew, I specialised in VCs from certain fields and these included trying to build a collection of VCs awarded to airmen during both the First World War and the Second World War. Today, for example, I own three of the six VCs that were awarded to fighter aces during the Great War.

As the collection grew, I became increasingly determined to put it on public display. I looked into the possibility of building a new gallery for my VC collection. After lengthy behind-the-scenes discussions, I was able to announce in July 2008 that I was donating £5 million for a new gallery at the Imperial War Museum. This would be used to house both my VC collection and the VCs owned by, or in the care of, the museum. After an incredible amount of hard work from my staff and the museum's staff, I am delighted to say that the new project – bearing my name – was unveiled on schedule in November 2010. It was opened by HRH The Princess Royal and, ever since, it has been enjoyed by hundreds of thousands of people. Admission to the gallery is free and I would urge everyone to visit it and to savour the gallantry of our bravest servicemen, including our airmen from the two world wars.

My VC collection on display at the Lord Ashcroft Gallery includes twelve 'flying VCs'. The first I bought was in November 1988 at a Christie's auction. It was the decoration that had been awarded to William Leefe Robinson, the first British pilot to shoot down a German airship over Britain during the First World War. In October 1989, I privately bought the VC that had been awarded to Roderick 'Babe' Learoyd for bravery during a pinpoint bombing raid over Germany in August 1940.

I only started to build up a collection of medals for gallantry in the air in the autumn of 1990. On 15 September, Sotheby's held a special aeronautical sale at the RAF Museum, Hendon, north-west London. The catalogue contained the decoration that had been awarded to William Rhodes-Moorhouse, the first ever VC awarded for action in the air. Among many other flying groups included in the same catalogue were a number of items which also took my fancy, namely 'Ginger' Lacey's Distinguished Flying Medal (DFM) and Bar, 'Pick' Pickard's Distinguished Service Order (DSO) and two Bars, and Distinguished Flying Cross (DFC), along with the DFMs to William Rich and Walter Ellis who had both flown with Learoyd on his VC mission, and the Military Cross (MC) to Sydney Dowse who had become a prisoner of war (PoW) and one of the men involved in the 'Great Escape'. Eventually, I bought all these medals and this set the ball rolling. After that sale, I was constantly on the lookout for outstanding flying gallantry groups, particularly those relating to the Battle of Britain and the 'Dambusters' raid. Today I own more than eighty groups of medals for gallantry in the air, including twelve VCs.

In 2009, I became involved in the appeal to have a permanent Bomber Command Memorial erected in Green Park, central London. I donated a substantial amount – more than £1 million – because I wanted to right a wrong. Rarely, if ever, can any group of servicemen have been more deserving of a memorial to their courage and self-sacrifice than members of RAF Bomber Command. I felt that a new monument would be a fitting tribute to men who helped to shape the world we live in but whose bravery, until now, has not been properly recognised.

Bomber Command consisted of some 125,000 volunteers from Britain, the Commonwealth and Allied countries who had to endure some of the most terrifying combat conditions of the Second World War. Indeed, Bomber Command was the primary British fighting force that took the war directly to Germany, destroying vital infrastructure and supply lines – but at a very heavy price. The average age of the aircrew was just twenty-two and the youngest were only eighteen. Three out of every five airmen became casualties and the more detailed statistics tell their own story: 55,573 men were killed, 8,403 were wounded and 9,838 were captured and held as prisoners of war. The losses of Bomber Command were greater than those of any other service – accounting for 10 per cent of all British fatalities – yet, perversely, its members have been the only Second World War servicemen not to have been publicly honoured by their country. During the war, no fewer than nineteen Victoria Crosses were awarded to men of Bomber Command and the recipients of the gallantry award included Guy Gibson, of 617 Squadron and 'Dambusters' fame. Among the various statistics that relate to the aircrews, one particular fact upset me greatly: half of the casualties from Bomber Command have no known grave (although they are commemorated on the Runnymede Memorial, near Windsor, Berkshire). One of the reasons that there had never previously been a permanent memorial to Bomber Command was that there was so much controversy after the war about the tactics used to bomb German cities. Inevitably this led to a large number of deaths and injuries among the civilian population. My view on this controversy is simple: the bravery of the RAF men should never be confused with the politics of their superiors. These airmen went to do their duty as they were ordered, and time and again they showed great courage to achieve their objectives.

The Bomber Command Association; John Caudwell, the entrepreneur; Richard Desmond, the publisher and business-man; and many others deserve praise for a successful £7 million appeal. On 28 June 2012, I was present when the Queen unveiled the memorial and I felt incredibly proud to see the project – also intended to be in memory of the civilian victims of the bombing – come to fruition while some Bomber Command veterans were still alive. It was a day full of emotion and one that I will never forget.

MEDALS FOR GALLANTRY IN THE AIR

Until early in the twentieth century there were no gallantry medals specifically for flying – because there was no flying. During the First World War, awards of the VC were for exceptional bravery in the face of the enemy, regardless of which member of the Armed Forces an individual served. This meant that VCs were awarded to members of the Army, the Royal Navy and the Royal Flying Corps and, after April 1918, to the RAF.

The RAF came into being on 1 April 1918 and remains the oldest independent air force in the world. By early 1918, it became clear that air power would play a significant role in future conflicts and, in turn, that many people would therefore display enormous gallantry in the air. With this in mind, shortly before the formation of the RAF, a committee was constituted by George V to advise the King on whether a special decoration was needed for the new service. After George V concurred with the committee that new decorations did need to be instituted, the King decided they should be 'brought out' for his birthday. The *London Gazette* recorded on 3 June 1918, the King's fifty-third birthday, that the Distinguished Flying Cross (DFC), Distinguished Flying Medal (DFM), Air Force Cross (AFC) and Air Force Medal (AFM) had been instituted. However, it was not until 17 December 1918 that the King signified his approval in writing, with a Royal Warrant instituting the four awards. Furthermore, it was not until

5 December 1919 that the warrant was published in the *London Gazette*.

According to the new clauses, the DFC was to be awarded to the RAF and other services for 'an act or acts of valour, courage or devotion to duty whilst flying in active operations against the enemy'. The decoration was originally awarded to officers of Britain and the Commonwealth. In the RAF, the award was initially made to commissioned officers and to warrant officers. During the Second World War, it was also awarded, among others, to Royal Artillery officers from the British Army who were serving on observation duties. Since the Second World War, the award has been made to Army and Royal Navy pilots. A Bar is added to the ribbon for holders of the DFC who receive further awards of the decoration. Since the DFM was discontinued in 1993, the DFC has also been open to other ranks beyond officers and warrant officers. However, since 1993 the DFC is no longer eligible to personnel from other Commonwealth countries. The DFC was awarded to a woman for the first time in 2008: to Flight Lieutenant Michelle Goodman. During the Great War, around 1,100 DFCs were awarded. Furthermore, seventy first Bars were awarded and three second Bars. During the Second World War, some 20,354 DFCs were awarded (more than any other decoration of the conflict). In addition, there were approximately 1,550 first Bars and forty-six second Bars. Finally, there were 964 honorary awards to aircrew from non-Commonwealth countries.

According to the 5 December 1919 Royal Warrant, the DFM was, like the DFC, awarded to the RAF and other services for 'an act or acts of valour, courage or devotion to duty whilst flying in active operations against the enemy'. A Bar was added to the ribbon for holders of the DFM who received further awards of the decoration. The DFM was awarded to other ranks, rather than commissioned officers. However, as stated above, in 1993 the decoration was discontinued. During the First World War, approximately 105 DFMs were awarded, and two first Bars. The Second World War saw 6,637 awards of the DFM, along with sixty first Bars. The only award of a DFM and second Bar was to Flight Sergeant Donald Kingaby in November 1941.

According to the 5 December 1919 Royal Warrant, the AFC was initially awarded to officers and warrant officers of the UK's Armed Forces, as well as personnel of other Commonwealth countries, for 'an act or acts of valour, courage or devotion to duty whilst flying, though not in active operations against the enemy'. After the Second World War, this was extended to include Army and Royal Navy officers. A Bar is added to the ribbon for holders of the AFC who receive further awards of the decoration. The decoration, along with the AFM, can be compared with the George Cross (GC), in that it is awarded for courage not in the face of the enemy. Since the AFM was discontinued in 1993, the AFC has also been open to other ranks as well beyond officers and warrant officers. However, since 1993 the AFC is no longer eligible to personnel from other Commonwealth countries. Approximately 680 AFCs were awarded during the Great War. During the Second World War, 2,001 decorations were awarded, with a further twenty-six first Bars. Wing Commander H. J. Wilson was awarded a unique second Bar in 1944 and a further fifty-eight honorary awards were made to the aircrew of non-Commonwealth countries.

The AFM was initially awarded to personnel below commissioned rank of the UK's Armed Forces, as well as personnel of other Commonwealth countries, for 'an act or acts of valour, courage or devotion to duty whilst flying, though not in active operations against the enemy'. A Bar was added to the ribbon for holders of the AFM who received further awards of the decoration. As already stated, the AFM was discontinued in 1993.

Back in August 1855, at the time of the Crimean War, Queen Victoria established a bravery award designated the Conspicuous Gallantry Medal (CGM), for petty officers and seamen of the Royal Navy, and non-commissioned officers and privates of the Royal Marines. As a result of the introduction of the VC, however, the CGM quickly fell into abeyance but, in July 1874, the Queen reinstituted the award to recognise acts of gallantry from the Ashantee War. In November 1942, George VI extended availability of the CGM to British and Commonwealth warrant officers and airmen 'for acts of conspicuous gallantry whilst flying in active operations against the enemy'. A highly prized decoration, second only to the VC – and, indeed, occasionally granted on the back of a recommendation for a VC – the CGM for services in the air is extremely rare, a little over 100 having been awarded up until the reorganisation of the honours' system in 1993, when it was discontinued.

The creation of gallantry medals solely for airmen did not, of course, prevent an aircrew member from being awarded other gallantry medals, particularly those decorations that ranked higher than the DFC, DFM, AFC and AFM. Aircrew have always, for example, been eligible for the VC for acts of supreme bravery along with other gallantry awards that were felt, for whatever reasons, to be more appropriate than medals for gallantry in the air.

Nineteen VCs were awarded to airmen for courage during the First World War and thirty-two VCs were awarded to airmen for gallantry during the Second World War. As air VCs have only, in practice, been awarded during the two world wars, this means that the total number of air VCs in existence is fifty-one. Of the fifty-one recipients of air VCs, twenty-five gave their lives during the action, or actions, which resulted in the award and six others were subsequently killed in (further) action. It is said that 'old men make wars, but young men have to fight them' and, if this is true, then the air VCs might be cited to back up the theory. Of the fifty-one airmen who received the VC, the oldest was thirty-four and the youngest just eighteen. All but six were in their early twenties and the average age was just twenty-four.

2

FIRST WORLD WAR VCS

Even before the first powered flight by the Wright brothers in December 1903, the military had been using manned balloons for observation purposes. So no sooner had the first powered flight taken place than many people were keen to see how the early aircraft could be adapted for a military use. In Britain, the Royal Flying Corps (RFC) was created by a Royal Warrant on 13 April 1912 and it superseded the Air Battalion of the Royal Engineers. When war broke out in Europe in August 1914, the RFC was extremely small. It had fewer than 1,400 men, most of whom went to France along with seventy-three aircraft, ninety-five support vehicles and a small number of manned balloons.

After the outbreak of the war, aircraft were initially seen as having value for reconnaissance. Early in the conflict opposing pilots who saw each other in the air largely ignored one other and went about their respective reconnaissance duties. Soon, however, the more aggressive pilots started taking to the skies with revolvers, grenades, rifles and other weapons to fire or hurl at the enemy. Next, machine guns were converted for use in aeroplanes and by 1915 the number of aerial combats was escalating rapidly. By early 1916, aircraft were becoming more sophisticated and the RFC had a marked air of supremacy by the start of the Battle of the Somme in July of that year. It had 421 aircraft, fourteen balloon and four kite-balloon squadrons.

By the end of the war, aircraft were being used to bomb targets and for other offensive purposes. These included the strafing of enemy infantry and emplacements, and the bombing of German military airfields and the strategic bombing of German industrial and transportation facilities. The Sopwith Camel was the most successful fighter aircraft, having accounted for more than 3,000 opponents. The early pilots took great risks and did not even have parachutes to use if their aircraft failed or were shot down.

On 1 April 1918, the RFC and Royal Naval Air Service (RNAS) were amalgamated to form a new service: the Royal Air Force (RAF), which was controlled by a new Air Ministry. In the final few months of the war, aircraft were playing a crucial role in supporting the ground offensive. By the end of the war, military experts were convinced of the need for aerial power: by 1919, a year after the war ended, the RAF had 4,000 combat aircraft and 114,000 personnel. With the advent of aerial combat, a new breed of heroes emerged, nineteen of whom were awarded the Victoria Cross (VC) in the Great War.

2ND LIEUTENANT (PROMOTED POSTHUMOUSLY TO LIEUTENANT) WILLIAM BARNARD RHODES-MOORHOUSE
Royal Flying Corps (RFC)
DECORATION: VICTORIA CROSS (VC)
GAZETTED: 22 MAY 1915

William Rhodes-Moorhouse was the first airman to be awarded the VC and few stories that lie behind Britain's most prestigious gallantry medal can have been more moving. For not only had Rhodes-Moorhouse written a 'first and final letter' to his recently born son, but he had also written a late postscript to it in which he predicted his death on the day of his final flight – a perilous mission from which he knew he was highly unlikely to return.

Rhodes-Moorhouse was born in London on 26 September 1887. His family were great adventurers: indeed, his grandfather, William Barnard Rhodes, became one of the first Englishmen to arrive in New Zealand in July 1836, having left his native Yorkshire. Rhodes, who was helped by his three brothers, amassed a fortune from farming and other business interests. This £750,000 – an enormous sum of money at the time – was eventually inherited by his half-Maori, adopted daughter, Mary Ann, after he died. She married a New Zealander, Edward Moorhouse, with whom she had four children, and their family was raised in England. Will, the couple's eldest son and a robust boy with fair hair and green eyes, was educated at Harrow, where he developed a taste for speed and an interest in the workings of the internal combustion engine. After school, he went to Trinity College, Cambridge, but here he neglected his studies for his love of engineering and his passion for racing motorcycles and cars.

By the time he was in his early twenties, Rhodes-Moorhouse was fascinated with the new sport of flying. He paid for flying lessons and became a pioneer airman, attracting large crowds when he flew from Huntingdon airfield, Cambridgeshire, at a time when a man in flight was still a sensational spectacle. With a friend, James Radley, he even produced a variation of the Blériot XI aircraft – the Radley-Moorhouse monoplane. He travelled to the USA in 1911, where he piloted a fifty-horsepower Gnome-engined Blériot to victory in numerous airspeed contests, thereby earning thousands of dollars in prize money. He continued to fly competitively on his return to

Britain, ending his peacetime flying career with a record-breaking, cross-Channel flight in 1912, which took place shortly after he married his wife, Linda, a school friend of his sister.

When war was declared, he volunteered for the RFC even though he had not flown for two and a half years. With a shortage of experienced pilots on the Western Front, Rhodes-Moorhouse joined 2 Squadron at Merville, France, on 21 March 1915. His squadron flew the Farnborough-designed Blériot-Experimental (BE) 2a and 2b, which were sturdy aircraft but had a maximum speed of just seventy mph at ground level. Rhodes-Moorhouse began with some familiarisation sorties, but soon had his baptism of German anti-aircraft fire at 7,500 feet over Lille. His pilot's logbook recorded that the top centre section of his aircraft was hit by a shell on 29 March. Four days later he wrote to his wife, describing the sound of anti-aircraft fire as 'first a whistle, then a noise like a terrific cough'. Poor weather meant he had few flights in the first two weeks of April, but from 16 April he was performing numerous highly dangerous missions. During one ninety-five-minute reconnaissance, his aircraft's wings and bracing wire were hit by shrapnel. His service did not go unnoticed by his superiors and he was recommended for promotion to substantive lieutenant.

The Germans conducted their first gas attack on Allied troops on 22 April 1915, and for the next four days they took the initiative in battles in and around St Julien and Ypres. On 26 April, the RFC was ordered to bomb the enemy's railway network to prevent reinforcements reaching the front lines. Rhodes-Moorhouse, who had been due some much-deserved leave, was sent to bomb the railway junction at Courtrai – one of three targets for four aircraft. He took off alone from

Merville at 3.05 p.m., having been asked to drop his 100-lb bomb from just below cloud level. However, after making the thirty-two-mile flight, he dropped right down to 300 feet to ensure a direct hit. He was greeted with a volley of rifle and machine-gun fire, and when he was directly over the target a burst of machine-gun fire perforated his aircraft's fuselage and smashed into his thigh. At the same time, fragments from his own bomb ripped through the wings and tailplane.

Rhodes-Moorhouse, badly wounded and in great pain, had two options: land behind enemy lines, receive urgent medical attention and become a prisoner of war (PoW); or try to limp back to his home airbase with his aircraft and valuable intelligence. Choosing the latter option, he dropped a further 200 feet to gain some extra speed and again encountered heavy fire from the ground. This led to two further wounds to his hand and abdomen. Nevertheless, he steered the aircraft towards his base, crossing the Allied lines over some Indian troops who looked up in awe and later asked for details of his courageous sortie to be translated into Hindustani. Just three days later, the daily bulletin to the troops stated that Rhodes-Moorhouse's mission had been a total success and 'would appear worthy to be ranked among the most heroic stories of the world's history'.

At 4.12 p.m., eyewitnesses saw Rhodes-Moorhouse's badly damaged aircraft approaching at a low height. He just cleared a hedge, switched off the engine and made a perfect landing. Two officers lifted him from the battered aircraft, which had ninety-five bullet and shrapnel holes. Rhodes-Moorhouse was taken to a nearby office, where he insisted on filing his report while his wounds were tended. He was then moved to a casualty clearing station in Merville, where it was discovered that a bullet had ripped his stomach to pieces. He was given painkillers but it soon became apparent that he was dying. Rhodes-Moorhouse showed his flight commander, Maurice Blake, a photograph of his wife and son, and asked him to write to them and his mother. He said that if he was awarded a Military Cross, it should go to his wife. After dozing briefly, he revealed: 'It's strange dying, Blake, old boy – unlike anything one has ever done before, like one's first solo flight.' Just after 1 p.m., he received Holy Communion and a note arrived informing him that he had been recommended for the Distinguished Service Order (DSO). At 2.25 p.m. on 27 April, with a recently delivered letter from his wife resting on his pillow and his friend Blake at his side, Rhodes-Moorhouse died. He was twenty-seven.

Back in Britain, he was instantly acclaimed as a hero. The *Daily Mail* noted: 'Such endurance is enough to make all of us ashamed of ever again complaining of any pain whatever. He was one of those who have never "done their bit" till they have done the impossible.' A squadron observer, Sholto Douglas, later Marshal of the RAF the 1st Baron Douglas of Kirtleside, wrote a letter of condolence to the pilot's widow: 'I do hope such courage will be recognised with a DSO although we all think a VC would be none too great a reward for such pluck and endurance.' It was obviously helpful to have such powerful supporters, but it was Blake's lobbying that secured the VC, and very swiftly: Rhodes-Moorhouse's award, for 'most conspicuous bravery', was announced on 22 May 1915, less than a month after his death. At the time, General Sir John French, the British commander, said the pilot had been responsible for 'the most important bomb dropped during the war so far'.

Before his mission, Rhodes-Moorhouse had written several

letters to his family, to be sent to them in the event of his death. One particularly touching one was to his four-month-old son Willie, in which he expressed his love and affection for his wife, with whom he stressed he had never had a 'misunderstanding or quarrel'. He urged his son always to seek the advice of his mother and hoped he would be an engineer and obtain 'a useful knowledge of machinery in all forms'. He also urged him to 'keep up your position as a landowner and a gentleman' (the family had acquired the sixteenth-century Parnham House and its estate near Beaminster, Dorset, before the war). Then, with an affectionate farewell, William Rhodes-Moorhouse signed what he described as his 'first and last letter' to his son. There was a poignant and astute postscript: 'I am off on a trip from which I don't expect to return but which I hope will shorten the War a bit. I shall probably be blown up by my own bomb or if not killed by rifle fire.' Unusually for the times, but at his own request (and possibly because he came from a well-off family willing to contribute towards the cost), Rhodes-Moorhouse's body was returned to Britain where he was given a funeral with full military honours.

The footnote to this tragic story is that Rhodes-Moorhouse's son went on to become a Battle of Britain pilot and actually served, from May 1940, at Merville, France, where his father had been killed in action twenty-five years earlier. After claiming twelve combat victories and being awarded the DFC, Willie Rhodes-Moorhouse's Hurricane was shot down in a dogfight over Kent on 6 September 1940. The body of the young officer, who died aged twenty-five, was recovered and his ashes were later interred beside his father at the family's Parnham estate.

CAPTAIN JOHN AIDAN LIDDELL
Army/Royal Flying Corps (RFC)
DECORATIONS: MILITARY CROSS (MC) AND
VICTORIA CROSS (VC)
GAZETTED: 18 FEBRUARY 1915 AND 23 AUGUST 1915

Aidan Liddell was born at Benwell Hall, Newcastle upon Tyne, on 3 August 1888. The eldest of four children born to a Justice of the Peace and his wife, Liddell was educated at Stonyhurst College, Lancashire, and Balliol College, Oxford. Scion of a wealthy Catholic family, he was a frail child and, at one point, his parents took him on a recuperative cruise to South Africa. At school, he earned the nickname 'Oozy' because he was always messing around with engines and chemicals. At Oxford, he took an honours degree in zoology, the only student to do so that year as it was a new subject. At just nineteen, and already with a passion for cars, Liddell was elected to the British Astronomical Association.

Early in 1912 and 'not wanting to be a slacker', he joined the Special Reserve of Officers of the 3rd Battalion, Argyll and Sutherland Highlanders. The following year, he took up flying, a pastime still in its infancy and one fraught with danger. He was promoted to lieutenant in July 1914 and captain the next month, when hostilities began. In early September, while out in France with his regiment, he was twice put on burial duty, writing in a letter home that life was 'nothing except noise and unpleasant smells and sights and jobs'. Matters did not improve: by mid-November he was noting in his diary that he had gone a month without a bath and seven weeks without a change of socks in the trenches, which had started to 'flow like a river' because of the early winter rains. On 26 November, he reflected: 'It's a war with no glamour or glory . . . modern weapons are too deadly, and the whole art of war has been altered . . . to a very slow and tedious and also gruelling business.' Yet he was a dedicated and brave soldier: one comrade told how Liddell had saved his life by helping him when he was wounded. His battalion was finally relieved on 11 December after he had spent forty-three consecutive days in the line. Two weeks later, he was present at the famous unofficial ceasefire on Christmas Day, writing to his old college: 'Most of our men and officers, including myself, went out and met them half-way, where we exchanged smokes, newspapers, and various souvenirs for over an hour.'

It was in January 1915, while on a week's leave in England, that Liddell learnt he had been awarded the MC for his work with the regiment's machine-gun section. His citation stated: 'For services in connection with Operations in the Field.' However, after rejoining the battalion, his frail health gave way and he was evacuated to England for a complete rest. After a period of recuperation, he obtained his Royal Aero Club Certificate and transferred to the RFC. Training at three British air bases followed, then he left for France on 23 July 1915 to join 7 Squadron at St Omer. He flew his first sortie on 29 July and his second, with 2nd Lieutenant Richard Peck as his observer, two days later. The men took off in an RE5 aircraft shortly before midday and arrived over Ostend at 5,000 feet. Heading for Bruges, they were suddenly fired upon from above by a German biplane. Peck returned fire with his Lewis gun, but then the RE5 lurched forward and rolled on to its back: one of the bursts of enemy fire had ripped through the side of the rear cockpit. Worse still, a bullet had hit Liddell's right thigh, exposing the bone, and he had fallen unconscious with shock. The aircraft began to drop to the ground as all loose objects in the cockpit, including weapons and ammunition, whistled past Peck's head. When the aircraft had fallen 3,000 feet, Liddell regained consciousness and righted it. However, the control wheel was half shot away and the throttle was shattered. Liddell, by then behind enemy lines, had a choice: he could either land and face inevitable capture and imprisonment or try to make it back to the Allied lines. He chose the latter option and scribbled a note to Peck saying that he intended to head for some sands west of Nieuport. Peck, though, indicated an Allied airfield near Furnes as a better option.

For half an hour, in appalling pain from his injury, Liddell flew the aircraft to safety, holding the broken control wheel in one hand and operating the rudder cables with the other. When they reached La Panne airfield Liddell made his approach on full engine power because of the broken throttle, switching it off before touchdown. He made a perfect landing, then refused to allow a group of Belgian airmen to move him until a doctor arrived. While he was waiting, he tied a tourniquet to stem the flow of blood and made a makeshift splint, and when he was finally lifted from the battered aircraft he even managed a smile for an attendant photographer. Later, staff at La Panne hospital battled to save his leg, but septicaemia set in and it was amputated.

Liddell's courageous deeds were well reported in Britain and he received many distinguished visitors while in hospital. On 3 August 1915 – his twenty-seventh birthday – he wrote a typically optimistic letter to his mother, saying he was being 'pampered' and 'everyone seems very pleased with my progress'. He also quoted a letter he had received from a Major Hoare, praising his actions: 'How you managed God only knows: but it was a magnificent effort . . . I cannot express to you the admiration we all have for you for what you did. You have set a standard for pluck and determination which may be equalled, but certainly will not be surpassed, during this War.'

Sadly, Liddell's cheerful optimism was misplaced. The blood poisoning had spread and, as his condition deteriorated, his mother was given permission to visit him. She managed to see him shortly before he died on 31 August. It was a month to the day after he had been wounded but he died in the knowledge that he had been awarded the VC, having been informed of this on 18 August. The award was officially announced on 23 August and the citation stated that his bravery had saved the life of his observer. It concluded with the words: 'it would seem incredible that he could have accomplished his task'. After his death, the Argylls issued a statement expressing just how much he would be missed: 'We all feel as if the light has gone out, the light of our Battalion. You see he was always bright. In snow, in muddy trench, or ante-room, he kept us laughing, and his influence will last . . . from the smallest drummer boy to the Colonel, this Battalion asks only to be given the chance to avenge Aidan's death.' More than 1,000 people wrote letters of condolence to his parents, among them Prince Alexander of Teck, the younger brother of Queen Mary, who praised Liddell for 'playing the game to the end'. Liddell's body was brought home on 3 September and the next day was interred in the Catholic section of Basingstoke Old Cemetery, Hampshire. Liddell's VC was presented to his father by George V at Buckingham Palace on 16 November 1916. By then Peck, his observer, had perished, too: he was killed on active service in Mesopotamia (now Iraq) on 10 March 1916.

MICHAEL ASHCROFT

LIEUTENANT (LATER CAPTAIN) WILLIAM LEEFE ROBINSON
Army/Royal Flying Corps (RFC)
DECORATION: VICTORIA CROSS (VC)
GAZETTED: 5 SEPTEMBER 1916

Billy Leefe Robinson acquired hero status after becoming the first airman to shoot down a German Zeppelin over the United Kingdom. Such was the acclaim for his achievement that, on a wave of public enthusiasm, he was awarded his VC in record time: little more than forty-eight hours after the event. Furthermore, he was the first man to be awarded a VC for an action in – or at least *over* – the United Kingdom.

Leefe Robinson was born on his father's coffee estate in Tollideta, South Coorg, India, on 14 July 1895. At school, he was never particularly academic but he was sporty. In December 1914, he was commissioned into the Worcestershire Regiment, and in March the following year he joined the RFC in France as an observer. However, he was invalided home after being wounded over Lille. By September, he had not only recovered but had qualified as a pilot and this led to postings to various Home Defence squadrons. In one letter home, he explained his passion for flying: 'You have no idea how beautiful it is above the clouds . . . I love flying more and more every day, and the work is even more interesting than it was.'

The Great War was the first conflict in which the civilians of Britain came face to face with indiscriminate death and destruction on a daily basis while the nation's fighting men were absent at 'the Front'. This was because of the German use of Zeppelin airships and Gotha bomber raids. Leefe Robinson had his first chance to shoot down one of these airships in

April 1916, but failed to do so. However, on the night of 2/3 September, he was given another chance. He took off from Sutton's Farm airfield in Essex in his BE2c 2963 aircraft at 11.08 p.m. on a routine 'search and find' operation. Leefe Robinson was accompanied by Lieutenant Fred Sowerby, his observer. Their first two hours, flying at 10,000 feet between the airfield and Joyce Green, were uneventful. However, at 1.10 a.m., he caught sight of a Zeppelin in two searchlight beams over Woolwich, south-east London. He set off in pursuit but lost it in the thick cloud.

Searchlights over Finsbury in north London had also spotted the airship – one of sixteen sent from Germany that night on a mass raid – and anti-aircraft guns opened fire on the Schütte-Lanz SL11. By this point, Leefe Robinson was desperately short of fuel but he gave chase and was joined, in another aircraft, by Lieutenants Mackay and Hunt. Tracer fire from the ground lit up the night sky but the airship unloaded its bombs, which enabled it to gain height. As Leefe Robinson closed in, he emptied two drums of ammunition into the airship, but it flew on unhindered: it seemed impregnable. He broke off but then made another attack from astern, firing his last drum into the airship's twin rudders. First, a reddish glow appeared inside the airship, then, moments later, it burst into flames. Thousands of Londoners looked up and cheered as the Zeppelin plunged from the sky.

Leefe Robinson landed back at Sutton's Farm at 2.45 a.m. after a gruelling patrol of three and a half hours. He was lifted shoulder high to the edge of the airfield but, despite being exhausted and numb with cold, was then ordered to write his report. His fitters were alarmed to see that part of the aircraft's central top wing and machine-gun wire guard had been shot away. After finishing his report, Leefe Robinson collapsed on his bed and fell asleep. As he slept, the ecstatic scenes of 'Zepp Sunday' were already under way all over London.

Leefe Robinson's exploits quickly made the headlines. For many people, it was the finest moment in the war so far. Photographs of the heroic pilot appeared in newspapers and magazines and he became an instantly recognised figure all over the country. He also received many honours and rewards, but his most cherished moment came when he was invited to Windsor Castle, where George V presented him with his VC on the same day that the sixteen crew members from the airship he shot down were buried. His VC had been gazetted just two days after his actions and he was presented with his decoration a mere three days after that. On the day his award was announced, the *Evening News* had bills all over London proclaiming: 'The Zepp: VC for airman'. Leefe Robinson was delightfully modest about his courage, telling well-wishers: 'I only did my job.'

In a letter to his parents dated 22 October 1916, Leefe Robinson reflected upon his fame and told how he had shot down the Zeppelin.

When the colossal thing actually burst into flames of course it was a glorious sight – wonderful! It literally lit up all the sky around and me as well of course – I saw my machine as in the fire light – and sat still half dazed staring at the wonderful sight before me, not realising to the least degree the wonderful thing that had happened!

My feelings? Can I describe my feelings? I hardly know how I felt as I watched the huge mass gradually turn on end, and – as it seemed to me – slowly sink, one glowing, blazing mass – I gradually realised what I had done and grew wild with excitement . . . As I daresay you have seen in the papers – babies, flowers and hats have been named after me also poems and prose have been dedicated to me – oh, it's too much! I am recognised wherever I go about Town now, whether in uniform or mufti – the city police salute me, the waiters, hall porters and pages of hotels and restaurants bow and scrape – visitors turn round and stare – oh it's too thick!

Leefe Robinson's good looks, fame and riches – including well over £4,000 in donations from well-wishers – also meant he was hotly pursued by young women. He was sent to France as a flight commander shortly after being awarded the VC, and in early 1917, while leading six of the new Bristol fighters, encountered Manfred von Richthofen leading a flight of five Albatros fighters. The short, fierce battle that followed led to four of the Bristols being shot down, including Leefe Robinson's. When he was taken prisoner, the Germans quickly realised who he was and made his life all the harder for it. After trying to escape four times in as many months, he was court-martialled and sentenced to a month in solitary confinement. Later, he was taken to the notorious Holzminden prisoner-of-war camp, in Lower Saxony. There he was one of the youngest and most brutalised prisoners – particularly after he briefly escaped – and his health suffered.

On 14 December 1918, following the end of the war, Leefe Robinson was returned from captivity but by then he was desperately weak. Subsequently he contracted influenza (during these times, illnesses such as this killed many servicemen who survived the fighting), his health deteriorated and he became delirious, reliving the horrors of his time in captivity.

On New Year's Eve, Leefe Robinson – one of the greatest heroes of the war – died, aged twenty-three. He is buried at the cemetery extension to All Saints churchyard in Harrow Weald, north-west London. Even today his name continues to be commemorated: in April 2010, to celebrate the 100th anniversary of the Great Northern Route extension that connects Grange Park to Cuffley, the First Capital Connect rail company named a Class 313 train *Captain William Leefe Robinson VC*.

SERGEANT THOMAS MOTTERSHEAD
Royal Flying Corps (RFC)
DECORATIONS: DISTINGUISHED CONDUCT
MEDAL (DCM) AND VICTORIA CROSS (VC)
GAZETTED: 14 NOVEMBER 1916 AND 12 FEBRUARY
1917

Thomas Mottershead earned the distinction of being the only non-commissioned officer (NCO) to be awarded the VC for aerial operations during the Great War. However, eventually succumbing to the serious wounds he received in battle, Mottershead never knew that he was to be honoured with Britain and the Commonwealth's supreme decoration for valour.

Mottershead was born in Widnes, Lancashire, on 17 January 1892. He was educated first at Simms Cross Council School in Widnes and, later, at Widnes Technical School. For the next three years, he studied engineering in which he received several qualifications. Both sporty and religious, he was apprenticed after leaving school as a fitter and turner. By studying in his spare time, Mottershead became a member of the Amalgamated

Society of Engineers and was employed by Camell Lairds in Birkenhead. He married his childhood sweetheart, Lilian Bree, on 10 February 1914 and the following year the couple had a son, Sydney Thomas. With his additional responsibilities, Mottershead travelled south and took a temporary job as a motor mechanic at a garage in Andover, Hampshire. Along with a friend, also from Widnes, he travelled to Portsmouth hoping to get a job in the naval dockyard but it was not long before the First World War broke out. With his friend, Frank Moore, Mottershead enlisted in the RFC on 10 August 1914. By then, an air mechanic 2nd class, Mottershead's first posting was to the Central Flying School, RAF Upavon, Wiltshire, where his wife and son joined him that September.

Mottershead was bright, eager and a quick learner: after three promotions he achieved the rank of sergeant on 1 April 1916 and his ambition to become a pilot came a step closer when he was accepted for training, starting his instruction in May 1916. His expert technical knowledge helped him become an excellent pilot and he quickly achieved the necessary qualifications. After a month of duties as a flying instructor, Mottershead was posted to France, along with three other NCOs, on 4 July. On 6 July, he reported to 25 Squadron at Auchel for operational duties. The squadron, a fighter/reconnaissance unit, was equipped with FE2b and FE2d two-seat 'pusher' aircraft (in which the propeller faces to the rear) and their duties were varied, including carrying out bombing sorties. The first Battle of the Somme was just a week old and the squadron saw action virtually every day. After being given an experienced observer-gunner and just two local flights to familiarise himself with the terrain, Mottershead was given an operational sortie. From his first mission, he showed great courage, carrying out a low-level bombing attack at 1,000 feet that destroyed a troublesome German anti-aircraft battery.

On 22 September 1916, Mottershead again showed immense bravery after being detailed to bomb the railway station at Samain. Initially, he dived to 1,500 feet to bomb and destroy an ammunition train, before flying low over another train and raking it with machine-gun fire. However, as he climbed away, his aircraft was attacked from behind by a Fokker Scout. Using all his manoeuvring skills, Mottershead eventually outfought the enemy aircraft and shot it down. For this action, he was awarded the DCM on 14 November 1916.

After being promoted to flight sergeant, Mottershead was posted to 20 Squadron, another FE unit and which was based at Clairmarais. For the next five months, he was on almost continual operational service but he was given two weeks' leave over Christmas 1916 which he spent with his family. He even found time to visit his former school and give pupils a talk on his work in France, before returning to 20 Squadron early in 1917. On 7 January 1917, Mottershead was the pilot of one of two FEs that were ordered to carry out a fighter patrol over Ploegsteert Wood, Belgium. When his aircraft was found to be unserviceable, he transferred to a reserve FE2d but he and his observer soon caught up with their fellow aircrew. No sooner had they got to the area above the wood than they were attacked by two Albatros Scouts. After becoming separated, the other crew managed to shoot down one Albatros. However, the second Albatros manoeuvred itself on to the tail of Mottershead's aircraft and opened fire at point-blank range. Bullets ruptured the petrol tank and the aircraft, which had a plywood fuselage, burst into flames. Mottershead's observer,

Lieutenant W. E. Gower, grabbed a fire extinguisher and tried to keep the flames from his pilot, but to little avail. Mottershead flew the stricken aircraft over the first line of Allied trenches and made for safe ground to the rear. Rather than make an immediate crash-landing, which would have endangered his observer's life, Mottershead circled a fairly flat field and headed his FE, by then trailing flames and smoke, into the wind in an attempt at a safer landing. However, as soon as the aircraft hit the ground, the undercarriage collapsed and the nose dug into the mud. Gower was thrown clear, suffering only cuts, bruises and shock, but Mottershead was pinned in his cockpit, with the engine close to crushing him and with blazing wreckage all around him.

Gower helped nearby soldiers to extricate the pilot from the burning wreckage. Despite dreadful burns to his back, hands and legs, Mottershead was able to speak to his rescuers, remaining cheerful and uncomplaining as he was taken for emergency medical treatment. For the next five days, surgeons desperately tried to save the pilot's life but Mottershead died on 12 January 1917, five days short of his twenty-fourth birthday. The next day he was buried, with full military honours, at Ballieu cemetery where every available man from his squadron paid his final respects. A day after the funeral, Captain G. J. Mahoney-Jones, the squadron's temporary commander, wrote to Mottershead's widow saying 'as we lifted the wreath and Union Jack from the coffin and laid it on the ground, we sorrowfully knew that we had laid to rest one of the bravest men who had ever fallen in war'.

On 12 February 1917, it was announced that Mottershead had been awarded a posthumous VC. His citation detailed how he had 'showed the most conspicuous presence of mind in the careful selection of a landing place, and his wonderful endurance and fortitude undoubtedly saved the life of his observer'. Gower was awarded the Military Cross (MC) for his bravery during the same incident. Mottershead's VC was presented to his widow by George V at an investiture in London's Hyde Park on 2 June 1917.

Furthermore, the town of Widnes started an appeal fund to provide for his widow and child and its residents gave generously to 'the wife and little son who, in life, were the Sergeant's special affections'. Nearly £1,000 – a small fortune in those days – was raised for the Mayor of Widnes Memorial Fund to Thomas Mottershead but, due to an administrative mix-up, the money never reached them. In fact, it was nearly half a century later that a diligent civil servant discovered the fund in council records. It was used to endow the Mottershead Scholarship at Widnes Technical College: a belated, but splendid, tribute to its former pupil. A street in Widnes – Mottershead Road – is also named in honour of this courageous, good-natured Lancashire lad who sacrificed his own life to save that of a comrade and friend.

2ND LIEUTENANT (LATER MAJOR) EDWARD MANNOCK

Army/Royal Flying Corps (RFC)/RAF
DECORATIONS: MILITARY CROSS (MC) AND BAR,
DISTINGUISHED SERVICE ORDER (DSO) AND
TWO BARS AND VICTORIA CROSS (VC)
GAZETTED: 17 SEPTEMBER 1917, 7 MARCH 1918, 3
AUGUST 1918, 16 SEPTEMBER 1918, 16 SEPTEMBER 1918
AND 18 JULY 1919

Edward 'Mick' Mannock was the highest scoring and most highly decorated British pilot of the First World War. He transformed himself from someone who initially came across as an arrogant and brash individual into one of the greatest legends in RAF history.

Mannock was born in Brighton, Sussex, on 24 May 1887, one of five children fathered by a tough Irishman who was a corporal in the 2nd Dragoons, Royal Scots Greys. As a child, Mannock was bright and an avid reader, but he suffered from a severe astigmatism in his left eye. Incredibly, given his later achievements as a pilot, he was virtually blind in this eye for the remainder of his life. His family was poor and so, after a brief education at St Thomas' School in Canterbury, Kent, until he was thirteen, he ended his education after his father abandoned the family. Mannock undertook a series of menial jobs before both he and his brother, Patrick, worked for the National Telephone Company.

Mannock was twenty-seven and working as a labourer in Turkey at the time the Great War broke out. When Turkey entered the war on Germany's side, he and some other British workers were imprisoned. In jail, he sang patriotic British songs, only to receive regular beatings from the Turkish guards for his perceived impertinence. When he tried to escape, he was put in solitary confinement and his health deteriorated – he had dysentery and suppurating sores – but eventually the American Consulate secured his release. Back in Britain, Mannock was initially listed as 'unfit for military duties' although at the same time he was obsessed with 'destroying Germans'. In July 1915, he re-enlisted in the Territorial unit of the Royal Army Medical Corps (RAMC), which he had first joined after leaving school. However, some of the requirements of the job – one of which was a duty to treat enemy prisoners – troubled him. For, after his experiences in the Turkish prison, he had no compassion for the Central Powers or their soldiers. On 1 April 1916, Mannock was commissioned as a 2nd lieutenant in the Royal Engineers. Then, a chance meeting with an old friend led to a discussion about flying and, in August 1916, 2nd Lieutenant Mannock transferred to the Number One School of Military Aeronautics at Reading, where he qualified as a pilot.

Posted to France in April 1917, he joined his first operational unit, 40 Squadron, at Treizennes. Unfortunately, he created a bad first impression among the squadron as a 'boorish know-all', and his first sortie, when he was badly shaken by anti-aircraft fire, reinforced this view. However, opinions soon started to change when, through brilliant flying, he pulled his damaged Nieuport Scout (a single-seater French fighter) out of a 'terminal' dive. On 7 May, he claimed his first success when he and five others shot down a kite balloon – a manned, gas-filled balloon used for reconnaissance – five miles behind German lines. On 25 May and 1 June 1917, he was convinced he had enemy 'kills', but he decided to bide his time until he could make a claim that was unquestionable. He did not have long to wait: the following week he sent an Albatros D.III crashing to earth from 13,000 feet.

On 17 September 1917, Mannock was awarded the MC when his citation stated: 'In the course of many combats he has driven off a large number of enemy machines, and has forced down three balloons, showing a very fine offensive spirit and great fearlessness in attacking the enemy at close range and low altitudes under heavy fire from the ground.' The very next month, Mannock was awarded a Bar to his MC. His citation stated: 'He has destroyed several hostile machines and driven others down out of control. On one occasion he attacked a formation of five enemy machines single-handed and shot one down out of control. On another occasion, while engaged with an enemy machine, he was attacked by two others, one of which he forced to the ground. He has consistently shown great courage and initiative.' Furthermore, Mannock was becoming a better team player, too: during one sortie he protected a promising young pilot, Lieutenant George McElroy. 'McIrish', as Mannock christened him, went on to become the tenth highest scoring pilot of the war, with forty-six victories.

Mannock had his last day with 40 Squadron on 1 January 1918, when he recorded his twenty-first official 'kill'. He next served, from March 1918, with 74 (Tiger) Squadron, flying to France on 30 March. In May, he was reduced to tears by the death of his protégé, Lieutenant Dolan, his wails of grief continuing long into the night. Afterwards, his comrades noticed a new bloodlust, but he never let it cloud his judgement in the air and his number of 'kills' rapidly escalated. He carried out a series of brilliant manoeuvres against his opponents: one 'kill' was described by Ira Jones, a fellow pilot, as 'a remarkable exhibition of cruel, calculated Hun-strafing'. However, amid all the success he remained a realist, never taking off without his revolver: 'to finish myself off as soon as I see the first sign of flames'.

In May 1918, he learned he had been awarded the DSO – a bestowal that was formally announced on 16 September. A Bar to his DSO followed – again it was not formally announced in the *London Gazette* until 16 September. On 21 June 1918, Mannock was promoted to major and chosen to succeed Major 'Billy' Bishop in command of 85 Squadron. However, a close friend noticed that his nerves seemed to be frayed as he left Britain for his new posting: 'He was in no condition to return to France, but in those days such things were not taken into consideration.' On 24 July, Mannock told his friend Ira Jones by telephone: 'I've caught up with Bishop's score now – seventy-two [including unofficial 'kills'].' Around 5 a.m. three days later, Mannock, flying with Lieutenant Donald Inglis, made his final 'kill' above Lestremme. Disregarding his own strict rule, he then made a couple of low passes over the wreckage, leading the inexperienced Inglis into a storm of small-gun fire from the German trenches. As they zig-zagged away from the scene, Inglis noticed a small bluish flame on his major's engine cowling. Then the left wing of Mannock's aircraft fell away and he plunged into a death spin. Inglis, showered in petrol from his own punctured fuel tank, made a crash-landing shortly afterwards. After being pulled from his battered aircraft, he announced: 'They killed him, the bastards killed my major. They killed Mick.' Mannock was dead at the age of thirty-one.

It later emerged that his body had been thrown out of the

aircraft – or he had jumped clear. Mannock may even have fulfilled his pledge to shoot himself at the first sign of flames. He was buried in an unmarked grave by a German soldier, who also returned Mannock's identity discs, notebooks and other personal effects. Mannock had, meanwhile, been awarded his third DSO but this and his two earlier awards were gazetted after his death. The citation for his second Bar, announced on 3 August 1918, stated: 'This officer has now accounted for 48 enemy machines. His success is due to wonderful shooting and a determination to get to close quarters; to attain this he displays most skilful leadership and unfailing courage. These characteristics were markedly shown on a recent occasion when he attacked six hostile scouts, three of which he brought down. Later on the same day he attacked a two-seater, which crashed into a tree.'

After the war, it was decided that Mannock's incredible and prolonged courage had not still been fully recognised. After much lobbying, largely by those who had served under him, the *London Gazette* announced his VC on 18 July 1919, nearly a year after his death. It recognised fifty official 'kills' but concentrated on his achievements in June and July 1918, concluding: 'This highly distinguished officer, during the whole of his career in the Royal Air Force, was an outstanding example of fearless courage, remarkable skill, devotion to duty and self-sacrifice, which has never been surpassed.' Edward Mannock, the recipient's wayward father, was presented with his son's VC by George V in the same month.

LIEUTENANT (LATER FLIGHT LIEUTENANT) ALAN JERRARD

Army/Royal Flying Corps (RFC)/RAF
DECORATION: VICTORIA CROSS (VC)
GAZETTED: 1 MAY 1918

Alan Jerrard was known affectionately as the 'Pyjama VC' and he had the distinction of being the only air VC during the prolonged war on the Italian Front. Furthermore, he was the only Sopwith Camel fighter pilot to be awarded the VC: by the end of the Great War, the Sopwith Camel was as well known to the British public as the Spitfire was during the Second World War.

Jerrard was born in Lewisham, south London, on 3 December 1897. He was educated at Bishop Vesey's Grammar School in Sutton Coldfield, West Midlands, where his father was headmaster. Later Jerrard attended Oundle School in Northamptonshire and Birmingham University. However, after only a matter of months at university, he volunteered to join the Army. On 2 January 1916, Jerrard was commissioned as a 2nd lieutenant into the South Staffordshire Regiment but he spent only a matter of months as an infantry subaltern before applying to be transferred to the RFC. At the time, Britain was short of pilots and training was quick: having reported for initial training on 23 September 1916, he was posted to RAF Narborough, Norfolk, on 5 December, where he fell ill as the unit was preparing for operations in France. Once fit again, he graduated as a RFC pilot on 14 June 1917. He showed above-average abilities in his further training and, on 2 July, he was promoted to lieutenant. Jerrard was then notified of his first operational posting and arrived at

19 Squadron, based at Liettres, France, on 24 July.

Jerrard's first operational patrol on 29 July ended ignominiously when, after failing to see the enemy, he lost contact with his formation and had to land at St Omer. His second operational patrol on 5 August was somewhat more eventful. Still inexperienced, he again lost contact with his formation and flew low to get his bearings. When he came across a large convoy of German transport vehicles, he raked the convoy with his machine-gun fire, causing several vehicles to burst into flames. After climbing to 10,000 feet through fog and low cloud, his engine cut out and he was forced to crash-land his Spad A8830 into a railway embankment near St Marie Cappel. Allied troops reached him and dug him out of the wreckage but Jerrard had suffered serious injuries, including a badly broken jaw and nose. After being invalided back to England, he was eventually declared fit for operational flying once again. On 22 February 1918, Jerrard arrived with his new unit, 66 Squadron, which was based in Italy. Just five days later, he claimed an enemy Berg single-seat Scout as shot down and out of control. Over the next month, he had more successes, shooting down an enemy observation balloon, claiming a pair of Berg Scouts (one of which crashed, the other damaged) and, finally, shooting down an Albatros Scout that also crashed.

On 30 March, Jerrard and two other pilots, one experienced, the other a novice, were given a sortie in three Sopwith Camels. There are some discrepancies over exactly who did what next but essentially they found themselves in a massive dogfight with at least nineteen enemy aircraft. According to the British pilots (and their account was disputed by their Austro-Hungarian opponents), Jerrard shot down three enemy aircraft and the other two pilots shot down a further three between them. Jerrard also launched a courageous attack, flying as low as fifty feet, on an enemy aerodrome, successfully shooting up aircraft as they tried to take off. Jerrard only retreated when ordered to do so by his patrol leader and he was then pursued by five enemy aircraft. However, by then wounded and with his aircraft damaged, he crash-landed west of Mansue aerodrome, where he was captured and later interrogated by the enemy. A combat report led to Jerrard being recommended for the VC and his award was announced on 1 May 1918, while he was still a prisoner of war (PoW). His citation described his dogfight and ended: 'Although apparently wounded, this very gallant officer turned repeatedly, and attacked single-handed the pursuing machines, until he was eventually overwhelmed by numbers and driven to the ground. Lt. Jerrard had greatly distinguished himself on four previous occasions, within a period of twenty-three days, in destroying enemy machines, displaying bravery and ability of the very highest order.'

Although the precise facts of the mission were unclear, one thing was certain: when Jerrard was captured he was wearing only his pyjamas beneath his bulky flying overalls. On the morning of 30 March, the weather had been unsuitable for flying and Jerrard thought he had been stood down for the day. When he was suddenly ordered to action, he had been asleep and had to dress rapidly, therefore pulling on his overalls over his pyjamas. Jerrard's chivalrous captors had sympathy for his predicament as a pyjama-clad prisoner and arranged for a note to be dropped behind Allied lines, requesting various items to be air-dropped for him. 66 Squadron arranged for two such packages for the twenty-year-old prisoner, containing everything from his military uniform to cigarettes and other clothing. Jerrard remained a PoW at Salzburg until the end of the war, when he was repatriated back to England.

Jerrard chose to stay in the RAF and, after his investiture at Buckingham Palace on 5 April 1919, he served with the RAF Murmansk detachment in Russia. He rose to the rank of flight lieutenant but, due to ill health, retired from the service in 1933. Jerrard died at a nursing home in Lyme Regis, Dorset, on 14 May 1968, aged seventy. Three days later he was buried with full military honours.

3

SECOND WORLD WAR – BATTLE OF BRITAIN FIGHTER PILOTS

The Nazi Blitzkrieg was utterly formidable and unlike any invasion the modern world had yet witnessed. It spread swiftly across parts of Europe with a force and an aggression that could not be countered. By the early summer of 1940, the Germans were on the north-west coast of France and looking across to England. It soon became clear that Britain was the next target, but as Winston Churchill told the House of Commons on 18 June 1940: 'Hitler knows that he will have to break us in this island or lose the war.' In the same speech, Churchill said that 'the Battle of France is over. I expect that the Battle of Britain is about to begin.'

The Battle of Britain was the air conflict that officially began on 10 July 1940 and ended on 31 October 1940. During this time, in order to make invasion a reality, Germany tried to gain air superiority over the RAF. Thus began the biggest aerial bombardment ever seen, initially targeting shipping convoys and ports. Later, the Luftwaffe switched its offensive capabilities to RAF airfields, factories and infrastructure and, eventually, terror bombing. Critically, it was the Luftwaffe's transfer to the latter activity that enabled Fighter Command to repair its damaged bases and thereby return to sustained fighter operations. British single-seater Spitfire and Hurricane fighters were often in combat with Messerschmitt and Focke-Wulf fighters, while the Germans also used Heinkel, Dornier and Junkers bombers in vast numbers. (NB These aircraft are abbreviated, in turn, as 'Me', 'Fw', 'He', 'Do' and 'Ju' for the remainder of the book.) In return, Bomber Command and Coastal Command, using Bristol Blenheims and other bombers, flew sorties against targets in France and Germany, with mixed success. Nearly 2,000 (the numbers varied) serviceable Allied aircraft lined up against more than 2,550 serviceable German aircraft but the RAF held out and changed the course of the war.

Churchill summed up the effect of the battle and the contribution of Fighter Command on 20 August 1940 when he told the Commons: 'Never in the field of human conflict was so much owed by so many to so few.' After his speech, the Allies' Battle of Britain pilots became known affectionately as the 'Few'.

To me, the Blitz was very much part of the Battle of Britain and so I make no excuses for including the write-up on Sergeant (later Flight Lieutenant) Bill Ripley in this chapter.

Pilot Officer (later Air Vice-Marshal) 'Johnnie' Johnson, Flight Lieutenant (later Air Chief Vice-Marshal) Harry Broadhurst, Squadron Leader (later Air Commodore) John Thompson, Flight Lieutenant (later Group Captain) Edward Wells, Flight Sergeant (later Squadron Leader) Charlton 'Wag' Haw, Sergeant Józef Jeka and Squadron Leader Manfred Czernin all served during the Battle of Britain. However, because they were largely decorated for their gallantry in other theatres later in the war, their write-ups appear in Chapter 4 (with the exception of Czernin's, which appears in Chapter 8).

FLIGHT LIEUTENANT (LATER GROUP CAPTAIN) JOHN WILLIAM CHARLES SIMPSON

RAF
DECORATIONS: DISTINGUISHED FLYING CROSS (DFC) AND BAR
GAZETTED: 25 JUNE 1940 AND 30 MAY 1941

John Simpson was born in Ramsay St Mary's, Huntingdonshire, in 1913. Aged twenty-one, he went to live in Australia, where he trained as a sheep farmer. However, he fell ill and returned to Britain by ship. It was on his voyage home that he met and became firm friends with Hector Bolitho, a writer. En route, Bolitho introduced him to the RAF at Suez. After working as Bolitho's secretary for a while, Simpson enlisted in the RAF on a short-service commission in January 1936. He was posted to 43 Squadron – 'The Fighting Cocks' – at RAF Tangmere, Sussex, in October that year, flying Hawker Fury fighters. After the outbreak of the Second World War, he switched to Hurricanes and found himself under the immediate command of Peter Townsend, who later singled him out for praise in his history, *Duel of Eagles*.

Simpson was involved in two early engagements and shot down his first enemy aircraft in February 1940, writing afterwards: 'I hit him fair and square in the wings and fuselage. One of his engines stopped and bits of metal flew off. He then disappeared into some wisps of cloud . . . he was burning well when he disappeared into the mist above the sea.'

However, on 20 February 1940 Simpson crash-landed and was injured, writing the next day to Bolitho: 'Last night I had the first crash I've had since I have been in the Service.

I am very lucky to be alive . . . I have told you, I think, how strong our Hurricanes are. My being alive is proof of that all right . . . I look pretty bloody as I've broken my nose and my cheekbone and I'm bruised to hell.' By May, he had fully recovered and was promoted to flight commander. On 9 May, he claimed the first Do 17 bomber to be shot down off the English coast. In early June, he saw action around Dunkirk after the withdrawal. His DFC was announced on 25 June 1940 and his citation stated: 'In June 1940, Flight Lieutenant Simpson led a section of aircraft in a squadron patrol over Northern France. During an engagement with a superior enemy force he succeeded in destroying three enemy aircraft. This officer has led his flight on every patrol, showing not only courage and skill in fighting, but also an excellent example by his confident and offensive spirit. He has personally accounted for seven enemy aircraft.' Simpson later received his award from the King with his arm still in a sling: the result of another combat that saw him parachute to safety from his stricken aircraft. During his descent his adversary circled him several times, before saluting him from his cockpit and heading home.

On 7 July, Simpson hit a Me 109 fighter, which, he reported, then turned and collided with one of two Me 110s that were attacking him. Simpson claimed a Me 109 shot down on 19 July, but he was shot down himself on the same day and received an injury to one of his legs. After baling out, he also broke his collarbone on landing.

At the end of the year, Simpson returned to his squadron. On 30 November, he claimed a Ju 88 bomber, which he listed as his tenth victory. The following month Simpson was posted to command 245 Squadron in Northern Ireland, where he claimed two night-time victories on 10 May 1941. The Bar to his DFC was announced on 30 May 1941 and his citation stated: 'This officer has displayed great skill and initiative both as a squadron commander and an individual fighter. He has destroyed 12 enemy aircraft, of which two have been shot down at night.' In fact, by this time Simpson had earned a thirteenth, and final, victory: he was flying over the Irish Sea to collect some spare parts when he intercepted and shot down a Do 17. Once again he received his award from the King who asked him: 'How many have you destroyed?' Simpson replied 'Thirteen, sir.' Then George VI asked: 'When did you get your DFC?' Simpson told him that it was in June the previous year and the King, showing a good memory, asked: 'Wasn't your arm in a sling?'

In June 1942, Simpson left his unit for a staff post but was taken ill with an abdominal abscess that required surgery. In November 1942, during the North African landings, he was based on Gibraltar as a wing commander. However, by January 1943, he had been promoted to group captain and was destined for a desk job. In 1943, Bolitho published his book *Combat Report*, based on Simpson's regular letters to him (the book was later republished under the title *Finest of the Few*). Bolitho had been serving with the Royal Air Force Volunteer Reserve (RAFVR) since the outbreak of the war.

Simpson remained in the RAF after the war but his health, which had often been poor, deteriorated and he died on 12 August 1949, aged thirty-six. Simpson, whose portrait was painted by the war artists Eric Kennington and Cuthbert Orde, is buried in St Andrew's churchyard, near Tangmere.

SERGEANT (FLIGHT LIEUTENANT) LIONEL SANDERSON PILKINGTON

Royal Air Force Volunteer Reserve (RAFVR)
DECORATION: DISTINGUISHED FLYING MEDAL
(DFM)
GAZETTED: 16 JULY 1940

Lionel Pilkington was born in Hull, North Humberside, in early 1919. He enlisted in the RAFVR in 1938 and, after qualifying as a sergeant pilot, he was posted to 73 Squadron, in which he flew Hurricanes. Pilkington began his combat flying in January 1940 when he was posted to Flight Lieutenant E. J. 'Cobber' Kain's legendary Red Section. Kain was the RAF's first fighter ace of the Second World War and, at the time of his death, aged twenty-one, in June 1940, was the RAF's top ace.

Pilkington's first engagement was with a He 111 bomber south of Longuyon, France, on 25 January. In a further engagement on 26 March, he fired all his ammunition in a protracted dogfight with Me 110s and Dorniers. An enemy aircraft hit his propeller, causing his aircraft to drop some 10,000 feet with a 'spluttering engine'. It was not until after the 'Phoney War', of September 1939 to March 1940 (the first eight months of the conflict in which there was a lack of major operations by the Western Allies), when Germany invaded the Low Countries in May 1940, that 73 Squadron embarked on a period of constant action.

During this hectic period, Pilkington kept a diary of his various flights. On 11 May, he wrote of action over Mourmelon, France, when flying a Hurricane: 'I get a Messerschmitt Me 110 but one also gets me! A cannon shot in the tailplane passes through the fuselage and out the other side! Bullets in the engine, shot away throttle control; cannot close throttle and bullet hits in cockpit, beside rudder bar. Land on [Rouvres] 'drome by cutting switches, rudder control wire practically sheared.' Charles Gardner, the war correspondent, witnessed Pilkington in action again on 13 May, when he shared a 'kill' of a Do 17 bomber. However, the enemy aircraft's rear gunner was a good shot and Pilkington wrote: 'We all came back very riddled.' Pilkington saw combat again the same evening against a brace of Heinkels, one of which was downed by his squadron leader. The next day, during an early morning patrol over the Sedan battlefront, Pilkington and a fellow pilot both damaged Do 17s. Pilkington saw that the aircraft he had hit lost large pieces of its starboard engine and that its windscreen was covered in oil. The Dornier made it back to base despite having three of its crew wounded. Later the same day, while one of six pilots on a similar patrol, Pilkington engaged seven Stuka bombers. However, they were 'ambushed' by Me 109s and two of the British pilots were shot down and killed. 'This is a hell of a blow to me. Hell!' Pilkington wrote. On 15 May, as the punishing schedule for 73 Squadron continued, Pilkington was again in the thick of the action. In his diary entry, he wrote: 'Panic take-off. First off, chase some Heinkels but do not catch them. Come back to base and chase five Dorniers. Get starboard engine then jettison bombs. Crossfire gets me in oil and patrol tanks, also glycol. Get back to drome, glycol tank melted and run into engine. Face slightly burnt and eyes sore from glycol. C.O. says a good show.'

In air battles over Lille on 19 May, Pilkington added another 'probable' to his tally, only to make a forced landing as a result of damage to his aircraft from return fire. 'Think I got a He.

111 but one of the rear-gunners gets my oil tank and I fly back. See three He. 111s doing dive-bombing 200 yards away; also run into 15 Me. 110s. Fly back in cloud and land at French bomber drome. Given a fine lunch.' The end of May saw the first of the pilots from 73 Squadron being recalled to the UK. Pilkington's DFM was announced on 16 July 1940 and his citation stated: 'For exceptional gallantry and devotion to duty in the air from January 1940, and especially from 10–15 May 1940, during which period this airman pilot displayed unflagging zeal and courage in the face of superior forces of the enemy. He has shot down five enemy aircraft.'

In the same month as his DFM was announced, Pilkington was posted to 7 Operational Training Unit (OTU) at RAF Hawarden, Cheshire, where he survived a collision with a student pilot. Unusually, on 20 September, during the height of the Battle of Britain, Pilkington was flying a cannon-armed Spitfire 1b when he intercepted and shot down a Ju 88 bomber over North Wales. Pilkington was commissioned into the RAFVR on 30 October 1940. Early in 1941, he was posted to 111 Squadron and became involved in offensive patrols and escorts. However, on 20 September 1941, he was shot down and killed by Me 109s over Hazebrouk, France. Aged twenty-two, Pilkington had been due to get married just six days later in Peterborough, Cambridgeshire, to his fiancée, Barbara Walker. He is commemorated on the Runnymede Memorial, near Windsor, Berkshire.

FLYING OFFICER (LATER WING COMMANDER) JOHN CONNELL FREEBORN

RAF
DECORATIONS: DISTINGUISHED FLYING CROSS (DFC) AND BAR
GAZETTED: 13 AUGUST 1940 AND 25 FEBRUARY 1941

John Freeborn held the distinction of flying more operational hours during the Battle of Britain than any other RAF pilot. He was already an experienced pilot by the time the battle commenced and, for his relentless bravery, he was also decorated by the USA and Poland. However, he had a disdain for authority and this led to many clashes with his superiors during his distinguished flying career. Late in his long life, Freeborn wrote his autobiography and was also the subject of a biography.

Born on 1 December 1919, the son of a Leeds banker, Freeborn was educated at the city's grammar school. Although bright, his dislike of what he saw as petty authority made him relieved to leave the school. At the age of eighteen, he enlisted in the RAF on a short-service commission early in 1938 and was flying solo after just four hours twenty-eight minutes' logged flying time, a little over half the average. His accuracy while flying in the air was more than twice the average during his training. Freeborn initially flew Gloster Gauntlets, but in October 1938 he joined 74 (Tiger) Squadron and from February 1939 he flew Spitfires.

On 6 September 1939, Freeborn took part in an action that was later dubbed the Battle of Barking Creek. In a tragic misunderstanding, two Hurricanes from 56 Squadron were intercepted and shot down by 74 Squadron, thereby becoming the first British victims of Spitfire 'friendly fire'. To his dismay, Freeborn shot down Pilot Officer Montague Hulton-Harrop, who thereby became the first RAF pilot to die in the Second World War. Freeborn and a fellow pilot were court-martialled on 7 October 1939, but were acquitted of any liability or blame, despite their squadron commander testifying against them. However, the incident led to a complete overhaul of Fighter Command's plotting system used to track Allied and enemy aircraft.

Freeborn put the tragedy behind him and, just months later, he was heavily engaged in the air fighting during the retreat of the British Expeditionary Force (BEF) to Dunkirk in May 1940. Over a period of just six days, the squadron accounted for nineteen enemy aircraft, including two shot down by Freeborn. During one combat, his Spitfire was badly damaged and he crash-landed on the beach near Calais but managed to get a lift home in a returning aircraft. During late May, Freeborn also claimed three enemy aircraft as 'probables'.

However, it was during the Battle of Britain that Freeborn repeatedly excelled, flying into action time and time again. On 10 July, the opening day of the battle, he shot down a Me 109 fighter over Deal, Kent. During the remainder of the battle, Freeborn shared a 'probable' Do 17 bomber on 24 July and shot down a Me 109 on 28 July, destroyed two Me 110s and a Me 109 and probably another on 11 August, destroyed a Do 17 on 13 August, destroyed another on 11 September and damaged a He 111 bomber on 14 September. His astonishing success on 11 August (three 'kills' and a 'probable') came when he flew four missions in eight hours.

At the height of the Battle of Britain – on 13 August 1940 – Freeborn was awarded the DFC. His citation stated: 'This officer has taken part in nearly all offensive patrols carried out by his squadron since the commencement of the war, including operations over the Low Countries and Dunkirk, and, more recently, engagements over the Channel and S.E. of England. During this period of intensive air warfare he has destroyed four enemy aircraft. His high courage and exceptional abilities as a leader have materially contributed to the notable successes and high standard of efficiency maintained by his squadron.' Just over a fortnight later, on 28 August, he was promoted to flight commander. In the same month, he was painted by Cuthbert Orde, the war artist.

On 17 November 1940, Freeborn shared a Me 109, while on 5 December he shot down two Me 109s, shared another and damaged a fourth. He then damaged Do 17s on 5 February and 4 March 1941. Freeborn was awarded the Bar to his DFC on 25 February 1941 and his citation stated: 'This officer has continuously engaged in operations since the beginning of the war. He has destroyed at least twelve enemy aircraft and damaged many more. He is a keen and courageous leader.' In 1941, he married Rita Fielder. After his long period with 74 Squadron, Freeborn was, in June 1941, posted to 57 Operational Training Unit (OTU) at RAF Hawarden, Cheshire, training pilots from overseas to fly Spitfires. Following America's entry into the war at the end of 1941, Freeborn was posted to the United States, where he instructed pilots and also tested US fighter aircraft.

He returned to operational flying in 1943, when he flew Spitfires with 602 Squadron. Here his role was to provide fighter escort to RAF bombers attacking shipping and port installations. On 1 June, Freeborn was given command of 118 Squadron, where he had a similar role. After Freeborn was promoted to become one of the RAF's youngest wing commanders, he spent the first six months of 1944 commanding No. 286 Wing, flying operations from southern Italy in support of the Allied armies. During this period, the RAF attacked German installations and convoys in the Balkans and provided defence for Allied convoys in Italian waters.

In late 1944, Freeborn returned to Britain, where he served out the remainder of the war, before leaving the RAF in 1946. After qualifying as a driving instructor, Freeborn joined Tetley Walker as regional director for one of their soft drinks brands. He took early retirement, and following the death of his wife in 1979, moved to Spain in the early 1980s. He married his second wife, Peta, in 1983. In 2000 they came back to Britain, settling in North Wales, but Peta died just a year later.

Although Freeborn had been cleared of any blame for the 'friendly fire' death in 1939, the victim, Montague Hulton-Harrop, always remained in his thoughts. Shortly before his death, Freeborn said: 'I think about him nearly every day. I always have done. I've had a good life – and he should have had a good life, too.' Freeborn died on 28 August 2010, aged ninety.

PILOT OFFICER (LATER FLIGHT LIEUTENANT) DORIAN GEORGE GRIBBLE
RAF
DECORATION: DISTINGUISHED FLYING CROSS (DFC)
GAZETTED: 13 AUGUST 1940

George Gribble was born in Hendon, north London, on 18 June 1919. However, he was brought up on the Isle of Wight, where he attended Ryde School. In March 1938,

Gribble enlisted in the RAF on a short-service commission. In December 1938, after training as a pilot, he was posted to 54 Squadron, a Gladiator unit based at RAF Hornchurch, Essex. Shortly after his arrival, the squadron was re-equipped with Spitfires. Gribble was confirmed to the rank of pilot officer on 7 March 1939.

54 Squadron went into action shortly after the German invasion of the Low Countries, and Gribble flew his first offensive patrol to Ostend on 16 May 1940. The previous evening, in an operational briefing delivered to the pilots in the officers' mess billiards room, Al Deere, the legendary New Zealand fighter pilot, had scanned the audience. Deere, who became an ace during the Battle of France and was eventually credited with twenty-two 'kills', recalled: 'The central figure was, as always, Pilot Officer George Gribble. Very English, very good looking and bubbling over with the enthusiasm of his twenty years, he epitomized the product of the public school; young yet mature, carefree yet serious when the situation required and above all possessing a courageous gaiety which he was later to display in abundance.'

On 24 May 1940, Gribble and his squadron were involved in a heavy combat with the Luftwaffe on their second patrol of the day. There was a large-scale dogfight over the Dunkirk–Calais sector in which Colin Gray, a New Zealand Battle of Britain pilot who was eventually credited with a remarkable twenty-eight 'kills', later recalled seeing 'nothing but black crosses hurtling around in all directions'. Gribble destroyed a Me 109 fighter after firing 1,700 rounds from a range of 250 yards. He later recalled: 'I saw my tracer crossing into his aircraft while he was on his back. He just fell into the ground . . .' However, Gribble's Spitfire was badly damaged the following day when his squadron was jumped by about a dozen Me 109s. Gribble carried out a forced landing on a beach near Dunkirk where he removed his radio equipment from the cockpit before finding passage home in a steamer bound for Dover.

54 Squadron was now due a rest: it moved to RAF Catterick, Yorkshire, on 28 May, and then returned to Hornchurch on 4 June. However, it would not be until July that it returned to front-line duties, when it began to play a full and active role in the Battle of Britain, flying from RAF Rochford, Essex, and RAF Manston, Kent. On 24 July, Gribble took part over North Foreland, Kent, in what Colin Gray described as a 'terrific dogfight'. Gribble claimed a brace of Me 109s destroyed, although these 'kills' were unconfirmed. The following day, when just five of 54's Spitfires joined in combat with two waves of Ju 87 bombers, escorted by about eighty Me 109 fighters, Gribble led Green Section. However, after two of their number had been shot down, 54's survivors were compelled to return to Manston. On 26 July, the squadron again moved to Catterick and on the same day Gribble was appointed flight commander of 'B' Flight.

Gribble's DFC was announced on 13 August 1940 and his citation stated: 'Since the outbreak of war, this young officer has taken part in most of the offensive patrols carried out by his squadron, including operations over the Low Countries and Dunkirk, and intensive air fighting over the Channel. Pilot Officer Gribble has led his section, and recently his flight, in a courageous and determined manner . . . This officer has personally destroyed three Messerschmitt 109's, and damaged many others.'

In early August, 54 Squadron returned to Hornchurch from

where, on 15 August, Gribble damaged a Ju 87 in a dogfight over Dover–Hawkinge sector. The enemy aircraft that Gribble hit was one of the thirty Ju 87s with a forty-strong Me 109 escort. Later the same day, he also destroyed a Me 109 and damaged a Do 17. In his combat report, Gribble wrote of chasing the Messerschmitt out to sea. 'I gave the enemy aircraft a longish burst from 350 closing to 250 yards. The enemy aircraft dived and then burst into flames . . .'

On 16 August, Gribble damaged a Me 109 east of Hornchurch. 'I managed to get in a long burst (10 seconds), opening at 300 yards and closing to 200 yards range. Smoke began to pour out of the machine and it went into a dive.' Two days later Gribble acted as 'Blue Leader' in 'B' Flight, and destroyed another Me 109. Furthermore, he also damaged a Me 110 and two He 111s, these being his first successes in Spitfire R6899 (the aircraft in which he flew continuously until early September). Of the Me 109, he wrote in his combat report: 'The enemy leader broke away down southwards. I followed him down; when the speed was 400 [mph] he pulled up gently, presenting an easy target. Then he levelled out, and I came within 100 yards, firing a long burst into the engine and cockpit. He burst into flames and went down slide-slipping and then on his back, out of control.'

On the afternoon of 20 August, Gribble took a massive risk, for which he was commended by his group commander, by pursuing nine Heinkels across to France. It was just the sort of daring deed that prompted Winston Churchill to make his famous tribute to the 'Few' on the same day. On 22 August, Gribble got a 'probable' Me 109 off Deal, having fired half of his ammunition into the enemy fighter at 100 yards' range. His combat report stated: 'This was just above sea level and the enemy pilot pulled back his stick and at 500 feet tried to do a flick stall – from which he could not possibly have pulled out.' Gribble damaged a Me 110 over the Dover–Folkestone sector on 24 August and later the same day he destroyed a Me 109 which, he reported 'was seen to crash west ofFaversham [Kent] by the searchlights'.

On 28 August, in 54's second patrol of the day and in a combat with thirty Dorniers that were heading for RAF Rochford, Essex, he destroyed one of the Me 109 escorts, followed by another of the same type later that afternoon. This was in an action against what Colin Gray described as 'a massive fighter sweep of Me. 110s and 109s'. On this occasion, Gribble closed to a range of just fifty yards, later reporting: 'I saw the pilot bale out.'

The 31 August proved a momentous day for 54 Squadron: it lost four Spitfires (though fortunately no pilots) and its airfield was bombed twice, once while the squadron was taking off. Yet Gribble and his number two hit back and 'managed to put paid to a 109 who had rather foolishly come down to ground level to see what he could find'. Gribble had also shot dead a cow, later explaining to Al Deere: 'In the course of our chase we crossed a meadow full of grazing cows and unfortunately I chose that moment to fire another burst. A cow was right in my line of sight and took the full blast. It went up vertically for about twenty feet, just as if someone had ignited a rocket tied to its tail, before plomping back to earth. I'll bet there's still a look of amazement on that cow's face when the farmer finds it.'

By this time, as Deere later admitted, 'Our morale was getting a bit low because there were only three of us left in the Squadron – George Gribble, Colin Gray and me – who had any combat experience. We had been there the whole time and were pretty tired. Each time we went up, there seemed to be more and more Germans up there.' Such was the pressure the experienced pilots were under that Gribble's logbook recorded no fewer than four patrols being flown on 1 and 2 September. On the second day, he shot down a Me 109 in a combat over Kent, the enemy aircraft crashing and its pilot being killed.

On 3 September, there was a temporary respite and his logbook recorded: 'Presented with the Distinguished Flying Cross by His Majesty King George VI at Buckingham Palace'. Gribble's combat experience was again to the fore on 27 October, when he damaged a Ju 88 in his final official Battle of Britain encounter.

On 6 November, he damaged an enemy aircraft south-east of Catterick when his score now stood at six and one shared destroyed, two unconfirmed destroyed, two 'probables' and at least nine damaged. By the time 54 Squadron returned to Hornchurch in February 1941, Gribble was the sole remaining member of its original wartime line-up.

For the next three months or so, Gribble took part in a series of cross-Channel offensive and convoy patrols until, on a bomber escort sortie on 4 June 1941, he was seen leading his section against two Me 109s, when his Spitfire was suddenly 'bounced' by further enemy fighters. Gribble was heard to say over his radio: 'Engine cut, baling out.' A fellow pilot saw his parachute going down into the sea, some twelve miles off the English coast. Boats got to the spot where Gribble hit the water but, despite searching for him for four hours, the pilot could not be found and he was presumed dead, only two weeks before his twenty-second birthday. In a letter to Gribble's mother dated 9 June, the squadron's CO wrote: 'George was an exceptional pilot and leader and also a very keen officer. He was also very entertaining in the Mess and most loved by all of us. The whole Squadron will miss a very gallant and brave gentleman for a very long time to come . . .'

On the same day, Gribble's girlfriend, who served in the Women's Auxiliary Air Force (WAAF), also wrote to the pilot's mother saying: 'I don't need to tell you how wonderful he was and how full of life, but I do want to tell you how loved he was by everyone, and to use his own expression – what a "whizzy-bang pilot".'

Al Deere wrote that Gribble 'typified more than any other the spirit of the Battle of Britain pilot', but perhaps his final epitaph should be the one from 54's Operational Record Book: 'Flight Lieutenant D. G. Gribble, D.F.C., was the last member of the old 54 [Squadron]. His exploits are recorded on nearly every page of this history. It only remains to be said that his personality was everywhere identified with the name of the Squadron and no one who knew or heard his happy laughter would ever forget the affection they felt from the first.' Gribble is commemorated on the Runnymede Memorial, near Windsor, Berkshire.

SERGEANT (LATER SQUADRON LEADER) JAMES HARRY LACEY
Royal Air Force Volunteer Reserve (RAFVR)/RAF
DECORATIONS: DISTINGUISHED FLYING MEDAL (DFM) AND BAR
GAZETTED: 23 AUGUST 1940 AND 26 NOVEMBER 1940

James 'Ginger' Lacey was quite simply one of the greatest fighter aces of the Second World War, including being the second highest scoring British fighter pilot of the Battle of Britain. By the end of the war, he was credited with twenty-eight enemy aircraft destroyed, five 'probables' and nine damaged. A talented pilot, a brilliant marksman and an authoritative leader, he was also understated and proud of his modest roots.

The son of a cattle dealer, Lacey was born in Wetherby, Yorkshire, on 1 February 1917. A bright pupil, he was educated at King James Grammar School in Knaresborough. At sixteen, Lacey became an apprentice chemist but, having succeeded in his intermediate exams, he brought his career in pharmaceuticals to a close. In 1937 he enlisted in the RAFVR and, having attended a sergeant pilots' course at RAF Scone, near Perth, Scotland, he was flying solo after less than seven hours in the air. In 1938, Lacey was appointed as an instructor at the Yorkshire Aeroplane Club yet, by Christmas of that year, he had succeeded in writing off one of his employer's aircraft. After completing 150 hours with the RAFVR, Lacey joined 1 Squadron on six weeks' attachment at RAF Tangmere, Sussex. On the outbreak of war, he was posted to 501 (County of Gloucester) Squadron, an Auxiliary Air Force unit based near Bristol. Lacey accompanied his new unit to France in support of the Advanced Air Striking Force during May 1940. Just three days after arriving in France, Lacey flew in action for the first time.

It had been intended for Lacey to fly number three in Red Section but, due to a small mechanical problem with his Hurricane, his aircraft was still on the ground long after his comrades had taken off. Eventually, he coaxed his aircraft into action but, rising to 20,000 feet, there was no sign of the rest of his section. Lacey then sighted a He 111 bomber at 10,000 feet but, before he could attack it, a Me 109 fighter appeared between his and the enemy aircraft. Without hesitation, Lacey started a full-bore 5,000-feet dive, descending to the sound of 'Oh Johnny' played by Jack Teagarden and his Orchestra on his radio system. After flying past the Messerschmitt going too fast to fire, he banked and climbed and went in for a second attempt, this time chasing and firing, destroying the enemy aircraft with a huge explosion. Next he shot away one of the wings of the Heinkel and, with 'Oh Johnny' coming to a close, headed for base. Once there, his CO was annoyed that he had not flown with the rest of the section and fellow pilots and ground crew were sceptical of his claims, especially as there had been no reports of enemy aircraft being destroyed.

However, Lacey's section was soon airborne again and, led by Flight Lieutenant Charles Griffiths, they attacked a formation of Me 110s. Individual dogfights took place and Lacey found himself pitted against a single enemy pilot. After banking inside his rival, he fired a two-second burst into the enemy aircraft's port-engine cowling. Two further bursts saw the aircraft go into a vertical dive and crash close to watching French troops. By the time Lacey rejoined the fray, he found himself in the middle of a defensive circle of Messerschmitts. Lacey dived so forcefully at lightning speed that he came close to lapsing into unconsciousness. Eventually, his Hurricane flipped through the perpendicular and came out of the dive flying inverted and level. Although dazed and shaken, Lacey returned safely to Bétheniville. By this time, his first two 'kills' had been verified by French gunners, leaving him credited with three enemy aircraft from his first day in action. This was extraordinary by any standards, and all before breakfast. Lacey was awarded the French Croix de Guerre for his bravery, later writing in his pilot's logbook: 'Some sort of French gong awarded for this morning's work. Cracking fine show.'

With 501 Squadron remaining in the thick of the action in France, it found itself bombed by more than fifty He 111s while at Boos airfield. Both Lacey and 'Cobber' Kain, the legendary New Zealand ace, sheltered in a dugout and it was only after they had emerged safely that they realised it was a submerged fuel dump. The squadron took off immediately and destroyed fourteen Heinkels without loss, Lacey scoring two more 'kills' while also leading Yellow Section. With the Battle of France drawing to a close, Lacey's squadron transferred to Le Mans.

Lacey had a close call after an inconclusive combat with a Me 109 over Le Mans on 9 June when, after a forced landing, his aircraft was thrown on to its back. As blood streamed down his face from a cut, water and petrol fumes filled the cockpit. Lacey managed to kick out the Perspex canopy. However, overwhelmed by fumes, he passed out, still in the cockpit, and was saved by French peasants who cut him free and took him to No. 1 Medical Receiving Station. As France capitulated, Lacey was ordered to Jersey and, two days later, back to Tangmere, Sussex. During the Battle of France, his squadron had claimed nearly sixty victories.

When the Battle of Britain began, the slim, fair-haired Lacey was twenty-three years old and already an ace, with a Mention in Despatches and a French Croix de Guerre. After two weeks at RAF Croydon, south London, the squadron was moved to RAF Middle Wallop, Hampshire, to re-equip. However, on 20 July, it was scrambled and ordered to defend a convoy off Jersey. After flying out over Portland Bill, they saw a horde of Ju 87 bombers, with Messerschmitt escorts, and went into battle. After Lacey spotted a Me 109 turning towards him, he broke hard and, after several decreasing inward turns, put a burst into the fuselage. He then followed the stricken aircraft down to finish it off. Next he engaged a Me 109 which was crossing his path at 90 degrees. As Lacey turned for a second attack, he saw that Flying Officer 'Pan' Cox was on the enemy's tail, finishing it off. Typically, Lacey put in no claim for the second 'kill', allowing his comrade his first victory.

Three days later, Lacey had another near miss when, after being caught in searchlights, 'friendly' anti-aircraft fire opened up on him during a night patrol, mistaking him for a He 111 that was also in the vicinity. Lacey had to spiral down to avoid being hit. His squadron now became based at RAF Gravesend, Kent, in the Biggin Hill sector, and prepared itself for the full onslaught of the Luftwaffe. On 12 August, the squadron took on thirty Ju 87s after its leader announced over the radio: 'Bastards at three o'clock.' Lacey hit an enemy aircraft with two quick bursts and saw it crash into the sea. At 4,000 feet, he engaged a second raider, killing the rear gunner with a burst of fire. After another burst of fire, the Ju 87 burst into flames. At midday, as the squadron confronted thirty Me 110s and twenty Me 109s, Lacey exhausted his fire on one of the Me 110s and saw the enemy pilot take to his parachute. Later the same day, the undercarriage of Lacey's Hurricane collapsed on the runway after landing.

On 15 August, Lacey damaged a Do 17 bomber; the next day he claimed a Me 109 as a 'probable'. On 23 August, Lacey's DFM was announced acknowledging his six 'kills' and praising his 'great determination and coolness in combat'. On 24 August, the day after his award was announced, Lacey flew a staggering eight times. At 10.30 a.m., he joined a combat involving thirty Do 17s and Me 109s. During his second flight of the day, he destroyed a Ju 88 and damaged a Do 215. However, during his fourth sortie, a bullet in his engine forced him down at RAF Lympne, Kent. Lacey had lunch in the mess, while his aircraft was repaired, and then embarked on four more sorties.

By now, the pressure of near-endless combats had started to unsettle Lacey: every time he heard the order to scramble, he ran to the back of the dispersal hut and threw up. Yet there was no respite and on 30 August, during his second flight of the day, he engaged Me 110s over Kent, claiming one as a 'probable'. He destroyed a He 111 on his third flight but it was his fifth flight that was the most memorable because it was filmed by a newsreel unit that had been given permission to work from Gravesend aerodrome. They filmed the CO announcing: 'Scramble! Bandits in Thames estuary!' before Lacey and his fellow pilots soared into action. The squadron quickly encountered an armada of enemy aircraft. In the ensuing combat, Lacey shot down a He 111 and damaged a Me 110. However, his aircraft then came under accurate fire and was hit in the engine and wings. Covered in oil, Lacey slid back the canopy and prepared to bale out, only to have second thoughts about plunging into the Thames. However, deciding he was high enough to glide back to Gravesend, Lacey opted to do just that and, to the delight of the film crew, he made a perfect, unpowered landing. The crew counted eighty-seven bullet holes in his aircraft.

On 31 August 1940, Lacey completed a highly successful month by destroying another enemy aircraft over Hornchurch, Essex. On 2 September, he shot down two more Me 109s and damaged a Do 215. Three days later, two more Me 109s fell to his guns. On 7 September, Lacey went on leave with fifteen confirmed victories to his credit. Six days later, he returned to find the squadron based at RAF Kenley, Surrey, where constant thick fog made flying conditions hazardous. On the day he returned from leave, 13 September, a He III dropped its bombs on Buckingham Palace and a volunteer was called on to try to shoot down the raider. Lacey took to the skies in search of the culprit, knowing the weather conditions meant he would probably be unable to land and would have to bale out of his aircraft. For two hours, Lacey was guided on to the He III's path by an air controller. As he approached the coast, the enemy aircraft slipped from the clouds and Lacey put a burst into the rear turret, killing the gunner. With the two aircraft flying just feet apart, enemy fire tore a gaping hole in the bottom of the cockpit in Lacey's Hurricane which ignited the glycol. However, Lacey's continuous fire had set both the engines of the enemy aircraft alight. While the He III, with its dead and wounded, later crashed in France, Lacey baled out of his stricken Hurricane and saw it crash into the ground near Leeds Castle, Kent. During Lacey's descent, he had to put out flames which had burnt his trouser legs to the knee. After landing, the new member of the Caterpillar Club (the name referred to the silky threads that made the original parachutes), for those who have successfully parachuted from a stricken aircraft, declined hospital treatment.

As the Battle of Britain reached its climax in mid-September, Lacey was again in the thick of the action. On 15 September, one of the heaviest days of fighting and which later became Battle of Britain Day, Lacey was attacked head-on by twelve Me 109s. He dived under them, pulling up sharply in a loop, and attacked the tail-end enemy aircraft while still upside down. His attack was successful and he saw the aircraft dive vertically in flames. His attack on a second Me 109 produced a white stream of glycol before making good his escape. At 7 p.m. the same day, he flew against the Luftwaffe's third wave of the day and, just an hour later, he shot down a Me 109 and a He 111. In his logbook, he wrote of the second attack: 'Certainly fooled this one!'

On 17 September, he single-handedly attacked fifteen Me 109s, but he was shot down and had to bale out. This time his Hurricane crashed at Winstead Court, Kent, and he later admitted he had been 'well and truly over-confident'. Yet he appeared unfazed by his latest brush with death, writing in his logbook: 'Quite pleasant to be shot down by fighters for a change.' By then, the Battle of Britain was in its final phase and the aerial combats were less frequent. Lacey, however, made sure he continued to leave his mark. On 30 September, he damaged a Ju 88 and on 7 October he claimed a Me 109 as a 'probable'. He destroyed Me 109s on both 12 and 26 October before, on the penultimate day of the battle, shooting down a Me 109 and damaging another. During the Battle of France and the Battle of Britain, Lacey had been shot down or forced to land an incredible nine times.

On 26 November 1940, Lacey was awarded a long over-due Bar to his DFM. His citation credited him with nineteen 'kills' and praised his 'consistent efficiency and great courage'. In the New Year, and already with twenty-three victories, Lacey was given a commission and promoted to acting flight lieutenant. Shortly afterwards 501 Squadron was converted to Spitfires and on 26 June 1941 he was appointed to the command of 'A' Flight.

The intriguing comments in Lacey's logbook for 7 July

failed to tell the full story. He wrote: 'Squirted at Ju. 88. Think I hit him. C.O. definitely hit him. Squirted at C.O. Definitely missed him.' In the height of a chase, Lacey had lost sight of the enemy aircraft and then fired on the Spitfire of his squadron leader, briefly mistaking it for the Ju 88. His CO apparently saw the funny side of this error. On 11 July, Lacey shot down a Me 109 and he damaged another on 14 July. On 17 July, he claimed a He 59 seaplane shot down and on 24 July, he claimed two Me 109s. This incident, however, saw him in yet another close shave after he was attacked as he homed in on Brest harbour, where he intended to attack two German ships. Two Me 109s had dived down from 31,000 feet and, after a frantic combat, Lacey ran out of ammunition. As the two enemy aircraft came in for the 'kill', Lacey pulled back the stick and his aircraft climbed almost vertically, seconds before the two 109s collided.

On 18 August, Lacey was posted to 57 Operational Training Unit (OTU) where he served as a flight instructor. The following year he returned to combat operations with 602 Squadron. On 24 March, Lacey tackled and damaged a Fw 190 over France and the following month he damaged two more. He was promoted to squadron leader in May and posted to 81 Group as Tactics Officer. In September, Lacey joined the experimental unit at Boscombe Down, Wiltshire, where he tested Hurricane equipment. November 1942 saw Lacey appointed as the Chief Instructor at No. 1 Special Low Attack Instructors' School at Millfield, Northumberland. Then on 26 March 1943, Lacey was posted overseas – to India.

There, Lacey joined 20 Squadron, in which he flew various aircraft, from Lysanders to Hurricanes. He also turned down a senior role in order to continue flying combat operations. On

23 November 1944, he took over command of 17 Squadron at Pale, Assam. On 14 December 1944, the squadron moved to Burma where it began its association with 3/1 Gurkha Regiment. Lacey raised morale among his men by allowing them to shave their heads Gurkha-style: he used unorthodox methods but had a reputation for getting things done. Christmas Day saw Lacey's squadron support the Gurkhas in their attack on the village of Kin, while his squadron also provided fighter escorts for Lord Mountbatten's visits to the front. On 29 January 1945, Lacey led the squadron in operations that resulted in the capture of Kabwet. His logbook entry displayed little remorse for his victims: 'Blew Jap soldier in half with 20 mm. Bags of gore. Loads of congrats from the General.'

Lacey scored his final victory on 19 February 1945 when he shot down a Japanese 'Oscar' Nakajima Ki. 43 – the only Japanese fighter he ever encountered in the air – with just nine rounds of cannon. After the fall of Rangoon, the squadron was withdrawn and re-equipped with Spitfire XIVs prior to the proposed invasion of Malaya. In the event, the Japanese surrendered on 15 August, but still the squadron was sent to Malaya before moving on to Japan in HMS *Vengeance*. Lacey then won the 'race' to put the first Spitfire above Japan, just beating 11 Squadron's CO into the air, and becoming one of only a small number of surviving combat pilots to be in the air on the first day of the war and the last. By this time, too, he had married a Wren in India on 8 July 1945: he and his wife, Sheila, had three daughters.

Lacey returned to Britain in May 1946 and remained in the RAF, reverting to the rank of flight lieutenant. In 1948, he became a fighter control specialist in Hong Kong. His retirement from the RAF in 1967 was marked by a fly-past of

Lightning jets and he was given the honorary rank of squadron leader. In civilian life, he became a flying instructor based at Bridlington, Yorkshire, and in 1968 he was appointed as a technical adviser for the film *Battle of Britain*. In his latter years, Lacey also ran a freight company.

The incomparable Ginger Lacey died on 30 May 1989, aged seventy-two. In September 2001, a plaque was unveiled at Priory church, Bridlington, in his memory.

PILOT OFFICER (LATER WING COMMANDER) HARBOURNE MACKAY STEPHEN

Royal Air Force Volunteer Reserve (RAFVR)
DECORATIONS: DISTINGUISHED FLYING CROSS (DFC) AND BAR, DISTINGUISHED SERVICE ORDER (DSO)
GAZETTED: 27 AUGUST 1940, 15 NOVEMBER 1940 AND 24 DECEMBER 1940

Harbourne Stephen, who was awarded three gallantry medals in just five months, was one of a small number of pilots to gain ace status with five victories in a single day.

Stephen, the son of a bank manager, was born in Elgin, Scotland, on 18 April 1916. He was educated between the ages of four and seven by a governess. Later he attended a school in Edinburgh and, finally, Shrewsbury School in Shropshire. His early career, after leaving school at fifteen, was in the newspaper industry: he was initially a copy boy with Allied Newspapers before moving on to the advertising staff of the *Evening Standard*. In April 1937, Stephen enlisted in the RAFVR in which he received his training. After achieving the required number of flying hours, he was given six months' leave of absence from his job in order to train with the regular RAF. In early September 1939, Stephen began training at 11 Group Fighter Pool at St Athan, South Wales.

After converting to Hurricanes, Stephen was posted to 43 Squadron – 'The Fighting Cocks' – at RAF Tangmere, Sussex, as a sergeant pilot. He and his squadron had their first encounter with the Luftwaffe on 28 March 1940 when he was flying in Yellow Section. After a He 111 was spotted, his section leader attacked and damaged the bomber before 43 Squadron shot it down. In April 1940, Stephen was commissioned and posted to 74 Squadron at RAF Hornchurch, Essex. On 24 May, Stephen shared in the destruction of a Henschel Hs 126 reconnaissance aircraft and also a Do 17 bomber. On 26 May, Stephen shared another Hs 126 and the following day he destroyed a Me 109 and shared a Do 17.

From July to December 1940, Stephen, by then twenty-four, was repeatedly in the thick of the action. On 28 July, he damaged a Me 109, while on 11 August he destroyed a Me 109 and also claimed a 'probable' Me 109 and a Me 110, and damaged two Me 109s and Me 110. On 13 August, he probably destroyed a Do 17 and on 27 August he was awarded the DFC and his citation stated:

> Since May, 1940, Pilot Officer Stephen has flown continuously with his squadron on offensive patrols, and taken part in numerous engagements against the enemy throughout the Dunkirk operations. He has also been engaged protecting shipping in the Channel and has taken part in intensive air operations over the Kentish coast. During one day in August, in company with his squadron, Pilot Officer Stephen

participated in four successive combats against large formations of enemy aircraft over the Thames Estuary and Channel and during these engagements he shot down five enemy aircraft. He has now destroyed a total of twelve enemy aircraft and has always displayed great coolness and determination in pressing home his attacks against the enemy.

On 11 September he destroyed a Ju 88 bomber and damaged a Me 109. On 1 October, he damaged a He 111 and four days later he shared a Do 17. On 20 October, he claimed a Me 109 destroyed and probably another, while on 27 October he destroyed another Me 109. On 14 November, Stephen destroyed three Ju 87s. The following day Stephen not only damaged a Me 109 but he was also awarded a Bar to his DFC when his citation stated that 'his courage and skill as a fighter pilot have been a great incentive to other pilots in his squadron'.

Stephen shared in the destruction of two Me 109s on both 17 and 30 October. On 2 December, he probably destroyed a Me 109 and three days later he shared in the destruction of another. On Christmas Eve 1940, Stephen was awarded the first immediate DSO of the war when citation stated:

One day in November 1940, Pilot Officer Stephen led a section of his squadron in an attack against an escorted formation of enemy bombers, three of which he destroyed. Later in the month he undertook a voluntary patrol in company with his flight commander and destroyed a Messerschmitt 109. This success brought the number of aircraft destroyed by members of his home station to the magnificent total of 600, and at the same time increased his own score to nineteen. His exceptional courage and skill have greatly enhanced the fine spirit shown by his squadron.

Stephen was posted to 59 Operational Training Unit (OTU) near Edinburgh on 11 January 1941, but this was later altered to a secondment to the Royal Aircraft Establishment, Farnborough, Hampshire. In late July 1941, Stephen took command of 234 Squadron at RAF Wittering, Cambridgeshire. On 12 August, he damaged a Ju 88 and on 15 October he shared in the destruction of a Me 109. Early in 1942, Stephen was posted to the Far East, where he was a wing leader at Dum Dum and Jessore, India. Later he commanded No. 166 Fighter Wing, went to HQ 224 Group, Fighter Ops, and then to Air Command South East Asia. During the war, Stephen claimed twenty-one victories, most of them during the Battle of Britain, but his official tally was nine and eight shared destroyed, four and one shared unconfirmed destroyed, three 'probables' and seven damaged.

After the war, and by then a wing commander, Stephen declined a permanent RAF commission and instead returned to his first love: newspapers. His first senior position was as manager of the *Scottish Daily Express*, the *Scottish Sunday Express* and the *Evening Citizen*. His move to Glasgow enabled him to continue his association with the RAF: in 1950 he was appointed commanding officer of 602 (City of Glasgow) Auxiliary Air Force Squadron. In 1956, Lord Beaverbrook, who owned the newspaper group, chose Stephen to oversee the rebuilding of his Scottish printing empire, though he later moved back to London as the general manager of the *Sunday Express* and *Sunday Graphic*. Stephen switched newspaper 'stables' in 1959 when he was appointed as general manager of the *Sunday Times*, where its new colour supplement was his brainchild. His next move was as managing director of the *Daily Telegraph*, where he launched the weekend colour magazine. Stephen, a keen fisherman, was made a CBE in 1985. Furthermore, he was a founder member and trustee of Raleigh International (the UK-based charity that offers youth of all nationalities and backgrounds the opportunity to fulfil their potential and challenge themselves in community and environmental projects), and a member of both the Council of the Royal Society for the Protection of Birds and of the Scientific Exploration Society. Married with two daughters, Stephen died in London on 20 August 2001, aged eighty-five.

SQUADRON LEADER (LATER GROUP CAPTAIN) THOMAS FREDERICK DALTON-MORGAN
RAF
DECORATIONS: DISTINGUISHED FLYING CROSS (DFC) AND BAR, AND DISTINGUISHED SERVICE ORDER (DSO)
GAZETTED: 6 SEPTEMBER 1940, 30 MAY 1941 AND 25 MAY 1943

Tom Dalton-Morgan was born in Cardiff on 23 March 1917 and he was educated at Taunton School, Somerset. He enlisted in the RAF on a short-service commission in August 1935 before being posted in November to 11 Flying Training School (FTS) at RAF Wittering, Cambridgeshire. A year later, Morgan joined 22 (Torpedo Bomber) Squadron. At the end of May 1939, he joined the Directorate of Training at the Air Ministry and, in June 1940, went for a refresher course at 6 Operational Training

Unit (OTU). He had little experience as a fighter pilot when, in the same month, he was appointed as flight commander of 43 Squadron – 'The Fighting Cocks'. The squadron was flying Hurricanes from RAF Tangmere, Sussex, and repeatedly confronted the Luftwaffe during the Battle of Britain.

Dalton-Morgan shared in the destruction of He III bombers on 12 and 13 July and, over the next three weeks, he accounted for at least four more enemy aircraft. On 13 August, Dalton-Morgan's aircraft was hit by crossfire and he had to bale out over Petworth, Sussex. After a local policeman found him with no badges or rank in evidence – he was wearing pyjamas under his flying suit – he was temporarily placed in a cell along with the German bomber crew that he had shot down. Dalton-Morgan had been slightly wounded during the incident but on 2 September he rejoined his squadron.

More success followed in September when he shot down three Messerschmitt fighters. However, on 6 September, he was wounded in the face and knee during an engagement and had to crash-land his Hurricane at Tangmere. The incident took place on the same day that he was awarded his DFC and the citation praised 'his great courage when his behaviour in action had been an inspiration to his flight'. Dalton-Morgan was promoted to acting squadron leader on 16 September 1940 and took command of 'The Fighting Cocks' after the death of Squadron Leader Caesar Hull. Shortly afterwards, the squadron, having suffered heavy casualties, was withdrawn north to rest.

After the Battle of Britain, Dalton-Morgan's primary task was to train new pilots, who largely served with squadrons in the south of the country. However, he was also tasked with establishing a night-fighter capability with the Hurricane. He succeeded in this project and, hunting alone, destroyed six enemy bombers, with three going down on successive nights on 6 and 7 May 1941. On 24 July, while again operating at night, he spotted a Junkers bomber, gave chase and intercepted it off the Isle of May, Scotland. Despite his engine failing and fumes filling his cockpit, Dalton-Morgan attacked it three times. However, no sooner had the enemy aircraft hit the sea than his own engine stopped. By then, too low to bale out, he made a masterly landing on the water, although in doing so his face hit the gun sight, causing the loss of two front teeth. His skill and bravery did not go unnoticed, with his station commander, Wing Commander H. Eeles, stating: 'I consider this to be a classic example of how a first-class fighter pilot can attack an enemy while his engine is failing, shoot it down, force land on the sea and get away with it.' On 30 May 1941, Dalton-Morgan was awarded a Bar to his DFC for his 'exceptional skill'.

On 2 October 1941, Dalton-Morgan scored another night victory off Berwick-upon-Tweed, Northumberland. In February 1942, after eighteen months in command – the longest spell by any of 43 Squadron's wartime commanding officers – Dalton-Morgan was finally rested, having by then shot down at least fourteen enemy aircraft and damaged many others. He worked as a fighter controller at RAF Turnhouse, near Edinburgh, Scotland, until returning to operational flying late in 1942, when he became leader of the Ibsley Wing. This role saw him in command of eight fighter squadrons and he was tasked with mounting long-range offensive sorties over northern France and providing escorts for tactical bomber squadrons. Yet still he was claiming successes of his own: he damaged a Me 109 in December and shortly afterwards shot down a Fw 190 and damaged another in a sweep over Brest.

Dalton-Morgan was awarded the DSO on 25 May 1943, which recorded his tally of victories at the time as seventeen.

With the US in the war, Dalton-Morgan was attached to the 4th Fighter Group of the US 8th Air Force because of his experience of escort operations. He flew more than seventy combat sorties with the group. In early 1944, he was promoted to group captain and he served as operations officer with the 2nd Tactical Air Force. Ahead of the Normandy landings in June 1944, Dalton-Morgan was involved in planning fighter and ground-attack operations. After the invasion, he moved to the French mainland. His CO at the time, later Air Marshal Sir Fred Rosier, said of Dalton-Morgan: 'It would be impossible to overstate Tom D-M's importance and influence on the conduct of fighter operations for and beyond D-Day.'

Just a month before the end of the war in Europe, Dalton-Morgan learnt that his only brother, John, who had also been awarded the DFC, had been shot down and killed flying a Mosquito aircraft. After the war, Dalton-Morgan remained with 2nd Tactical Air Force before becoming a senior instructor at the School of Land/Air Warfare at RAF Old Sarum, Wiltshire. Later he commanded the Gütersloh Wing, flying Vampire jets, before taking command of RAF Wunstorf, Germany. In his pilot's logbook, Dalton-Morgan is recorded as having claimed twenty-two enemy aircraft, along with ten 'probables' and twelve damaged (his official tally was, however, fourteen confirmed and three shared).

He was made an OBE in 1945 and the following year President Harry Truman awarded him the US Bronze Star. On leaving the RAF in 1952, Dalton-Morgan joined the UK/Australian Joint Project at Woomera, where he managed the weapons range for the next thirty years. He eventually retired in Australia although he made regular visits to Britain. Dalton-Morgan died on 18 September 2004, aged eighty-seven, on the eve of the annual Battle of Britain anniversary service that he had been due to attend. He had been married twice, and had two children from his first marriage and six from his second. He was an exceptional pilot but, arguably, an even greater leader. In an article on leadership written after the war, one of his former pilots said of Dalton-Morgan: 'He had awesome charisma; some sort of special aura seemed to surround him. He was the epitome of leadership.'

SERGEANT (LATER FLIGHT LIEUTENANT) JAMES RUSSELL CAISTER
RAF
DECORATION: DISTINGUISHED FLYING MEDAL (DFM)
GAZETTED: 13 SEPTEMBER 1940

James 'Bill' Caister was born in October 1906. He entered the RAF in 1925 as an aircrafthand but subsequently qualified as a pilot. Before the Second World War, he served in Palestine with the rank of sergeant. Shortly after the opening of hostilities in September 1939, Caister, who had an easy-going nature, was posted to 603 (City of Edinburgh) Squadron, a Spitfire unit which was then commanded by Squadron Leader Lord Douglas-Hamilton. The author David Ross describes Caister as a 'well built, tough Scot who liked to box and frequently sparred with ground crew'.

During the first eleven months of the war, 603 Squadron was based at three Scottish RAF bases: Turnhouse, Dyce and Montrose. From early in the war, the squadron was in action and it claimed its first victory over the Firth of Forth as early as October 1939. During the so-called 'Phoney War', Caister saw plenty of action.

On 9 January 1940, he became involved in the search for an enemy bomber off Aberdeenshire. He succeeded in locating the He 111 and engaged it but his guns were frozen up with ice and would not fire. However, half an hour later 603's Red Section relocated the enemy aircraft and brought it down in the sea. On 7 March 1940, Caister shared in the destruction of a He 111 some seventy miles off the Scottish coast, after which only the enemy radio operator was subsequently rescued. On 10 March 1940, Caister shared in the destruction of an enemy aircraft off Fraserburgh and on 16 April 1940 he shared in the destruction of a Do 17.

Once the Battle of Britain got under way, Caister saw even more action and July 1940 was particularly hectic. On 3 July 1940, he shared in the destruction of a Ju 88 bomber off Stonehaven, Aberdeenshire, with the enemy aircraft being seen by the local coastguard to crash into the sea. Just three days later, Caister shared in the destruction of a Me 110 brought down by 603's Red Section 100 miles north-east of Aberdeen. On 12 July 1940, he shared in the destruction of a Heinkel following a further combat over Aberdeen: the bomber crashed into the town's newly completed ice rink. On 18 July 1940, Caister severely damaged a Ju 88 which was attacking a convoy off Aberdeen. During a combat on 19 July 1940, his Spitfire was damaged in combat but he managed to land at Turnhouse. On 30 July 1940, Caister destroyed a He 111 twelve miles west of Aberdeen.

On 30 August 1940, Caister claimed a He 111 destroyed, while on 2 September 1940 he flew alongside Richard Hillary in a morning patrol over RAF Hawkinge, Kent, and in an evening patrol over Hornchurch, Essex, when he claimed a brace of Me 109s. The next day he claimed a Me 109 destroyed after a ten-second burst of fire at less than 250 yards' range. On this occasion, his combat report stated:

When on patrol with No. 603 Squadron, 12 or more Me. 109s dived on the Squadron from above, a few miles east of Manston [Kent]. Six Me. 109s broke away east from below and did not enter the engagement. I attacked from astern one Me. 109 and after a few seconds burst it steeply climbed; closing up with a long burst I saw the enemy aircraft out of control. I had fired a few seconds burst at close range and broke off, and almost stalled. Turning away from the enemy aircraft I had attacked, I fired a few seconds burst at another Me. 109 almost dead ahead. This machine did not break off but passed me within a few yards distance. There appeared to be six streams of fire coming from the enemy aircraft. I did not observe any damage. I saw at least two and perhaps a third explosion on the water, either bombs or aircraft crashing. I noticed an aircraft in my mirror, but I was too far away for it to start firing. Spiralling down in a steep dive I lost it, and being short of petrol I refuelled at Manston, taking off immediately and returned to base.

On 4 September 1940, Caister shot down a Me 109 off Dunkirk, with the enemy pilot being wounded but rescued from the sea. Two days later, however, he was shot down by the German pilot Hauptmann Hubertus von Bonin after a running combat over the Channel and was forced to crash-land in Occupied France. Due to damage to his aircraft's hydraulics system, he could not get his undercarriage down yet he still made a perfect landing in a meadow near Guines in northern France, thereby, unfortunately, giving the Luftwaffe an intact example of the Spitfire. Caister, then thirty-four and recently commissioned, had a brief meeting with von Bonin in the mess at Guines, after which he was taken away to spend the rest of the conflict as a prisoner of war (PoW). Having recently married, he would not see his new bride for nearly five years.

Caister was a PoW when his DFM was announced on 13 September 1940 and his citation began: 'This airman has been concerned in the destruction of six enemy aircraft and has consistently shown himself to possess a very fine sense of air discipline and spirit in attack. By his everlasting good humour and keenness, he is a refreshing influence in his flight.'

During his captivity, Caister was held for part of the time at Stulag Luft III, the scene of the famous 'Great Escape'. He was liberated in May 1945 and he left the RAF in June 1946 in the rank of flight lieutenant. Caister died in 1994, aged eighty-seven.

FLYING OFFICER (LATER WING COMMANDER) HOWARD CLIVE MAYERS
Royal Air Force Volunteer Reserve (RAFVR)
DECORATIONS: DISTINGUISHED FLYING CROSS (DFC) AND BAR, AND DISTINGUISHED SERVICE ORDER (DSO)
GAZETTED: 1 OCTOBER 1940, 13 FEBRUARY 1942 AND 28 JULY 1942

Howard Mayers was born in Sydney, Australia, on 9 January 1910. After being educated in his home country, he attended

Jesus College, Cambridge, where he became a member of the University Air Squadron in 1929. Mayers was a company managing director until, after the outbreak of hostilities, he was commissioned as a pilot officer in the RAFVR on 11 March 1940.

Mayers' first operational posting on 3 August 1940 was to 601 (County of London) Squadron, a Hurricane unit based at RAF Tangmere, Sussex. As a new member of the 'Millionaires' Squadron', so called because its pilots were considered to come from wealthy and privileged backgrounds, he soon found himself in the thick of the action, flying Hurricanes, during the Battle of Britain. His pilot's logbook records that on 8 August he 'shot down ME 109 South of St Catherine Point'. On 12 August, it recorded: 'Shot down 2 JU 88 near Brighton and 1 ME 110.' The following day, Mayers wrote: 'Shot down ME 110 off Portland. Hurricane hit by cannon . . . baled out found by Archie [Sir Archibald Hope] and rescued.' Mayers later expanded on his ordeal in an interview for the *Evening News* in which he said the strike on his aircraft 'felt like a tornado'.

He added:

I felt a pain in my right side and leg, felt the engine stop, heard hissing noises and smelt fumes. My first reaction was to pull back the stick but there was no response. The next thing I remember was falling through the air at high speed and feeling my helmet, flying boots and socks torn off. Lack of oxygen must have dulled my senses as the combat ended at 19,000 feet and my parachute opened just above the clouds at 7,000 feet. At about 5,000 feet, between two layers of clouds, an Me 110 fired at me while being chased by a Hurricane. I landed in the sea three miles from Portland – 200 yards from a German pilot. After twenty minutes I saw a Hurricane searching the bay and recognised it as my Flight Commander, Flight Lieutenant Hope. He guided a Motor Torpedo Boat to our position.

Mayers received treatment at Portland Hospital for shrapnel wounds but was back flying just three days later, when he recorded in his logbook: 'Shot down 3 JU 87's over and near base. Bombed.' On 26 August, he wrote: 'Dog fight with ME 109. Damaged or shot down.' By 18 August, his experiences were becoming even more hair-raising: 'Bombed while taking off . . . Sgt. Wooley's machine burnt on aerodrome.' While flying from RAF Debden, Essex, Mayers was involved in further aerial combat: 'Attacked JU 88. Damage not ascertained . . . attacked alone about 30 DO 17 over London Docks. Shot down 1 DO 17 and probably another DO 17.' In early September 1940, Mayers returned to Tangmere where, on 3 September, he and a comrade attacked a Do 17, causing smoke to come from the aircraft. The next day, he shot down a Do 215 off Brighton and listed a Me 110 as a 'probable' half-share having attacked it with a comrade. On 6 September, his aircraft was attacked: 'S.B. [starboard] main plain hit by cannon from ME 109 making a tremendous hole. Got back to base.' Later, he inserted a photograph of his comrade standing in the hole.

After moving with the squadron to a new base at Exeter in Devon, Mayers recorded some good news: 'Archie, Griers and self awarded D.F.C.' The announcement of the award came on 1 October – after Mayers had shot down two further enemy aircraft. His citation stated: 'This officer has participated in a number of interceptions and has destroyed seven enemy aircraft and possibly three others. During a recent engagement, a cannon shell passed through the port wing of his aircraft making a hole four feet in diameter, but Flying Officer Mayers succeeded in bringing his aircraft safely to base. He has displayed great courage and fighting spirit.'

On 7 October, Mayers was shot down again in what proved to be his last operational flight of the Battle of Britain. He wrote in his log: 'Shot down by ME 110 over sea. Force landed near Lyme Regis. Turned over. Wounded. Glycol tank hit. Invalided to Torquay.' Yet again, Mayers was soon out of hospital and living up to his reputation as a 'gentleman flyer' in the air and on the ground. His logbook for 8 November stated: 'C.O. Gilbert and I flew in formation for party at Tangmere. Consumed 137 bottles of champagne.'

In December 1940, Mayers moved with his squadron to RAF Northolt, Middlesex. By February 1941, their main role was to escort Blenheim bombers over France. On 10 February, he and others escorted six Blenheims to Calais where they were involved in combat and lost a pilot when two British aircraft were shot down. The *Evening Standard* later reported on the incident:

During a recent RAF offensive sweep over occupied France, states [the] Air Ministry, a Flight Lieutenant [Mayers] saw another Hurricane burst into flames. The pilot baled out and came down in the Channel. The Flight Lieutenant turned to fly down the Channel to find help, and in a few moments sighted a Motor Torpedo Boat. He then dived down to the boat and flew out in the direction of the pilot. At first the boat crew could not understand, so he turned back and dived again, almost to sea level. This time the message was understood, and the motor boat followed the Hurricane as it led the way to the rescue.

After Mayers moved with the squadron to RAF Manston, Kent, he was shot down a third time. On 4 May 1941, he wrote: 'Shot down by 3 or 4 ME 109. Baled out at 20 grand [thousand feet] N. of Dover. Fearn [a comrade] also shot down.' At the end of May, Mayers' time as a flight commander with 601 Squadron came to an end when he was posted to first Malta and then Egypt.

In July 1941, Mayers took command of 94 Squadron, Ismalia, Egypt (Hurricanes) and the following month was afforded a lively 'welcome' when his base was heavily bombed by Ju 88s with the loss of three Hurricanes. It was when he moved to Ballah in September 1941 that he claimed his first enemy aircraft with his new squadron: 'Self attacked JU 88 for some 15 minutes. It eventually crashed in flames on Ataea Mountains. One bullet through my rad [radiator] and cockpit.' When he moved with his squadron again – to the Western Desert – Mayers was promoted to acting wing commander in November 1941. He and his squadron were heavily involved in bomber escorts over El Adem and Sidi Rezegh and were often involved in strafing German armoured columns. In December 1941, Mayers and the squadron did a great deal of operational flying around Tobruk, Libya. At the end of the month, he was, yet again, exceptionally brave in an incident that, despite the gallantry award citation putting it five days later, is believed to have taken place on Boxing Day. The citation for a Bar to his DFC stated:

This officer has led his wing on a large number of sorties during the Libyan campaign. His mastery of tactics and skilful planning of operations have contributed largely to the many successes obtained. One day in December, 1941, during a machine gun attack against an enemy column, Wing Commander Mayers observed a member of his formation shot down by anti-aircraft fire. When the attack was concluded, he skilfully landed near the crashed aircraft and, although enemy vehicles were approaching, coolly waited for his comrade to reach him. Putting him in the seat, Wing Commander Mayers clambered in on top of him and took off as the enemy neared the aircraft. He finally flew safely to base. This officer has always shown great courage and leadership. He has destroyed at least 11 enemy aircraft.

Mayers, with typical modesty, recorded this in his logbook as: 'Mackay shot down by A.A. Fire. Landed and picked him up in my Hurricane.'

On 25 April, he was appointed wing leader 239 Wing (Kittyhawks) and on 12 May his squadron intercepted up to twenty Ju 52 transport aircraft and two Me 110s fighters. In an incredibly successful attack, they destroyed thirteen of the former and one of the latter. One newspaper reported: 'The operation was led by an Australian born Wing Commander [Mayers] D.F.C. and Bar, who shot down one Ju 52. The rest of the bag was well spread being shared by British, Australian and Canadian pilots . . . In brilliant sunshine the enemy aircraft was sighted "right on the deck" about 50 feet over the sea. Immediately, the R.A.F. fighters went into attack, and, in a few moments, the first JU 52 plunged blazing into the waves. One fighter pilot said: "For the next 15 minutes I haven't seen anything like it. One after another at half-mile intervals the JUs crashed in flames."' The fighter ace's last entry in his logbook was for 8 July 1942: 'Got ME 109f confirmed.' On 20 July, Mayers had shot down an enemy aircraft when he was himself shot down, force-landing in the Qattara Depression. Spitfire pilots searched for Mayers and found his aircraft but there was no sign of him. He had been recommended for his DSO before his last flight and it was announced on 28 July 1942. The recommendation for his award praised his leadership and stated: 'Wing Commander Mayers has commanded a wing since April 1942. He is an expert on bombing and machine gun attacks, whilst his tactical knowledge has contributed much to the success of long-range fighter operations . . . Wing Commander Mayers has displayed gallantry and great devotion to duty in the direction of recent intensive operation.'

Mayers was apparently taken as a prisoner of war (PoW) but the exact circumstances of his death are not known. It is believed by some that he was lost when a ship carrying prisoners to Sicily was sunk in the Mediterranean by British fighter aircraft. However, another theory is that he was on a Ju 52 transport aircraft, which was taking him to a PoW camp in Italy, when it was shot down by an Allied aircraft. Either way, it looks as though an Allied pilot was, inadvertently, responsible for the death of one of the great aces of the Second World War. Mayers is commemorated on the Alamein Memorial in Egypt and on the Canberra War Memorial in Australia.

FLIGHT SERGEANT (LATER SQUADRON LEADER) PERCY FREDERICK MORFILL
RAF
DECORATION: DISTINGUISHED FLYING MEDAL (DFM)
GAZETTED: 5 OCTOBER 1940

Percy 'Ronnie' Morfill was born in Gosport, Hampshire, on 11 December 1914. The son of a publican who had served in the Royal Marines, he attended Bishop Wordsworth School in Salisbury, Wiltshire. After leaving school, Morfill sat the entrance exams to join the RAF as an apprentice. His results were the highest gained in Wiltshire, earning him public praise from the Air Ministry. Morfill enlisted in the RAF on 3 September 1933 at Halton, Buckinghamshire. After passing out as a metal rigger in September 1933, he was posted to Fleet Air Arm in Gosport. Morfill volunteered for pilot training, was successful and began flying in January 1936. From 1936 to 1938, he served in 65 Squadron as a sergeant and was a member of its aerobatics' team, which was flying Gladiators. He learnt flying skills that would stand him in good stead once war broke out. No doubt, too, he received some useful tips from his fellow aerobatics team member Bob Stanford Tuck, who went on to become a highly decorated wartime fighter pilot.

In May 1940, Morfill was posted to 501 (County of Gloucester) Squadron and, after Germany invaded Holland and Belgium, he went to France with his unit where he was promoted to flight sergeant. The unit suffered a tragedy on 10 May, its first day in France, when one of the two Bristol Bombay troop carriers stalled on landing: nine officers and men were killed, including the adjutant. They were all buried in a local cemetery but just three days later enemy bombs intended for the airfield fell in the cemetery, the explosions disinterring the bodies. The subsequent reburial of the corpses was as gory as it was bizarre. Morfill, however, was soon into his stride during the Battle of France, shooting down a Me 110 over Tourteron on 11 May and a He 111 over St Hubert the following day. On 14 May, he shared in the 'kill' of a Do 17 over Bétheniville.

As the war progressed, Morfill continued to fly with distinction, including many sorties with his friend, the legendary 'Ginger' Lacey. Collectively, this squadron was responsible for destroying a large number of German aircraft, while at the same time helping to cover the retreat of the British Expeditionary Force and its eventual evacuation from the beaches of Dunkirk. During the Battle of France, Morfill flew thirty-three sorties and claimed two victories.

With the German occupation of France, the squadron was forced to withdraw to the Channel Islands. When the enemy closed in on the islands, too, Morfill and some fellow stragglers managed to escape from Jersey on a fishing boat even though the vessel was repeatedly attacked by German bombers. Morfill eventually arrived back in England in June where he rejoined his squadron, which by then was stationed at RAF Gravesend, Kent. From so-called 'Hell's Corner', British pilots, day after day, fought off wave after wave of German bombers and fighters, 501 Squadron flying more sorties and losing more pilots than any other squadron.

On 20 June, the squadron moved to RAF Croydon, south London, under the new command of Squadron Leader H. A. V. Hogan. On 4 July, 501 moved again, this time to Middle Wallop, Hampshire, where it concentrated on night-fighter patrols. On 26 July, the squadron returned to Gravesend in the path of the Luftwaffe raids on London. Here 501 were in the so-called 'Biggin Hill sector', with 32, 600 and 610 Squadrons. Morfill had many scrapes with death but none more so than on 18 August. In a series of dogfights over Kent, seven of the squadron's Hurricanes were shot down. Two pilots were killed, three others were injured but two, including Morfill, baled out of their aircraft and landed without any injuries.

Morfill's DFM for his gallantry was announced on 5 October 1940 and his citation stated: 'Flight Sergeant Morfill has served with the squadron since 5th May, 1940, and has taken part in most patrols. He has shown skill and calmness in combat and ability to seize the best opportunity to strike at the enemy (7 destroyed, 2 probably destroyed or damaged). His general steadiness and flying ability has been praiseworthy.' Eventually, between 18 June and 31 October 1940, Morfill flew 215 sorties, claiming eight enemy shot down. In June 1941, and by then a warrant officer, Morfill was posted to 58 Operational Training Unit (OTU) as an instructor, before being commissioned the following year. In 1944, he was posted to Southern Rhodesia, to the Central Flying School (CFS) at Norton.

After hostilities ended in 1945, Morfill returned to Britain. Initially, he served at the Air Ministry but in 1947 he was posted to the Ministry of Aircraft Production on Bomber Research and Development. Later he was given an extended commission and went to CFS at Little Rissington, Gloucestershire, where he flew Vampires. A spell based in Cardiff followed before he became the Chief Flying Instructor at the University Air Squadron at St Andrews University,

Scotland. Next came a posting to HQ, 63 Group, at RAF Hawarden, Cheshire, where he undertook a gliding course. It was here that, after ten years as a flight lieutenant, Morfill was promoted to squadron leader in 1953. After leaving the service in February 1958, he undertook a course with Wingards, a motor accessory firm, with whom he remained until retiring in 1977. Morfill then moved to West Sussex, where he died in Chichester in April 2004, eight months short of his ninetieth birthday.

FLIGHT LIEUTENANT (LATER WING COMMANDER) CHRISTOPHER FREDERICK CURRANT
RAF
DECORATIONS: DISTINGUISHED FLYING CROSS (DFC) AND BAR, AND DISTINGUISHED SERVICE ORDER (DSO)
GAZETTED: 8 OCTOBER 1940, 15 NOVEMBER 1940 AND 7 JULY 1942

The son of a hatter, Christopher 'Bunny' Currant was born on 14 December 1911 in Luton, Bedfordshire. He was educated at Rydal School, North Wales, and joined the RAF on 27 January 1936. Currant served with 46 and 151 Squadrons flying Gauntlet fighters. It was while training as a pilot that his fellow airmen began calling him 'Bunny', a nickname which remained with him for the rest of his life. Currant subsequently converted to Hurricanes in January 1939. During the period January–March 1940 he carried out numerous convoy patrols and survived an engine failure on 15 March when he was forced to land at North Weald, Essex. He next joined 605 (County of Warwick)

Squadron at RAF Wick, Caithness, Scotland, and was commissioned on 1 April 1940.

On 10 April 1940, Currant intercepted and attacked a He 111 bomber that crashed into the sea. However, Currant himself crash-landed at Wick later that night. For the remainder of April, he carried out many patrols. At the end of May, he flew down to RAF Hawkinge, Kent, and carried out patrols over Calais and Boulogne. Then he crash-landed, almost disastrously, in Fruges, France, having previously shot down a Heinkel and attacked two more. Currant subsequently hitchhiked to Calais and reached Hawkinge at 10 p.m. before going to hospital in Folkestone.

On 23 May, Currant wrote to his parents from his hospital bed at the Officers' Ward, Military Hospital, Shorncliffe, Kent. The letter provides a wonderful insight into his robust character:

Dear Mother & Father & all, Heigh ho! Heigh ho! We do get about these days don't we? My little story is long but amusing. You must excuse the writing, I can only just see what I'm doing because of a black eye – what a beauty – and a busted nose, apart from that I'm as fit as can be. I hope to be out again in a couple of days. Yesterday morning we did an early morning patrol over Northern France and the Channel – we saw plenty of activity in various forms and then all returned intact. At 11am we took off again twelve of us and we made for Arras. Unfortunately before we got there we rather lost each other in cloud layers and only five of us arrived together over Arras. Here we were subjected to very accurate AA [anti-aircraft] Fire – pretty to watch but too close for a quiet snooze so I and another lad nipped into some cloud for protection. When we came out the other three had disappeared so had the AA bursts much to our relief. Then I met three Heinkel Bombers or they met me anyhow they were in the process of bombing – funnily all the bombs fell in a field in open country but it annoyed me to see them and so I waded into them and knocked one down in 5 seconds and then played 'catch me – hit me' with the other two. I hit the oil tank of one brute but he had the last laugh as his oil smothered my aircraft. I couldn't see a thing and my aircraft was rather shot about now and in due course the engine refused to play anymore. Most irritating . . . and 6,000 feet over the German lines. I headed North gliding down – turning the clouds black and blue . . . By now streams of steam from a bust glycol tank and volumes of black smoke from my oil tank were belching out, and I must have looked a pretty sight. I hit the ground on my tummy – the aircraft's belly is more precise – and then either my face hit the gun-sights or the gun-sights hit me and there I was all alone by my little self in the middle of a ploughed field – somewhere in France. Such a nice new Hurricane – and with great glee I took out a box of matches – got at the petrol tank, sprinkled liberally and then lit same and retired immediately. A beautiful blaze and the dear old thing had gone.

I gathered up my gear and walked across the field to a cottage where I met a number of French peasants. They were terribly kind and patched me up and poured large quantities of rum and wine down me. After about an hour in this cottage I set off determined to get to the coast and England if it took me years.

Before leaving I asked for a dictionary which they kindly gave me and with this and my gear I was on my way. I was carrying my helmet, sidcot [flying suit], life-jacket and parachute and thus burdened and bloody I walked 5 miles into a small hamlet. Stopped here for 10 minutes for another sup of rum – then I proceeded to stop every refugee car I could and eventually got a lift – as far as St Omer. Thousands of refugees thronged all the roads, some going North and some South. All stared at me and crowded round and jabbered continually. They were all emphatic that the Germans were just over the hedge a few fields away, full of rumour and unfounded facts – all absolutely untrue.

The French people lose all dignity and resource in an emergency, panic easily and whine continually. I have no time for them at all – they've no guts – excellent when their troops are advancing but abject cowards in retreat. It was most depressing. At St Omer I scrounged another lift – town empty and recently bombed – and so on to Calais – buildings here still burning from bombing that morning. My luck was in as a boat was just leaving for Dover. At 9pm I walked into the Mess at Hawkinge after ten hours of varied fortunes – very tired but with tail up. I have had an anaesthetic and the operation on my fractured nose – it should be nearly straight by now.

I shall be out of here this Saturday and hope to set some leave and shall see you all then.

My love to all.

Christopher

Currant resumed flying on 10 June at RAF Drem, East Lothian, Scotland. For the rest of the month and through July, he carried out many patrols and exercises. However, the next month there was even more activity and on 15 August his squadron intercepted eighty He 111s, of which he shot down two and damaged a further two. Currant was promoted to acting flight lieutenant on 5 September 1940 and his pilot's logbook carries brief details on his huge involvement in the Battle of Britain.

Currant was awarded the DFC on 8 October 1940 and his

citation stated: 'This officer has led his flight with great skill and courage in air combats in the defence of London. He has destroyed seven enemy aircraft and damaged a number of others. His splendid example and fine fighting spirit have inspired the other pilots in his flight.'

Just a month later, on 15 November 1940, Currant was awarded a Bar to his DFC and his citation stated: 'Since September, 1940, this officer has personally destroyed six enemy aircraft and damaged several others, bringing his total to thirteen. He has led his flight, and on occasions his squadron, with great success, and shows a sound knowledge of tactics against the enemy.'

Currant transferred to 52 Operational Training Unit (OTU) at RAF Debden, Essex, where he worked as an instructor. He was promoted to acting squadron leader on 23 June 1941. On 14 August of the same year, Currant was promoted to command 501 Squadron at RAF Ibsley, Hampshire, where he carried out numerous patrols. In September 1941, Currant essentially played himself – though with a fictitious name – in the film *The First of the Few*, starring David Niven and Leslie Howard. On 9 March 1942, he received a head injury during combat and was forced to land at RAF Lympne, Kent, where his aircraft overturned. Currant was taken to Folkestone Hospital to have metal removed from his head. In late March, he was transferred to an RAF rehabilitation centre at the Palace Hotel, Torquay, Devon.

It was on 10 March 1942, while recuperating from his injuries, that he wrote another entertaining letter to his parents:

Dear Mother and Father,
Shades of May 1940 waft by with the breeze from my window

only this time it's the back of my face and not the front – Folkestone seems to have small reaction for me but not I for Folkestone (I don't think that's sense).

History does repeat itself, but not in all details . . . Again I got mixed up with the filthy Hun only this time, it was 4 to 1 – in their favour and they were fighters and not unfortunately fat-lazy bombers.

I was roughly over the same spot as before – Furges near St-Pol, and where angels fear to tread – I stepped in and out again – with 3 very angry Germans after my blood – they nearly got it too but just not quite, and I'll bet they're cursing themselves now. They certainly hit me and the aircraft – funny what an awful row metal makes when it goes into all the wrong places. But my skull was tougher than their metal and although it went in the back of my head, it met my skull and bounced off and came out again.

I pushed everything forward and spent the next five minutes hurling myself down to the French fields in the craziest way I know with those three persistent Huns pouring lead at me the whole time – I shot over the French sand dunes near Boich at 0 feet at some fantastic speed opened [up] and those three little Huns gave it up as a bad job and flew away.

The first time I've even said a little prayer at 450 miles per hour but speed doesn't have anything to do with it really – I throttled back and flew across the calm bluish sea and took careful stock. Surprising how wet I was and it wasn't all sweat I found. I turned my oxygen full-on in the hopes that at least I'd remain conscious until I'd surfed that water – at last Rye loomed up and another little prayer whispered its way up to the Heavens. I was beginning to feel fairly groggy by now so searched quickly for Lympne which I found at the second attempt.

I put my wheels down, flaps down, seat down, tightened my straps hand back and motored gently in to land. I touched down quite softly and then the thing I was half expecting and half-dreading occurred – the aircraft was so shot-up that the under-carriage collapsed. Down went the nose and Spitfire and self did a perfect somersault – I ducked instinctively and found myself upside down on the cool grass of England – all very pleasant but I couldn't get out and again a prayer whispered its way out but a much bigger one this time with not a little fear that the wretched thing would catch fire. After what seemed ages some exhausted airmen got me out – and I think we all said – 'Thank God'.

I know I said 'good show chaps' and collapsed on to a stretcher. They humped me into the sick bay and a young F/O [Flying Officer] Doctor made me comfortable with bags of rugs and hot tea – I lay there about 40 minutes, wondering how bad my wound was and hoping like hell that I was alright. Doc kept taking my pulse and told me I was fine and of course I didn't believe him and of course I was alright really as it happened. Another ambulance drove me to hospital and they whisked me into the theatre – gave me a real anaesthetic and then really got down to brass tacks. The surgeon spent an hour mucking about – I didn't pass out, felt perfectly, but it's wonderful what a nurse's hand can do – bless them.

And here I am as large as life half sitting up and feeling fit except for a bit of a throb.

I don't know how long I shall remain here, not long I hope. My love and thoughts to all.

Christopher

In May and June 1942, Currant carried out a number of fighter sweeps and on 23 June he was promoted to acting wing commander. The following day he was put in command of RAF Ibsley, Hampshire. On 7 July 1942, Currant was awarded the DSO and his citation stated:

> Squadron Leader Currant is a most courageous pilot and a brilliant leader. His untiring efforts and outstanding ability have been reflected in the splendid work accomplished by the squadron which he commands. One day in March, 1942, he was wounded in the head during a sortie. Despite this, he flew his aircraft safely back to base. Following a short enforced rest, he returned to operational flying with renewed vigour. Squadron Leader Currant has destroyed at least 14 and damaged many more enemy aircraft.

On 24 August 1942, Currant was put in charge of RAF Zeals, Wiltshire, and he was given the task of forming No. 122 Wing of Spitfires. He then led his wing on a variety of offensive operations against enemy transport and aircraft, over France and the Low Countries. Currant, who had commanded a squadron with many Belgian pilots, was awarded the Belgian Croix de Guerre on 9 April 1943 and, on 24 January 1944 he was forced to crash-land due to undercarriage hydraulic failure. On D-Day, he led his wing over the Normandy beachhead, but late in 1944 he took a break from his combat role to carry out a four-month lecture tour of the eastern states of America. On his return, Currant was posted to the Netherlands to 84 Group Control Centre. There he was engaged on target allocation for tactical air operations in support of the advancing Allied armies.

Currant remained in the RAF after the war. Among his posts were three years in Washington, DC, on the staff of the

Joint Chiefs of Staff and a year in London at the Ministry of Supply dealing with guided missiles. Currant was then invited to Norway as British adviser to the Royal Norwegian Air Force Staff College. Although intended to be a three-year posting, the Norwegians asked him to remain for another year before awarding him the Order of St Olaf on 30 September 1960.

Currant retired from the RAF in 1959 and the following year joined Hunting Engineering at Luton, Bedfordshire, where he worked in research and development on weapons for the RAF for a further fifteen years. He also umpired at professional tennis tournaments, including Wimbledon. Currant died in Taunton, Somerset, on 12 March 2006, aged ninety-four. He was survived by his wife, Cynthia, whom he had married in 1942, and their three sons and a daughter.

FLIGHT LIEUTENANT (LATER WING COMMANDER) ATHOL STANHOPE FORBES

RAF
DECORATIONS: DISTINGUISHED FLYING CROSS (DFC) AND BAR
GAZETTED: 22 OCTOBER 1940 AND 4 NOVEMBER 1941

Athol Forbes, a flight commander with the newly created 303 (Polish) Squadron, survived the war despite being wounded three times in combat. He was the squadron's highest scoring British pilot with seven victories and two 'probables' during the Battle of Britain. Despite having cemented his own status as an ace commanding Blue Section, Forbes' number three had even greater success: Sergeant Josef František amassed seventeen victories in the same period, becoming the top ace for the Battle of Britain.

Forbes was born in Hanover Square, central London, on 4 April 1912. He was educated at Dover College, Kent, before joining the RAF on 25 November 1935 on a short-service commission. After completing his flying training, he was posted to the School of Army Co-operation, RAF Old Sarum, Wiltshire. When 303 Squadron was formed on 2 August 1940, Forbes was one of three RAF officers, including the CO, Squadron Leader Ronald Kellett, to serve alongside their Polish compatriots. All three men were pre-war pilots with plenty of flying hours but little combat experience. In contrast, the cadre of thirteen Polish officers and eight NCO pilots, alongside 135 Polish ground staff, had largely seen plenty of combat in the defence of their homeland and the fall of France. The squadron, based at RAF Northolt in Middlesex, became fully operational on 31 August and Forbes' first combat was on 5 September when 303 was scrambled to engage Ju 88 bombers with their Me 109 fighter escorts.

Forbes' first combat report gave a good account of the action close to London, as well as a taste of what was to come:

I was Blue 1. I lost Red Leader when he became involved with Me 109s and just beyond AA [anti-aircraft] fire. I saw five Vics [a type of flying formation] of 3 Ju 88s formed in a Vic. I led into the attack, Blue 2, F/O [Flying Officer] Lapkowski broke from the section to settle some Me 109s. Blue 3, Sgt. Frantisek, saw a Me 109 attacking a pilot who had just baled out of a Spitfire, and shot it down. He then caught up and followed me to attack the bombers. I took No. 3 and he took No. 2 of the rear most section. After an attack from dead astern, I attacked head-on to the starboard quarter. A shower of oil came from the starboard engine, covering my machine. I attacked the starboard engine and this time from astern, and it burst into flames. I had expended all my ammunition. I pulled up to watch, but a Me 109 got on to my tail and I saw tracer on my port side. I broke away to the starboard and dived to the ground and so home.

In this initial action, Forbes was credited with a Ju 88 destroyed and his comrades were credited with six further 'kills'.

Forbes' next day was even more eventful: he shot down a Me 109 before attacking another that was on the tail of a Hurricane. Forbes delivered a short, successful burst and saw the aircraft plunge out of control. However, he then received strikes to his petrol tank and through his Perspex windshield that left him blinded by petrol. He dived for home only to crash-land as he was overcome by fumes. Forbes ignored his minor injuries to be airborne the next day when he was again wounded in combat with Me 109s, this time being forced to land in Essex. On 11 September, Forbes shot down two Do 17 bombers but was wounded for a third time before landing his damaged Hurricane at Heston aerodrome, west London. His final 'kills' with 303 Squadron were He 111 bombers, the first on 26 September and the second the next day.

The success of 303 as a squadron was nothing short of incredible. Even though it joined the fray two months after the start of the Battle of Britain, it had one of the highest number of enemy aircraft destroyed and one of the highest 'kill'-to-loss ratios.

Forbes was posted to 66 Squadron on 17 October 1940, just five days before his DFC was announced. The citation stated:

'This officer is a splendid leader and has contributed materially to the many successes obtained by his squadron. He has displayed great keenness in pressing home his attacks against the enemy and has destroyed seven of the aircraft.' At the end of the year, Forbes was also awarded the Polish honour of the Virtuti Militari (5th class). He was one of only three British officers from 303 Squadron decorated by the Poles.

Having converted to Spitfire IIs, Forbes' combat success continued in early 1941. On 25 January 1941, he claimed a shared He 111 before a Me 109 'kill' on 20 August. In October 1941, Forbes was posted to HQ 10 Group, by then with the rank of acting squadron leader. He was awarded the Bar to his DFC on 4 November 1941 and his citation stated: 'Squadron Leader Forbes has always shown the greatest keenness to engage the enemy and has undoubtedly contributed materially to the high standard of operational efficiency of the squadron. At his own request he has been permitted to make long flights out over the sea, alone in an endeavour to engage enemy aircraft.'

From 11 April 1942, Forbes was stationed at 224 Group, Calcutta, India. In October that year, he was appointed to command No. 165 Wing and did so with success during the Arakan operations of 1943. It was for this meritorious service that he was awarded the OBE on New Year's Day 1944 when his recommendation stated:

This officer was in command of the forward fighter wing during the Arakan operations and displayed outstanding leadership and administrative ability. He was responsible for opening up and making operationally complete six advanced airfields from which he operated his own squadrons and frequently additional squadrons from the rear. When forced to retire, Wing Commander Forbes continued to operate until the last possible moment and then successfully evacuated every member of his equipment including fuel and oil.

On 6 August 1943, Forbes was posted to Headquarters 222 Group, India, and later 221 Group, Imphal (also in India).

After the war, Forbes remained in the RAF until 1948 and he later became operations manager of Cameroons Air Transport Ltd. He eventually settled in Alcester, Warwickshire, and died in hospital in nearby Stratford-upon-Avon on 18 August 1981, aged sixty-nine.

FLIGHT LIEUTENANT (LATER GROUP CAPTAIN) ROBERT WARDLOW OXSPRING
RAF
DECORATIONS: DISTINGUISHED FLYING CROSS (DFC) AND TWO BARS, AIR FORCE CROSS (AFC)
GAZETTED: 8 NOVEMBER 1940, 18 SEPTEMBER 1942, 16 FEBRUARY 1943 AND 1 JANUARY 1949

Robert Oxspring was born in Sheffield, Yorkshire, on 22 May 1919, and was the son of a distinguished First World War pilot of the same name. Indeed, his father was awarded the Military Cross (MC) and Bar before being wounded in action in a mid-air collision with a fellow British pilot on 30 April 1917. Oxspring Jnr enlisted in the RAF in March 1938 on a short-service commission and was appointed acting pilot officer on 7 May. In his autobiography, *Spitfire Command*, Oxspring says that as a youngster, and because of his father's exploits, he had an 'obsession' with flying. Oxspring joined 66 Squadron in the

December of that year and, after training, he was ready to take up an aircraft alone. In his autobiography, he writes: 'On 2nd February 1939 the great day came. I strapped into Spitfire K9802 for my first solo hour of what was ultimately to total 1488 hours in most marks of Spit up to the 22.'

Oxspring started operational flying in July 1940 and quickly earned a reputation as a distinguished pilot: he was one of the 'Few' selected by Fighter Command to have their portrait drawn by Cuthbert Orde, the war artist, sitting for it on 9 December 1940. Oxspring, who was usually known as Bobby, Bob or 'Oxo', flew throughout the Battle of Britain and was promoted to flying officer on 3 September 1940. He was shot down by a Me 109 over Kent on 25 October 1940. After eventually baling out, Oxspring's parachute lines became tangled and he hurtled towards the ground convinced that he would break both his legs, or even die. In his autobiography, he writes:

These quandaries inspired a sudden devout Christianity as I earnestly sought Divine Guidance to steer me towards a friendly tree or lake which might just cushion the impending impact. Fortune smiled and provided me with a whole wood just north of Pembury, and after a dodgy float over some high-tension cables I crashed down through the foliage of an enormous tree. I covered my face with my arms as I went through the branches, and the canopy caught on the top of the tree leaving me suspended like a yoyo some twenty feet up. I managed to swing to one side and clamber up on to a branch still tied up in my harness. I didn't have long to wait before a number of the splendid and alert Home Guard arrived to the rescue and whisked me away to the Kent and Sussex General

Hospital for a check-up. There the super medical staff gave me a sympathetic going over, produced a most welcome four fingers of brandy and pronounced me fit for further adventures.

His DFC was announced in the *London Gazette* on 8 November 1940:

One day in September, 1940, Flight Lieutenant Oxspring was engaged on an offensive patrol with his squadron. Whilst acting as rear guard, he sighted and engaged several Messerschmitt 109s 3,000 feet above. After driving them off, he led his section in an attack against a large formation of enemy bombers and succeeded in destroying a Dornier 17 at short range and also in damaging two Heinkel 111s. He has at all times led his section with skill and determination, and has destroyed six enemy aircraft.

Oxspring became a flight commander in 41 Squadron and went on to command 91 Squadron at RAF Hawkinge, Kent, and, later, 72 and 222 Squadrons and No. 24 Wing. He was awarded a Bar to his DFC on 18 September 1942 and his citation stated: 'This squadron commander has rendered much valuable service. His skill, whether in attacks on the enemy's ground targets and shipping or in air combat, has been of a high order. He has destroyed at least 7 enemy aircraft.' Oxspring married the following month.

After transferring to North Africa with 72 Squadron, Oxspring is believed to have shot down the renowned German ace, Anton Hafner, on 2 January 1943. Boosted by his own run of success in the skies, he went on to lead his squadron as it became the highest scorer in the North African theatre. He was awarded a second Bar to his DFC on 16 February 1943 and his citation stated: 'During initial operations from forward airfields in North Africa Squadron Leader Oxspring led his formation on many sorties. He destroyed 1 enemy aircraft, bringing his total victories to 8. His outstanding devotion to duty and fine fighting qualities have been worthy of high praise.'

By the time hostilities ceased, his total claims were thirteen enemy aircraft destroyed plus one 'shared', two 'probables', thirteen damaged and four V-1 flying bombs destroyed. The latter 'kills' were usually accomplished by the pilot tipping the wings of the unmanned V-1 to force it down in open ground, a highly risky strategy. Oxspring was somewhat surprised to survive the war, writing in his autobiography:

The day before VE Day I strapped on a Spitfire for a carefree sortie of aerobatics. I had reason to celebrate. Notice arrived from the Air Ministry that I'd been granted a permanent commission in the RAF, so my future was secure. I could scarcely believe that I was still in one piece after six years of war and still flying my faithful Spitfire. Other pilots whose operations started on Spitfires transferred their allegiance to alternative fighters of excellent wartime design, among them the Typhoon, Mustang and Tempest. Thanks to the dedicated engineers at Supermarine and Rolls Royce, the Spitfire remained Queen of the sky. Circumstances had aligned my embattled survival with her ever increasing performance.

Oxspring remained in the RAF after the war and, on 31 October 1946, he was awarded, by royal decree, the Dutch Vliegerkruis (also known as the 'Dutch Flying Cross'), an award that appeared in the *London Gazette* on 10 January 1947. He was promoted to substantive squadron leader on 1 August 1947. Oxspring also received the AFC on 1 January 1949, after leading a team of 54 Squadron Vampires to Canada and the USA. At the time, he and his men had the honour of flying the first jet aircraft across the Atlantic. Oxspring retired from the RAF with the rank of group captain, having been station commander of RAF Gatow, Germany. He settled near RAF Cranwell, Lincolnshire, and died on 8 August 1989, aged seventy. For many years after his death, his medals were on display at RAF Cranwell. They were eventually sold at auction with some interesting memorabilia, including his RAF pilot's logbooks and Caterpillar Club badge. The Caterpillar Club is an informal association of those of any nationality who have successfully parachuted from a stricken aircraft, so called because the strings of the parachute are made from silk.

SERGEANT (LATER FLIGHT LIEUTENANT) WILLIAM THOMAS EDWARD ROLLS
Royal Air Force Volunteer Reserve (RAFVR)
DECORATIONS: DISTINGUISHED FLYING MEDAL (DFM) AND DISTINGUISHED FLYING CROSS (DFC) GAZETTED: 8 NOVEMBER 1940 AND 4 DECEMBER 1942

Bill Rolls was born in Edmonton, north London, on 6 August 1914. He won a scholarship to The Latymer School, also in Edmonton, in 1925. After leaving school, Rolls worked as a building engineer's apprentice in his uncle's firm, while at the same time earning extra money making leather coats and golf jackets. In March 1939, he enlisted in the RAFVR and, after training, he gained his pilot's 'wings' in July of the same year. He was mobilised as a sergeant pilot at the outbreak of hostilities and then attended another training course, this time at South Cerney, Gloucestershire. In June 1940, Rolls, who was by then married with a baby daughter, was posted to 72 Squadron, based at RAF Acklington, Northumberland, to fly Spitfires. In his memoir, *Spitfire Attack*, Rolls wrote of his joy at hearing the news: 'The Spitfire was the finest aircraft in the world as far as I was concerned.' His operational career took off when the squadron moved to RAF Biggin Hill, Kent, on the last day of August. Rolls further commented: 'I did know one thing – we were now at war with a capital W . . . It was obvious that the German High Command were out to destroy our airfields especially the fighter ones, as a prelude to the Invasion of Great Britain. It was up to us to stop the bastards from doing it.'

Rolls was soon playing a full part in the Battle of Britain. On 2 September, only his second day at Biggin Hill, Rolls claimed his initial two victories: a Me 110 fighter and a Do 17 bomber, both the result of combats over Maidstone, Kent. Two days later, Rolls claimed another brace of enemy aircraft – Ju 87 bombers – in combats over Ashford and Tunbridge Wells, both in Kent. However, the next day, one of his five sergeant pilot friends was killed. Rolls wrote of the distress and how the remaining four fulfilled a promise that, if one of them died, the others would drink his health and, having ordered the victim's favourite drink, share it among them. On 11 September, Rolls added another Do 17 to his tally, along with a 'probable', both in combats over Tunbridge Wells.

However, his Spitfire was badly shot up the next day, 12 September, in a further combat. Rolls recalled:

When I landed back at Croydon, and having taxied to our dispersal point, I saw the holes in the cockpit; one of the instruments had been smashed too. Then I saw the holes on the other side of the cockpit and wondered how I had got hit both sides at the same time. I soon found out because before I could get out of the cockpit, I saw a metal rod coming through one of the holes and an airman on my wing put his hand on the rod and pushed it through the other side of the cockpit. The rod was now four inches from my Mae West [life jacket] at chest height. The airman then said: 'Sergeant, do you realise that one ten-thousandth of a second later that bullet would have gone straight through your heart.'

On 14 September, Rolls claimed a Me 109 destroyed in combat west of Canterbury, Kent, after seeing the enemy aircraft crash-land in flames near Bethersden. Four days later, Rolls returned from a combat mission with his own aircraft damaged again, including holes in the cockpit and his life jacket. On 20 September, Rolls claimed his final victim in the Battle of Britain: another Me 109 destroyed after a fifteen-minute combat. Rolls regarded this as his most memorable combat because he had been due to go on leave the next day. 'So I had to win this one,' he wrote:

I dived out of the sun on to its tail and waited till it started to climb before I pressed the tit to fire. I let it have about three seconds fire and the 109 did a stall turn to starboard and I followed it. I saw a large black piece break away from the side of the cockpit on the port side. I got it in my sights again as it turned and let it have another four sec burst. This time I saw the smoke and what appeared to be oil and water come from underneath it. It turned to dive and as it did I let it have a final burst when the whole lot of the cockpit dropped away and the rest dropped down towards the cloud.

Rolls was recommended for an immediate DFM and his commanding officer wrote: 'This N.C.O. pilot, whose first experience of squadron flying of any kind began on 19 June 1940, when he joined this squadron, has proved in a very short space of time to be an excellent war pilot. His record since the Squadron's arrival in this sector on 31 August 1940, being six and a half enemy aircraft confirmed destroyed, one probably destroyed and one damaged . . .' Rolls' happiness at his decoration, formally announced on 8 November 1940, was sadly marred soon afterwards by the death of his young daughter, Carole, who had been suffering from a heart defect.

After being rested as an instructor at two bases, Rolls returned to operational duties in October 1941 with an appointment to the recently formed 122 (Bombay) Squadron, a Spitfire unit based at RAF Scorton, Yorkshire. In the spring of 1942, his squadron moved to Hornchurch, Essex, where Rolls quickly rediscovered his earlier good form during cross-Channel sweeps. By then promoted to a pilot officer, Rolls claimed a Fw 190 fighter destroyed over St Omer–Audruicq on 17 May, together with a 'probable' on the same occasion. His combat report stated:

I was the Wing Commander's No 2 (Red 2) and went down with him when he attacked the Fw. 190s. I got in a two seconds burst at one Fw. 190 which came past me from port to starboard and saw white smoke issuing from it. I followed it in a dive down to 11,000 feet approximately, the range closing from about 200 yards to 50 yards, giving it about a two seconds burst of machine-gun and cannon. Very shortly afterwards the enemy aircraft exploded in mid-air and an undercarriage leg and wheel came past over my port wing. I claim this enemy aircraft as destroyed. I pulled out of my dive at 3,000 feet and started climbing to 10,000 feet approximately, S.E. of Gines, but shortly after saw another Fw. 190 very close to my tail. I went into a very steep turn and after about a turn and a half got to his tail, managing to get a two seconds burst (machine-gun only) from about 15 degrees port I saw white smoke coming from what appeared to be the port wing root but could not observe further as I was overshooting. This combat, however, was seen by Flight Lieutenant Thomas of 64 Squadron, who states this enemy aircraft was completely out of control going down over and over 'very sloppily', obviously finished and not worth going after to make sure. In view of his confirmation, I claim this aircraft as a 'probable'.

In a head-on attack on 2 June, with more Fw 190s over Le Crotoy, Rolls added a half-share and another 'probable' to his score. Rolls was posted to RAF Debden, Essex, a few weeks later and was told to prepare for passage to Malta in 126 Squadron.

Rolls embarked at Greenock, Scotland, in the aircraft carrier HMS *Furious* and ended up accompanying the famous 'Pedestal' convoy to Malta. On 11 August 1942, he also led a section of Spitfires from the flight deck of *Furious* to Luqa, Malta. This difficult and daring mission was known as Operation Bellows. Yet again, Rolls enjoyed great success in combat: he added nine victories to his total in just over two months of operational flying. The first of these victories was a Ju 88 bomber off Linosa on 13 August when Rolls wrote in his pilot's logbook how he saw 'a pattern of strikes zig-zag along the fuselage. I ran out of ammo. By this time the 88 was pouring black smoke at 1,800 feet from both engines and it dived nearly vertically into the sea.' His second victory was a Dornier flying boat off Capo Passero, Sicily, on 19 September when the aircraft was seen with 'a red-orange glow within' before it disappeared in a white splash in front of Rolls.

During the famous 'October Blitz' over Malta, Rolls distinguished himself yet again, bringing down seven enemy aircraft in a fortnight. His first victim was a Reggiane 2001, which crashed into the sea after a combat on 11 October. After the Italian pilot baled out, Rolls circled him in his rescue dinghy but he refused to return the airman's wave. The next day Rolls claimed a Ju 88 over Grand Harbour, Valetta, when he wrote of the combat: 'I saw one of the Ju. 88s I had fired at diving down. I put a final burst into it and it almost fell to pieces . . . I followed to 4,000 feet and thought I saw two bale out. I did not see what had happened to the others I had hit since I was too busy getting out of the mass of aircraft flying around . . . I saw Ju. 88s burning and going down all over the place.' On the same day, Rolls claimed two Macchi 202s, one that blew up in mid-air and the other that crashed into the sea off Gozo. On 14 October, Rolls claimed another enemy aircraft in a head-on attack: 'I saw my cannon shells hit the leading aircraft; its port engine blew up and the aircraft went down.' Two days later, he claimed a Ju 88, which came down in the sea east of Grand Harbour. His final victory from this period came on 26 October when Rolls claimed another Me 109, attacking at 8,000 and 4,000 feet: the aircraft was hit and went into a vertical dive from 2,000 feet, pouring black smoke.

Rolls, who had been serving as flight commander from mid-August, was in hospital when news of his DFC was announced on 4 December 1942. He had received serious leg and foot injuries when a wall, earlier damaged by a bomb, collapsed on him, forcing him to be evacuated to the UK via Gibraltar. The recommendation for his decoration stated: 'As Flight Commander, he has shown outstanding leadership and determination especially during the present operations. He has led his Flight with great courage and skill as a result of which enemy bomber formations turned back on two occasions. He is a first class fighter pilot and a leader who gets the best out of pilots.'

In early 1943, Rolls was appointed to the Air Ministry's publicity branch, giving lectures and talks at various 'Wings for Victory' events. In September of that year, he was sent to the Air Armament School at RAF Manby, Lincolnshire, for a lengthy course. Afterwards he was appointed as a specialist armament officer with 12 Group, and later he was attached to the bombing analysis unit. He was demobbed early in 1946. During the war, Rolls had flown more than 400 hours in Spitfires and claimed seventeen 'kills'. After the war, he was appointed as a films officer in the scientific advisers' division of the Ministry of Works. Later Rolls moved to the Department of Scientific and Industrial Research headquarters in London, as an exhibition officer, where his work involved designing and producing exhibitions for Olympia and Earl's Court. In 1960, he was appointed as senior information officer responsible for the production of RAF training films. Rolls lived in Westcliff-on-Sea, Essex, where he produced around 150 films, and was promoted to director, before retiring because of ill health in

September 1975. It was only after he suffered a heart attack that Rolls, encouraged by comments from his medical team, decided to write his memoirs. Rolls' book, *Spitfire Attack*, was published in 1987 and he wrote: 'It was suggested that I had a ghost writer to help me write the book, but I had many real ghosts helping me every time I sat down to the typewriter.' Rolls died in July 1988, aged seventy-three.

PILOT OFFICER (LATER SQUADRON LEADER) BRYAN VINCENT DRAPER
Royal Air Force Volunteer Reserve (RAFVR)
DECORATION: DISTINGUISHED FLYING CROSS (DFC)
GAZETTED: 24 DECEMBER 1940

Bryan 'Ben' Draper was born in Barry, South Wales, in early 1916 and joined the RAFVR in April 1938. He gained his pilot's 'wings' in October 1939 and was commissioned as a pilot officer on 10 December 1939. Draper arrived at 11 (F) Group Pool, St Athan, South Wales on 28 December. However, after learning to fly Spitfires, he was posted to 74 (Tiger) Squadron, based at RAF Hornchurch, Essex, on 14 February 1940.

On 20 May 1940, the squadron began operational flying over France at the time of the battle for and the evacuation of Dunkirk. Within a week, the squadron had lost five pilots although Draper had enjoyed a great deal of success. He shared a 'kill' when he was in Blue Section and the leader of Red Section targeted a He III bomber some thirty miles inland from Dunkirk. Draper wrote in his pilot's logbook: 'By the time I could close range E/a's [enemy aircraft's] port engine was on fire . . . I fired a three second burst into fuselage and broke away . . . When I next saw E/a he was crashing into a field.' Four days later, Draper wrote of another offensive patrol:

Red 2 and myself attacked a Heinkel which was lagging behind the others and Red 2 went in first to deliver his attack. When he broke away the port engine of E/a was smoking. I then attacked and fired one burst into the fuselage at about 250 yards followed by a burst in each engine. The rear gunner stopped firing and both engines were smoking badly and the E/a started losing the formation and dropping height . . . E/a not seen to crash as AA [anti-aircraft] fire and cross fire from Heinkels very severe. Position last seen three miles S.E. of St Omer.

In June 1940, the squadron regrouped and the next month it became heavily involved in the Battle of Britain. On the first day of the battle, 10 July, Draper damaged a Me 109 fighter in the morning and a Do 17 bomber in the afternoon. He wrote:

I was Yellow 2 on patrol over Deal and Dover and received orders to intercept a raid off Margate. Red and Blue Sections took off from Manston [Kent] at 1037hrs and enemy aircraft were sighted at 1100hrs and a dogfight ensued. One enemy aircraft positioned himself on Yellow Leader's tail and I opened fire on this E/a from 300 yards from slightly above and behind and put four bursts of one second into him. I could see the bursts going into enemy aircraft around the engine but had to exercise care so as not to hit Yellow Leader. The enemy aircraft started diving vertically with white trail of steam or smoke following him but I was unable to follow him down as by that time there were several other enemy aircraft to be attacked. I then saw an enemy aircraft below and coming towards me. I dived to attack but by the time I was in position for a deflection attack I was in an over the vertical dive. I fired three short bursts at him and then had to break away in order to avoid collision. Having climbed up again the enemy were just breaking off the fight so after firing one very short burst at the straggler . . .

Draper's report of the afternoon incident told how the squadron was confronted with an enemy formation of more than 100 aircraft:

I was Yellow 2 in A Flight 74 Squadron guarding a convoy 5 miles off Dover when it was attacked by enemy bombers escorted by two layers of fighters ranging in height from 4,000 feet to 12,000 feet. I, in company with Yellow 3, climbed above the top layer of fighters which were Me. 109s. We then split and each attacked an enemy aircraft. I fired a short burst at 30% deflection into one enemy aircraft which promptly half-rolled and dived. I then found I was surrounded and so climbed into cloud at 14,000 feet and altered course. When I came down I found myself over an enemy aircraft at which I fired a burst from above. The other fighters again wheeled to attack me so I once again climbed into the clouds. When I again came below the cloud I found myself in a favourable position to make a diving attack on the Dornier 17s. I came down in a 60 degree dive and put a three or four second burst into one bomber which emitted smoke from the starboard engine and then climbed steeply again to avoid the fighters. When I again looked down I saw three parachutists descending towards the sea which I took to be the crew of the Do. 17. I again dived and put another burst into another Dornier . . . and again climbed above the top layer of fighters.

There were many days when Draper engaged the enemy more than once. For example, on 14 September 1940, he spotted and engaged a Me 110, which proved inconclusive. However, within twenty minutes he got his victory over another enemy aircraft as detailed in his log: 'At 1405 while doing a wide sweep to port I sighted a Ju 88 emerging from cloud almost below me. I half-rolled and fired at it from behind and above and then fired another burst into the starboard motor from almost line astern. E/a answered the fire from the top rear turret but at my second burst the starboard wing dropped and E/a spiralled into a dense cloud to starboard.' On 29 September 1940, Draper reported: 'Patrol. 1 Ju 88. Found him over the sea & shot the living Jesus out of him.'

In October, the squadron moved to RAF Biggin Hill, Kent, where Draper's high success rate continued. On 17 October, he shot down one Messerschmitt and gained another 'probable'.

I was Yellow 3 when 74 Squadron intercepted about 60 Me. 109s in the vicinity of Maidstone-Gravesend area at 26,000 feet. In the first encounter a Me 109 crossed my sights at about 200 yards range . . . I fired a three second burst which hit him in the engine and a cloud of mixed black and white smoke streamed back . . . I then saw seven Me 109s flying in line astern southwards and getting into position behind and slightly above the rear most one I shot him down in flames before he realised my presence . . . I tried south again I spotted about twelve Me 109s proceeding towards the coast below and in front of me. I tried to repeat my previous tactics but they saw me before I could attack and turned to attack me. As I was at their height and alone I sprayed one quick burst at the front two which swerved to starboard and enabled me to break off combat.

On 20 October, Draper engaged with more than thirty enemy aircraft over south London and Kent. He wrote: 'Shot Down 4 Miles West of Sevenoaks By Another Blasted 109. He Shot Away My Oil Rad [radiator]. Holes in Engine & Stbd. [starboard] Elevator. The Bastard.' Draper's aircraft was a write-off but he was soon back in the skies in a new Spitfire.

November 1940 saw yet more success for the squadron when it destroyed twenty-six enemy aircraft. Draper shot down a Me 109 over Littlehampton, Sussex, on 11 November 1940. However, the pinnacle of Draper's flying career came three days later when he shot down and destroyed three Ju 87s and damaged another. He wrote:

I was Yellow 1 when we were ordered to intercept a formation of 50-80 E/a over Deal at 15,000 feet. I got onto one Ju 87's tail and gave him a short deflection burst after which pieces fell from his port wing root and engine cowlings and I left him going down almost vertically . . . I then attacked another '87 which burst into flames after a two second burst. I then saw a Me 109 at which I fired a short burst which damaged him slightly but he disappeared into cloud ... I then attacked a third Ju 87 which I saw crash into the sea after two or three second burst.

The following day, 15 November, Draper claimed what was to be his final victory of the war, a Me 109, over the Littlehampton area.

Draper's DFC was announced on Christmas Eve 1940 when his citation stated: 'Since December, 1939, Pilot Officer Draper has participated in numerous engagements against the enemy. He has displayed great skill and determination as a fighter pilot and has destroyed seven enemy aircraft.'

December 1940 also saw Draper posted to Central Flying School at RAF Upavon, Wiltshire, on an instructors' course. He then went on to instruct at RAF College Cranwell, Lincolnshire, before being posted in a similar capacity to Canada. The news of his foreign posting was recorded in Draper's logbook as: 'Canada Blast It!!' Draper was promoted to flight lieutenant on 10 March 1942. He returned to England in December 1943 and undertook a conversion course in Mosquitos. In January 1945, he was posted to join up with his new unit, 45 Squadron, in India. The following month, when based at Kumbhirgram, he was tasked with flying ground attack missions against the Japanese in support of the Burma campaign. On 28 February 1945, while en route to attack a Japanese target, his Mosquito was seen to break up in mid-air – the aircraft crashed into the ground and no one was seen to bale out beforehand. Draper, by then a squadron leader, and his navigator were both killed. Draper, who died aged twenty-eight, just three weeks after the birth of his son, was buried at Taukkyan War Cemetery, Rangoon, Burma.

SQUADRON LEADER ALAN FRANCIS ECKFORD
RAF
DECORATION: DISTINGUISHED FLYING CROSS (DFC)
GAZETTED: 24 DECEMBER 1940

Alan 'Shag' Eckford was born in Thame Park, Oxfordshire, on 6 February 1919. He was educated at King Edward VI Grammar School, Birmingham, before being awarded an engineering scholarship to Loughborough College. In November 1938, aged nineteen, he enlisted in the RAF on a short-service commission. After completing his training, he joined 32 Squadron, a Hurricane unit based at RAF Biggin Hill, Kent, in September 1939. Eckford flew his first patrols in December 1939, but it was not until the first four months of the New Year that he was involved in a significant increase in operational activity: numerous defensive and convoy escort sorties being carried out as well as a good deal of battle practice.

In mid-May 1940, 32 Squadron began encountering the Luftwaffe, having been ordered to France. Eckford quickly claimed his first victory, a Do 215 bomber at 16,000 feet over Le Cateau. A few days later 32 Squadron returned to Biggin Hill and flew around ten operational patrols over the Manston sector of Kent before the end of the month. In early June 1940, Eckford was posted to 242 Squadron, a Canadian unit that was taking heavy casualties in France. Eckford arrived at Châteaudun on 8 June and quickly became embroiled in the squadron's punishing operational agenda. He flew several offensive sorties before moving to a new airfield at Le Mans. The following day, after a fierce combat, he brought down a Me 109 over the Seine–Rouen sector.

The offensive patrols continued over Nantes, St Nazaire and elsewhere until, on 18 June, 242 Squadron was withdrawn from France. Two days later, its weary pilots flew into RAF Coltishall, Norfolk, to meet their new commanding officer, the legendary – and legless – Acting Squadron Leader Douglas Bader, who ended all speculation about his own flying capabilities by putting on a spectacular thirty-minute session of low-level aerobatics right over the airfield. Within little more than a week, Bader reported to his superiors: '242 Squadron now operational as regards pilots but non-operational repeat non-operational as regards equipment.' However, by early July, following a successful meeting regarding equipment supply, Bader reported back: '242 Squadron now fully operational.'

On 10 July, Eckford shot up a He III bomber, off Yarmouth, Norfolk, in one of 242's first interceptions since returning to England. He wrote:

I took-off [as Green Leader, 'B' Flight] at 0725 hours to patrol a convoy 12 miles S.E. of Yarmouth. On reaching the convoy, I noticed flashes from a destroyer's guns, then shell bursts. Two bombs dropped close to the ship and then I saw a Heinkel climbing N. from 1200 feet, my section being at 4000 feet. I followed the E.A. [enemy aircraft] into cloud and lost sight of him until I saw him again about a minute later. I opened fire from astern and above at 300 yards, noticing tracer from the top gun which stopped when I fired. I expended all of my ammunition in one burst, but the E.A. broke away in the cloud. I saw it when I emerged, climbing S.E., leaving a trail of white smoke . . .

Eckford took part in another seven operational sorties over the next fortnight, but on 24 July he was posted back to 32 Squadron, still based at Biggin Hill. By then, with the Battle of Britain in full swing, the daily demands on Fighter Command were formidable. In fact, on the day after arriving at Biggin Hill, Eckford flew three operational patrols, a daily tally that was repeated four more times that month. It was here, towards the end of July, that a cameraman captured some highly evocative images of the Battle of Britain, notably the shattered pilots of 32 Squadron, including Eckford, resting between scrambles. If July was busy, then August was even busier, with 32 Squadron's pilots undertaking a vast number of patrols. On 18 August, Eckford claimed his first 'double whammy': Ju 88 and Do 17 bombers. Alfred Price, the author, featured the latter aircraft's fate in his *Royal Air Force Yearbook* article, 'Death of a Dornier':

> Early on the afternoon of 18 August, as a formation of 27 Dornier Do. 17s of Kampfgeschwader 76 were running in to bomb the airfield at Kenley [south London], the Hurricanes of No. 32 Squadron moved into position for a head-on attack. As he closed on the enemy aircraft, Pilot Officer Alan Eckford worked out his attack plan: 'The bombers were stepped up, in close formation. I remember thinking as I was approaching the formation, that if I opened fire at the first one and then gradually lifted my nose and kept the button pressed, several would have to pass through my fire.'

The plan failed to take into account the tremendous closing speed of the opposing forces.

Eckford had time for only a short burst at the Dorniers,

Right: 2nd Lieutenant (promoted posthumously to Lieutenant) William Rhodes-Moorhouse was the first airman to be awarded the VC after being fatally wounded in a daring attack on a railway junction at Courtrai in German-occupied France in April 1915. He is pictured three years earlier in the cockpit of his Breguet aircraft.

RAF MUSEUM

Right: Captain Aidan Liddell of the Royal Flying Corps, photographed on the Western Front in July 1915 during his previous service with the Argyll and Sutherland Highlanders. In August 1915, shortly after transferring, Liddell was awarded the VC for flying his badly damaged aircraft back to an Allied airfield despite horrific injuries. He died days after the decoration was announced.

IWM (Q56193)

Below and right: Lieutenant (later Captain) William Leefe Robinson was awarded the VC in September 1916 after becoming the first airman to shoot down a German Zeppelin over the UK. He is pictured both sitting on the fuselage of his BE2c aircraft after a crash-landing and (centre, left arm half raised) being hailed as a hero by his fellow airmen after the Zeppelin incident.

RAF MUSEUM

RAF MUSEUM

Lieut. W. L. Robinson, VC.
red by his fellow airmen after destroying Zeppelin Contr on

Above: Major Edward 'Mick' Mannock was the highest scoring and most highly decorated British pilot of the First World War. Awarded a posthumous VC, he was feted by the *Sunday Dispatch* newspaper after being shot down and killed in July 1918.

Below left: Lieutenant (later Flight Lieutenant) Alan Jerrard, who served in the Army and the Royal Flying Corps during the Great War, was known affectionately as the 'Pyjama VC'. The only airman to be awarded the decoration during the war on the Italian Front, he was wounded, forced to crash-land at Mansue, Italy, and captured. He was wearing his pyjamas beneath his flying overalls because he had been ordered into action at short notice in March 1918.

Left: Sergeant Thomas Mottershead had the distinction of being the only non commissioned officer (NCO) to be awarded the VC for aerial operations during the Great War. Pictured in his Royal Flying Corps uniform, he received his decoration for crash-landing his blazing aircraft in January 1917, thereby saving his observer's life Mottershead, however, died from his severe injuries five days later.

Above: Flight Lieutenant (later Squadron Leader) James 'Ginger' Lacey (centre) and other officers from 501 Squadron are all smiles after he was presented with an Australian parachute. Lacey, who was the second highest scoring British fighter pilot of the Battle of Britain, was awarded the DFM and Bar in August and November 1940.

Below left: Flight Lieutenant (later Group Captain) John Simpson, a fighter pilot serving with the RAF during the Second World, is grinning despite his wounds after being awarded the DFC by George VI. Simpson's initial decoration in June 1940 was followed by a Bar to his DFC in May 1941.

Below right: Flying Officer (later Wing Commander) John Freeborn had the distinction of flying more operational hours than any other RAF pilot during the Battle of Britain. He was awarded the DFC in August 1940 and a Bar to the decoration in February the following year.

IWM (CH8977)

Top: Bank manager's son Pilot Officer (later Wing Commander) Harbourne Stephen, a brilliant and daring fighter pilot, was awarded three gallantry awards in just five months in 1940. The DFC and Bar, awarded in August and November, were followed by the DSO on Christmas Eve.

Above left: Wing Commander (later Group Captain) Tom Dalton-Morgan is pictured in March 1943 while leading the Ibsley Wing from RAF Harrowbeer in Devon. Dalton-Morgan, who claimed twenty-two victories during the war along with ten 'probables', was awarded the DFC and Bar in September 1940 and May 1941, followed by the DSO in May 1943

Above right: Sergeant (later Flight Lieutenant) James 'Bill' Caister was awarded the DFM in September 1940 for bravery during the Battle of Britain. By the time that his decoration was announced, he was a prisoner of war having been shot down and forced to crash-land his Spitfire in German-occupied France.

Above left: Flying Officer (later Wing Commander) Howard Mayers, a Hurricane pilot from Sydney, Australia, was awarded three gallantry awards between October 1940 and July 1942, the same month that he was shot down and taken as a prisoner of war. Mayers was killed in an Allied attack while being transported to a PoW camp in Italy.

Below left: Sergeant (later Flight Lieutenant) Bill Rolls was awarded the DFM in November 1940 for his courage during the Battle of Britain. He was awarded the DFC in December 1942 for bravery while defending the besieged island of Malta. In October 1942, Rolls had shot down seven enemy aircraft in just a fortnight.

Above right: Flight Lieutenant (later Wing Commander) Christopher 'Bunny' Currant, the son of a hatter, was awarded the DFC and Bar in October and November 1940, before being awarded the DSO in July 1942. Twice hospitalised by injuries from enemy fire, he spent his recovery time writing letters containing surprisingly upbeat accounts of his exploits to his parents.

Below right: Squadron Leader (later Group Captain) Robert Oxspring stands on the wing of his Spitfire at RAF Hawkinge, Kent, in May 1942, while he was in command of 91 Squadron. He was awarded the DFC and two Bars between November 1940 and February 1943, before being awarded the AFC in January 1949 for his work with the RAF in Canada and the USA.

Above: Squadron Leader Alan 'Shag' Eckford (far right) was awarded the DFC in December 1940 after shooting down six enemy aircraft. His citation praised him for his courage, skill and 'great keenness in his attacks'.

Below left: Pilot Officer (later Squadron Leader) Bryan 'Ben' Draper, a Battle of Britain fighter pilot, was awarded the DFC in December 1940 after destroying seven enemy aircraft. He and his navigator were shot down and killed in February 1945 while flying his Mosquito to attack a Japanese target in support of the Burma campaign.

Below right: Sergeant (later Flight Lieutenant) Michal Maciejowski was nicknamed 'Mickey Mouse' by his British comrades because they struggled to pronounce his Polish surname. He was awarded the DFM in February 1941 and the DFC in November 1942.

Right: Wing Commander (later Air Vice-Marshal) James 'Johnnie' Johnson is greeted by his faithful Labrador, Sally, after returning from a sortie in his Spitfire during 1945. Johnson, the top-scoring British flying ace of the war with thirty-three confirmed victories, was awarded five gallantry decorations between September 1941 and July 1944.

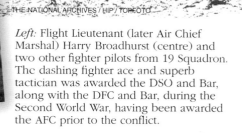

THE NATIONAL ARCHIVES / HIP / TOPFOTO

RAF MUSEUM

Left: Flight Lieutenant (later Air Chief Marshal) Harry Broadhurst (centre) and two other fighter pilots from 19 Squadron. The dashing fighter ace and superb tactician was awarded the DSO and Bar, along with the DFC and Bar, during the Second World War, having been awarded the AFC prior to the conflict.

Right: Flight Lieutenant (later Group Captain) Edward 'Hawkeye' Wells sits in the cockpit of his Spitfire at RAF Kenley, Surrey, in November 1941. Given his nickname because he was a brilliant shot in the air, Wells was awarded the DFC and Bar in August and November 1941, before being awarded the DSO in July 1942.

IWM (CH5061)

Above: A photograph of Sergeant Józef Jeka rests on the open pages of his log book detailing his experiences, including being shot down and seriously injured, from late 1940 and early 1941. The Polish fighter pilot served courageously with the RAF and was awarded the DFM in February 1942.

Below left: Squadron Leader Eric 'Jumbo' Genders was awarded the DFM in April 1942, the same month that he was commissioned as a pilot officer. In September 1942, he was shot down close to Greece, but he survived twenty-one hours in the sea before swimming to land. Genders was awarded the AFC in January 1949, but was killed while working as a test pilot the following year.

Below right: Flying Officer (later Flight Lieutenant) John Hancock (right) stands with a fellow pilot from 64 Squadron in front of a Spitfire at RAF Hornchurch, Essex. He was awarded the DFC in July 1942 but, having claimed eight victories, he was shot down and killed over Normandy in June 1944. A Bar to his DFC followed the next month.

before he had to push hard on his stick to avoid colliding with his victim. Once he was past the enemy formation, he looked back and saw the bomber he had attacked pull into a drunken half-roll before falling into a spin. Eckford was back in action for the remainder of the month and on 26 August he shot up a He III.

In mid-September, Eckford was posted to 253 (Hyderabad) Squadron at RAF Kenley, Surrey. On his first day, he took part in two scrambles while, after a hectic fortnight or so, he became involved in four separate scrambles and patrols. Furthermore, on 27 September, Eckford claimed his first victory with the squadron, a Me 109 over Kent. He later wrote in his combat report: 'I dived vertically on the E.A. and opened fire at about 300 feet above, observing my tracer entering the machine. The engines started to give off a little white smoke, and the E.A. lost height. I delivered another quarter attack from the port side and broke away upwards. I then attacked from astern, closing to 50 yards and firing at that range, breaking away just behind as the E.A. exploded. The wreckage fell 500 feet into a field . . .'

By October, Eckford had no energy left to enter the nature of his daily sorties in his pilot's logbook, a series of dittos under the word 'Patrol' from the 9th onwards having to suffice. He flew four times on 11 October, flew a night patrol over London four days later ('Don't volunteer when tight again!'), and destroyed another Me 109 over Kent on 30 October when his combat report stated:

I attacked the second E.A. of the front pair and saw my tracer entering the fuselage and he turned away and dived. I then attacked the last E.A. with a stern attack. He climbed with a left hand turn which I had no difficulty in following. After firing a burst of 4–5 seconds I observed white smoke coming out, then a little black smoke with flame. The E.A. dived vertically and I followed him through the cloud, the E.A. being slightly faster in the dive. I came out of the cloud at about 3000 feet and saw the wreckage burning in a field about 4 miles south of Meopham, near Gravesend. The pilot had baled out and when I approached [in the air] he held his hands up.

Yet it was November that proved to be Eckford's most successful period, with one destroyed, one shared destroyed, two 'probables' and a 'damaged'. A patrol on the 22nd produced positive results, Eckford sharing in the destruction of a Do 17 and in the damaging of another, both over Newhaven, Sussex. The next day a brace of Me 109s met comparable fates, the first of them a confirmed victory following a combat six miles south-west of Cap Gris Nez. His combat report stated:

I attacked the last E.A., who was slightly below me, attacking from the beam, changing to astern, range 100 yards. After two bursts of 5 and 3 seconds, the E.A. half-rolled and dived, turning vertically. I was able to counter this evasive action easily and observed flame and smoke. I gave the E.A. a further 5 seconds at 80 yards, as the E.A. straightened out of its dive, and observed that he was well on fire. I then had to take evasive action, as the other 5 E.A. had dived in line astern behind me, and I returned home at 10,000 feet crossing the coast at Dungeness. The E.A. had yellow noses up to the cockpits, and bright grey camouflage.

With the second 109, which was assessed as a 'probable', Eckford engaged it in an afternoon sortie over the Maidstone–Biggin Hill sector, later writing in his combat report: '. . . I noticed one E.A. coming towards me and turned on his tail quickly. We then dived steeply straight for the cloud, and I fired three bursts of 2, 4 and 5 seconds approximately. The enemy aircraft disappeared into the cloud emitting white smoke.'

Eckford was informed that he was to be awarded the DFC on the following day (24 November) and his squadron retired for a few days' rest. Returning south in early December, he flew another night sortie, over Sevenoaks, on the 21st, three days before his DFC was announced on Christmas Eve when his citation stated: 'This officer has displayed great keenness in his attacks against the enemy both in France and in England. His courage and skill, often in the face of odds, have enabled him to destroy six enemy aircraft.' The New Year found the squadron allocated to a good deal of convoy escort work, in addition to section scrambles and an increasing number of night operations, work that Eckford undertook for the remainder of his time with 253, latterly as a flight commander.

However, in November 1941, Eckford was posted to 55 Operational Training Unit (OTU) at Usworth, near Sunderland, where the CO and chief instructor was Dennis 'Hurricane' David, the famous ace. Eckford returned to the operational scene with 64 Squadron at RAF Hornchurch, Essex, in May 1942, having converted to Spitfires. Participating in a number of offensive operations the following month, he transferred to 154 Squadron in July. That month, among other offensive sweeps, he flew on a 'Rhubarb' operation (owing their name to fighters or fighter-bombers which took advantage of thick cloud to fly low across the Channel) to Etaples, France, in which sortie his wing leader, the ace 'Paddy' Finucane, was lost. Casualties were high, too, on a bomber escort mission to St Omer at the end of the month, Eckford noting in his logbook the loss of thirteen of fifty-four aircraft.

Eckford was credited on 19 August 1942 with damaging a Do 217 and a Fw 190 over Dieppe during Operation Jubilee, his score being further improved by a 'probable' Fw 190 five miles south of Dover on the 27th. He had been flying on an air sea rescue mission, when sector control warned of a pending attack by inbound enemy aircraft from Cap Gris Nez. Eckford reported:

A few minutes later Red Section was attacked from behind by two Fw. 190s. I turned to port and made a beam quarter attack on one E.A. which was firing at a Spitfire of my section. I observed strikes on the underside with cannon shells and the E.A. gave off a stream of white smoke, diving towards Dover. I was then forced to take evasive action as another E.A. was close behind me, and I did not see the first one again. Yellow 1 saw the E.A. giving off white smoke and diving. I carried out two further attacks on enemy aircraft with M.G. only, but observed no results.

Two more offensive sweeps were flown over France that month, but September and October proved to be non-operational, partly a result of the squadron having to prepare for its onward journey to North Africa, via Gibraltar, that November. Arriving at Maison Blanche, Algiers, on 8 November, 154 Squadron went quickly into action in support of the Allies' North African landings, Eckford and fellow pilots busying themselves in the defence of the harbour of Algiers and covering the Army moving rapidly east. On the 12th, having moved to an airfield at Djidjelli, the squadron was allocated to escort a formation of American C 47s carrying paratroops for the capture of the harbour at Bone. Halfway there, a Do 217 bomber was spotted, and Eckford and his wing leader, Group Captain P. H. 'Dutch' Hugo, shot it down between them.

The following day, over Djidjelli, Eckford shared a Ju 88 with two other pilots and destroyed another, but was forced to make a crash-landing after the latter combat. He was wounded by flying debris in December during an attack by Me 109s on his airfield. In the New Year, however, he returned to a busy round of operations, participating in numerous sweeps and bomber escort missions until March 1943, when he was appointed to the command of his old 242 Squadron. Between then and late May, when victory in Tunis was celebrated, he led 242 on many sorties. Returning to the UK in mid-June 1943, Eckford was employed at the Air Ministry for the remainder of the war, being promoted to substantive squadron leader in July 1944.

Eckford was demobilised in February 1946, by which point he was credited with eight/nine victories, three shared destroyed, two/three 'probables' and five damaged. Little is known of his life after the war, although he is believed to have retired to Norfolk. He died in 1991, aged seventy-two.

SERGEANT (LATER FLIGHT LIEUTENANT) MICHAL KAROL MACIEJOWSKI

Polish Air Force/RAF

DECORATIONS: DISTINGUISHED FLYING MEDAL (DFM) AND DISTINGUISHED FLYING CROSS (DFC) GAZETTED: 17 FEBRUARY 1941 AND 15 NOVEMBER 1942

Michal Maciejowski was born in Poland in the town of Gródek Jagdowski on 29 October 1913. He learnt to fly at nineteen, after joining the Polish Air Force. Maciejowski was initially posted to a fighter squadron and served as an instructor before being transferred to a bomber squadron. In late 1939, during the fall of Poland, he was ordered to fly to Romania. He was interned there for a short time before travelling by sea to Syria, where he arrived in January 1940. Another journey by ship took him to Marseilles in southern France. From there, he was sent to the Polish air base at Lyons for posting to a fighter squadron. However, when France too fell, he flew to Britain and was posted to RAF Eastchurch, Kent. His initial brief was to learn English and to familiarise himself with British aircraft. It was here that he became known affectionately as 'Mickey Mouse' because his British comrades found his name too difficult to pronounce.

In August 1940, after training on Hurricanes, Maciejowski was posted to III Squadron at North Weald, Essex, and in October 1940 he was transferred to 249 Squadron. On 15 October 1940, he was involved in what he later called an 'embarrassing moment' when he could not find his trousers as he 'scrambled' at 5 a.m. After a dogfight over Kent, his engine failed and he later wrote:

I glided toward mother earth and landed in a meadow near an army barracks. A few farmers and army personnel came and thought that I was a German pilot in a stolen Hurricane. With my command of pidgin English, I made myself understood and gave them my squadron number and airfield. We became friends when it was confirmed that I was a Polish pilot. Later that afternoon the mechanic fixed whatever was wrong – I took off, and was on duty with the same aircraft later the same day.

Maciejowski's exploits in the air soon left an impression: he claimed a Me 109 fighter destroyed on 29 October and two more 'probables' on 7 November. On 28 November, he claimed another 'probable' before destroying Me 109s on 5 December, 10 January 1941 and 10 February 1941. Upon the formation of 317 (Polish) Squadron on 22 February 1941, Maciejowski was posted to the unit where he claimed a 'probable' Ju 52 bomber on 22 May.

Maciejowski was awarded the Polish Cross of Valour and Bar on 1 April 1941 having already received the DFM on 17 February 1941. The award was based on the recommendation from Wing Commander F. V. Beamish, of RAF North Weald, Essex, which stated: 'This Pilot NCO has proved to be a cool and determined fighter pilot who always shows a calm yet extremely resolute intention of destroying the enemy. His courage and example are admired by all ranks. He has destroyed five enemy aircraft besides damaging several others.'

On 15 July 1941, Maciejowski was awarded a second Bar to his Cross of Valour but there were still many more adventures to come. On 30 December 1941, he claimed two Me 109s destroyed and on 5 May 1942 he was awarded the Virtuti

Militari (5th class). In June, Maciejowski was commissioned and on the 19th he saw heavy combat action over Dieppe: claiming a Ju 88 and a Fw 190 destroyed and a Do 217 shared destroyed. On 25 August, he was posted to 58 Operational Training Unit (OTU) Grangemouth, Stirlingshire, Scotland, as an instructor. On 15 November 1942, Maciejowski was awarded a third Bar to his Cross of Valour and also the DFC. The latter award was based on the recommendation from Group Captain A. S. Adnams, of RAF Northolt, Middlesex, which said:

> This officer fought with an English Squadron in the 'Battle of Britain' and then joined his present Squadron. Recently commissioned, he was the outstanding victor of the Polish Wing in the operations over Dieppe on 19th August, 1942. In this operation he brought his personal score up to 9½ enemy aircraft destroyed and one probably destroyed, by the destruction of an enemy bomber and an enemy fighter aircraft, sharing in the destruction of a further enemy bomber. Since the award of the Distinguished Flying Medal, he has destroyed a further 4½ enemy aircraft, and he has at all times shown the greatest determination to engage and destroy the enemy.

Maciejowski returned to operational flying on 23 March 1943, when he rejoined 316 Squadron at Northolt. He probably destroyed a Fw 190 and damaged another on 4 May and on 11 June he destroyed a Me 109. Having survived every encounter with an enemy aircraft, he was, ironically, finally brought down over Occupied France in a mid-air collision with a fellow Allied pilot on 9 August 1943. Maciejowski was forced to bale out at 23,000 feet and suffered his only injury of the war: part of his ear was torn off and then frostbite set into the wound. He was taken prisoner of war (PoW) and held at Stalag Luft III, where he took part in tunnelling for the 'Great Escape'. However, he was not one of those who exited the tunnel and he was instead repatriated in May 1945.

Maciejowski was a real character and, in their book about Stalag Luft III, *Escape to Danger*, Paul Brickhill and Conrad Norton devoted a chapter to him. They wrote:

> The nickname [Mickey Mouse] was remarkably apt because it conveyed all the sense of a diminutive knight errant, chockful of guts, skill and a puckish, appealing wit – which was Mickey all over. He was a bare 5ft. 4ins., topped by a close-fitting cap of dark, wiry hair, and built like a baby tank, sprouting knotty muscles from hefty shoulders and slightly bandy legs . . . He has eleven and a half victories, three probables and several damaged, and his fighting career was quite spectacular until a stroke of fiendish luck put him behind the wire.

Even though Maciejowski's wartime flying ended on 9 August 1943, he still emerged as Poland's seventh highest scoring ace for the Second World War. All of his 'kills' were made while operating from Britain and many were fighter aircraft. Maciejowski returned to flying duties in June 1945 and attended a refresher course at 16 Flying Training School (FTS), Newton, Nottinghamshire. From there, he was posted on 11 November to 309 Squadron based at RAF Coltishall, Norfolk. Maciejowski remained with the squadron until it was disbanded on 6 January 1947. Unlike many of his fellow Polish pilots,

Maciejowski did not return to his homeland after the war. Instead, he settled in Britain and changed his surname to Manson.

After the war, he wrote of his early days flying with the RAF: 'What I remember most of those days was fast-flowing adrenaline, scores of eager young men, some boys of bigger hearts than their awareness of the danger of a short life, quiet sadness and continuity of efforts and purpose of those who survived.' Maciejowski rejoined the RAF in June 1951 and flew as a test pilot until, in 1958, he was ruled to be too old to fly. However, the RAF remained loyal towards him and offered him ground duties: he chose catering because he 'wanted to learn to cook'. In 1963, Maciejowski formally transferred to the catering branch and three years later he was put in charge of supply in Aden, in the Middle East, during the troubles. By 1970, he was running the RAF Transit Hotel in Malta. Maciejowski retired as a flight lieutenant in 1972 and emigrated to Winnipeg, Canada, where he enjoyed a full and happy retirement. He died on 16 April 2001, aged eighty-seven.

SERGEANT GEORGE ATKINSON
RAF
DECORATION: DISTINGUISHED FLYING MEDAL
(DFM)
GAZETTED: 7 MARCH 1941

Although little is known of George Atkinson's early life, we do know that he enlisted in the RAF straight from school as an apprentice at RAF Halton, Buckinghamshire. He passed out as a metal rigger in 1934 and served overseas with 47 Squadron at Atbara and Khartoum in Sudan. He began his flying training in September 1937 before joining 151 Squadron the following year as the unit began to receive its first Hurricanes. Atkinson was posted to Blue Section and the squadron took part in defensive patrols early in the Second World War before covering the evacuation at Dunkirk. The squadron flew missions over northern France during May and June 1940, before taking part in the Battle of Britain.

Atkinson was present when 151 Squadron was involved in its first engagement of the Second World War. It happened at around 11 a.m. on 17 May 1940 when the squadron was patrolling the Lille–Valencie area of northern France. When two enemy aircraft were spotted to the south-east, Red Section went to investigate leaving Blue and Yellow sections to give top cover. The enemy were identified as Ju 87s bombers and Red Leader ordered an attack. More enemy aircraft joined in and so Blue and Yellow sections were also ordered to attack. A massive fight took place in which the squadron claimed ten victories. Atkinson claimed an enemy aircraft damaged, although his own aircraft was holed.

The next day the same nine pilots from 151 Squadron were airborne when a massive battle took place between another Hurricane squadron and twenty Me 109s over Vitry, France. Shortly afterwards, Blue Section engaged two He 111 bombers, after which Atkinson became separated from his comrades and encountered three He 111s which he attacked, seeing one go down with its port engine on fire. Atkinson eventually landed at Le Touquet, where he could not immediately refuel, and rejoined his squadron the next day. On 21 May, the squadron was acting as an escort for a squadron of Blenheim bombers that was targeting a railway junction south-east of Boulogne. Atkinson identified and engaged a Henschel Hs 125, which he shot down. The next day, he destroyed a Ju 87 as the squadron escorted three Ensign transport aircraft taking fuel and ammunition to Merville, France.

After yet another engagement on 29 July 1940, Atkinson submitted a combat report detailing how the squadron had encountered enemy aircraft trying to dive-bomb five Allied ships near Felixstowe, Suffolk. He described attacking Me 110s:

> The E.A. [enemy aircraft] were on our port side, and I selected one, and using an almost beam attack, allowed full deflection for the first burst. The deflection I varied for the second and third bursts – very slightly. After the second burst, I perceived a thin trail of black smoke coming from the E.A. port engine. After the third burst, the smoke increased to a thick black trail, and the E.A. turned East, and was last seen losing height rapidly. I attempted to attack another E.A. but ammunition was finished.

Throughout August 1940, 151 Squadron took part in intense fighting as, time and again, heavy formations of German bombers and fighters were sent to the southern counties of Britain. On 13 August, during a frantic engagement, Atkinson was shot down over the English Channel in a major combat with Messerschmitt fighters. However, he baled out and came down in the sea where he was picked up by an air sea rescue launch.

Atkinson's DFM was announced on 7 March 1941 after the recommendation for his award stated:

> Sergeant George Atkinson has served with No. 151 Squadron for over 16 months, and except for a period in hospital after

he had been shot down, has been in action with them on all possible occasions. His devotion to duty and keenness maintained over this long period of day fighting are of an exceptionally high order and in night fighting, he is continuing to set an example of the highest order. He has shot down two aircraft and probably three others.

Atkinson's decoration was the only DFM awarded to his squadron for a Battle of Britain pilot.

Atkinson then flew Spitfire 1s on a detachment to RAF Stapleford Tawney, Essex, before being posted to RAF East Fortune, Scotland, as an instructor and, later, to 96 Squadron (Defiants). From October 1943 to December 1944, he was posted to Canada as an instructor on Mosquitos. Atkinson flew his last flight – in a Mosquito from 54 Operational Training Unit (OTU) – on 1 March 1945. His aircraft fell into a spin from a low-level roll and crashed into a field near Pallinsburn House, Northumberland. The aircraft exploded and Atkinson and a comrade were both killed close to the house, which was being used as a convalescent hospital. Atkinson was buried in Links Cemetery, south of Blyth, Cumbria.

SERGEANT (LATER FLIGHT LIEUTENANT) WILLIAM GEORGE RIPLEY
RAF
DECORATION: DISTINGUISHED FLYING MEDAL (DFM)
GAZETTED: 13 MAY 1941

Bill Ripley was born in Emsworth, Hampshire, in 1912 and enlisted in the RAF in February 1940 as an airman. He trained as a wireless operator and air gunner before, on 20 August 1940, joining 604 Squadron, based at RAF Middle Wallop, Hampshire. Having qualified as a radio observer, Ripley was paired with Flying Officer Roderick 'Rory' Chisholm.

During the Battle of Britain, Ripley and Chisholm formed a formidable combination undertaking numerous day and night patrols in Beaufighters: long-range heavy fighters. However, it was for the latter that the pair became most celebrated, establishing a reputation as one of the best-known Home Defence night-time partnerships of the Blitz.

After the pair had claimed five 'kills' of He 111 bombers in March and April 1941, Chisholm was recommended for a DFC and Ripley for a DFM. The latter's recommendation from Wing Commander H. Appleton, the Officer Commanding 604 Squadron, stated: 'Sergt. Ripley, W. G., has been with this Squadron since 10th August, 1940. He has been Radio Operator Air Gunner with Flying Officer Chisholm for most of his period of service with this Squadron, and has been instrumental in the confirmed destruction of five enemy aircraft with a further one which is certainly damaged, if not destroyed.'

Two of these 'kills' were achieved on the night of 13/14 March 1941, a success described by Chisholm in his memoir *Cover of Darkness* as 'sweet and very intoxicating'. The first of them crashed into the sea:

On that night there was an almost full moon and the weather was very fine. We had been flying for more than an hour when we were put on to a bomber that was going back empty. We were overtaking fairly well, and by the time we passed over Bournemouth were about a mile behind. We closed a bit more and Ripley, my observer, got a close radar contact over to the left. I turned to the left, and I could hardly believe my eyes, for there was another aircraft about a hundred yards away and on the same level . . . I pressed the firing-button. There was a terrific shaking and banging, and to my surprise I saw flashes appearing, as it seemed, miraculously on the shape in front of me. Pieces broke away and came back at me. I kept firing, and it turned away to the right slowly, apparently helplessly and obviously badly damaged . . . and then I saw a lick of flame coming from the starboard engine. It grew rapidly, and enveloped the whole engine and soon most of the wing. The machine turned east and started to go down slowly; it looked by now like a ball of flame. We followed it down from 11,000 feet until, minutes later, it hit the sea, where it continued to burn. It was said the crew baled out, but none was found . . .

Ripley's DFM was announced on 13 May 1941. The total of five 'kills' during the Blitz achieved by Chisholm and Ripley was only surpassed by John 'Cats Eyes' Cunningham and his radar operator, Sergeant Rawnsley. Ripley was promoted to warrant officer in March 1942 and he was commissioned as flying officer in January 1943. However, while serving as a flight lieutenant with 141 Squadron, Ripley died on 16 November 1943, aged thirty, from serious injuries received when his aircraft crashed shortly after take-off. His body was later interred in Havant and Waterloo (Warblington) Cemetery in Hampshire.

Chisholm survived the war and later dedicated his memoir, which traced the development of night fighting, to Ripley and two other fallen comrades, writing that they 'flew with me and brought about the success I describe'.

4

SECOND WORLD WAR
– OTHER FIGHTER PILOTS

'By itself, the air war does not make sense,' wrote R. J. Overy in the introduction to his book The Air War. *'There were few battles in the Second World War fought only by aircraft. Even fewer can be said to have had any decisive strategic effect. This is not to say that aircraft were not important in the war. Each of the combatant powers wanted to gain command of the air – an overwhelming supremacy designed to neutralize and destroy enemy air power while subjecting the enemy to continuous air attack. Yet such command was not expected to bring the war to an end by itself. Command of the air was a necessary component in the successful execution of naval and military strategies. But it was these strategies, involving the movement of ships and men, and the occupying of land, that won the day. Air power had a complementary rather than an autonomous role to play.'*

For the British and Allied pilots and aircrew, the Battle of Britain did not end on a definitive day. They fought many battles in the skies above Britain after 31 October 1940, the day the Battle of Britain is officially deemed to have ended. The role of fighter pilots continued for another five years beyond this date when they took the fight to the enemy in all theatres of war.

FLIGHT LIEUTENANT (LATER AIR CHIEF MARSHAL) HARRY BROADHURST

Army/RAF
DECORATIONS: AIR FORCE CROSS (AFC),
DISTINGUISHED FLYING CROSS (DFC) AND BAR,
DISTINGUISHED SERVICE ORDER (DSO) AND BAR
GAZETTED: 1 FEBRUARY 1937, 2 JANUARY 1940,
29 SEPTEMBER 1942, 4 JULY 1941 AND 19 DECEMBER
1941

Harry Broadhurst was a dashing fighter ace and a superb aerial tactician before becoming, aged thirty-eight, the youngest air vice-marshal in the history of the RAF. The brilliant military career of 'Broady', as he was affectionately known, spanned thirty-five years during which there were few dull moments.

Broadhurst was born in Frimley, Surrey, on 28 October 1905. He was educated at Portsmouth Grammar School, Hampshire, before being commissioned into the Royal Artillery in 1926. However, later the same year he found his true vocation when he was transferred into the RAF. From 1926 to 1928 he served with 11 Squadron, which was based at RAF Netheravon, Wiltshire, and which was equipped with Horsley and Wapiti bombers. From 1928 to 1931, Broadhurst served with the squadron on the North West Frontier. His return to the UK saw him posted to 41 Squadron, a Bulldog fighter unit based at RAF Northolt, Middlesex, from 1931 to 1933. From 1933 to 1936, Broadhurst served with 19 Squadron (Bulldogs) based at RAF Duxford, Cambridgeshire. Before the Second World War, he was a regular performer at the Hendon Air Pageants in north-west London, where he led an aerobatics team that was roped together by its wingtips. Broadhurst was also one of the best shots in the RAF and won the Brooke-Popham Trophy three years running. He was appointed chief instructor of 4 Flying Training School (FTS) (Egypt) in 1937 and on 1 February that year was awarded the AFC. In January 1939, he was appointed to the command of 111 Squadron and soon after the outbreak of the war he was in the thick of the action.

Broadhurst's first 'kill' came in poor weather on 29 October 1939 when he intercepted and shot down a He 111 bomber. His DFC, for this incident, followed just over two months later on 2 January 1940. His citation stated:

> He [Broadhurst] stated that the weather conditions were unfit for formation-flying and yet, despite the rain and clouds at ground-level, he took off alone, flying blind by means of instruments. Emerging above the clouds and endeavouring to clear an iced-up windscreen, he sighted the enemy aircraft. Squadron Leader Broadhurst attacked and caused it to turn on its side and dive vertically into cloud close to sea level. In following it down he narrowly escaped from crashing into the sea. On his return weather conditions had not improved, and it was only at the third attempt that he was able to regain the aerodrome.

In the same month, Broadhurst was appointed station commander of RAF Coltishall, Norfolk, at a time when the airfield was still under construction. Soon afterwards he volunteered for a vacant wing commander's position in France and in May 1940 he was appointed to command No. 60 Wing in Lille. Broadhurst flew a Hurricane 1 during the German Blitzkrieg when he destroyed a Me 110 near Arras. Then, as France fell, he also collected the personnel of No. 61 Wing and brought them home under his own command. Next he was appointed station commander at RAF Wittering, Cambridgeshire, serving in 12 Group. Broadhurst led the Wittering Wing with 229 Squadron for the first time on 19 June 1940. As the Battle of Britain unfolded, Broadhurst became an adherent of the 'Big Wing' concept of meeting the incoming Luftwaffe with a greater strength of aircraft. His Wittering Wing made thirteen operational sorties over 11 Group's airfields and Broadhurst himself was able to take part in operational sorties with 1 Squadron, which qualified him for the Battle of Britain clasp. Even as early as 1940, Broadhurst was regarded within the RAF as 'one of the three most resourceful brains among the senior pilots in Fighter Command'.

Broadhurst's appointment to the command of RAF Hornchurch, Essex, saw him come into his own as one of the great fighter–leaders of the war. It was while leading the Hornchurch Wing that his personal victory tally grew apace: on 25 February 1941, Broadhurst destroyed a Me 109 as well as claiming another 'probable'. On 3 May 1941, while flying as leader of 611 Squadron in a wing sweep over Le Touquet, Broadhurst added another 'probable' and another damaged, then a Me 109 destroyed at Cap Gris Nez on 17 June. His logbook report for the day stated:

I flew at 18,000 ft over the bombers and their escorts as they crossed the French coast. I made a wide sweep and again crossed the bombers from east to west over the Channel, when one Me. 109 moved in from the south and 200 ft above to attack Red 3 on the starboard quarter. I ordered Red 3 to break outwards, which he did . . . The Me. 109 turned to follow whereupon I swung in, fired a full deflection shot from the beam in a short burst at 200 yards range. The e/a [enemy aircraft] flew through my fire and then spun out of its turn and went straight down.

On 21 June 1941, Broadhurst destroyed a Me 109, stopping its engine and killing the pilot. On the same sortie, he overcame mechanical problems and a persistent opponent before successfully attacking from beneath the enemy aircraft. He wrote: 'My aircraft became covered with bits of aluminium, oil and glycol, and the e/a dived into the ground near Calais Marck aerodrome.' At the end of June, Broadhurst was promoted to group captain and in early July he took part in seven operational sorties in eight days. On 3 July, on his second trip of the day, Broadhurst claimed a Me 109 destroyed and a Me 109 'probable' over St Omer. It later emerged that Broadhurst had probably been responsible for a bizarre victory over one of Germany's greatest fighter aces, Wilhelm Balthasar, who had been credited with forty-four victories. For, on 3 July, Balthasar had taken a new Me 109 on a test flight when he was 'jumped by Spitfires'. It was the stresses caused by his evasive manoeuvres that caused his wing to collapse, resulting in him crashing to his death.

On 4 July 1941, Broadhurst was again in the thick of the action: he destroyed two Me 109s, but his wingman was killed during a battle over Lille. Broadhurst was himself wounded in the ferocious fighting, suffering injuries to his backside that required surgery. This meant that when he had to attend an RAF Air Officer Commanding (AOC) meeting at Uxbridge, Middlesex, he had to kneel gingerly on the back seat of the car. Broadhurst received little sympathy from Douglas Bader, the legendary fighter ace, who playfully slapped him on the backside and said: 'Hello, hello. Running away from the Hun again?'

Broadhurst had received his injuries on the day that his DSO was announced and his citation stated: 'His ability, keenness and outstanding powers of leadership have been an inspiration to all and have contributed materially to all the successes obtained by the squadrons under his command.' Broadhurst's final victory of 1941 came on 27 September when he destroyed a Me 109 six miles inland from Mardyck, northern France. He also damaged another Me 109 off Cap Gris Nez on 1 October. From October to November 1941, Broadhurst went on a lecture tour of the US, where he met Generals Carl Spaatz and Ira Eaker. Shortly after his return from the US – on 19 December 1941 – Broadhurst's Bar to his DSO, announced on the same day, detailed how he had been in action over northern France:

On the return journey, he was attacked by a force of 6 Messerschmitt 109s but, by brilliant tactics, Group Captain Broadhurst fought them off and, it is believed, destroyed 2 of them before the engagement was terminated some 15 miles north of Gravelines. Although his aircraft was damaged by the enemy's fire, Group Captain Broadhurst flew it safely back to this country. Since being awarded the Distinguished Service Order in June, he has destroyed 8 and probably destroyed a further 4 enemy aircraft. He has set an example worthy of the highest traditions of the service.

In May 1942, Broadhurst handed over command at Hornchurch to become Senior Air Staff Officer (SASO) at 11 Group. However, he continued to fly combat missions and in August 1942 he returned to the Hornchurch Wing to lead it during the Dieppe raid. On 2 December 1942, he claimed a 'probable' Me 109 off Gravelines. Broadhurst, who destroyed a Fw 190 fighter and damaged three more, also devised a better strategy of using Spitfires to operate in pairs to see off the increasingly effective enemy aircraft.

Broadhurst's final tally for the war was thirteen destroyed, seven 'probables' and ten damaged, all claimed before the end of August 1942. The following month, he was appointed SASO to Air Officer Commanding (AOC) Western Desert. This promotion meant, however, that he could not take part in operational flying because he had access to highly secret information, which could possibly have been extracted from him under torture. The Bar to Broadhurst's DFC was announced on 29 September 1942 when he was praised for his daring actions during the Dieppe raid when he flew alone for some eight hours in an area of hostile patrols. His citation stated: 'His skill and gallantry were of the highest order.'

In early 1943, Broadhurst was appointed to the command of the Desert Air Force, at the same time becoming the youngest air vice-marshal in the RAF's history. He proved to be an astute tactician, firmly believing that fighter-bomber pilots could provide greater support to the land forces if they understood the battle ground better, including the whereabouts of enemy tanks and armour. Broadhurst believed, too, in the value of more planned, set-piece attacks rather than simply strafing opportunity targets.

Broadhurst was in northern Africa at a crucial time when the Eighth Army had driven Rommel's Afrika Korps from Alamein back to Tunisia and when General Leclerc had advanced his Free French forces up from Lake Chad in the south. Furthermore, the British First Army and the Americans were pressing in from Algeria. With the Germans caught in Tunisia and with their backs to the sea, Broadhurst sent in his fighter aircraft and fighter-bombers on 10 March 1943 to support Leclerc, whose advance was being halted by the 21st Panzer Division. Broadhurst's Hurricane flew successful missions with 'Billy' Burton, the wing leader, reporting: 'We must have hit the NAAFI because I came back with my air filter full of razor blades.' Ten days later, with Montgomery's forces advancing on the Mareth Line, the Desert Air Force continued its assault. Indeed, on 22 March alone, Broadhurst's crews flew nearly 620 'unquestionably effective' sorties.

Broadhurst was determined to concentrate on well-planned, precision attacks and, knowing that Montgomery's forces were advancing with a wide 'left hook', he concentrated his aerial attack, in an unprecedented manner, on the nights of 24/25 and 25/26 March, on the enemy's rear. Furthermore, he concentrated on transport and telephone communications, thereby echoing the Luftwaffe's successful tactics in France during 1940. After 'softening up' the enemy, Broadhurst's *coup de grâce* was a surprise daytime assault on the main enemy positions on 26 March when, at 3.30 p.m., three formations of light and medium bombers launched a simultaneous pattern-bombing attack. This was immediately followed up with an attack by fighter-bombers on the lowest heights. Gun positions that were holding up the Allied armour from advancing were specifically targeted, with great success, while a strength of two and a half squadrons was maintained in the area with fresh relays of aircraft arriving at fifteen-minute intervals.

Just half an hour after the start of the air offensive, the infantry attacked under cover of a heavy barrage. They were able to creep forward at the rate of 100 feet per minute and, within two and a quarter hours, the enemy defences at the most difficult position were overwhelmed and the British armour was able to break through the Mareth Line. Such was the confidence that Montgomery now had in Broadhurst that he insisted on the Desert Air Force following him, first to Sicily with Operation Husky and then to north-west Europe for Operation Overlord. In fact, Broadhurst flew into Pachino, Sicily, from Malta in his own Spitfire two days after the island had successfully been invaded. On mainland Italy, Broadhurst ensured that there was huge cooperation between the armies and air forces. He used systems of attack in which pilots were in radio contact with forward observation posts in order to be directed straight on to enemy targets. The US recognised Broadhurst's achievements in North Africa by awarding him the Legion of Merit on 27 September 1943 for 'exceptionally meritorious conduct', and the citation ended with praise for his 'combative spirit and outstanding leadership'.

In early 1944, Broadhurst returned to the UK and in March he was appointed to the command of 83 Group in the new 2nd Tactical Air Force. At his headquarters in Redhill, Surrey, Broadhurst worked alongside Lieutenant General Miles C. Dempsey to ensure the group worked closely with the British Second Army during the Normandy landings of June 1944. 83 Group operated some ten wings: twenty-nine Spitfire, Mustang and Typhoon squadrons, plus five Air Observation Auster squadrons. Before the D-Day landings, the group carried out intensive fighter sweeps, attacks on V-1 construction sites and reconnaissance. On D-Day itself, the initial echelon of the group went ashore from fighter control ships. Typically again, on 10 June, Broadhurst flew his personal Spitfire to new headquarters at Creully and at this point 83 Group was controlling all RAF units ashore. Within days, however, the group switched to its intended function of cooperating with the Second Army, which it supported for the rest of the war. As a commander, Broadhurst had proved himself to be exceptionally bold, creative and original. He remained in command of 83 Group until the end of the war.

After the war, he continued his distinguished RAF career and was appointed air officer in command of administration at Fighter Command from 1945 to 1946. After a host of other senior positions and a knighthood, Broadhurst was promoted to air chief marshal in February 1957. His final service appointment was Commander, Allied Air Forces, Central Europe, from 1959 to 1961. After retiring from the RAF in March 1961, Broadhurst also held a number of senior positions within the aviation industry, ending up as a director of the Hawker Siddeley Group Ltd – of which he had previously served as managing director – from 1968 to 1976. Air Chief Marshal Sir Harry Broadhurst GCB, KBE, DSO and Bar, DFC and Bar, AFC, died on 29 August 1995, aged eighty-nine. He married twice, having a daughter with each of his wives.

SQUADRON LEADER (LATER AIR COMMODORE) JOHN MARLOW THOMPSON

RAF

DECORATIONS: DISTINGUISHED FLYING CROSS (DFC) AND BAR, DISTINGUISHED SERVICE ORDER (DSO) AND AIR FORCE CROSS (AFC)

GAZETTED: 6 SEPTEMBER 1940, 4 DECEMBER 1942, 14 MAY 1943 AND 1 JANUARY 1952

John Thompson was born in Keynsham, near Bristol, on 16 August 1914. After attending Bristol Grammar School, he received a short-service commission into the RAF in March 1934 and was quickly christened 'Tommy'. After finishing his pilot training on 4 March 1935, he was posted to 29 Squadron based at RAF North Weald, Essex. By 1937, he was a flight commander with 151 Squadron and showing potential as a fine pilot and a strong leader. Furthermore, he was an excellent sportsman, earning a fearsome reputation for his exploits in the boxing ring and on the rugby field. After the outbreak of the Second World War, Thompson was promoted to squadron leader and in January 1940 he took command of 111 Squadron, which was equipped with Hurricane fighters.

As the German attack developed in April and May 1940, 111 Squadron, which was based at Drem in Scotland, was involved in heavy fighting. In May, Thompson took part in patrols over France in which he claimed a Me 110 fighter destroyed and another 'probable', as well as a He 111 bomber 'probable'. However, in this latter engagement on 19 May 1940, Thompson was shot down by escorting Me 110s over Valenciennes, France. After making a crash-landing in a field, he was helped by British soldiers and returned to England on a ship from Boulogne. Thompson was soon back in the air and on 31 May he possibly destroyed a Me 109 and on 11 June he destroyed a Me 109, as well as damaging another and damaging a Ju 88 bomber. On 10 July and 11 August 1940, Thompson damaged a Do 17 bomber, and on 13 August he destroyed a Do 17 and damaged another. On 15 August, he destroyed a Do 17 and a Me 110 and probably a Me 109, while the next day he destroyed a Do 17.

During the summer of 1940, Thompson had excelled himself taking part in both the Battle of France and the Battle of Britain. He was awarded the DFC on 6 September 1940 and his citation stated: 'This officer has commanded a squadron since January, 1940, and has operated over various areas in Northern France. He has taken part in nearly every patrol and, under his leadership, eighty-one enemy aircraft have been destroyed, twelve probably destroyed and at least forty-four damaged. He has, himself, shot down eight and damaged at least six enemy aircraft.'

Thompson was posted to HQ 11 Group as a controller on 5 October 1940 but he returned to operations on 30 June 1941, taking command of 131 Squadron at its re-formation at RAF Ouston, near Newcastle upon Tyne. The squadron had a high proportion of Belgian pilots and, after it became operational in October, Thompson was posted to RAF Valley on Anglesey, North Wales, on 13 November. With him came twelve Belgian pilots and Thompson's role was to form and command 350 Squadron, which he led until he was posted for a rest in March 1942.

The next phase of Thompson's career saw him posted to Malta on 25 July 1942. On 5 August, he was appointed as temporary commander of Ta Kali Spitfire Wing. However, from 27 August until 27 December 1942, he led the Hal Far Wing and from 28 December 1942 until 10 June 1943 he led the Luqa Wing. These roles gave Thompson the distinction of commanding all Malta's Spitfire wings over a period of just ten months. Furthermore, he had personal successes in the air during this period, too: he shared a 'probable' Ju 88 on 27 August, destroyed a Me 109 on 11 October, damaged another on 12 October and, finally, destroyed a Ju 88 and damaged a Me 109 on 14 October. It was during his time in Malta that the Bar to his DFC was announced on 4 December 1942. Further honours also followed during this period: he was awarded the Belgian Military Cross (1st Class) on 1 January 1943 and the DSO on 14 May 1943 and his citation stated:

> This officer has a fine operational record. He fought in France and later took part in the Battle of Britain. For the past 9 months, he has been engaged in flying operations from Malta, playing a prominent part in the defence of the island during a period of intense air attacks. Latterly, Wing Commander Thompson has led formations of fighter-bombers in numerous successful attacks against port installations, factories, airfields and other targets. By his great skill and brilliant leadership, Wing Commander Thompson has contributed in a large measure to the excellent results obtained.

During the latter part of the war – and, indeed, during the first twenty years of the subsequent peace – Thompson specialised in air defence duties, including the challenges of introducing jet-propelled aircraft. He was awarded the AFC on 1 January 1952 and, by this stage a group captain, was made a CBE on 1 January 1955. By 1957, Thompson was commanding officer at

RAF Leeming, Yorkshire, becoming the Director of Air Defence at the Air Ministry in December 1958. His last appointment was at HQ Military Air Traffic Organisation in 1962 where he served until he retired, with the rank of air commodore, in September 1966, after a distinguished thirty-two-year career in the RAF. However, afterwards his expertise in air defence matters was acknowledged by consultancies with several developing air forces. Indeed, immediately after retiring from the RAF, Thompson was general manager at Airwork Services in Saudi Arabia from 1966 to 1968. He also proved to be an excellent golf club secretary, holding the post for three years at Moor Park in Hertfordshire and for eleven years at the famous Monte Carlo Golf Club. Thompson, who had married in 1938 and had two children, retired to Sussex in 1983. Air Commodore Thompson CBE, DSO, DFC and Bar, AFC died in Brighton on 23 July 1994, aged seventy-nine.

SQUADRON LEADER (LATER GROUP CAPTAIN SIR) DOUGLAS ROBERT STEUART BADER*

RAF

DECORATIONS: DISTINGUISHED SERVICE ORDER (DSO) AND BAR, DISTINGUISHED FLYING CROSS (DFC) AND BAR

GAZETTED: 1 OCTOBER 1940, 15 JULY 1941, 7 JANUARY 1941 AND 9 SEPTEMBER 1941

Douglas Bader was arguably the most famous British pilot of the Second World War. He was immortalised in the book and

---

* *Bader's gallantry and service medals are not part of my collection. His story, however, features in the Channel 5 television series.*

film *Reach for the Sky*, which chronicled an extraordinary life and career during which he was one of Britain's most successful fighter aces despite a crash in December 1931, while attempting aerobatics, which cost him both his legs. The disability did not prevent him being credited with twenty victories, four shared victories, six 'probables', one shared 'probable' and eleven enemy aircraft damaged. When he became a prisoner of war (PoW), the Germans eventually had to confiscate his tin legs to prevent him trying to escape.

Bader was born in St John's Wood, north London, on 21 February 1910. The second son of a civil engineer and his wife, he spent his first two years living with relatives on the Isle of Man because his father was working in India. Bader then went to live with his family in India for a year before they settled down in London from 1913. Bader's father died in 1922 from injuries received in the First World War; his mother remarried (her new husband was a clergyman) and the family settled in Yorkshire. At St Edward's School in Oxford, Bader showed an aggressive nature and shone at sport, notably rugby. After being accepted as a cadet at RAF Cranwell, Lincolnshire, in 1928, Bader continued to shine at sport, including by then boxing and hockey, but he showed a rebellious streak, too, and was warned about his conduct. He took his first instructed flight on 13 September 1928 and, after just eleven hours fifteen minutes of flying time, he flew solo on 19 February 1929. Bader was commissioned as a pilot officer into 23 Squadron, based at RAF Kenley, Surrey, on 26 July 1930. Here, flying Gloster Gamecocks and Bristol Bulldogs, he flew a number of highly dangerous stunts. On 14 December 1931, while training to defend his pairs' title at the forthcoming 1932 Hendon Air Show, Bader carried out some stunts in a Bulldog above

Woodley airfield, Berkshire. When the tip of his left wing touched the ground, he crashed and was badly injured. At the Royal Berkshire Hospital in Reading, one of his legs was amputated above the knee, the other below the knee. Bader's entry in his logbook later stated: 'Crashed slow-rolling near ground. Bad show.' During a long convalescing period, Bader received a pair of artificial legs that enabled him to drive a modified car, play golf, dance and . . . fly. He was passed fit for active service but the RAF reversed this decision in 1933. Invalided out of the RAF, he took an office job with a petroleum company, now part of Shell, and married Thelma Edwards, a barmaid he had met in a pub while convalescing, on 5 October 1933.

As the Second World War loomed, Bader angled for a posting and eventually regained a medical categorisation for operational flying in November 1939. On 27 November 1939, nearly eight years after his accident, Bader flew solo once more, turning his biplane upside down at just 600 feet. He was back doing what he loved best and from February to May the following year he practised formation flying air tactics and took part in sea convoys. Soon he was promoted to section leader but he suffered a setback when, due to an error, he crashed his Spitfire on take-off and received a serious head wound. Bader was soon promoted to flight commander of 222 Squadron and took on the rank of flight lieutenant. It was with 222 Squadron that Bader tasted his first combat. On 1 June 1940, while patrolling the coast near Dunkirk, he shot down a Me 109 fighter. More 'kills' soon followed, including five claimed in a single day. Bader was posted to command 242 Squadron, as a squadron leader, on 28 June 1940. At the Hurricane unit based at RAF Coltishall, Norfolk, Bader stamped his personality on the unit during the Battle of Britain, scoring his first 'kill' with his new squadron – a Do 17 bomber – on 11 July 1940. Throughout August and September, Bader was repeatedly in action and a supporter of the 'Big Wing' tactic to combat the oncoming Luftwaffe with a greater strength of aircraft.

For his service during the Battle of Britain, Bader was awarded the DSO on 1 October 1940 and his citation stated: 'This officer has displayed gallantry and leadership of the highest order. During three recent engagements he has led his squadron with such skill and ability that thirty-three enemy aircraft have been destroyed. In the course of these engagements Squadron Leader Bader had added to his previous successes by destroying six enemy aircraft.' On 7 January 1941, his DFC was announced and his citation stated: 'Squadron Leader Bader has continued to lead his squadron and wing with the utmost gallantry on all occasions. He has now destroyed a total of ten hostile aircraft and damaged several more.'

In March 1941, the same month that his portrait was painted by war artist Cuthbert Orde, Bader was promoted to wing commander and was one of the first wing leaders. Stationed at RAF Tangmere, Sussex, he was in command of 145, 610 and 616 Squadrons. Throughout the summer of 1941, he led his wing of Spitfires on sweeps and bomber escort duties over north-western Europe. As a wing leader, he was entitled to have his initials painted on his Spitfire, which he did: 'D-B' led to his radio call sign of 'Dogsbody'. After many dogfights with Me 109s, Bader was awarded the Bar to his DSO on 15 July 1941 – the day he claimed one enemy fighter aircraft destroyed and another damaged. His citation stated: 'This officer has led his wing on a series of consistently successful sorties over enemy territory during the past three months. His high qualities of leadership and courage have been an inspiration to all. Wing Commander Bader has destroyed 15 hostile aircraft.'

Between 24 March and 9 August, Bader had been relentless in his pursuit of the enemy, flying sixty-two fighter sweeps over France. However, on 9 August, while patrolling over the French coast, he ran out of luck in pursuit of twelve Me 109s. After diving on them too fast and steeply, he became separated from his section after levelling out at 24,000 feet. He spotted three pairs of Me 109s in front of him and attacked, destroying one with a short burst of fire. After hitting a second enemy aircraft, he banked and decided to head for home, only to suffer an apparent mid-air collision with another aircraft. With his fuselage, tail and fin gone from behind him, he lost height and descended into a spin at around 400 mph. After jettisoning the cockpit canopy and releasing his harness pin, he found himself trapped by one of his prosthetic legs. As he plunged towards the ground, Bader gambled on releasing his parachute and saw the leg's retaining strap snap under the strain as he pulled free.

As a PoW, Bader was treated with respect by the Germans: a drop-off was arranged to replace his lost leg. 'Leg Operation' took place on 19 August 1941, when a new artificial limb was dropped by parachute to St Omer, a Luftwaffe base in Occupied France. While in hospital, Bader tried to escape but he was betrayed by a staff nurse and later found at a nearby safe house. It was while Bader was in the early stages of being a PoW that the Bar to his DFC was announced on 9 September 1941 when his citation stated: 'This fearless pilot has recently added a further four enemy aircraft to his previous successes; in addition he has probably destroyed another four and damaged five hostile aircraft. By his fine leadership and high courage Wing Commander Bader has inspired the wing on every occasion.' On 18 August 1942, after further escape attempts, Bader was sent to the Colditz Castle where he remained until 15 April 1945, when he was freed by the advancing US Army, but not before assisting in some successful escapes.

Bader returned to Britain a war hero: in June 1945, he was given the honour of leading a victory flypast of 300 aircraft over London. On 1 July 1945, he was promoted to temporary wing commander. Later, after initially deciding to pursue an RAF career, he was promoted to temporary group captain. However, his affection for the RAF waned after the war and he retired on 21 July 1946 to take a job with Royal Dutch Shell, which had taken him on after his 1931 accident. He worked as chairman of Shell Aircraft Ltd until retiring in 1969, after which he toured scores of countries. His fame had grown worldwide after his biography, *Reach for the Sky* by Paul Brickhill, was published in 1954. Brickhill concluded: 'I agree with those who class him as the best fighter leader and tactician of World War II (and one of the best pilots). Also I know of no fighter tactician so outstanding in other wars.' Two years later, in a film of the same name, Kenneth More starred as Bader. On 2 January 1956, Bader was made a CBE for services to the disabled.

Bader's first wife died of throat cancer on 24 January 1971 and he remarried two years later, on 3 January 1973. He and his second wife, Joan Murray, lived in the Berkshire village of Marlston. He flew for the last time on 4 June 1979, having recorded 5,744 hours and 25 minutes' flying time. As a fighter pilot, he attributed his success to three basic rules: if you had height, you controlled the battle; if you came out of the sun, the enemy could not see you; and if you held your fire until you were close, you seldom missed. Many more honours and tributes followed, including a knighthood in June 1976. Douglas Bader died, aged seventy-two, from a heart attack when returning from an RAF dinner at London's Guildhall on 5 September 1982. On 9 August 2001, the sixtieth anniversary of Bader's last combat sortie, a bronze statue of him was unveiled by his widow, Joan, at Goodwood motor circuit in West Sussex.

SERGEANT (LATER FLIGHT LIEUTENANT) GARTRELL RICHARD IAN PARKER
RAF
DECORATIONS: DISTINGUISHED SERVICE MEDAL (DSM), DISTINGUISHED FLYING CROSS (DFC) AND BAR, AIR FORCE CROSS (AFC)
GAZETTED: 1 JANUARY 1941, 24 NOVEMBER 1944, 10 FEBRUARY 1945 AND 10 JUNE 1948

Gamekeeper's son Gartrell 'Sailor' Parker was born on 26 November 1918 in Harberton, Devon. He was educated at King Edward VI Grammar School in nearby Totnes. He enlisted in the RAF, aged just fifteen, in September 1934 and served at the School of Army Co-operation and 59 (Army Co-operation) Squadron at RAF Old Sarum, Wiltshire, from 1936 to 1938, qualifying as a wireless operator. From January to March 1938, he served with 3 Anti Aircraft Co-operation Unit (AACU) at Hal Far on Malta. Next he served in Gibraltar before returning to Malta in August 1938. Parker then trained as an air gunner and he was due to return to Britain in September 1939 for sergeant pilot training. However, the outbreak of the Second World War scuppered this plan and he was instead posted to 830 Squadron, Fleet Air Arm, also based at Hal Far.

Parker served as a sergeant and air gunner in the unit's Swordfish Torpedo bombers and he was involved in numerous combats. On 16 October 1940, Parker qualified for the Goldfish Club (for those who have successfully parachuted, or ditched, into the sea from a stricken aircraft) when his Swordfish aircraft landed in the sea after engine failure. Parker and his pilot, Sub Lieutenant Thompson, were picked up by a Sunderland flying boat aircraft some seven hours after ditching into the water. Parker was involved in the successful Catania raid of 5 July 1940, the Tripoli raid of 21 December 1940 and the Palermo raid of 10 January 1941. He was awarded the DSM on 1 January 1941 and his citation stated: 'In his capacity as air gunner he has accompanied his Squadron on four raids on enemy bases, and a successful attack on an enemy convoy at night, during all of which he has shown considerable skill and initiative.' This was one of only an extremely small number of DSMs awarded to the RAF.

While later serving with 800X Flight and flying Fulmar aircraft, Parker took part in night sorties over Sicily. After being commissioned in October 1941, he returned to Britain the following month. Parker became a gunnery instructor for short periods at 7 Air Gunnery School near Porthcawl, South Wales. He was based there before and after attending Gunnery Leaders' Course 32 at Central Gunnery School (CGS) at RAF Chelveston, Northamptonshire. After pressing hard to be allowed on a pilots' course, Parker was sent to Cambridge 22 Elementary Flying Training School (EFTS), going solo for two hours after being taught to fly in Malta. In September

1942, he was posted to Caron 33 EFTS in Canada before being switched to Calgary 37 Service Flying Training School in November. While in Canada, he managed to talk his way out of being made an instructor but after returning to Britain in March 1943 he was selected for instructor training. The decision was made on the grounds that, at just twenty-four, he was too old for day fighters. Having trained on single-wing aircraft, Parker took a course to enable him to instruct on twin-engine aircraft. During this period, it became clear that Parker had exceptional night vision and he passed selection for night fighters. His training finally ended in March 1944, having qualified on Blenheims, Beauforts and Beaufighters.

Parker was now posted to 219 Squadron as a flight lieutenant and he converted to Mosquitos. It was here that he acquired the nickname 'Sailor' because of his earlier service with the Fleet Air Arm. His brilliant talents as a night-fighter pilot brought a series of combat successes over an eight-month period. His missions were, however, fraught with danger as his combat report from 10/11 August revealed:

I was patrolling 20 miles S.W. of Le Havre under LEGION Control at Angels [altitude measured in units of 1,000 feet] 10 and was informed that there was a bogey [enemy aircraft] about 20 miles to the N.E. of me. Ordered to vector 080° and gain angels to 15, bogey turned out to be 3 bogies flying in line astern at 15,000 feet slowly losing angels. Ordered to vector 040° and a little later to vector 340°, almost immediately obtained contact at 8 miles slightly to starboard and my Navigator took over the interception. Visual obtained at 4 miles range, closed to 2 miles and e/a [enemy aircraft] identified as a Ju88 which was corkscrewing. Closed to

200 feet, 270 indicated air speed, and identity being confirmed gave e/a a short burst from 5° starboard as e/a was jinking to starboard. Starboard engine immediately exploded and caught fire, e/a rolled starboard onto its back and went down beneath me, the flames spreading to the fuselage, it finally spun into the sea, still burning 10 miles S.W. of Le Havre . . . Ordered immediately to vector 080° angels 7 and given bogey range 4 miles. Immediately obtained contact on weaving target travelling east and slowly losing height. Navigator took over interception and we closed to 1500 feet when visual was obtained dead ahead. Closed to 50° and identified a FW 190 fitted with long range belly tank. Height 6000 feet, 250 indicated air speed, dropped back to 100 feet and fired two short bursts from dead astern, strikes being observed on fuselage and wing roots during first burst and belly tank immediately blew up on firing second bursts. Mosquito was covered with flaming petrol – Ultra Violet lighting failed and Airspeed Indicator went u/s [unserviceable]. Mosquito burnt for 4 or 5 seconds and we stalled losing height, but regained control at 5,000 feet, aircraft was a little sluggish on rudder control, but we finally settled down and cockpit lighting (U/V) came on and Airspeed Indicator worked again eventually. E/a was observed to be burning on the ground about 15–20 miles south of Le Havre . . .

Parker had survived a close scrape with death. When he landed back at RAF Bradwell Bay in Essex, his aircraft was found to have Category 'A' damage: the port-side rudder was burnt off and most of the fabric burnt off the nose, port side of the fuselage and the tailplane. By destroying a brace of enemy aircraft on three occasions, Parker came to the attention of the

British press which duly wrote about his exploits.

Parker's DFC was announced on 24 November 1944 after the recommendation for his award stated: 'This officer has flown on over 50 operational sorties involving 170 hours night flying, during which he has destroyed 5 enemy aircraft at night, probably one and damaged another, and on one occasion bringing back safely a badly damaged aircraft. He has also destroyed 6 flying bombs at night. At all times this officer has shown the utmost keenness and courage to seek out and destroy the enemy.'

The Bar to Parker's DFC was announced less than three months later – on 10 February 1945 – after the recommendation for his award stated: 'Since his last award F/Lt. Parker has destroyed four enemy aircraft at night. On 24th December 1944 he destroyed two enemy aircraft north of Arnhem in the same night, and on 22nd January 1945, he again destroyed two enemy aircraft in the same night east of Venlo. All these four aircraft (two Ju. 188 and two Ju. 87) were destroyed on their way to their target before they had bombed.'

Parker's squadron commander added:

He has shown skill and courage of a high order and his keenness to seek out and destroy the enemy has been infectious to other members of his Squadron. On one occasion, after a combat, at night he brought his aircraft back although it had been on fire for several minutes and the control surfaces badly damaged. He has operated over Normandy Beachhead, Dutch, Belgian and German Battle Areas, and also for a short time against Flying Bomb attacks on London when he shot down five Flying Bombs into the sea.

Parker had amassed a total of nine 'kills', one 'probable' and one damaged in under eight months of combat flying. He was one of only a small number of pilots to be confirmed as a 'double ace'. In addition to his traditional victories, he destroyed five, or six, V-1 flying bombs.

After the war, Parker became a test pilot at the Royal Aircraft Establishment in Hampshire and he was twice assessed as an 'exceptional' test pilot. In June 1947, he received a King's Commendation for Valuable Service in the Air and he was awarded the AFC in June 1948. Later he left the RAF to join the General Aircraft Company as its deputy chief test pilot. After a merger of his company in January 1949, Parker carried out the same role for Blackburn Aircraft. At this stage, flying was Parker's hobby as well as his job: he took second place in the 1952 King's Cup and Kemsley Air Races, and came second in the 1953 Goodyear Trophy and third in the Siddeley Trophy and Welsh Air Derby. Parker was also a keen shot, gardener and raconteur. He entered the 1955 International Aerobatic Competition at Baginton in the West Midlands and during his service flew around 200 aircraft types. In October 1960, he was forced to eject from the first prototype Buccaneer XK486, thereby qualifying for the Caterpillar Club for those who have successfully parachuted from a stricken aircraft. However, in February 1963, at the age of forty-four, Parker and his observer, Gordon Copeland, were killed when their Buccaneer crashed at RAF Holme-Upon-Spalding-Moor, Yorkshire, during a test flight.

FLIGHT LIEUTENANT (LATER GROUP CAPTAIN) EDWARD PRESTON WELLS

Royal New Zealand Air Force (RNZAF)/RAF
DECORATIONS: DISTINGUISHED FLYING CROSS (DFC) AND BAR, DISTINGUISHED SERVICE ORDER (DSO)
GAZETTED: 7 AUGUST 1941, 6 NOVEMBER 1941 AND 28 JULY 1942

Edward Wells, known by his comrades as 'Hawkeye' because he was a brilliant shot, had the distinction of being the first UK-based pilot to engage the Italian Air Force. He was regarded by his peers as 'the finest shot in the air' having, even before the Second World War, established himself as a crack shot with a rifle.

The son of a farmer, Wells was born in Cambridge, New Zealand, on 26 July 1917. He was educated at the local high school before working on a farm. In October 1938, he applied for a short-service commission in the RNZAF. He was accepted in mid-April 1939, but was not called up until 26 October. After pilot's training, Wells sailed for the UK on 7 June on RMS *Rangitata* and was posted to 7 Operational Training Unit (OTU), based at RAF Hawarden, Cheshire, soon after his arrival in Britain. After converting to Spitfires, he joined 266 Squadron at RAF Wittering, Cambridgeshire, on 26 August. On 2 October, he was posted to 41 Squadron at RAF Hornchurch, Essex.

In combat, both during and after the Battle of Britain, Wells soon left his mark. He claimed a Me 109 fighter on 17 October and a 'probable' Me 109 twelve days later. His first confirmed 'kill' came on 2 November and, nine days later, he became the first British-based fighter to engage the Italians when he chanced on some Fiat CR 42s over the Channel. On that day, 11 November, Wells damaged a CR 42 and probably destroyed a Henschel Hs 126 reconnaissance aircraft. On 27 November, Wells destroyed another Me 109 and on 22 January 1941 he damaged a He 111 bomber.

In March 1941, Wells joined 485 Squadron, the first all-New Zealand fighter squadron, scoring its first success on 5 July when he shot down a Me 109 whilst escorting Stirling bombers over Lille. On 7 August 1941, Wells was awarded the DFC for showing 'the greatest courage and determination'. He damaged a Me 109 on 16 August and destroyed another three days later. On 7 September, he probably destroyed another Me 109 and he definitely destroyed one on 18 September, along with two more on 21 September. Wells probably destroyed yet another on 2 October. On 6 November 1941, having completed forty-six sorties over enemy territory, he was awarded a Bar to his DFC when he was described as 'a splendid leader and a most skilful fighter pilot'.

Wells was promoted to squadron leader and took command of 485 Squadron on 22 November. When the German battleships *Scharnhorst* and *Gneisenau* slipped out of Brest on 12 February 1942, 485 was one of the squadrons sent to attack the enemy fighters defending the German ships. Wells found no fighters to engage so instead led an attack, through intense flak, on an E-boat (German torpedo boat), causing it to sink.

Wells shot down a Fw 190 fighter on 16 April, another on 24 April and damaged a third the following day. On 5 May 1942, he was promoted to wing commander and appointed to lead the Kenley Wing. On 24 May, he damaged a Me 109 and on 20 June he destroyed a Fw 190. Wells was awarded the DSO on 28 July 1942 for 'courage and inspiring leadership'.

Wells was finally rested in August 1942, after two years' continuous fighting. By this point, he had carried out 133 sweeps over enemy-occupied territory, probably more than any other pilot in Fighter Command. Wells was sent back to New Zealand, where he could have resettled in an important wartime role but he rejected the opportunity, preferring to return to Europe. He travelled back in March 1943 via the United States, where he visited aircraft factories and addressed workers. He was sent on a course at the RAF Staff College on his return, after which he again took over the Kenley Wing. In 1943, Wells married Mary de Booy, who, three years earlier, aged seventeen, had escaped in a fishing boat with her parents and sister from Nazi-occupied Holland.

Wells led the Kenley Wing until November, when he went to 11 Group, responsible for fighter aircraft training. In March 1944, Wells returned to operations as leader of the Tangmere Wing when he was equipped with the latest mark of Spitfire. He destroyed a Messerschmitt night fighter on the ground and led his wing on many sweeps over northern France during the build-up to D-Day. He later led the Detling and West Malling Wings before being rested in November 1944. Next he was posted to the Central Fighter Establishment to command the Day Fighter Leaders' School.

Among Wells's large band of admirers was 'Johnnie' Johnson, the most successful British fighter pilot of the Second World War. Johnson considered the New Zealander to be the 'complete Wing Leader and the finest shot and most accurate marksman in Fighter Command'. He was officially credited with shooting down twelve enemy aircraft but his tally was almost certainly considerably higher. Wells was released by the RNZAF in February 1947 and took up a permanent commission in the RAF, being given various appointments involved with fighter aircraft operations. In 1954, he took command of the air defence radar station at RAF Bawdsey, Suffolk. After serving with the Joint Planning Staff, Wells retired from the RAF in June 1960 as a group captain.

After farming near Woodbridge in Suffolk, in 1975 Wells moved to Spain, from where he travelled around the world gathering species of sub-tropical fruit. Over the years, he received many awards from the Spanish authorities for his fruit-growing and his studies into fruit diseases. Wells died on 4 November 2005, aged eighty-eight. His wife, with whom he had two children, had died four years earlier.

PILOT OFFICER (LATER AIR VICE-MARSHAL) JAMES EDGAR JOHNSON
Royal Air Force Volunteer Reserve (RAFVR)/RAF
DECORATIONS: DISTINGUISHED FLYING CROSS (DFC) AND BAR, DISTINGUISHED SERVICE ORDER (DSO) AND TWO BARS
GAZETTED: 30 SEPTEMBER 1941, 26 JUNE 1942, 4 JUNE 1943, 24 SEPTEMBER 1943 AND 7 JULY 1944

'Johnnie' Johnson not only flew in more than 700 Spitfire combat missions during the Second World War but he was also the top-scoring British flying ace of the conflict with thirty-eight confirmed victories. Furthermore, he was awarded a staggering three DSOs and two DFCs as well as other decorations both from home and abroad. Unlike many top pilots who preferred to concentrate on their own flying,

Johnson was an inspirational leader of men and trained, encouraged and led scores of Allied pilots.

The son of a policeman, Johnson was born on 9 March 1915 in Barrow upon Soar, Leicestershire, and educated at nearby Loughborough Grammar School. Later he attended Nottingham University, where he graduated as a civil engineer in 1938. Despite taking flying lessons at his own expense, he applied unsuccessfully for the part-time Auxiliary Air Force (AAF). His second application to the AAF was also unsuccessful, as was his initial application to the RAFVR. As tension mounted in Europe, Johnson enlisted in the Leicestershire Yeomanry cavalry. However, the RAFVR began to expand in early 1939 and his earlier application was reactivated. In August 1939, having already undergone part-time training, he was called to full-time service with the rank of sergeant. By the time Johnson completed the course, he had eighty-four hours' flying logged. During pilot's training, where he learnt to fly Spitfires, he was selected for a commission and appointed a probationary pilot officer. After a brief stop-off with 19 Squadron, Johnson was posted to 616 (South Yorkshire) Squadron, which had been part of 11 Group. Yet his time here was interrupted by an old rugby injury, which he aggravated flying, and this required him to have his collarbone broken and reset.

In December 1940, Johnson returned to 616 Squadron based at RAF Kirton in Lindsey, Lincolnshire, joining 'A' Flight and often flying as Hugh 'Cocky' Dundas's wingman. In combat with an enemy Dornier, Johnson initially fired too soon but he learnt from his mistake and played his part, along with Dundas, in damaging the aircraft during a further attack, sending it limping back to Holland. 616 Squadron was posted back to 11 Group in February 1941, joining 145 and 610 Squadrons flying Spitfires at RAF Tangmere, Sussex. The following month, the legendary Douglas Bader was appointed wing leader and he chose Johnson to fly alongside him, at the same time passing on many useful tips.

In May and June 1941, 616 Squadron flew low-flying 'Rhubarb' operations. Bader's search for the perfect flying formation saw him adopt the 'Finger Four' in which Johnson was largely responsible for protecting Dundas. This restricted Johnson's personal score but on 26 June 1941 he got his first 'kill' in a dogfight. Johnson later wrote:

> I was dead line astern of the Messerschmitt and hit him behind the cockpit with the eight machine-guns. As the range closed I contrived to spray the 109 with bullets and the Pilot half rolled on to his back and jettisoned his hood . . . I hammered him once more. A shapeless bundle fell away from the Messerschmitt and when I circled to watch it I saw the parachute break open. Feeling a deep exultation at this sight, I drove the Spitfire round in a steep, tail clearing turn . . .

Johnson now started flying regular sweeps – one of nine pilots chosen for the role – and his score soon escalated. Flying as number one of a two-aircraft section, Johnson destroyed two enemy aircraft on 6 and 14 July, having already damaged one on 4 July. On 21 July, he claimed a shared 'kill' but on the same day he lost his wingman, Sergeant Mabbett, a tragedy that affected him greatly. On 23 July, he damaged yet another Messerschmitt and on 9 August he was flying in the operation when Bader was shot down. Johnson made another 'kill' before he and others volunteered to search for their leader over the

French coast. However, five days later the news arrived that Bader was a prisoner of war (PoW). Johnson continued to add to his score with a Me 109 'probable' on 21 August, a half Me 109 'probable' on 4 September and two Me 109s destroyed on 21 September. Shortly after Bader was shot down, Johnson wanted to show the wing was still very much up for the fight, embellishing his Spitfire with the words: 'BADER'S BUS COMPANY, STILL RUNNING'.

On 30 September 1941, Johnson's DFC was announced after the recommendation for his award stated: 'Pilot Officer Johnson has taken part in 46 sweeps over enemy territory. He has at all times by his cheerful courage been a great asset to the Squadron. He has the following enemy aircraft to his credit: 4.5 Destroyed, 2 Probables, 1.5 Damaged.' At the same time, Johnson was appointed as commander of 'B' Flight. However, by then the character of 616 Squadron was changing: a dozen pilots had been lost between mid-June and mid-August 1941 and by 1942 it was neither a Yorkshire nor an auxiliary squadron. Furthermore, with many young, foreign pilots in its ranks, Johnson was the sole survivor of the 1940 pilots. On 15 April 1942, he opened his account for the year with a Fw 190 damaged close to Le Touquet even though he was flying an outclassed Spitfire V.

The Bar to Johnson's DFC was announced on 26 June 1942 after the recommendation for his award stated:

Flight Lieutenant Johnson was awarded the D.F.C. in September 1941 and since that date he has taken part in 22 Sweeps over enemy territory and also carried out two 'Rhubarb' operations. He has destroyed a further 2 Me 109Fs and on 16 April damaged one Fw. 190. Added to this, Flight

Lieutenant Johnson has always shown outstanding qualities of leadership and carried out an enormous number of Convoy Patrols. Although most of these patrols have been without incident, he has led his Flight in a manner that has been an inspiration to the Pilots under his command, and his cheerful countenance at all times has done much to foster a high morale in the Squadron.

Johnson was appointed to the command of 610 (County of Chester) Squadron, based at RAF Coltishall, Norfolk, in July 1942 and was given the rank of acting squadron leader. 610 Squadron was part of 12 Group, but Johnson wanted it to be part of 11 Group for the 'shooting season'. Initially, Johnson and the men under his command had to accept shipping reconnaissance and convoy patrols but then came the opportunity for them to make their mark: the Combined Operations raid on Dieppe, codenamed Operation Jubilee. Early on 19 August, the squadron took off to provide top cover for 411 (Royal Canadian Air Force) and 486 (Royal New Zealand Air Force) Squadrons, which had been tasked with preventing enemy aircraft from attacking the Allied ground forces. For Johnson and others involved in the thick of the fighting, it was to be an unforgettable day of relentless and daring aerial combat action. While still some three miles off the French coast, Johnson saw up to fifty Fw 190s and Me 109s jockeying for position some 2,000 feet or more above his squadron. Climbing swiftly, his squadron went to meet the advancing aircraft almost head-on. Johnson managed to get on the tail of a Fw 190 at around 11,000 feet and, after a brilliant manoeuvre, hit the enemy aircraft from behind with accurate fire, forcing it to crash into the sea. Along with two other airmen, Johnson also shot down a Me 109, which crashed into the sea, before getting into what he later assessed was his hardest dogfight of the war.

Johnson said of the combat:

> We sparred for about a minute and I tried my usual tactic of trying to turn inside the enemy, but after a couple of turns I was making no headway, and, in fact, he was gaining on me! Although I held the Spitfire in the tightest of vertical turns, the enemy pilot was still closing and it was only a matter of time before he had me in his sights. Stick over and well forward, I plunged into a near vertical dive to try and escape him. At ground level I pulled into another steep turn with the 190 still with me, and as I gauged my height above the ground and watched the roof tops I caught a glimpse of the Dieppe promenade, of stationary tanks, the white casino, and a deserted, littered beach. Then I made my bid to throw him off a short distance .off shore, where I could see a Navy Destroyer surrounded by a cluster of smaller ships. We had been briefed not to fly near them because the Royal Navy always opened fire on friend and foe alike. Flat out and at sea level I raced towards the Destroyer, slammed down on the nose and headed out to sea. I broke hard to the left and searched for the 190, but, happily he was no longer with me.

610 Squadron returned to 12 Group after Dieppe, where it resumed routine duties. Johnson still hoped for a posting to 11 Group, but, to his disappointment, the squadron was dispatched to RAF Castletown, Caithness, Scotland. Early in 1943, after a relatively quiet early winter, 610 rejoined the Tangmere Wing. On 13 February 1943, Johnson claimed a

'probable' but shortly after that the squadron lost no fewer than five pilots in a week to Fw 190s. Although Johnson was due to be rested, he had made himself indispensable so, instead, he was promoted to wing commander and given command of the Kenley Wing (403 and 416 Squadrons, Royal Canadian Air Force), which were re-equipped with Spitfire IXs. At this stage, he also adopted the call sign 'Greycap' and, despite expert advice that it would be safer to change it periodically, kept it for the rest of the war. As a wing leader, he took the privilege of substituting the Spitfire's three initials for his own 'JE-J', even though he was again warned that this would attract unwanted attention from the enemy.

Johnson's DSO was announced on 4 June 1943 after the recommendation for his award stated:

On 13 May [1943], in the morning, while top cover to a force of bombers, Wing Commander Johnson led the wing with outstanding success. They were heavily engaged by a superior force of enemy Fw. 190s, but fought their way home without loss, destroying four enemy fighter aircraft in the afternoon, while escorting a large force of Fortresses [heavy bombers] deep into France. A further three were destroyed, one falling to Wing Commander Johnson, while the bombers were guarded with success. On 14 May, Wing Commander Johnson destroyed another enemy fighter and led the wing on another successful escort of Fortresses, with three enemy aircraft destroyed. Wing Commander Johnson's personal score now stands at 13 destroyed, 3 probably destroyed and 6 damaged ... He is an outstanding Wing Leader and in my opinion his leadership expressed in his cheerful, forceful personality is largely responsible for the high morale and success of the Kenley Wing. Wing Commander Johnson puts the success of his wing first on all occasions. His personal victories have been inevitable in view of his outstanding ability as a Fighter Pilot. He has now led the Kenley Wing on 33 occasions.

The Canadian pilots thrived under his leadership and, over that spring and summer, shot down more than 100 enemy aircraft on 140 missions over north-west Europe. As a mark of their respect for their wing commander, they asked Johnson to put up 'CANADA' shoulder flashes, a request with which he complied. In August 1943, the month after Johnson claimed his twentieth victory, Kenley Wing became No. 127 Wing, 83 Group, 2nd Tactical Air Force.

The first Bar to Johnson's DSO was announced on 24 September 1943 after the recommendation for his award stated:

Since the citation of the award of the D.S.O. to this Officer on 17 May, he has completed 41 offensive sorties, during which he has personally destroyed a further 7.5 enemy aircraft while damaging another. During the same period the Wing under his leadership has destroyed 27, probably destroyed 3 and damaged 30. This is considered to be a magnificent effort for [a] two months' period and is due in large part to the skilful leadership and relentless determination to engage the enemy displayed by this Wing Leader.

In September, Johnson was ordered off operations to a staff job at RAF Uxbridge, Middlesex. Here he worked with the US Air Force coordinating escorts but he continued to 'keep his eye in' by occasionally flying with Spitfire IX and XII combat units.

March 1944 saw Johnson appointed wing commander of No. 144 Wing, which comprised 441, 442 and 443 Squadrons, Royal Canadian Air Force. By then, with twenty-five official victories, his score was closing in on the total of 'Sailor' Malan, the famed South African RAF fighter pilot, who was no longer flying operationally. This ensured great media interest in his activities. The initial task of his new wing was to maintain air supremacy during Normandy landings and then to convert to a ground-attack role. Yet Johnson kept his personal score ticking over: he claimed a Fw 190 on 5 May 1944 and another victory later in the same month. In late May, Johnson moved to RAF Ford, Sussex, part of the invasion build-up area. On 5 June, the day before the D-Day landings, his wing was instructed to protect part of the invading force's eastern flank from air attack. On D-Day itself, Johnson led his men on several sorties over the invasion beaches. The landings went so well that by 8 June, he was ordered to make a sweep before taking his wing to the first Allied landing ground in France: Croix-sur-Mer, near Caen. The first Spitfire landed at 1.30 p.m. on ground prepared by RAF Commandos and within half an hour all the wing's Spitfires had been serviced and refuelled, ready for another sweep before the return flight to Ford.

Johnson shot down a Fw 190 on 16 June and a Me 109 on the 22nd. When two more fell to his guns on 28 August, his official tally had drawn equal with Malan's thirty-two 'kills'. He destroyed two more Me 109s on 5 July and was feted in the press. Typically, Johnson suggested Malan's achievements were superior since he had flown from 1940 to 1941, when he had less protection in the air and was frequently out-numbered by the enemy. Johnson's second Bar to his DSO was announced on 7 July 1944 after the recommendation for his award stated:

> This Wing Leader was cited for the award of a Bar to his Distinguished Service Order on 14.8.1943. He has since then led 127 and 144 Wings in a further 107 hours of operational flying on 64 sorties . . . These Wings have in this 100 hours of his leadership destroyed 34 enemy aircraft and damaged 13. Personally he has accounted for 6 aircraft destroyed and one damaged of this total. His score is now 28 destroyed. He did a non-operational tour as Wing Commander Plans at No. 11 Group H.Q., leaving to form 144 Wing at its arrival in this country from Canada with no operational experience. He has, in two and a half months, succeeded in bringing it to absolutely first line standard with a record of 17 destroyed to date. This result could only have been achieved by a leader who combines the complete confidence and respect of his Pilots, combined with an untiring patience and energy on his part. These qualities Wing Commander Johnston has invariably displayed with the result that all Pilots working under him have been able to benefit from his vast operational experience to the maximum effect.

Yet still his tally mounted: on 23 August 1944 he shot down two Fw 190s, but his aircraft was also hit. He took off in another Spitfire to continue the combat but this time collected flak shrapnel in its tail. On 27 September, Johnson collected his final victory, shooting down a Me 109 at Rees am Rhein, Germany. In March 1945, Johnson was promoted to group captain and was also given the command of No. 125 Wing which had been equipped with new Spitfire XIVs. Johnson's verdict on the aircraft was that it was a 'nice, fast flying machine but it's not a Spitfire any more'.

Before and after the end of hostilities, Johnson was given numerous decorations by other Allied countries. He was awarded the American DFC on 18 January 1944, as well as the Belgian Order of Leopold and Belgian Croix de Guerre in January 1947. After the war, Johnson was given the task of organising a victory show over Denmark. He then continued to serve in Germany until 1946 before serving in Canada and the US. After the outbreak of the Korean War in 1950, Johnson was posted to the US Far East Forces for a three-month tour of active service. Johnson flew Douglas B-26 Invaders up to the Yalu River to photograph, by day and night, North Korean-held territories, being rewarded for his courage with the US Air Medal and Legion of Merit. After returning to the RAF, Johnson took responsibility for setting up the first Sabre fighter aircraft wing in Germany. He was appointed Deputy Director of Air Operations at the Air Ministry in 1954 and three years later became the commanding officer of RAF Cottesmore, Rutland, the base of the first V-Bomber Wing. In June 1957, Johnson flew one of the RAF's last operational Spitfires to RAF Biggin Hill, Kent, to found the Battle of Britain Memorial Flight. The 1950s saw him become an author, too: in 1956 he published his autobiography, *Wing Leader*. The 1960s saw more promotions: to air commodore in 1960 and to air vice-marshal in 1963, when he was posted to Aden as Air Officer Commanding (AOC) Air Forces Middle East. Furthermore, Johnson was created a Companion of the Order of the Bath (CB) in June 1965, on top of his earlier Commander of the British Empire (CBE) announced on New Year's Day 1960.

Johnson retired in 1966 and, afterwards, worked for British, Canadian and South African companies, as well as founding the Johnnie Johnson Housing Trust, which he established in 1969 to provide homes for thousands of elderly and disabled people.

Johnson died on 30 January 2001, aged eighty-five. I purchased his medals in London in December 2001 for a 'hammer price' of £210,000, then the world-record price for an RAF group at auction.

FLIGHT SERGEANT (LATER SQUADRON LEADER) CHARLTON HAW
Royal Air Force Volunteer Reserve (RAFVR)/RAF
DECORATIONS: DISTINGUISHED FLYING MEDAL (DFM) AND DISTINGUISHED FLYING CROSS (DFC)
GAZETTED: 23 JANUARY 1942 AND 17 OCTOBER 1944

Charlton 'Wag' Haw was born in York on 8 May 1920. As a child, he wanted to be a pilot after enjoying a flying circus joyride at the age of ten. Haw enlisted in the RAFVR in Hull, Humberside, before the Second World War and started flying early in 1939. He was called up on 1 September 1939 as the global conflict was beginning.

After finishing his pilot training, Haw was posted on 21 June 1940 to his first operational unit: 504 Squadron based at RAF Wick in Caithness, Scotland. After the start of the Battle of Britain on 10 July 1940, Haw took part in thirty-five sorties, nineteen daylight patrols and sixteen interceptions. In his pilot's logbook for 14 September, he referred to an attack on seventy Me 109 fighters. On 27 September, his squadron shot down six enemy aircraft including a Me 110 that was Haw's 'kill'. On the same day, he was shot down in combat, although he was unhurt, crash-landing his Hurricane.

On 22 June 1941, Hitler launched Operation Barbarossa – the invasion of Russia. Within three weeks the Red Army was in full-scale retreat, leaving the Allied military leaders to ponder their next move. Winston Churchill was well aware of the gravity of the situation, particularly that the ice-free Russian port of Murmansk should not be lost to the Axis powers as it was essential for the passage of Allied convoys. Churchill dispatched two squadrons of Hurricanes to help protect the port and by mid-August the 'Murmansk Expedition' was fully under way.

Germany, however, was equally aware of the strategic importance of Murmansk. As the German Army fought to take the port, the Luftwaffe attempted to destroy Murmansk's defences from the air. However, the Germans took an unexpected beating in the air from the now combined British and Russian forces, with the Battle of Britain experience of Haw and others proving invaluable. Not a single Russian bomber was lost when it was escorted by RAF fighters, yet fifteen German aircraft were shot down for the loss of one Hurricane pilot, with Haw responsible for at least three of the 'kills'. On 23 January 1942, Haw was awarded the DFM and his citation stated: 'Flight Sergeant Haw has displayed admirable qualities as a fighter pilot.'

Haw was the top-scoring fighter pilot of the Hurricane Wing in Russia and his efforts were much appreciated by the Soviets. On 31 March 1942, he was one of just four RAF servicemen to be awarded the Order of Lenin. Written praise conferred on Haw included these words from Russian Vice-Admiral A. Golovko: 'Your Manliness, heroism and excellent mastery in Battles of the Air have always assured Victory over the enemy. I wish you new Victories in Battle against the common enemy of all progressive nations i.e. German Fascism.'

In 1943, Haw took on two senior roles: from February he commanded 611 Squadron based at RAF Biggin Hill, Kent, and from November he commanded 129 Squadron, based at RAF Hornchurch, Essex. On 17 October 1944, he was awarded the DFC and his citation stated: 'Squadron Leader Haw is now on his third tour of operations and has throughout shown great courage and eagerness to engage the enemy. He is an exceptional squadron commander and a very keen leader.' Haw survived the war and was later praised by Flight Lieutenant Joe Leigh, of 129 Squadron, who said: 'Wag led well. He was a good squadron commander and he was a good Squadron Leader and there is a difference. He led us well on all our shows.'

Haw, who was also a talented boogie-woogie piano player, wrote of his flying experiences: 'Looking back on it all I suppose one could really say that if you wanted, as I wanted, to be a pilot, particularly a fighter pilot, it was just a schoolboy's dream.' After the war, Haw remained in the RAF. He commanded 65 Squadron from 1946 to 1948 and retired in 1951. The Russians never allowed 'Wag' Haw to forget that he was 'a hero of the Soviet Union' and he was their guest at various special functions in London and Moscow.

Haw, aided by his first wife, was landlord of the Blacksmith's Arms at Adversane, West Sussex, from 1952 to 1958, a role he later described as a 'six-year-working holiday', adding: 'We came out of there with the same amount of money in the bank as we did when we went in to it but we had a hell of a six years. I shall never forget it.' He later ran a pet-food and boarding-kennels business at Farnham, Surrey, and in recent years made dolls' houses and toys. Haw died on 27 November 1993, aged seventy-three, and was survived by his second wife, Audrey.

SERGEANT JÓZEF JEKA
Polish Air Force/RAF
DECORATION: DISTINGUISHED FLYING MEDAL (DFM)
GAZETTED: 19 FEBRUARY 1942

Józef Jeka was born in Tupaldy, Poland, on 6 April 1917. He enlisted in the Polish Air Force, aged twenty, in 1937. After the German invasion of Poland, he escaped through Europe to Britain, arriving early in 1940. Jeka completed his training with 15 Elementary Flight Training School (EFTS) in Redhill, Surrey, and arrived at 6 Operational Training Unit (OTU), RAF Sutton Bridge, Lincolnshire, on 1 August 1940. Jeka converted to Hurricanes and joined 228 Squadron at RAF St Eval, Cornwall, on 31 August 1940.

On 15 September 1940, Jeka had his first combat when he shot down a Me 110 fighter before damaging a second one. Further successes soon followed: Jeka shot down two He 111 bombers on 26 September and he destroyed a Ju 88 bomber on 7 October. However, on 5 November Jeka was shot down by Me 109s and baled out over Wimborne, Dorset. He suffered serious injuries and was taken to the Army Hospital in Shaftesbury. He made a good recovery and, on 15 February 1941, he joined 306 (Polish) Squadron at RAF Ternhill, Shropshire, where he converted to Spitfires. On 17 June 1941, he claimed a Me 109 destroyed, before damaging another on 27 June and destroying another on 16 August.

Jeka was commissioned in November 1941 and went to 58 Operational Training Unit (OTU), RAF Grangemouth, Stirlingshire, Scotland, as an instructor. His DFM was announced on 19 February 1942 after the recommendation for his award stated: 'This Sergeant fought last Autumn with an English Squadron destroying five enemy aircraft, probably destroying 2 more and shared in the destruction of another. With No 306 (Polish) Squadron he has taken part in many offensive sweeps over France in the course of which he has destroyed one enemy aircraft and damaged another. At all times he has shown the greatest courage and determination to inflict losses on the enemy.'

On 29 May 1942, Jeka rejoined 316 Squadron serving with them again for almost a year. On 24 May, 1943, he was posted to 308 Squadron but in August of the same year he returned to 316 Squadron, now based at RAF Northolt, Middlesex. On 19 August, Jeka shot down a Fw 190 fighter and damaged another. In December 1943, having completed his tour, Jeka was posted to 18 Armament Practice Camp. He remained there for four months until rejoining 308 Squadron on 30 March 1944. On 21 May, shortly before the D-Day landings, Jeka was shot down over Occupied France. Yet, remarkably, this courageous pilot evaded capture by the Germans and was hidden by the French Resistance for two months at a house near the village of Flixecourt on the Somme. Jeka managed to rejoin his unit on 11 September 1944. He again moved to 306 Squadron in November that year and took command of the squadron on 25 May 1945, a role he retained until after the war. Jeka was highly decorated by his home country between 1941 and 1945: he was awarded the Virtuti Militari (5th class), the Cross of Valour with three Bars and the Cross of Merit, with swords.

Jeka relinquished command of his squadron in May 1946 and was posted to 58 Polish Resettlement Unit. Later he served in Germany and the US. It was during his latter posting that Jeka was recruited by the Central Intelligence Agency (CIA), which, because he was a brilliant pilot and a stateless citizen, considered him perfect material for its various secret missions. At one point, President Eisenhower ordered that no US citizens were to undertake clandestine flights so that his country could deny all knowledge of a mission if it was discovered by the targeted country.

In 1949, Jeka resigned his RAF commission and was subsequently put on the highly secretive U2 spy plane programme. He became the first Pole to fly at Mach 2 (twice the speed of sound). It is understood that he was also selected and trained to parachute into Soviet territory to capture a MIG 15 jet and fly it to a UK base. However, the plan was apparently shelved when Lieutenant Kum Sok, a twenty-one-year-old North Korean Air Force pilot, helpfully landed a fully fuelled and armed MIG 15 in South Korea and handed it over to the US Air Force.

By 1958, the CIA had turned its attention to Indonesia, in particular its communist training camps. The CIA established a small squadron of B-26 bombers and P-51 Mustang fighters in Indonesia. In April 1958, the US commenced Operation Black Deniable, a mission to strike enemy targets on Sumatra and Sulawesi. On 13 April, Jeka had been detailed to bomb the airport of Makassar in southern Sulawesi. However, shortly after take-off, his B-26B bomber, which had been painted black for the mission, inexplicably crashed into trees shortly after take-off from Mapangaet airfield. Captain Jeka, aged forty-one, and his two crew perished in the accident and their bodies were swiftly flown back to the US. Death certificates were issued giving the correct date of death but the place of death was altered to: 'test area, Washington D.C.'. Jeka's body was later interred in the Newark-on-Trent Cemetery in Columbia, South Carolina.

FLIGHT SERGEANT (LATER SQUADRON LEADER) GEORGE ERIC CLIFFORD GENDERS

Royal Air Force Volunteer Reserve (RAFVR)/RAF
DECORATIONS: DISTINGUISHED FLYING MEDAL (DFM) AND AIR FORCE CROSS (AFC)
GAZETTED: 7 APRIL 1942 AND 1 JANUARY 1949

Eric 'Jumbo' Genders was born in Oldham, Lancashire, on 15 February 1920. The only son of an employee of the Great Central Railway, he and his family moved to Doncaster, Yorkshire, where Genders attended Doncaster Grammar School. Genders, who was from a deeply religious family, left school at sixteen and shortly afterwards started work at the general manager's office of the London and North-Eastern Railway in Doncaster. He enlisted in the RAFVR on 27 July 1939 and was called up two months later on the outbreak of war. After undergoing pilot training, he was posted as a sergeant to 245 Squadron in Northern Ireland, where he was awarded his pilot's 'wings' on 9 August 1940. In November 1940, Genders joined 73 Squadron, based at RAF Debden, Essex, and was embarked on HMS *Furious*, an aircraft carrier, for the west coast of Africa. On arrival, one of his first jobs was to fly one of the squadron's Hurricanes to Egypt, where the British were suffering a shortage of both aircraft and pilots. He joined 33 Squadron at the Fuka satellite airfield where the youthful, fair-haired and clean-living Genders acquired the nickname 'Jumbo'. In early 1941, and after further training at 70 Operational Training Unit (OTU), Genders was posted with 33 Squadron to Greece.

It was in the Mediterranean theatre that Genders quickly proved himself to be an exceptional fighter pilot. On 15 April 1941, there was a surprise dawn attack on the RAF's base at Larissa, Greece, by some twenty Messerschmitts. In the ensuing one-sided combat, two British pilots were shot down and killed but Genders flew his Hurricane brilliantly to avoid becoming the third victim. He described this incident – his first time in action – in a letter to his parents:

> I was at about 7,000 feet a few miles from the aerodrome when I heard over the wireless that enemy aircraft were circling the aerodrome, so I flew back quickly and saw seven or eight 109s at my own height. I climbed 100 feet then dived among them. I aimed at one from behind at 250 yards and the pilot must have realised he was being fired at because he did a sharp turn to the left and, turning inside him, I hit his engine with a beam shot. The pilot then baled out and, seeing another 109 coming head on at me, I opened fire at him and then we had passed one another. I got under him and he over me. All the 109s were then coming at me from all directions, so I manoeuvred quickly and in doing so I jammed one of the aircraft controls, but the enemy fighters must have been running short of petrol because they all went off home.

During an enemy raid on shipping at Piraeus, Genders claimed three Ju 87 bombers, while it is also thought that he brought down the Me 109 flown by Hauptmann Franz Lange, the commander of II/JG 77. Genders' success continued over Crete: on 3 May 1941, the enemy launched a twenty-five-aircraft attack on shipping in Suda Bay. Genders claimed two Ju 88s shot down and a further two damaged, thereby becoming the tenth most successful Allied pilot in the Mediterranean theatre.

After being evacuated from Greece, 33 Squadron was re-formed in Egypt. During this time, Genders became heavily engaged over the Libya–Egypt border, particularly during operations Brevity, Battleaxe and Crusader. His success continued as he shot down two Fiat G50 fighters on 17 June and, on 22 November, he shared in the destruction of a Savoia SM79 bomber and single-handedly damaged a Ju 88. As well as his combat victories, Genders flew on numerous ground-strafing sorties: on one occasion he set three enemy trucks alight with his first burst of fire. In April 1942, he was commissioned as a pilot officer and during the same month – on 7 April – he was awarded the DFM. The citation stated: 'This airman has taken part in operations over Greece, Crete and the Western Desert with great courage and determination. In the course of these operations he has destroyed at least 7 enemy aircraft and damaged several others. He has set an excellent example to junior pilots in the squadron.'

Genders' next appointment was in May 1942 to 103 Main-tenance Unit in Aboukir on the Mediterranean coast of Egypt. He then went on to serve as a test pilot on many different aircraft types. This was a challenging role and included becoming involved in further combat experience. One of the most formidable projects allocated to Genders was to fly a modified Spitfire V, which had been stripped of all unnecessary equipment in the hope that it could match altitudes to engage the Luftwaffe's Ju 86 reconnaissance aircraft. So as to be given their best chance of achieving the aim, the Spitfire V was fitted with only two fifty-inch machine guns. However, whereas the German reconnaissance aircraft had pressurised crew quarters, the adapted Spitfire had no such luxury, and temperatures were capable of dropping to 67 degrees below zero. Genders fought his first high-altitude battles on 26 and 27 June, damaging two Ju 86s. By then, two other talented airmen, Flying Officer G. W. H. Reynolds and Pilot Officer Gold were carrying out similar experimental projects. Together they were known affectionately as 'The Three Musketeers of Strato'.

On 6 September 1942, Genders succeeded in destroying a Ju 86, but a letter home, dated four days after the incident, also revealed that his engine had cut out.

I did this [baled out] at 1,000 feet and the parachute opened quite quickly, but I did not have time to get any sensations of the descent, as I had to get the release gear ready for when I hit the water. I do not think I went under the water. I got rid of the parachute harness as quickly as possible and then blew my Mae West [life jacket] up. We did not fill our Mae Wests on the ground as any air in them expands to about six times its volume at very high altitudes, and this would explode the thing.

When I had blown my Mae West up, I discarded my helmet, shoes and socks, but to have got my flying kit off I would have had to have taken off my Mae West, and, as this is put on like a jacket, I do not think I would have got it on again, so I had to keep my flying suit on. When I was in the water, I realised I was in an awful fix. I was ten or more miles from the coast and I thought my only hope was for a searching aircraft to find me. I learned later that 12 aircraft searched for me and I saw five of these. Two of them had come fairly near to me but they had not seen me although I splashed around as much as possible.

After the aircraft that were looking for me disappeared, I became very despondent. But I thought of one of your sentences in a letter, 'God who has protected you for so long will continue to do so.' I decided I would try to swim to shore even if it took me several days. I was on my back with my Mae West supporting my head, and I did a kind of back stroke with my arms and scissors kick with my legs. The swimming kept me warm but my movements seemed very slow and I soon became tired, my arms particularly. I wondered if it was a hopeless task and then realised nothing is impossible to God, and I recollected hymn No. 10 we had at a service I attended at Athens. I seemed to get renewed strength after that and continued swimming all the afternoon and night. At about 8.30 in the morning I saw telephone posts on shore and I finally got to land about 10 o'clock. I had been in the water 21 hours.

Two Greeks who had been out shooting birds then saw and helped Genders. He was granted a week's sick leave but was soon back in action at the height of the Battle of El Alamein, bringing down a reconnaissance Ju 88 on 21 October. This was to be his last claim and, for the rest of the war, he continued as a test pilot in the Middle East.

Post-war, Genders attended the Empire Test Pilots' School, then based at RAF Cranfield, Lincolnshire, in January 1946. Subsequently posted as a squadron leader to the Royal Aircraft Establishment at RAF Farnborough, Hampshire, in May, he continued his valuable work, and was rewarded with the AFC in the New Year's Honours of 1949. Genders was employed in testing the DH 108, Britain's first supersonic jet, also known as the 'Flying Wing'.

Only three such aircraft were ever built, one claiming the life of Geoffrey de Havilland, the son of the famous aircraft manufacturer, when it exploded over the Thames Estuary in September 1946, and the other two, on being released into service, the lives of their respective RAF pilots, one being Genders. An eyewitness to the disaster at Hartley Whitney, Hampshire, on 1 May 1950 described how he saw the DH 108 'whirling head-over-heels and the windmilling, wing tip over wing tip . . . like a sheet of paper caught in a sharp, unsteady breeze'. Another witness saw Genders bale out at around 200 feet, but 'instead of falling clear he stopped several feet from the plane, and swung round apparently attached to it'.

Genders, who had recorded more than 3,000 flying hours, had been due to marry just a few weeks later. The *Evening News* recorded the story of the crash on its front page with the headline: 'Hush-hush jet blows up'. Later a memorial cross was erected close to the scene of the crash by the mother of Genders' godson, Stuart Munro. The inscription read: 'To the memory of Sqn Ldr G.E.C. Genders A.F.C., D.F.M. killed here in a flying accident May 1st 1950 aged 30 years. He gave his life that others might live.'

Pauline Shacklock (née Genders) ends her excellent forty-page booklet, a tribute to her relative, with the words: 'Today, when air travel is so widely used both for business and pleasure, we tend to take the safety of flying very much for granted. However, we should never forget the Test Pilots, including Eric, who undertook the arduous and often dangerous work of testing experimental aircraft, which has contributed so much to the safety of air travel which we all enjoy today.'

PILOT OFFICER (LATER GROUP CAPTAIN) STEFAN WITORZENC

Polish Air Force/Royal Air Force Volunteer Reserve (RAFVR)
DECORATION: DISTINGUISHED FLYING CROSS (DFC)
GAZETTED: 1 JUNE 1942

Stefan 'Steve' Witorzenc was born in Lida, Poland, on 15 January 1908. In 1929, he entered the Polish Air Force College in Deblin, graduating three years later with the rank of 2nd lieutenant. His flying duties began with 3 Air Force Regiment in Poznań and, after completing a course at the Advanced Flying School in Grudziądz, Witorzenc joined 132 Fighter Squadron. In 1935, he was posted as a flying instructor, a job he held until the outbreak of the Second World War in 1939.

Witorzenc was put in command of a unit to defend his airfield and the Deblin region of Poland. However, with limited manpower and outdated equipment it was a hopeless task against the might of the Luftwaffe. Nevertheless, equipped only with P7 fighter aircraft, the Polish pilots bravely managed to break up the formations of enemy aircraft attacking their homeland. They even destroyed one enemy aircraft and damaged two others. On 7 September 1939, Witorzenc's Advanced Flying School was evacuated to an airfield near Sokal before being diverted later to an airfield near the Polish–Romanian frontier. On the night of 17/18 September, the unit was forced to cross into Romania. The following month Witorzenc left

Romania and travelled by sea to southern France, where he was stationed at Salon.

Witorzenc arrived in Britain late in 1939 with some 2,000 pilot hours' flying experience in single-engine aircraft. On 27 January 1940, he was commissioned as a pilot officer in the RAFVR, where he became known as 'Steve' to his British comrades. He had responsibility for training at RAF Eastchurch, Kent, but this role was interrupted when Germany attacked France and the Low Countries before directing its attentions on Britain. After a short conversion course to Hurricanes, Witorzenc was posted to 501 (County of Gloucester) Squadron at Gravesend, Kent, and it was not long before he made his mark. On 15 August, he shot down two Ju 87 bombers and three days later, over Whitstable, he shot down the Me 109 fighter of German ace Horst 'Jacob' Tietzen, who had twenty-seven 'kills' to his name. On 2 September, Witorzenc shot down a Ju 88 and nine days later shared in the destruction of a Do 215 bomber.

On 22 November 1940, Witorzenc was transferred to 306 (Polish) Fighter Squadron and appointed flight commander. He received the first of many gallantry awards – the Polish Virtuti Militari (5th class) – on 21 December 1940. On 21 May 1941, Witorzenc was transferred to 302 (Polish) Fighter Squadron where he was promoted to squadron commander on 27 May. His success in the air continued unabated: on 4 September, he shot down a Me 109. Witorzenc was awarded the Polish Cross of Valour on 30 October 1941 and on 24 November took command of No. 2 (Polish) Fighter Wing. His DFC was announced on 1 June 1942.

On 25 November 1942, Witorzenc was appointed liaison officer to 11 RAF Fighter Group. From 24 April 1944, he was chief instructor at 61 Operational Training Unit (OTU). On 7 January 1945, he took over the command of 25 (Polish) Elementary Flying Training School (EFTS) at RAF Hucknall, Nottinghamshire, before commanding No. 131 Fighter Wing for more than a month from 1 June 1945.

Witorzenc was released from the Polish Air Force in January 1947 and returned to live in Poland the following year. In 1957, he was again called up for military service, serving as the commandant of the Air Training Centre at Modlin. He later lived in Warsaw and became President of the Polish Air Force Association. Witorzenc died on 31 December 1994, aged eighty-six, and he was posthumously decorated with the Commander's Cross of the Order of Polonia Restituta.

SERGEANT (LATER SQUADRON LEADER) GEORGE FREDERICK BEURLING*

Royal Air Force Volunteer Reserve (RAFVR)/Royal Canadian Air Force (RCAF)
DECORATIONS: DISTINGUISHED FLYING MEDAL (DFM) AND BAR, DISTINGUISHED FLYING CROSS (DFC) AND DISTINGUISHED SERVICE ORDER (DSO)
GAZETTED: 24 JULY 1942, 4 SEPTEMBER 1942, 16 OCTOBER 1942 AND 3 NOVEMBER 1942

George 'Screwball' Beurling, the so-called 'Falcon of Malta', was the most successful Canadian fighter pilot of the Second World War. His career was made possible by his utter determination to become a fighter pilot after being initially rejected

---

* *Beurling's medals are not part of my collection. His story, however, features in the Channel 5 television series.*

by the RCAF because of his lack of academic qualifications. He had to overcome numerous other difficulties before eventually serving with the RAF on the besieged island of Malta where, at one point, he shot down an incredible twenty-seven German and Italian aircraft in just fourteen days.

Beurling was born in Verdun (now part of Montreal), Quebec, on 6 December 1921. The son of a Swedish farmer and an English mother, he had an early fascination with flying. He first took the controls of an aircraft aged just eleven and, five years later, was flying solo. He left school to work for an air freight company in Gravenhurst, Ontario, and soon had his commercial pilot's licence. Beurling was imprisoned for a few months for illegally crossing the border to the United States in order to join the 'Flying Tigers' (the 1st American Volunteer Group of the Chinese Army). Beurling's rejection by the RCAF came shortly after the outbreak of the war. Only just short of his eighteenth birthday, Beurling was also denied permission by his parents to join the Finnish Air Force, which was fighting the Soviets in the 'Winter War'.

Undeterred, he embarked on a merchant ship bound for Glasgow and travelled through U-boat (German-submarine) infested waters in an attempt to join the RAF. When asked for his birth certificate, Beurling admitted it was still in Canada. He had to make the return journey by sea to fetch it and then returned to present it to the same recruitment officer. In September 1940, Beurling was finally accepted into the RAF. Despite some clashes with authority, he was sent to an Operational Training Unit (OTU) at RAF Hawarden, Cheshire, in September 1941. There he came under the influence of the great 'Ginger' Lacey, who described him as 'a wonderful pilot and an even better shot'. Throughout his

195

military career, Beurling's flying and shooting skills were aided by his exceptional eyesight.

In December 1941, Beurling was posted as a sergeant pilot to 403 Squadron, where he flew his first combat mission and spent a relatively uneventful four months escorting bombers on sweeps across the English Channel. In late spring 1942, Beurling joined 41 Squadron, based in Sussex, and his third mission, a sweep over Calais on 1 May, proved eventful. As 'tail-end Charlie', his Spitfire became detached from his flight and he was attacked and hit by German fighters. Despite half his guns being out of action, he fired a short burst at a Fw 190 fighter, which exploded in mid-air. Two days later, he broke from his flight after spotting a lone Fw 190. Beurling claimed the fighter as destroyed over Cap Gris Nez, but was reprimanded for attacking the target without permission. After volunteering for a posting overseas, Beurling was dispatched to Malta with 249 Squadron, landing on the island on 9 June 1942. Soon he had been given a new nickname, 'Screwball', a word he had a habit of using.

On his third day on Malta, Beurling and three other Spitfire pilots from 249 Squadron intercepted eight Me 109s. Although Beurling claimed to have blown the tail off one enemy aircraft, no one saw it hit the ground so he was credited with only a 'damaged'. The citations to his four gallantry medals, all awarded during five dizzy months in 1942, tell the story of his incredible success on Malta where he became an ace after claiming five 'kills' in just four days up until 10 July.

He was awarded the DFM on 24 July 1942 and his citation stated: 'Sergeant Beurling has displayed great skill and courage in the face of the enemy. One day in July, 1942, he engaged a number of enemy fighter aircraft which were escorting a formation of Junkers 88's and destroyed one fighter. Later during the same day he engaged 10 enemy fighters and shot two of them down into the sea, bringing his total victories to eight.'

On 30 July 1942, he was commissioned as a pilot officer. Less than five weeks later, he was awarded a Bar to his DFM and his citation, announced on 4 September, stated: 'Since being awarded the Distinguished Flying Medal in July, 1942, Sergeant Beurling has destroyed a further 9 enemy aircraft, bringing his victories to 17. One of his exploits was the destruction of 4 enemy fighters in one day; during these brief combats he also damaged a further 2 hostile aircraft. His courage and determination are a source of inspiration to all.'

Yet the stress of daily combats, along with poor rations and dysentery, took their toll. Beurling was bedridden for much of August and September, gaining only one and a half victories in the former month. On 25 September, he claimed to have downed three German fighter aircraft, but he was deemed to have 'overclaimed'. Beurling was awarded the DFC on 16 October 1942 and his citation stated:

Since being awarded a Bar to the Distinguished Flying Medal, this officer has shot down a further 3 hostile aircraft, bringing his total victories to 20. One day in September, 1942, he and another pilot engaged 4 enemy fighters. In the ensuing combat, Pilot Officer Beurling destroyed 2 of them. As a relentless fighter, whose determination and will to win has won the admiration of his colleagues, this officer has set an example in keeping with the highest traditions of the Royal Air Force.

Despite his heroics in the air, Beurling was not universally popular: he was a complex and driven character. A teetotaller and non-smoker, he dedicated himself to aerial combat but was a loner both on the ground and in the air. His superiors and his fellow airmen were unimpressed, too, by his disdain for teamwork. He was, however, acclaimed for his 'situational awareness' in the air and for his daring exploits, including his ability to 'toss his Spitfire' into violent combat manoeuvres. Like many other successful Spitfire pilots, Beurling fired late – at 250 yards or less – when less experienced pilots would be breaking away. However, for all his talents, Beurling was not invincible: he was shot down four times over Malta, the last time on 14 October, which would prove to be his final flight over the island. Beurling, who had serious shrapnel wounds, was hospitalised and sent back to Britain on 31 October 1942. Even then there was more drama: the B-24 transport aircraft in which he was flying crashed into the sea off Gibraltar and Beurling was one of only three survivors, while fifteen others perished.

While in Malta, Beurling's total of twenty-seven 'kills' was far more than any other RAF pilot during the campaign. On 3 November 1942, it was announced that he had been awarded the DSO and his citation stated: 'This officer's skill and daring are unexcelled.' After a short spell back in Britain, Beurling was sent to Canada and was the guest of honour at a parade in Verdun, when he met Prime Minister Mackenzie King. Once again, his unconventional approach caused difficulties and he embarrassed the RCAF by saying how much he enjoyed killing people. Beurling was hospitalised for several weeks as a result of his war wound from Malta and his general poor health. His work promoting the sale of war bonds, which he did not enjoy, had one major benefit: in Vancouver he met Diana Whittall, who was to become his wife. Back in Britain, Beurling was posted as a gunnery instructor to 61 Operational Training Unit (OTU). Less than two weeks after being posted to the Central Gunnery School on 27 May 1943, Beurling was accidentally shot during a mock dogfight, baling out of his Spitfire after the engine caught fire. On 1 September 1943, he transferred to the RCAF and was posted to 403 Squadron. That month he shot down a Fw 190, but his disciplinary problems soon resurfaced and, although he was promoted to flight lieutenant, he was also threatened with a court martial for stunt-flying a Tiger Moth. Later he was transferred to No. 126 Wing HQ and then to 412 Squadron, where he was grounded, for stunting and lack of teamwork, before his last 'kill' – a Fw 190 – on 30 December 1943.

In his autobiography, *Malta Spitfire*, published in 1943, Beurling admitted that flying was an obsession. 'Ever since I can remember, airplanes and to get them up in the free sky had been the beginning and end of my thoughts and ambitions,' he wrote. In April 1944, Beurling returned to Canada and was given an honourable discharge that October. His career had ended, Beurling holding the rank of squadron leader, with thirty-one confirmed 'kills', one shared and nine 'damaged'. Despite a later attempt to join the US Army Air Force, his wartime flying was over.

By early March 1945, his marriage had ended, too, and after the war he struggled to adjust to civilian life. In 1948, he was recruited by the Israeli Air Force to fly P-51 Mustangs. However, en route to his new job, he crashed his transport aircraft while landing in Rome. His tenth crash, on 20 May 1948, was to be his last, occurring amid suspicions of possible sabotage. Beurling died, aged twenty-six, and the incident also claimed the life of Leonard Cohen, another Malta-based RAF pilot.

When Beurling's estranged widow failed to claim his remains, the coffin was held in a warehouse for three months. Eventually, he was buried in a Protestant cemetery beside the Pyramid of Cestius in Rome. However, in November 1950, fully two and a half years after his death, Beurling's coffin, draped in the blue and white Israeli flag, was flown to Haifa airport in northern Israel. Here he was given a military funeral and he was reinterred in a military cemetery at the foot of Mount Carmel. 'The Falcon of Malta' had finally been given a farewell fit for a hero.

PILOT OFFICER (LATER FLIGHT LIEUTENANT) ALLAN JOHN HANCOCK
RAF
DECORATIONS: DISTINGUISHED FLYING CROSS
(DFC) AND BAR
GAZETTED: 28 JULY 1942 AND 13 OCTOBER 1944

John Hancock was born in Lahore, pre-Partition India, on 26 April 1918, although his family originally hailed from Wallingford, Berkshire. He enlisted in the RAF early in the summer of 1940 when he was twenty-two. He attended Elementary Flying Training School (EFTS) at Marshalls Flying School, Cambridge, and Initial Flying Training School (IFTS) in nearby Peterborough. Throughout his training, Hancock was graded 'above average' and, after attending 56 Operational Training Unit (OTU) in December 1940, he was posted to 213 Squadron early the following month as a sergeant. Hancock flew a Hurricane off the deck of HMS *Furious* to Takoradi, Ghana, and, from there, across Africa to Egypt. In June 1941, he saw action with 80 Squadron over

Syria before, later in the year, starting operations over the Western Desert in North Africa.

On 10 June 1942, shortly after being commissioned, he was wounded in the arm and leg over the Western Desert. The incident was noted in the citation for his DFC, awarded on 28 July 1942, which stated: 'This officer has shot down five enemy aircraft and damaged a further two during recent operations in the Western Desert. In a combat in June, 1942, Pilot Officer Hancock sustained a bullet wound in the arm. Despite the intense pain and the loss of much blood he flew his aircraft to the nearest landing ground and, although in a semi-conscious condition, made a perfect landing.'

After returning to the UK, Hancock began a second tour with 64 Squadron at the end of March 1943. By then, he was flying Spitfires, undertaking thirty-three sweeps with his unit. Hancock was posted as a flight commander to 129 Squadron on 23 September 1943, where he was flying Mustangs. Hancock was shot down and killed by flak over Normandy on 22 June 1944, aged twenty-six. By this point, he had claimed at least eight victories.

On 13 October, 1944, almost five months after his death, Hancock was awarded a Bar to his DFC and the citation stated: 'Since being awarded the Distinguished Flying Cross this officer has completed many operational sorties during which he has destroyed two enemy aircraft, damaged others, bringing his total to seven destroyed. Flight Lieutenant Hancock is [was] an inspiring leader.'

FLIGHT SERGEANT (LATER FLIGHT LIEUTENANT) KAZIMIERZ WÜNSCHE

Polish Air Force/RAF

DECORATIONS: DISTINGUISHED FLYING MEDAL (DFM) AND DISTINGUISHED FLYING CROSS (DFC)
GAZETTED: 15 NOVEMBER 1942 AND 26 MAY 1945

Kazimierz Wünsche was born in Poland on 5 June 1919 and started flying with the Polish Air Force on 1 September 1936. At the outbreak of the Second World War in September 1939, he was serving with the III Escadra. On 8 September, he shared in the destruction of a Henschel Hs 126 reconnaissance aircraft. After the fall of Poland, Wünsche escaped to Romania. He then moved to France where he flew in combat operations from 2 March to 18 June 1940. He arrived in Britain in midsummer and joined 303 Squadron on its formation at RAF Northolt, Middlesex, on 12 August 1940.

An experienced pilot, he soon saw success in the skies, destroying Me 109 fighters on 31 August and on 5 September. He had a 'probable' on 6 September but three days later he was shot down by a Me 109 in combat over Beachy Head, Sussex. Wünsche baled out with slight burns and was admitted to Hove Hospital in Brighton, while his Hurricane crashed and burnt out.

Wünsche was decorated by his home country: his Virtuti Militari (5th class) was announced on 23 December 1940. During 1941, he had more combat success: he destroyed a Me 109 on 23 June 1941 before being awarded the Polish Cross of Valour on 10 September 1941. Wünsche then shared in the destruction of two Ju 88 bombers on 3 July 1942 and on 20 August 1942 was awarded a Bar to his Cross of Valour. His long tour of duty ended on 6 September 1942 when he was posted to 58 Operational Training Unit (OTU) at RAF Grangemouth, Stirlingshire, Scotland, as an instructor. His DFM was announced on 15 November 1942 and was based on the recommendation from Squadron Leader J. Zumbach, the commanding officer of 303 Squadron, which stated: 'F/Sgt Wünsche has showed exceptional skill as a fighter pilot and his fearlessness and determination in combat have been outstanding.'

Wünsche was commissioned in December 1942 and rejoined 303 Squadron, by then based at RAF Debden, Essex, on 17 March 1943. On 1 October 1943, he was posted for duties at the Polish Air Force depot in Blackpool, Lancashire. On 20 October 1943, Wünsche was awarded a second Bar to his Cross of Valour. On 18 April 1944, he joined 315 Squadron at RAF Coolham, Sussex. He became a flight commander on 6 December and was awarded a third Bar to his Cross of Valour on 30 December 1944. Wünsche stayed in the squadron until 24 August 1945, when he was posted to RAF Coltishall, Norfolk, on staff duties. He was awarded the DFC on 26 May 1945 and released from the RAF in December 1946, when he was serving as a flight lieutenant. Wünsche was repatriated to Poland and died there in 1980, aged sixty.

NAVAL KAPITAN PAVEL DMITRIEVICH KLIMOV
Soviet Air Force
DECORATION: DISTINGUISHED FLYING MEDAL (DFM)
GAZETTED: HONORARY AWARDS TO ALLIED AIRMEN WERE NOT GAZETTED

Only four DFMs were awarded to Russian airmen during the whole of the Second World War. One of them went to Dmitrievich Klimov, of the 2nd Guards Fighter Aviation Regiment of the Soviet Air Force. Born in Baku, the capital of Azerbaijan, on 7 February 1920, Klimov graduated from the Bakinsk Industrial Institute in 1939 and joined the Naval Air School. It was after Germany invaded Russia on 22 June 1941 that Klimov made a name for himself as a fearless and talented fighter pilot. After attending various other training and military posts, Klimov joined the famous 2nd Guards Aviation Regiment in January 1942. He was posted to the Air Force of the North Sea Fleet. Initially, he flew P-40 Kittyhawks but his unit was re-equipped with P-39 Aircobras in April 1943.

On 31 October 1942, twenty German bombers attacked the strategically important Russian port of Murmansk. Klimov and just one other fighter pilot rose to meet them but they quickly engaged the enemy and with great success. Klimov shot down one bomber in his first attack and two others subsequently.

Decorations came thick and fast in 1942 and 1943 for this tenacious and ruthless airman. On 31 November 1942, he was decorated with the order of the Red Banner. On the same day, he celebrated his decoration by becoming the first pilot in the

Northern Fleet to destroy a bomber at night when he shot down two Ju 88s during an enemy raid on Murmansk. His DFM followed soon afterwards: of the four DFMs awarded to Russian airmen, two were to fighter pilots. Klimov was the highest scoring Soviet ace to receive the medal.

By the summer of 1943, he was a junior lieutenant and flight leader and, on 24 July of that year, he was appointed a Hero of the Soviet Union. His recommendation noted that, between September 1942 and April 1943, he had completed 306 sorties, fought thirty-three air battles and shot down eight enemy aircraft (five bombers and three fighters).

Klimov's stature and fame grew and grew. In December 1943, he graduated from the flight commander's course and was appointed deputy squadron commander of the 2nd Guards Fighter Aviation Regiment, Air Force, Northern Fleet. In January 1945, he was promoted to commander, a position he retained until the end of the war. By the cessation of hostilities, Klimov had flown more than 350 missions, fought in fifty-two air battles and had been wounded three times. He was given a final tally of twenty-seven 'kills', of which sixteen were shared. His other decorations included the Order of Lenin.

After the war, Klimov remained in the military, graduating from the Air Academy in 1951 and from the General Staff in 1959. He retired in 1970 with the title of an Honoured Air Force Pilot of the USSR and became a colonel in the Reserves. In civilian life, Klimov lived in Moscow, where he worked as a chief engineer on hydrometeorology and the protection of the environment. He died in 1999, aged seventy-nine.

SERGEANT (LATER FLIGHT LIEUTENANT) EDWARD MILES SMITH

Royal Air Force Volunteer Reserve (RAFVR)
DECORATIONS: DISTINGUISHED FLYING MEDAL
(DFM), DISTINGUISHED FLYING CROSS (DFC)
AND BAR
GAZETTED: 27 JULY 1943, 21 JANUARY 1944 AND
26 OCTOBER 1945

Edward 'Bulls Eye' Smith, who was born in 1922, was educated at Wakefield Grammar School in Yorkshire. In 1942, he enlisted in the RAFVR and was posted for training.

In April 1943, Smith was posted for operational duties to 141 Squadron (Beaufighters) at the same time as Howard Kelsey (later wing commander DSO, DFC and Bar). The two men went on to form a formidable partnership that lasted for more than two years until almost the end of the Second World War. Kelsey was the pilot and Smith the navigator and radar operator. Later, the squadron, including Smith and Kelsey, converted from Beaufighters to Mosquitos. Together the two men flew on seventy-three operational sorties, primarily involving night intruder and bomber escort roles. They flew mainly over heavily defended German cities and large towns including Berlin, Dortmund, Cologne, Stuttgart, Kessel, Aachen and Munich, as well as the industrial Ruhr. The two men claimed nine enemy aircraft destroyed, one 'probable', two damaged and three destroyed on the ground, as well as a large number of locomotives destroyed on the ground.

Later in the war, the pair were posted to 169 and 515 Squadrons, with Smith being promoted to flight lieutenant and Kelsey serving as the commanding officer in December

1944. The success of Smith's career is best told through the recommendations that led to his three decorations. He was awarded the DFM on 27 July 1943 after the recommendation for his decoration stated:

Sergeant Smith joined No. 141 Squadron with his pilot, Flying Officer Kelsey, on the 5th April 1943, from No. 51 O.T.U., having shown more than average promise on his various courses. This was proved within a fortnight of joining the squadron when he safely navigated his pilot on a 'Ranger' operation in difficult weather over the Brest Peninsula, resulting in the severe damaging of a locomotive. On the 22nd June, 1943, on his second special intruder trip (an operation entirely new to the squadron), he navigated his pilot over Germany and succeeded in pinpointing the objective. By his coolness and direction, he assisted Flying Officer Kelsey in the destruction of an ME. 110, and in returning safely to Base. Three nights later, on this crew's next intruder operation, he warned his pilot of an impending attack by another ME. 110 and, by his promptitude and instruction, materially assisted in turning the tables on the enemy aircraft and destroying it. Despite his youth, in the short time he has been in an operational squadron, his diligence and application have proved him one of the most able and conscientious navigators and he has set an example to others many years his senior.

Less than six months later, on 21 January 1944, Smith, by then a pilot officer, was awarded the DFC after the recommendation for his decoration stated:

On the 16th August, 1943, near Paris, Pilot Officer Smith brought his Pilot into a position which enabled him to attack three enemy night fighters in formation. The first, a JU88, was sent down in flames to explode on the ground. Then an ME110 went diving off, hit in many places and with its starboard engine on fire, probably destroyed. The attack was pressed home until the third, another JU88, was damaged with cannon and machine gun hits as it peeled off with flashes from its starboard engine. On 24th December, 1943, after a long and difficult chase, in which the Navigator's skill and quickness of mind in directing his Pilot was of paramount importance, this crew attacked and destroyed a JU88 in the Duren area. The combat had brought the aircraft over the Aachen defences which opened up with great accuracy and intensity. Although the Beaufighter was hit and damaged and the port engine was running very badly, Pilot Officer Smith with great coolness assisted his Pilot to bring the aircraft safely back to base over 200 miles of enemy territory and sea. This last combat brings this crew's score up to four enemy aircraft destroyed, one probably destroyed and one damaged, and since his last award Pilot Officer Smith has completed fourteen sorties over enemy territory.

The Smith–Kelsey partnership was finally broken up in June 1945 when Smith was posted to 85 Squadron. The Bar to Smith's DFC was awarded on 26 October 1945 after the recommendation for his decoration stated:

Since being awarded the D.F.C. in January 1944, F/Lt Smith has taken part in a further 48 offensive sorties as Radio Navigator over enemy territory. He has assisted in destroying a further five enemy aircraft, damaging four others, and has successfully attacked many ground targets of which sixteen were locomotives. These sorties included close bomber escort to Berlin, Nuremberg, Leipzig, and other heavily defended targets with 141 Squadron. On one occasion over Berlin, he so directed the interception of a fast weaving F.W. 190, that the pilot was able to destroy the enemy after a long chase. Latterly, F/Lt Smith has been engaged on low level bomber support with 169 and 515 Squadrons. He has carried out many intruder patrols on enemy airfields and freelance ranger sorties to Prague and Breslau. Whilst with 515 Squadron, he has been detailed on two occasions to divert the attention of the intense light flak defences of the Kiel Canal against his own aircraft, or by engaging them at very close range to silence the guns so that minelayers could complete their work without loss. On another occasion as Marker Navigator he has marked and assisted in directing fire raids from very low level on enemy airfields. All F/Lt Smith's duties have been carried out with great determination and frequently in the teeth of intense opposition from the enemy. He has at all times continued to work with coolness and skill, displaying exceptional tenacity of purpose.

It is not known what happened to Smith after the war.

MICHAEL ASHCROFT

MAJOR (LATER BRIGADIER GENERAL) ROBIN OLDS*
US Air Force
DECORATION: DISTINGUISHED FLYING CROSS (DFC)
GAZETTED: HONORARY AWARDS TO ALLIED AIRMEN WERE NOT GAZETTED

Robin Olds was a legendary character within the US Air Force both during and after the Second World War. As an established ace with a combined total of sixteen 'kills' from the 1939–45 war and the Vietnam War, he had both a formidable presence with his swashbuckling style, and a distinctive look with his towering frame and handlebar moustache (sported only in Vietnam). In the words of Stephen Coonts, the bestselling American author: 'Robin Olds is probably the greatest aerial warrior America ever produced.'

Olds was born in Honolulu, Hawaii, on 14 July 1922. He came from a military family: his father, Robert, was a captain (eventually a major general) in the US Army Air Corps and had been an instructor pilot in France during the First World War. Olds was the eldest of four boys (two of them half-brothers) and he spent much of his boyhood in Hampton, Virginia, where he attended both local elementary and high schools. Flying was in his blood: when his mother, Eloise, died when he was four, he is said to have asked his father if she was in heaven with all the aeroplanes. He first took the controls, aged eight, when his father piloted an open-cockpit aircraft. In

---

* *Olds' medals are not part of my collection. His story, however, features in the Channel 5 television series. Each hero's introductory panel lists only British and Commonwealth gallantry awards.*

210

1939, Olds enrolled at Millard Military Prep in Washington, DC, already set on a career as a fighter pilot.

When the Second World War broke out, Olds, just seventeen, attempted to join the Royal Canadian Air Force, but his father refused to sign his enlistment papers. From Millard, Olds won a place at West Point, the US military academy in New York that he hoped would lead to him becoming a military aviator as well as advancing his passion for American football. Indeed, he was an aggressive and talented footballer, representing the US Army versus the Navy in front of 100,000 fans on 29 November 1941, just eight days before the Japanese attack on Pearl Harbor. From the attack onwards, Olds wanted to qualify as quickly as possible to fly in combat. He eventually received his pilot's 'wings' on 30 May 1943, having completed fighting training with 329th Fighter Group, based in Glendale, California. By early 1944, Olds was part of the cadre assigned to build up the newly activated 434th Fighter Squadron and its parent 479th Fighter Group, based at Lomita, California. Soon, in Olds' own words, 'I was on my way', bound for the war in Europe in the USS *Argentina* on 3 May 1944. The 479th arrived at RAF Wattisham, Suffolk, via Scotland, on 15 May 1944 and went into combat eleven days later.

Olds, who flew one of the new P-38 Lightning fighter aircraft, was promoted to captain and became a flight commander and, later, a squadron leader. On 14 August 1944, following a bridge-bombing mission to Montmirail in France, Olds shot down his first enemy aircraft: a pair of Fw 190 fighters. On 25 August, while on an escort mission to Wismar in Germany, Olds pursued a Me 109 fighter for ten minutes before shooting it down. As he fired, both his engines cut out

211

but he dived away, and, despite damage to his own aircraft from enemy fire, he restarted his engines. Soon after he was involved in a dogfight with an enemy aircraft which he shot down – and he claimed another on the way home. Despite only being in theatre for just over three months, he had become an ace, aged just twenty-two – and the first ace of the 479th Fighter Group. Olds later wrote of his feelings that night: 'Life was sweet . . . Nothing could erase the feeling of complete aliveness coursing through my body, nor the exaltation in my soul.'

In mid-September 1944, 479th Flying Group converted from the Lightning P-38 fighter to the Mustang P-51. On 6 October, he shot down a Fw 190 during a fierce aerial battle near Berlin in which he was nearly accidentally shot down by his own wingman. On 9 November 1944, he completed his first tour of duty, having accrued 270 hours of combat time and with six confirmed 'kills'.

Two months' leave in the US was followed by a second tour at RAF Wattisham, Suffolk, beginning on 15 January 1945. On 9 February 1945, the same day that he was promoted to major, he claimed his seventh 'kill', south-east of Magdeburg, Germany, downing a Me 109. Five days later, he claimed three more victories, two Me 109s and a Fw 190 (the latter was later changed to a 'probable' by the authorities). His final 'kill' of the war came on 7 April 1945 when, while on an escorting mission to Lüneburg, Germany, he pursued and destroyed a Me 109.

In the same month, Olds destroyed six German aircraft on the ground during successful attacks on two German airfields and later wrote: 'Five of these were on the sixteenth, when we had great fun on a "freelance" mission to the Reichersberg, Kirchen, and Eferding airdromes. The squadron destroyed twenty-one aircraft and damaged seven at those 'dromes that day. Göring's Luftwaffe was largely crippled by this time. The mighty Huns had fallen to their knees under the daily Allied onslaught. By the end of the month, we knew it was all over.' On 8 May 1945, Nazi Germany collapsed and by the end of the summer Olds was heading home to a hero's welcome, officially credited with twelve German aircraft shot down and eleven and a half destroyed on the ground. Olds was widely decorated: as well as his US Silver Star, Legion of Merit and DFC, he was awarded the British DFC, for 'his great skill, bravery and aggressive leadership'. He was also awarded the French Croix de Guerre.

After the war, Olds decided to embark on a career in the USAF. He was assigned to the first jet squadron and was a member of the USAF's first jet aerobatic team. He returned to England in October 1948 under a USAF–RAF exchange programme and joined the RAF's 1 Squadron flying Meteor jet fighters from RAF Tangmere, Sussex. Six months later, Olds took command of 1 Squadron, the first foreigner to command an RAF unit in peace time. More senior postings followed, but it was during the Vietnam War that Olds once again rose to prominence, this time both for his skills as a pilot and a tactical leader. Olds was widely recognised as the outstanding fighter leader during the campaign in South East Asia.

On 30 September 1966, shortly after being promoted to colonel and by then forty-four, Olds took command of the 8th Tactical Fighter Wing (TFW) – the 'Wolfpack' – based at Ubon in Thailand. It soon became apparent that his views on tactics did not always accord with accepted practices and fighter pilot training. Confident of his own judgement, Olds set about introducing a new approach towards the feared

North Vietnamese MiG fighters. Forever unconventional, Olds placed himself on the flight schedule as a 'rookie' pilot under officers junior to himself and challenged them to train him properly because he would soon be leading them.

On 2 January 1967, Olds, who by then was flying the F-4C Phantom, led his wing over North Vietnam against the enemy's new aggressive MiG 21s on Operation Bolo, which would later be recognised as one of the most successful air battles of the Vietnam War. His ambitious plan was to simulate a bomber formation using their tactics, radio call signs and electronic counter-measures – then spring an aerial ambush on the enemy. He timed the attack to arrive in the area where the MiGs would be returning to their airfields short of fuel.

In poor weather, Olds and his formation of Phantom F-4Cs soon caught some enemy fighters and launched two air-to-air missiles against one of them, resulting in the MiG 21 exploding in mid-air. The pilots of the 8th TFW gained the advantage and they eventually shot down seven of the enemy, suffering no losses. Olds' tactics, and the aggressive spirit he had imparted to his crews, gave them a huge psychological advantage over the North Vietnamese Air Force, which became wary of the American's superior fighters after their losses.

Olds destroyed another MiG on 4 May 1967 and, two weeks later, he was leading his wing during one of the USAF's biggest raids north of Hanoi when he shot down two more, making him the most successful fighter pilot during the early years of the Vietnam War. Olds was now a legendary ace, with sixteen 'kills' (twelve from the Second World War and four from Vietnam). For his courage and leadership in Vietnam, Olds received many more decorations, including the Vietnam Air Force's Distinguished Service Order.

When Olds left Vietnam in October 1967, he had flown 152 combat missions; his predecessor had flown twelve over a similar period of time. His wing had accounted for twenty-four aerial victories, a total unsurpassed by any other during the war. On completion of his one-year tour of duty in Vietnam, Olds was promoted to brigadier general and became the commandant of cadets at the US Air Force Academy at Colorado Springs, Colorado. In February 1971 he became the Director of Aerospace Safety, but was soon restless to return to flying operations in Vietnam. Olds, who by then had a reputation as a heavy drinker and for being rebellious, offered to drop a rank to take command of a fighter wing. However, when this request was refused, he decided to retire. In his autobiography, *Fighter Pilot: The Memoirs of Legendary Flying Ace Robin Olds*, he wrote: 'On June 1, 1973, I retired from the United States Air Force exactly thirty years after graduating from West Point. The ceremony was simple and subdued. The next day we took off in a caravan of cars driving back across the country to the little ski town of Steamboat Springs. When the Rocky Mountains came into view once in Colorado, I knew I was finally home. It was the home I would never leave.' After retiring, Olds was in great demand as a public speaker. In 2001, he was inducted into the US National Aviation Hall of Fame, when he became the only person to be enshrined in the National Aviation Hall and the College Football Hall of Fame.

Olds' lifestyle meant his personal relationships often suffered. He was married in 1947 to Ella Raines, an actress. The couple, who had two daughters and a son (who was stillborn), separated in 1975 and divorced the following year. Olds married his second wife, Morgan Sellers Barnett, in 1978 although they too later divorced. Olds died in Steamboat Springs, Colorado, on 14 June 2007, aged eighty-four.

MAJOR (LATER COLONEL) FRANCIS STANLEY GABRESKI*

US Air Force
DECORATION: DISTINGUISHED FLYING CROSS (DFC)
GAZETTED: HONORARY AWARDS TO ALLIED AIRMEN WERE NOT GAZETTED

Francis 'Gabby' Gabreski was the top American fighter ace in Europe during the Second World War. He was credited with twenty-eight 'kills' during the war and then added six and a half more during the Korean War. This made him one of only seven US pilots who became an ace in two separate wars.

The son of Polish parents who had emigrated to the US in the early 1900s, Gabreski was one of five children born in Oil City, Pennsylvania, on 28 January 1919. His father, Stanley, owned and ran a grocery store, frequently working twelve-hour days. Gabreski's parents were ambitious for their son and they were delighted when he won a place at Notre Dame University in Notre Dame, Indiana. During his first year at university, Gabreski became interested in flying and took lessons, accumulating six hours' flying time (although his instructor doubted he had 'the touch to be a pilot'). During his second year at university, Army Air Corps recruiters visited the campus. Gabreski, who was keen to avenge the seizure of

Gabreski's medals are not part of my collection. His story, however, features in the Channel 5 television series. Each hero's introductory panel lists only British and Commonwealth gallantry awards.

Poland by Germany on 1 September 1939, enrolled into the military and reported for duty in July 1940. After earning his pilot's 'wings' in March 1941, he was commissioned into the Army Air Corps as a 2nd lieutenant. Soon he was off to his first assignment, sailing aboard the SS *Washington* for Hawaii where he served with the 45th Fighter Squadron of the 5th Fighter Group based at Wheeler Air Base. In Hawaii, Gabreski not only trained as a pilot but he met his future wife, Catherine 'Kay' Cochran, with whom he eventually had three sons and six daughters. The couple became engaged shortly after the Japanese attack on Pearl Harbor on 7 December 1941. Gabreski was shaving at the time of the attack and, although he managed to take off in a Curtiss P-36 fighter, he was too late to engage the departing raiders. In September 1942, Gabreski left Hawaii for Washington, DC, where he was promoted to captain, after he offered to serve as a liaison officer to the Polish squadrons serving with the British RAF.

In October 1940, Gabreski reported to the US 8th Air Force's VIII Fighter Command in East Anglia. Gabreski was invited to join 315 Squadron, an RAF fighter unit manned by Poles. In all, he flew twenty missions with the squadron, flying a Spitfire to escort bombers and engaging in combat once. On 27 February 1943, he rejoined the US 8th Air Force and became part of the 56th Fighter Group under Lieutenant Colonel Hubert 'Hub' Zemke. He was assigned to the 61st Fighter Squadron and flew P-47 Thunderbolt fighters, which were more cumbersome than Spitfires. In May, Gabreski was promoted to major and the following month he took charge of his squadron, causing resentment because he had leapfrogged two senior pilots to get the post (both of whom were lost in combat on 26 June 1943).

Gabreski's first 'kill' came on 24 August 1943, when he shot down a Fw 190 fighter near Dreux, France. At 27,000 feet, he had spotted seven enemy aircraft 10,000 feet below and preparing to attack some Allied bombers. Gabreski led his four-strong flight down behind the Fw 190s and kept firing on the German flight leader until he was just 250 yards away, then witnessed the aircraft plunge to the ground. His aggressive, often selfish, flying style soon meant he had further victories. He became an ace on 26 November 1943, when the 56th (which eventually scored an incredible 677 aerial victories over Europe) was tasked with covering the withdrawal of B-17s that had bombed Bremen, Germany. The P-47s arrived to find the bombers under heavy attack and in the ensuing combat with Me 110s Gabreski scored his fourth and fifth 'kills'. However, he had a close brush with death on 11 December 1943 when a 20mm cannon shell, fired from a Me 109, lodged in his engine without exploding, but it destroyed his turbocharger. Gabreski gambled on staying in his stricken aircraft and successfully restarted the engine at a lower altitude where the turbocharger was not required.

Throughout the winter of 1943/4, Gabreski's victory tally grew slowly but surely. By 27 March 1944, he had earned eighteen 'kills' and was third in the 'ace race'. In April, the 56th moved to RAF Boxted, Essex, where he was promoted to lieutenant colonel. Gabreski got to the top of the 'ace race' league table when he achieved his twenty-eighth victory on 5 July. The loner, originally from 315 Squadron, had become the top American ace in the European theatre. Stardom brought him a succession of public relations events, including a planned trip back to the US to sell war bonds. When already packed for the trip home, during which he intended to get married, Gabreski impulsively volunteered for 'one last mission'. Returning from a relatively uneventful sortie, he led his flight down to attack some parked He III bombers. However, he misjudged his second attacking manoeuvre, clipping the Thunderbolt's propeller on the ground. With a damaged aircraft, he was forced to crash-land. Although he evaded capture for five days, and was by then exhausted and hungry, he was eventually picked up. After being interrogated, Gabreski was sent to Stalag Luft I camp. He was freed when Soviet forces liberated the camp in April 1945.

His official wartime record was 166 combat sorties, with twenty-eight aircraft destroyed in air combat and three more on the ground. He married his fiancée in America on 11 June 1945. After ninety days' recuperative leave, he resumed his military career as a test pilot. However, this did not prove rewarding. He left the service in April 1946 and worked for Douglas Aircraft for a year, selling DC-6s in South America. On 7 April 1947, he rejoined the Army Air Forces with the permanent rank of lieutenant colonel. He was promoted to full colonel on 11 March 1950.

Gabreski flew combat again during the Korean War, after awaiting the birth of his fourth child. On 17 June 1951, as deputy wing commander with the 4th Fighter Inceptor Wing, he took part in his first combat sortie of the Korean War. On 8 July, flying a F-86 Sabre, he shot down a MiG 15 just south of the Yalu River. As the commander of the 51st Fighter Inceptor Wing from November 1951, Gabreski brought new tactics to the conflict, and on 1 April 1952 he once again shot down a MiG over the Yalu River. This meant he became the 51st's first jet ace. On 12 April 1952, his score for the conflict rose to six and a half 'kills'. As he approached his 100-mission limit, he stopped logging them, fearing he would be sent home. Although this tactic worked for a month, Gabreski was eventually grounded and ordered home on 4 June 1952 as the highest scoring living ace from the war. He returned to a hero's welcome, including a ticker-tape parade in San Francisco and a meeting with President Truman. After a series of operational and staff jobs, Gabreski retired from the military on 31 October 1967. During a brilliant career, he had flown more than 260 combat missions. He was repeatedly honoured by his country, his decorations including the Distinguished Service Medal, Distinguished Service Cross, Silver Star with Oak Leaf Cluster and the Distinguished Flying Cross (DFC) with twelve Oak Leaf Clusters. His foreign decorations included the DFC from Britain.

For the twenty years after leaving the military, Gabreski worked for Grumman Aircraft, finally retiring in 1987. His autobiography, *Gabby: A Fighter Pilot's Life*, was published in 1991. Gabreski died in Huntingdon, New York, on 31 January 2002, three days after his eighty-third birthday.

5

SECOND WORLD WAR
– BOMBER AIRCREW

The RAF had three major combat commands for most of the war: RAF Fighter Command, which was tasked with the defence of the country and then taking the fight over to Occupied Europe and elsewhere; RAF Bomber Command, which operated the bombers that were used to attack enemy targets; and RAF Coastal Command, which was used to protect Allied shipping and to attack enemy shipping and U-boats (German submarines).

After the outbreak of the Second World War in September 1939, Franklin D. Roosevelt, President of the then neutral US, urged both sides to confine their air raids to military targets. Britain, along with France, agreed to this request provided that 'the same rules of warfare will be scrupulously observed' by all opponents. Afterwards, Britain restricted its bombing to military targets and to ports and railways of military importance. However, this policy was abandoned on 15 May 1940, the day after the German blitz of Rotterdam. The first attack under the new policy took place on the night of 15/16 May 1940, when ninety-six bombers set off to attack numerous targets east of the Rhine. Of these, only twenty-four were believed to have hit their targets but the strategic bombing campaign of Germany had begun.

For the rest of the war, Britain showed a commitment to strategic bombing, in general, and the use of long-range bombers, in particular (the latter were intended to take the war to the enemy in its homeland). Strategic bombing of industrial and, later civilian, targets became highly controversial both during and after the war. It is estimated that the bombing of German cities claimed between 300,000 and 600,000 civilian lives. However, the aircrew of Bomber Command also experienced heavy casualties.

Bomber Command consisted of some 125,000 volunteers from Britain, the Commonwealth and Allied countries who had to endure some of the most terrifying combat conditions of the Second World War. Indeed, Bomber Command was the only British fighting force that took the war directly to Germany, destroying vital infrastructure and supply lines – but at a heavy price. The average age of the aircrew was just twenty-two and the youngest were only eighteen. Three out of every five airmen became casualties and the more detailed statistics tell their own story: 55,573 men were killed, 8,403 were wounded and 9,838 were captured and held as prisoners of war (PoWs). The losses of Bomber Command were greater than those of any other service – accounting for 10 per cent of all British fatalities – yet, perversely, its members have been the only Second World War servicemen not to have been publicly honoured by their country. During the war, no fewer than nineteen VCs were awarded to men of Bomber Command. Three of these VCs form part of my collection of medals for gallantry in the air.

ACTING FLIGHT LIEUTENANT (LATER SQUADRON LEADER) KENNETH CHRISTOPHER DORAN

RAF
DECORATIONS: DISTINGUISHED FLYING CROSS (DFC) AND BAR
GAZETTED: 10 OCTOBER 1939 AND 30 JANUARY 1940

Kenneth Doran earned his place in the history books of the Second World War for three distinct reasons: he was responsible for dropping the first Allied bombs of the conflict and he was the first recipient during the war of both the DFC and Bar.

Doran was born in Mill Hill, north London, on 14 September 1913 and was educated at St Albans School, Hertfordshire. He was given a short-term commission into the RAF on 23 October 1935, aged twenty-two. As an acting flight lieutenant, Doran was in a Mark IV Blenheim bomber when, on 4 September 1939, he led an attack by fifteen aircraft that was conducting the first aerial offensive of the war. Their target was the *Admiral Scheer* and other enemy ships that had been located that morning by a reconnaissance aircraft at Schillig Roads, Wilhelmshaven, Germany. Only ten of the fifteen Blenheims, from 110 and 107 Squadrons, made it to the target area. This operation led to the first DFC of the war, announced on 10 October 1939, and Doran's citation stated: 'In face of heavy gunfire and under extremely bad weather conditions he pressed home a successful low attack with great determination.'

However, it was Cajus Bekker's *Luftwaffe War Diaries* which give a more detailed account of the first attack of the war:

The first three Blenheims formed into line ahead, and with short intervals between them flew straight for the German battleship. The fourth and fifth machines broke way to port and starboard and climbed briefly into cloud. They were to attack the ship from either side and disperse the enemy defensive fire . . . So, at least, was the plan the British had worked out. A lightning attack on their victims from all sides, by five Blenheims, and at mast height, and all within eleven seconds . . . [Acting Flight Lieutenant] Doran writes: 'We saw the matelots' washing hanging out around the stern [of the *Admiral Scheer*] and the crew idly standing about on deck. However, when they realised our intention was hostile they started running around like mad.

Before a shot could be fired the first bomber was on them. Just missing the mast, it screamed diagonally over the after-deck. Two heavy bombs crashed onto the ship. One dug itself in and came to rest; the other bounced along the deck, then rolled overboard into the water. No explosion! Then at last the flak began firing angrily at the retreating Blenheim. Almost at once the second was upon them with the same results as the first. One bomb plummeted into the sea with a great fountain of water just a few yards from the gunwale – an especially dangerous spot for a delayed-action bomb, for it could work like a mine and hole the ship below the waterline.

But now at Schillig Roads all hell had broken loose. Over a wide area, lines of tracer laced the air, as over a hundred flak barrels – from the ships and from the numerous batteries ashore – concentrated their fire on each aircraft as it dived out of the cloud . . . The five Blenheims of 107 Squadron fared worse. Attacking somewhat later than Doran's 110 Squadron, they bore the whole brunt of the now fully alerted defences.

Only one of them returned; the others were all shot down. As one Blenheim fell it crashed sideways into the bows of the cruiser *Emden*, tearing a large hole and causing the war's first casualties in the German Navy.

Four days after the attack, Doran and his crew reported to RAF Uxbridge, Middlesex, and, in recognition of their first blow against the enemy, they were presented to George VI. Within little more than three months of Doran's DFC being announced, and by then with the rank of acting squadron leader, he received a Bar to his DFC, again the first of the war. The citation for the award, announced on 30 January 1940, stated:

> This officer was the leader of a formation of bomber aircraft which was attacked by enemy fighter aircraft over the North Sea during January 1940. By his clever tactics and gallant leadership he successfully maintained a close defensive formation throughout the engagement, two of the enemy fighters being compelled to break off the fight, a third being shot down in flames into the sea, and the remainder eventually abandoning the attack. Although one of our aircraft was lost and a second returned to its base, Squadron Leader Doran showed a great determination in leading the remaining aircraft a distance of about 130 miles further on to his objective.

Few, if any, RAF pilots, had started the war more impressively but Doran's luck ran out on 30 April 1940 when he was shot down on a raid to Stavanger. He was forced to bale out of his aircraft and was taken prisoner of war (PoW): he would remain one for the next five years. After his release, Doran wrote about his frustrations of being a PoW:

Medals on the chest or bullet in the belly: this was the usual philosophy in our squadron when war started in 1939. Nobody considered the third possibility: as prisoner of war . . . So when I was shot down I was amazed and very angry that this sort of thing was happening to me. It was all wrong: this sort of thing only happened to the other chap. I was even more amazed later when I came to, in a German first-aid post, with no clothes on and firmly strapped to a stretcher. Apparently I had been fished out of the North Sea by a German flying boat and I was prisoner of war. This was brought home more forcibly when a Luftwaffe doctor spoke the words that all PoWs remember so clearly: 'For you the War is over'. This meant complete reorientiation. In story books prisoners escape. It was only the other chap who remained a prisoner. The German was being stupid. Of course the War was not over for me. I would escape, return to England and dine out for a month on the strength of my experiences. However, until I got some clothes escaping must be rather impractical, but plans must be made without delay. After all the war might finish before I managed it.

A few days later I was flown from Stavanger to Oslo in a Junkers 52; this was obviously my chance. All I had to do was hold a gun to the pilot's head and force him to fly to England. This is what happens in films. However, 20 armed German soldiers were also on the aircraft, and one sat behind me with a dirty big gun in his hand pointing it at me. Perhaps after all, this was not the right moment. I must choose a better time. On arrival at Oslo I was escorted to the Hotel Bristol by two

Germans in a staff car. Again the big effort was put off. In the Hotel Bristol, which had been taken over by the Luftwaffe as their HQ in Norway, I was taken to a room on the sixth floor and the door was shut behind me. It was eleven o'clock at night. This was the big chance. Looking out of my sixth floor window, the ground seemed a very long way away indeed. The traditional method of knotting blankets together would not get me very far. A subterfuge must be used. First, I banged on the door. It was eventually opened by a German who shouted something unintelligible. I said: 'Good night' and shut the door. I waited an hour then put the master plan into action.

First, tie the blankets together: not very effective, as most of the blankets were used up in the knots and left very little to hang out of the window. Then open the window and move the bed under it. Tie one end of the blankets to the bed and dangle the other end out of the window. The scene was all set. All I had to do was break a window to attract the attention of the guards and then hide in the wardrobe. The guards would then come in and think that I had escaped out of the window, and rush away to look for my body on the ground outside. I would then walk calmly through the door and out of the building. The first part went as planned. I broke the pane of glass with some difficulty and hopped into the wardrobe. I heard the door open and the sound of several people with heavy boots milling around. This went on for some time. Then someone else came into the room and everyone stamped their feet and stood still. After a few minutes' noisy discussion the door of my wardrobe slowly opened and a German officer with a greatcoat over his night-shirt and wearing pince-nez spectacles gazed at me curiously and said: 'Why are you in this cupboard? Do you not like the bed?' I had no adequate reply, but let it be understood that in England people frequently slept in cupboards. Never mind, there will be another opportunity. It is only the other chap who remains a prisoner; or is it?

Doran also later tried to escape through a lavatory window in Copenhagen airport while being transported to a PoW camp, but he was caught by guards. Eventually, he escaped through the wire from one of the Stalag Luft camps but then he was caught by police near the German city of Rostock. It is known that Doran was involved in digging tunnels in at least three PoW camps, including Stalag Luft III, but he never made a successful escape and he was repatriated on 9 May 1945. Doran became an air attaché in Tel Aviv and The Hague after the war, before eventually retiring from the RAF in 1961. He then worked as an adviser with the Ministry of Overseas Development on national youth services. During this time, he toured Kenya, Botswana, Ethiopia and Fiji. However, on 3 March 1974 Doran, aged sixty, and his wife were on board Turkish Airlines flight 981, which crashed into a forest at Ermenonville shortly after taking off from Paris, killing all 346 passengers and crew on board. At the time, it was the worst air disaster in aviation history. The names of Doran, who was returning from holiday to his job as an air attaché in Turkey, and his wife appear on the Ermenonville Memorial in Paris.

FLYING OFFICER (LATER AIR CHIEF MARSHAL SIR) BASIL EDWARD EMBRY
RAF
DECORATIONS: AIR FORCE CROSS (AFC), DISTINGUISHED SERVICE ORDER (DSO) AND THREE BARS, DISTINGUISHED FLYING CROSS (DFC)
GAZETTED: 1 JANUARY 1926, 13 SEPTEMBER 1938, 30 APRIL 1940, 20 AUGUST 1940, 20 JULY 1945 AND 22 JUNE 1945

Basil Embry, whose six gallantry medals were awarded over a period of nearly twenty years, was one of the finest pilots and tacticians ever to serve in the RAF. He led from the front and, even after he was captured by the Germans early in the Second World War, he managed to escape, successfully evading the enemy for two months in Occupied France. He eventually made it back to Britain in order to play an active part in the war for a second time.

Embry was born in Barnwood, Gloucestershire, on 28 February 1902. While at Bromsgrove School, Worcestershire, he developed an interest in aviation. In March 1921, just days after his nineteenth birthday, he enlisted in the RAF on a short-service commission as a pilot officer, training at RAF Netheravon, Wiltshire. After gaining his pilot's 'wings' in April 1922, he applied for an overseas posting and in August of the same year he joined 45 Squadron in Iraq. He served there with distinction for five years, with both 45 and 30 Squadrons. Embry made an impression with his enthusiasm, professionalism and energy and, on New Year's Day 1926, he was awarded the AFC. His citation stated: 'This officer has invariably pushed through to his objective in order to collect urgent cases of sick [and wounded] in spite of every imaginable difficulty and under exceptionally adverse weather conditions, and in doing so has displayed high courage and zeal in addition to the utmost skill in flying, navigation and air pilotage.' In 1927, after being promoted to flight lieutenant, Embry returned to Britain and became an instructor at the Central Flying School, Middlesex. In 1934, he was posted to India, arriving in March of that year and being promoted to squadron leader the following year. During five years in India, he took part in the North West Frontier operations of 1935 and the Waziristan campaigns of 1937 and 1938. It was for his courage during the second of the Waziristan campaigns that he was awarded the first of his four DSOs on 13 September 1938 after the recommendation for his decoration stated:

The success of the Shami Pir Operations was largely due to this officer's initiative as a commander, quite apart from his exceptional flying ability and complete disregard of personal danger. During the Kharra Operations he was largely responsible for the heavy casualties to the enemy; and the resulting comparatively few casualties in our troops. Throughout all recent operations his Squadron was remarkable for a sustained very high standard of performance and general efficiency both in the air and on the ground.

Embry was promoted to wing commander early in 1939 and he returned to Britain for a staff appointment in the Air Ministry. After the outbreak of war in September 1939, Embry took over the command of 107 Squadron, a Blenheim bomber unit based at RAF Wattisham, Suffolk. Embry led a three-aircraft formation on a reconnaissance sortie into Germany on 25 September. However, they were attacked by German fighter aircraft and Embry's aircraft suffered serious damage to the wings, fuselage and the tyre of one of the main wheels. Embry carried out a single-wheel landing on his return to Wattisham. Throughout the remainder of 1939 and into early 1940, Embry carried out numerous reconnaissance flights as well as attacking targets, including U-boats (German submarines).

RAF photo reconnaissance revealed on 6 April 1940 that a substantial German naval force, including the battleships *Gneisenau* and *Scharnhorst*, was at anchor off Wilhelmshaven. This led to Embry and his crews becoming heavily involved in attacking the German fleet. On 30 April 1940, Embry was awarded a Bar to his DSO and his citation stated:

In April, 1940, Wing Commander Embry led a squadron of twelve aircraft in an attack on Stavanger aerodrome and seaplane base. He successfully completed his task and returned to his base, with the whole squadron, despite the failure of one of his engines before he reached his objective. Again, two days later, he led his squadron in another attack on Stavanger, which was also a success, and very valuable photographs were taken. During this flight he suffered from frost-bite. The satisfactory results achieved were due, primarily, to the courage, determination and fine leadership of this officer.

Embry and his crews had, in fact, taken part in ten raids in eight days on Stavanger from their base in Lossiemouth, Scotland.

On 10 May, Germany invaded the Low Countries and soon Embry and his crews were once again in the thick of the battle.

On 12 May, he led 107 Squadron, in company with 110 Squadron, to attack two bridges crossing the Albert Canal at Maastricht. After being savaged by ground flak and jumped by numerous Messerschmitts, the two squadrons lost seven Blenheims while another two aircraft from 107 Squadron were forced to crash-land at Wattisham. Indeed, close examination of the squadrons' surviving Blenheims revealed that every one had suffered shell or bullet strikes. Over the coming days, Embry and his crews – facing overwhelming odds – repeatedly helped to assist the British Army in its retreat to Dunkirk. It was for his leadership and courage during this time that Embry received a second Bar to his DSO, which was announced on 20 August 1940. His citation stated: 'During the operations over the Low Countries and France, Wing Commander Embry continued to display an extremely high standard of leadership and resolution in carrying out all tasks allotted to his squadron, raising its morale to a high level and setting an example to the other squadrons in his group. He has shown a high sense of duty and determination.'

However, by this point, Embry had been on quite an 'adventure'. On 26 May 1940, after returning from his last sortie of the day, he was ordered to take command of RAF West Raynham, Norfolk, with promotion to group captain. The next day he led his squadron for the final time with his successor in support but all did not go according to plan. As Embry attacked German troops advancing on Dunkirk, he made his bombing run into heavy flak and received a direct hit to his aircraft. His air gunner was killed and the Blenheim was soon out of control, leaving him and his navigator with no choice but to bale out. Embry landed behind enemy lines near St Omer and was marched away to a prisoner-of-war (PoW) camp along with other captives. When he saw a sign reading 'Embry, 3 km', he took it as a good omen and seized the opportunity to break away, roll down a bank and escape. For the next two months, he evaded capture and eventually made it back to Britain via Spain and Gibraltar. A full account of these dramatic nine weeks and five days is told by Anthony Richardson in his book *Wingless Victory*.

Embry spent the next two months on sick leave before being posted as senior administrative officer to No. 6 Group. This appointment was short-lived and he soon reverted back to being a wing commander, serving with Fighter Command. Embry initially led a wing comprised of 151 and 264 Squadrons. However, in December 1940, he was given command of a sector at RAF Wittering, Cambridgeshire, a post he filled for ten months. His next appointment was to the Desert Air Force in North Africa but, on his return to Britain in March 1942, he went back to commanding the Wittering sector. Embry was appointed as senior air staff officer at No. 10 Group, Fighter Command, in early 1943 but in May of the same year he switched to the command of No. 2 Group, Bomber Command. By then, he had reached the rank of acting air vice-marshal and was in command of some ten squadrons operating a variety of aircraft. As part of his belief in leading from the front, he issued orders that all station commanders should fly two or three operations every month. From late 1943 to May 1944, his group – which had been re-equipped with Mosquitos – was involved in attacking V-1 rocket sites. The group also developed a reputation for precision bombing and, on 18 February 1944, in Operation Jericho, it bombed Amiens prison, liberating hundreds of French patriots, many of whom were awaiting execution by the Gestapo.

Under the pseudonym 'Wing Commander Smith', Embry took part in many other precision attacks, including the successful raid on the Gestapo headquarters in Odense, Denmark, on 17 April 1945: his final operational sortie of the war. Embry was awarded the DFC on 22 June 1945 and his citation stated:

> On three occasions within recent months, Air Vice Marshal Embry took part in air attacks on Gestapo Headquarters. The targets were at Aarhus, Copenhagen and Odense respectively. In the first operation complete surprise was achieved and the attack proved highly successful. At Copenhagen the operation was also well executed and success obtained. At Odense, the target was cleverly camouflaged, making the task on hand even more difficult. In spite of this, several runs were made over the target, which was finally attacked with great precision. In these hazardous missions, Air Vice-Marshal Embry pressed home his attacks with a skill and gallantry in keeping with his outstanding reputation.

Embry was also made a Companion of the Order of the Bath (CB) on 1 January 1945 and knighted on 3 July 1945, as well as being Mentioned in Despatches four times during his military career.

After the war, Embry remained in the RAF and one of his first tasks was to coordinate a fund for those people in the occupied countries who had helped British aircrew evade capture and escape back to their homeland. The group became known as the RAF Escaping Society and Embry soon had more than £20,000 in its coffers, eventually becoming its chairman for the next decade. In 1945, he was appointed as the

RAF's director general of training and in July 1947 he was promoted to substantive air vice-marshal. From April 1949 to April 1953, he served as Officer Commanding-in-Chief, Fighter Command, attaining the rank of air marshal from January 1951. Such was his seniority that he represented the RAF at both the funeral of George VI in 1952 and the coronation of Queen Elizabeth II the following year. Embry was appointed as Commander-in-Chief, Allied Air Forces Central Europe, in July 1953 and promoted to air chief marshal in December that year. He was appointed a Knight Grand Cross of the Order of the Bath (GCB) on 2 January 1956 and on 26 February of the same year brought the curtain down on his distinguished military career.

Within months, however, Embry had emigrated to New Zealand and by the end of 1956 had written and published his memoirs, *Mission Accomplished*. He was soon uprooting himself once again and this time moved to Australia where he farmed successfully in the bush. Embry died on 8 December 1977, aged seventy-five.

SERGEANT (LATER PILOT OFFICER) SIDNEY BEN FULLER
RAF
DECORATION: DISTINGUISHED FLYING MEDAL (DFM)
GAZETTED: 6 AUGUST 1940

Sidney Fuller was born in Chiswick, west London, in 1915. He enlisted in the RAF as a boy apprentice in 1931 and, having qualified for his pilot's 'wings', was later posted to 144 Squadron flying Hampden bombers from RAF Helmswell, Lincolnshire.

After the outbreak of the Second World War, Fuller flew in operations which took him over Hamburg, Aachen, Reims, the Dortmund–Ems Canal and Schillig Roads.

However, it was for a daring low-level attack with special bombs and mines that Fuller was awarded the DFM. In what was described as an 'almost zero feet attack' – in reality from somewhere between 50 and 100 feet – on 20 July 1940, Fuller targeted the German battleship *Admiral Scheer* and other warships at Wilhelmshaven.

The recommendation for his gallantry award stated: 'He carried out this attack from a few feet above the docks and placed his mine correctly in the face of a terrific barrage of gunfire and searchlight glare from the whole of the defences. His aircraft was hit but by skill and determination, he brought it safely home across the North Sea. On his way back, he went out of his way to attack the aerodrome at Borkum with machine-gun fire. This N.C.O. has shown conspicuous courage and devotion to duty on many previous occasions when he pressed home his attack with the same determination.' German records revealed that two bombers crashed in the town and three nearby, all shot down by local flak. Fuller was awarded the DFM on 6 August 1940.

Subsequently commissioned, Fuller mainly flew Mosquito patrols over the Bay of Biscay from April 1942 to February 1943, However, at 11.12 p.m. on 2 February 1943 Fuller, aged twenty-eight, was killed in a collision with another British aircraft at 10,000 feet over the Southampton area. Flying Officer Mountain, who was in the same aircraft as Fuller, and the two airmen in the other aircraft all baled out safely. Both aircraft crashed and burst into flames and Fuller's body was found in the wreckage of his aeroplane near RAF Thorney

Island, then Hampshire but now in West Sussex. Fuller is buried in a churchyard in Minster-in-Sheppey, Kent.

PILOT OFFICER (LATER SQUADRON LEADER) JAMES YOUNG MALLEY
Royal Air Force Volunteer Reserve (RAFVR)
DECORATIONS: DISTINGUISHED FLYING CROSS (DFC) AND BAR, DISTINGUISHED SERVICE ORDER (DSO)
GAZETTED: 21 NOVEMBER 1941, 23 JULY 1943 AND 26 OCTOBER 1945

Farmer's son Jim 'Zulu' Malley was born in 1918 and educated at Dungannon Royal School, Northern Ireland. After working in the civil service, he enlisted in the RAFVR as a navigator and bomb aimer and was posted as a pilot officer to 149 Squadron (Wellingtons) in 1941. On his first tour of operations, Malley flew in the Wellington 'F-for-Freddie' (later of the film *Target for Tonight* fame). The 35th and last mission of his first tour was to Berlin on 2 November 1941, from which many aircraft failed to return.

Malley was awarded the DFC on 21 November 1941 after the recommendation for his decoration stated:

P/O Malley has been employed as an Observer in this Squadron for the last six months. His ability as a navigator cannot be disputed, as he has successfully attacked the primary target on the majority of his raids, and some of the best night photographs taken by this Squadron during the past six months are due to his outstanding ability and the perfection of his training of the crew. On several occasions this Officer and his Captain have spent up to two hours trying to locate the primary target and then being unable to locate the primary target have flown at a very low altitude to find a railway and then followed it until an important junction has been reached when systematic bombing has been carried out. His determination to attack the primary target or, under conditions of adverse weather, a target of major importance, is an example to the other observers in the Squadron. The standard he has set is the perfection peak to be aimed at, and by his example he has assisted considerably our war effort.

A Bar to his DFC was awarded on 23 July 1943 for his service in the Middle East as a flight lieutenant in the Liberator aircraft of 178 Squadron. The recommendation for his award stated:

F/Lt. Malley has now completed 487 hours operational flying in the European and Middle East theatre of war. His work in this Squadron both on the ground as Navigation Officer and in the air has been most praiseworthy. His cool determination in attacking the target in adverse weather conditions and in the face of heavy opposition has made his work outstanding and an excellent example for his fellow squadron members. On the 6th Aug. 42 he was Navigator (B) in the leading aircraft of a formation which attacked shipping in Tobruk harbour [Libya] in daylight. Despite intense anti-aircraft fire he achieved excellent results.

In the final year of the war, the number of his sorties and the danger of Malley's missions became even more intense. As a master bomber and squadron leader in 139 Squadron, in Mosquito aircraft, he raised his tally of operational sorties to an astonishing total of 127, no fewer than twenty-seven of them having been to Berlin – surely a record in the annals of Bomber Command history?

He was awarded the DSO on 26 October 1945 after the recommendation for his decoration stated:

> Throughout this lengthy period [of his tour] he has had many arduous experiences and many times has his aircraft been hit by flak. Invariably his courage, coolness and accurate navigation under the most difficult circumstances have largely contributed to the successful completion of his task, and safe return to base. In spite of his long operational career, and numerous harrowing experiences he has never tired, and his keenness to operate and his courage and tenacity at all times have been a shining example and a source of confidence and pride to the whole Squadron.

Writing after the war, Malley recalled: 'I flew 127 missions in all. We didn't know our last [mission] was going to be our last because at that time we were supposed to lead a daylight raid to Berlin with the whole of Bomber Command and the Americans but luckily peace came a few days before. Then I wasn't allowed to go out to Japan.' He said of his crews: 'We were always friends. That was the best part. I don't remember targets and hits anymore, but I remember that the crew were always friends.'

After the war, Malley rejoined the civil service and, during the 1960s, held a senior post in the private office of Terence O'Neill, the Prime Minister of Northern Ireland (1963–70). A man who enjoyed fishing, shooting and gardening, Malley died on 5 June 2000, aged eighty-two.

SERGEANT (LATER SQUADRON LEADER) GEOFFREY FRANK KEEN
RAF
DECORATIONS: DISTINGUISHED FLYING MEDAL (DFM) AND CONSPICUOUS GALLANTRY MEDAL (CGM)
GAZETTED: 30 JANUARY 1942 AND 23 APRIL 1943

Geoffrey 'Chuffo' Keen was born in Chesham, Buckinghamshire, in March 1916. He was the son of a corporal serving in the Royal Engineers and he was only fifteen months old when his father, who had never seen his infant son, was killed in action in June 1917. A pupil at Dr Challoner's Grammar School in Amersham in Buckinghamshire, Keen played amateur football for Maidenhead United before the Second World War. Aged twenty-four, and having already served an apprenticeship as a printer, he enlisted in the RAF in August 1940. He trained as a wireless operator/air gunner on Whitley bombers prior to joining 51 Squadron, based at RAF Dishforth, Yorkshire, in April 1941.

The next month, he commenced his operational tour starting with a mission to the German city of Kiel on 3 May; he then returned to the same target a few nights later. On 18 May, his aircraft crashed while landing at Dishforth, but all the crew survived. There were more hair-raising incidents to come: on the night of 6 August 1941, as he returned from Frankfurt, he and his crew were forced to bale out over the Norfolk town of East Dereham as a result of severe icing. During his tour, he took part in three sorties to Cologne and two each to Berlin, Bremen, Dortmund, Frankfurt and Hamburg. On 21 November 1941, Keen was recommended for the DFM by Wing Commander 'Pick' Pickard, having completed twenty-nine sorties and some 200 hours of operational flying time. His citation, dated 30 January 1942, stated: 'During the many raids in which he took part, some of them to extreme range, he always showed the highest qualities of courage, keenness and determination. His knowledge and capabilities as a Wireless Operator are of a high order and on one occasion after a raid on Stuttgart, his skill and steadiness in obtaining wireless navigational aids was solely responsible for bringing his aircraft back to Base after it had become hopelessly lost.'

Despite being rested at an Operational Training Unit (OTU), Keen was called upon to take part in the '1,000-bomber raids' against Cologne and Essen from May to July 1942, both of them as a wireless operator in Whitleys. His rear gunner later portrayed a vivid picture of the raid on Cologne on the night of 1/2 June 1942 when he wrote:

The whole city was a mass of flames and over the intercom everyone was using superlatives – ordinary words failed to express our amazement. The northern part of Cologne's defences were throwing everything but Panzer Divisions into the sky and the searchlights enhanced the already panoramic scene. For about two minutes just before we bombed we were caught in searchlights and subjected to some intense A.A. [anti-aircraft] fire. In the middle of this I distinctly remember Geoff [Keen] calling me up from the front, 'How are you doing back there Kidda?' – hell was I glad to hear someone talk who was on my side; I thought all the Jerries in Jerryland were firing at me alone . . . The skipper did a steep turn to give us all a good view of the inferno before we headed home.

241

Despite nominally being rested, Keen took part in another large-scale attack against Düsseldorf on the last night of July 1942.

In January 1943, Keen returned to full-time operations with 427 (Royal Canadian Air Force) Squadron, operating Wellington aircraft from RAF Middleton St George, Co. Durham. A sortie to Lorient in German-occupied France took place in late January and twice more in February. On 5 March he was involved in a raid on Essen. On the night of 12/13 March 1943, Keen flew over the city in his CO's aircraft. He was sitting just four feet away from Pilot Officer R. J. Heather, when his Canadian navigator was killed outright by a splinter from a shell exploding close to the aircraft. As the navigator collapsed and died on top of the bomb aimer, the scene in the aircraft was one of chaos: glycol poured out from a damaged tank, choking fumes filled the front of the aircraft and the oxygen supply began to fall. Yet, in spite of the weight of the dead navigator, the sickly smell of the oil fumes and the lack of oxygen, the bomb aimer calmly continued to give directions to his captain and released his bombs over the target.

'The oxygen supply seemed to give out completely and we were all on the point of passing out,' said the captain later. 'I found that the aileron control [controlling roll] had been damaged and, after we had bombed, we staggered about the sky, going down to 10,000 feet to get some air.' It was not until they were able to breathe more freely that the rest of the crew became aware that Keen, too, had been hit. 'His right foot had been shot clean off,' said the captain in a press release later issued by the Air Ministry. 'But without complaint he went to his damaged radio set and tried to get it working. Until we reached England, he remained at his set, trying to repair it, and even managed to help me with the navigation.' In fact, Keen had lost only part of his foot.

Wireless communications between the captain and the rear gunner had been cut, but the latter somehow still managed to give directions to the former, who was able to take evasive action and shake off an enemy Junkers night fighter. Eventually, the damaged Wellington managed to reach an airfield in the south of England and make a safe landing.

Afterwards, Keen was put forward for the VC. The recommendation, written by Wing Commander D. H. Burnside, his squadron commanding officer, was endorsed by the group captain commanding the station. It stated: 'I consider this N.C.O.'s superb display of courage and devotion to duty whilst seriously wounded fully merits an award of the Victoria Cross.' Air Vice-Marshal G. E. Brookes, of 6 Group, agreed with the assessment, saying: 'This case is considered to be an outstanding example of coolness and tenacity of purpose on the part of this N.C.O. when seriously wounded, and demanding courage of the highest order. An award of the Victoria Cross is recommended.' However, the RAF Awards Committee eventually decided the CGM would be a more fitting award and the decoration was announced on 23 April 1943 when his citation stated: 'His courage and fortitude in such circumstances were of the highest order.' Wing Commander Burnside himself received a Bar to his DFC, and the bomb aimer, Pilot Officer R. J. Hayhurst, and air gunner, Pilot Officer D. B. Ross, were awarded DFCs.

Keen, who was soon also commissioned as a pilot officer, was hospitalised for several months, but rejoined 427 Squadron that summer. He did not, however, return to operations until

1944, when he flew sorties to Le Mans on 7 March, Le Cliton on 18 May, and the Falaise Gap on 14 August. He was released from the RAF as a squadron leader at the end of 1946.

Keen resettled in Buckinghamshire after the war and, despite the disability of losing part of one foot, he played football and cricket to a good standard. He became a teacher and ended up as headmaster of St Leonard's village primary school, Buckinghamshire. It is not known what happened to him after his retirement.

ACTING FLYING OFFICER (LATER ACTING WING COMMANDER) DAVID SCOTT SHEARMAN WILKERSON
Royal Air Force Volunteer Reserve (RAFVR)
DECORATIONS: DISTINGUISHED FLYING CROSS (DFC) AND DISTINGUISHED SERVICE ORDER (DSO)
GAZETTED: 13 MARCH 1942 AND 23 MAY 1944

David 'Wilkie' Wilkerson was born in Walthamstow, north-east London, on 20 May 1917, but his family soon moved to nearby South Woodford. From 1925 to 1932, he attended Forest School, Snaresbrook, north-east London. After leaving school, he worked for W. H. Hill, a City book publishing company. As a young man, Wilkerson, the younger of two brothers, was a talented pianist and a Scout leader: he ran the 17th Epping Forest Cub Pack.

On 20 January 1940, Wilkerson enlisted in the RAFVR and, on 20 September of the same year, he embarked on his first solo flight – a cross-country adventure in a Tiger Moth lasting seventy minutes. After training in Britain and Canada,

Wilkerson was promoted to pilot officer on 11 April 1941 and, on 17 May, he was posted to 58 Squadron at RAF Linton-on-Ouse, Yorkshire. He initially flew localised familiarisation air tests but on 28 May he undertook his first operation as second pilot in a raid on Kiel. That spring and summer Wilkerson had various postings on day and night flying but on 15 September he was posted to 35 Squadron, his flight commander being Flight Lieutenant Leonard Cheshire, who went on to be awarded the Victoria Cross and was one of the most decorated British pilots of the war. On 22 October 1941, after attacking the German city of Mannheim, Wilkerson was injured when his aircraft crash-landed back at his base, the starboard undercarriage having collapsed. However, he quickly recovered and, just four nights later, he and his crew bombed Hamburg. After test flying the new Halifax MkII bomber, Wilkerson was involved in the attempt on 18 December to destroy two enemy battleships at the port of Brest. The official report of the incident richly praised his actions in helping a fellow pilot, Wing Commander Robinson, who, after being hit, was forced to ditch into the sea sixty miles off the English coast. Two of his flight remained in the vicinity to protect him, despite the risk of further enemy attack. The report concluded: 'This reflects much credit to the pilotage of the two captains concerned, Flying Officer Wilkerson and Sergeant Williams who agreed that Wilkerson should remain circling the ditched aircraft and crew in the dinghy. This he did for half an hour and remained in the vicinity communicating by wireless to air/sea rescue stations and did not depart until he was satisfied that everything had been done to ensure the safe recovery of the crew.'

Flight Lieutenant R. C. Rivaz was the rear gunner in the

stricken aircraft and, after the war, he wrote a book, *Tail Gunner*. Of Wilkerson, he remembered:

> Wilkie was a tall, dark-haired, loose-limbed fellow . . . and the first impression a stranger might have of him could be that he was rather an irresponsible, carefree and vague individual. But on closer acquaintance it would be seen that he had one of the kindest, gentlest and most sympathetic and thoughtful natures any man could possess . . . He has the knack of inspiring confidence in every member of his crew . . . When flying he is always perfectly calm and I cannot imagine anything disturbing him.

For nearly two years from January 1942, Wilkinson was involved heavily in training pilots as well as test flying, but he also took part in many operations. On 13 March 1942, he was awarded the DFC and his citation stated: 'As a pilot, and captain of aircraft, this officer has shown outstanding ability and keenness and he has succeeded in reaching and bombing his objectives with unfailing regularity and success. Flying Officer Wilkerson has attacked a wide range of enemy targets, including Berlin, Nuremberg, Kiel and Essen, besides other industrial centres and dockyard towns. He took part in 2 daylight raids on the enemy warships at Brest, and in spite of fierce opposition, carried out his attacks with the utmost skill and determination. Flying Officer Wilkerson has proved himself to be a courageous captain.'

Part of Wilkerson's duties involved test flights with various bomb loads – often one or two 4,000-lb bombs and four mines. On one exercise, Wilkinson's Halifax II aircraft suffered a partial hydraulic failure with loss of brakes on the ground.

On board was a concerned Royal Navy officer who asked Wilkerson: 'Can you land one of these aircraft with a 4000-lb bomb and no brakes?' Wilkerson replied: 'We are about to find out.' He landed the aircraft without incident. By then a flight lieutenant, Wilkerson took part in the first '1,000-bomber raid' – to Cologne – on 30 May 1942, returning safely despite a failed port outer engine. On 5 June, and by now a squadron leader, he left 35 Squadron to take command of 158 Conversion Flight. His role was to oversee the switch from Wellington to Halifax II bombers. On 15 November 1943, now a wing commander, he was posted to become second in command of 51 Squadron at RAF Snaith, Yorkshire. Wilkerson, who was hugely popular with his men, also set about creating a new 578 Squadron, which officially came into existence on 14 January 1944.

Wilkerson's DSO was announced on 23 May 1944 and his citation stated: 'This Officer has completed many sorties on his second "tour" of operations. He has displayed high powers of leadership, great skill and determination, qualities which have earned him much success. He is a devoted and zealous Squadron Commander, whose great drive and tactical ability have contributed in a large measure to the high standard of operational efficiency of the Squadron.' Yet there were more acts of bravery to come and the next night he led twenty-three aircraft to attack Aachen, a railway town which was a major communications link between Germany and France. On the night of 5/6 June, ahead of the D-Day landings, Wilkerson led an attack on Montfleury. One of his rear gunners, C. W. Adams, later recalled of Wilkerson that night: 'He created a feeling of excitement among us. Although not being told specifically that this was support for the invasion of Europe, we were as good as told, and knew from experience, what was to occur on this historic day. Like the rest of the Squadron's aircrews he did not want to miss this trip.'

However, on 16 September 1944, tragedy struck. After an overnight visit to RAF Rednal, Shropshire, Wilkerson was in an American-built light bomber, a Martin Baltimore, when it inexplicably crashed shortly after take-off, killing two of the passengers, Wilkerson himself and a major from the South African Air Force. At just twenty-seven, the man who had more than 1,200 hours of flying, and who had survived forty-seven operational sorties against the enemy, was dead. In November 1944, the USA awarded Wilkerson a posthumous Silver Star: only thirty-four Silver Stars were awarded to the RAF during of the Second World War. Countless other posthumous tributes to Wilkerson included one from Flight Lieutenant G. Sanders DFC, of 578 Squadron, who said: 'Winco Wilkie, a prince among men. Brilliant pilot, wonderful squadron commander. Led by example and a great sense of humour. He was indeed a very special man. I have a lot to thank him for and am very much richer for having known him.' At the request of his family and former comrades, Wilkerson's body was returned to Selby, Yorkshire, to be buried near his beloved 578 Squadron airfield. His memory is perpetuated by memorials in Burn Chapel and Selby Abbey, the former also in Yorkshire, and at Tedsmore, Shropshire.

Most of my information on Wilkerson comes from a splendid appraisal of his life by Hugh Cawdron in his book *Based at Burn MkII*. Wilkerson was Cawdron's Cub Master and became the seven-year-old's 'hero and friend for the next eight years and beyond' after the two met in 1936. The book contains many fascinating extracts from letters that Wilkerson wrote to Cawdron during the war. Knowing of the friendship between the two men, after her son's funeral Wilkerson's mother handed the then fifteen-year-old Cawdron a parcel containing her son's Scout uniform. Cawdron later wore the uniform 'until it disintegrated' but he still retains a precious part of it, the small leather-handled sheaf knife which 'Akela' always wore on his belt.

2ND LIEUTENTANT (LATER AIR COMMODORE) ARTHUR MOSTYN WRAY
Army/Royal Flying Corps/RAF
DECORATIONS: MILITARY CROSS (MC), AIR FORCE CROSS (AFC), DISTINGUISHED FLYING CROSS (DFC) AND BAR, DISTINGUISHED SERVICE ORDER (DSO)
GAZETTED: 16 AUGUST 1917, 1 JANUARY 1919, 30 MAY 1924, 10 APRIL 1942 AND 24 AUGUST 1943

Arthur 'Father' Wray was decorated five times for gallantry, the span of his active service and the combination of his decorations contributing to a unique career in the annals of RAF history. Left with a permanent limp as a result of wounds received in the Great War, Wray was cast from a similar mould to Douglas Bader: nothing would stop him from flying. Hence his AFC in 1919 and first DFC for gallantry on the North West Frontier in the 1920s. Like Bader, too, he loathed red tape, was unorthodox and prone to invoking his superiors' displeasure, though it is just such spirited warriors who win battles and wars, particularly when they take great care of their less experienced charges. Thus Wray, in action in the Second World War, time and time again ignored orders to remain grounded so as to accompany his young bomber crews on their first operational sorties, knowing full well that his wounds received in the Great War would have prevented him from baling out of a stricken aircraft.

Wray was born in Brighton, Sussex, in August 1896. The son of a pioneer missionary to central Africa, he was educated at Monkton Combe School in Bath. Aged eighteen, he left mid-term to join the Army after the outbreak of the First World War. In February 1915, he was appointed a temporary 2nd lieutenant in the 9th (Service) Battalion, East Kent Regiment. In early 1917, he was seconded to the recently formed Royal Flying Corps as a flying officer.

Having gained his pilot's 'wings', in April 1917 Wray was posted to France with 29 Squadron, which was operating in Nieuport Scouts. The average life expectancy for a flyer at this time was just three weeks. Yet Wray, as was his wont, quickly made his mark, as the recommendation for his MC makes clear:

Lieutenant Wray joined No. 29 Squadron on 24 April 1917, and during the short time he has been here his conduct on at least four occasions has been conspicuously gallant. While on offensive patrol on 13 May 1917, he attacked and fired at four Albatros Scouts single-handed. He drove down three and crashed a fourth (confirmed). On 19 May 1917, he attacked a hostile balloon at O18C [grid reference]. He fired at it at very close range, and drove it down. The Observers were seen to jump out with parachutes. Again, on 20 May 1917, while on offensive patrol over Douai, he attacked two Albatros Scouts single-handed. He crashed the first – E.A's [enemy aircraft's] wings being observed to fall off as it went down – and drove down the second. On 28 May 1917, while on offensive patrol, he attacked a hostile two-seater biplane at close range south of Arras. Almost immediately after attacking, he was severely wounded in the knee, and his thigh was fractured. In this state this gallant officer – though his machine fell for several thousand feet completely out of control – eventually managed to bring it to Wagnonlieu, where he was observed to make a perfect landing without damaging his machine. He is 20 years of age, and was a very efficient and capable officer . . .

Wray's MC was announced on 16 August 1917, while he was recovering from the serious injuries mentioned in this recommendation. Indeed, it was after he landed from this operation that his left kneecap was, somewhat gruesomely, found in his flying boot. Surgeons gave Wray a choice: with surgery, the knee joint could be repaired so that he would be able to walk relatively normally, but with a leg too stiff to enable him to pilot an aircraft; or, without surgery, his knee would retain a degree of flexibility that should make flying possible but leave him lame for life. To no one's surprise, Wray elected to go for the latter: from then on he had a noticeable limp, which became worse as he grew older. After being invalided home, Wray's wound developed 'serious septic complications' and he saw no more action for the rest of the war. However, he was back in the air in April 1918 at 55 Training School after which he wrote: 'First flip for ten months. O.K.' It was for his work later the same year, as a pilot instructor at the School of Aerial Fighting in Ayr, Scotland, that he was awarded his AFC on New Year's Day 1919.

By then, Wray was committed to a career in the newly formed RAF. In January 1920, he was posted to India where he served a short stint with 114 Squadron in Ambala, flying Bristol fighters. Next, and by then with 28 Squadron, he became involved in the Waziristan operations. Between 1920 and 1924, he took part in operational reconnaissance, photographic trips and bombing raids. It was for his courage in Waziristan, combating the revolt against British rule, that Wray was awarded the DFC for 'distinguished services' on 30 May 1924.

By this time, he was back in Britain having joined 15 (B) Squadron in January 1924 operating from the Aircraft Experimental Establishment at RAF Martlesham Heath, Suffolk. This posting was followed by a long-standing appointment as a pilot at the Armament and Gunnery School at RAF Eastchurch, Kent. By his early thirties, Wray was commanding 407 Fleet Fighter Flight, based in Lee-on-Solent, Hampshire. Most pilots were at least a decade his junior and he was given the nickname 'Father', which stayed with him for the rest of his RAF career. Wray was promoted to squadron leader in October 1933 and, during the same year, he flew to St Paul's Walden, Hertfordshire, for the funeral of one of his pilots, Rodney Clarkson, who had been killed in a road accident. After the service, Wray met Clarkson's sister, Margaret, for the first time. They were married at the same country church the following year. In 1935, Wray received his first squadron command: 43 Squadron, the famous 'Fighting Cocks'. Next, Wray moved to Fighter Command headquarters and, after the outbreak of the Second World War, to bombing schools in Wales and Cumbria.

In November 1941, Wray was appointed as station commander of RAF Hemswell in Lincolnshire where, among other units, he was in charge of two Polish squadrons. By then aged forty-five, and walking with a stick, he was protective of his young airmen – and had even less time for red tape. Survival rates for pilots were low and, if morale dipped, Wray would fly with a young crew to their target and back without first getting permission – on at least two occasions he was seriously reprimanded for his actions. Wray also learnt some Polish so as to be able to encourage them, on one occasion bringing the house down when he read them a fighting speech from Winston Churchill that he had written down in phonetic Polish.

On 10 April 1942, Wray was awarded a Bar to his DFC when he was praised in the recommendation as 'a very gallant officer, with a fine spirit of leadership'. On 24 July 1942, he was awarded the Virtuti Militari (5th class), Poland's prestigious military honour. 'He was the finest kind of Englishman,' said one Polish pilot.

In May 1943, Wray became an air commodore and commander of 12 Base, which comprised the bomber stations of Binbrook, Waltham and Kelstern, all in Lincolnshire. From his headquarters at Binbrook, he was responsible for eighty Lancaster bombers. Binbrook was also the home of 460 Squadron, Royal Australian Air Force. At a time when it was almost unheard of for a base commander – let alone one of his age – to fly on operations, Wray flew one of the 740 bombers which attacked Hamburg in one of the most devastating raids of the war. He won the admiration of the Australians – and the DSO. His decoration was announced on 24 August 1943 after the recommendation for his award stated: 'By his keenness to operate against the enemy, his skill as a Captain of Aircraft, his personal courage and complete disregard of danger, he has set a very fine example to all the Squadrons under his command.'

By 1944, the RAF was losing about 265 heavy bombers and

nearly 2,000 men a month. Inexperienced crews were the most vulnerable and Wray continued to be hugely protective of them, often standing on the runway to see them off. At one point, Wray and a friend who commanded another squadron flew with their men on a daylight raid, even though Wray had been refused permission to fly just hours earlier. His companion was shot down and, although Wray survived, he was read the riot act: 'You know too much to risk being captured. No more operational flying.'

Wray retired at fifty in 1946. He settled with his wife and their three children in Pitney, Somerset, where he spent the next decade running a small farm. However, it was always a financial struggle and he was forced to give it up. Wray next worked with ex-servicemen through local branches of the Royal Air Forces Association and the Royal British Legion. His love of flying remained with him but it was too expensive a hobby to pursue. However, in 1961, he discovered the Devon and Somerset Gliding Club at Dunkeswell, near Exeter. Despite by now being sixty-five, he took to the skies for the first time in fifteen years and became enchanted with silent flight. He embraced his new hobby and was a regular at the club in his battered tweed hat and corduroy trousers. In 1964, he became one of the oldest pilots to earn the international 'Silver C' badge. He then determined to get his 'Gold C' qualification, which required a 300-kilometre (186-mile) cross-country flight. Time and time again he failed in his attempt to make the distance until he finally succeeded in 1972, aged seventy-five. He died in April 1985.

The year after Wray's death a tribute to him appeared in *Reader's Digest* in which Squadron Leader Douglas Sutton, DFC, recalled a flight he had made with Wray to bomb

Stuttgart, one of Germany's most heavily defended cities, on 15 March 1944, as a young sergeant pilot with only seven hours' flying experience. With Wray at the controls, the navigator misread the flight plan and managed to get them lost but he insisted on completing the mission through a barrage of intense flak, teaching his young crew various techniques to avoid being hit. 'By the time we landed back at Waltham that night, I had decided that Air Commodore Wray was the most remarkable man I had ever known,' said Sutton. 'I was not alone. For so many of us who flew with Bomber Command in the Second World War, "Father" Wray was unforgettable. Repeatedly risking his own life to shepherd novice crews half his age through their baptism of fire, he increased immeasurably our chances of returning from raids. Beyond doubt, I owed him my own survival.'

There is an adage within the RAF: 'There are old pilots, and bold pilots, but no old, bold pilots.' 'Father' Wray was the exception to the rule.

FLYING OFFICER (LATER SQUADRON LEADER) RALPH VAN DEN BOK
Royal Air Force Volunteer Reserve (RAFVR)
DECORATIONS: DISTINGUISHED FLYING CROSS (DFC) AND TWO BARS
GAZETTED: 4 AUGUST 1942, 24 NOVEMBER 1942 AND 26 OCTOBER 1945

Ralph Van den Bok was born in London in 1907. The son of a Dutch father and Australian mother, he attended Dulwich College in south-east London. When the Second World War began, he was working at the London Stock Exchange. In 1940, he applied to join the RAFVR, and was granted a commission as a pilot officer on probation in July of that year. After training as a wireless operator/air gunner, Van den Bok joined 408 (Goose) Squadron of the Royal Canadian Air Force (RCAF) with whom he flew thirty operations. The squadron was a Hampden unit that operated out of RAF Balderton, Nottinghamshire.

In August 1941, Van den Bok was promoted to flying officer and he continued to serve with 408 Squadron. It was partly for his bravery during a failed attempt to sink *Scharnhorst*, the German battleship, that he was awarded the DFC on 4 August 1942. The recommendation for his award stated:

Flying Officer Van den Bok has taken part in 29 sorties, a large number of them being carried out against heavily defended targets, and pressed home with determination and resolve. He has participated in repeated attacks on Mannheim, Duisberg, Huls, Bremen, Kiel and Hamburg, returning from seven different sorties in aircraft severely damaged by enemy A.A. [anti-aircraft] fire. As a Wireless Operator he has been responsible on many occasions for his aircraft's safe return in bad weather.

He was the Wireless Operator/Air Gunner on a Hampden which made a low-level attack on the *Scharnhorst* during the battleship's flight from Brest. The whole aircraft was severely damaged by *Scharnhorst*'s A.A. defences: included in this damage was the radio installation: this Flying Officer Van den Bok repaired and re-established communication with his base. While carrying out the repair he observed an enemy fighter stalking his aircraft which by this time was in no condition to face an engagement. By following Flying Officer

Van den Bok's evasive directions, his captain was able to shake off the fighter. While this officer was detached from the Squadron on a course he obtained 48 hours leave in order that he might take part in the Squadron's effort against Rostock. Last autumn he took part in the Squadron's daylight attacks on enemy targets in occupied France . . . Throughout his cool steadfast courage has been an example that the Wireless Operators have been eager to emulate.

However, what was not mentioned in the recommendation for his first DFC was that his captain, a New Zealander, D. S. N. 'Tinny' Constance, attacked the enemy battleship from about 800 feet, or indeed the fact that one projectile came through the fuselage – right between Van den Bok's legs – and out through the roof. This all happened on 12 February 1942, the day of a major naval engagement, the famous 'Channel Dash'.

Van den Bok was awarded a Bar to his DFC for bravery when, on returning from a target, his Hampden was shot down over German-occupied Europe by an enemy night fighter piloted by top-scoring ace Hauptmann Wilhelm Herget. His aircraft crashed at Boussu-lez-Walcourt, Belgium. His pilot, Wing Commander J. D. Twigg, and Flight Lieutenant I. Maitland, DFC, were killed, but Van den Bok, who was wounded in the leg by a piece of shrapnel, and Flight Lieutenant G. C. Fisher, both evaded capture during three weeks in enemy-occupied territory. Van den Bok was duly elected to membership of the Caterpillar Club, for those who have successfully parachuted from a stricken aircraft.

The recommendation for his Bar, announced on 24 November 1942, stated:

Since the beginning of his tour on operations, commencing 22 August 1941, Flying Officer Van den Bok has taken part in 25 sorties over enemy territory against very heavy enemy defences. Targets he has attacked are Duisberg, Essen, Bremen, Mannheim, Düsseldorf, Huls, Cologne, Rostock and Flensberg. On his last trip to Saarbrücken on 28 August 1942, on returning from the target, his aircraft was attacked by enemy aircraft and shot down over Belgium. He sustained a wound in his leg by the entry of a piece of flak and despite physical suffering due to his wounded leg, he was able to travel some 3,000 miles through enemy territory to escape capture and arrived in Gibraltar in less than three weeks. Under a calm and quiet manner he has a fine offensive spirit in action which inspires confidence in his fellow aircrew.

Having trained as a pilot, Van den Bok's second Bar to his DFC was announced on 26 October 1945 following a number of radio counter-measure operations in Flying Fortresses. The recommendation for his award stated:

This officer has operated with No. 214 Squadron 16 times on his second tour, in which number is included the last Bomber Command attack in the Berlin area and the last operation by that Command in Europe. His attention to detail and planning, and his outstandingly good captaincy, have been responsible for the seemingly effortless manner in which he has operated against many targets well known for the strength of their defences. His enthusiasm for operations was in no way diminished by his experiences in evading capture after being shot down by flak over occupied Belgium after 29 sorties on his first tour. He has always been anxious to fly on every possible occasion when his duties as Flight Commander would permit. Despite his personal keenness for operational flying, he has, however, devoted a large amount of time to the instruction of new captains and crews, and has always been tireless in his efforts to improve the operational and training efficiency of his flight and the Squadron as a whole.

Only forty-six British and Commonwealth aircrew were awarded the DFC with two Bars during the whole of the Second World War. Van den Bok left the RAF in 1950 to work for Standard Oil (Esso) but was seriously injured (he lost a leg) in the Lewisham train disaster in south London in 1957. Van den Bok died in Whiteparish, Wiltshire, on New Year's Day 1973, aged sixty-five.

SQUADRON LEADER KEITH FREDERICK THIELE
Royal New Zealand Air Force (RNZAF)
DECORATIONS: DISTINGUISHED FLYING CROSS (DFC) AND TWO BARS, AND DISTINGUISHED SERVICE ORDER (DSO)
GAZETTED: 11 AUGUST 1942, 28 MAY 1943, 8 MAY 1945 AND 14 APRIL 1943

Keith 'Jimmy' Thiele was born in Christchurch, New Zealand, on 25 February 1921. One of six children born to a postman and his wife, Thiele worked as a reporter on the *Star-Sun* in Christchurch after leaving school. On 1 December 1940, he enlisted in the RNZAF and began his pilot training the following month at Harewood, Christchurch. Thiele gained his pilot's 'wings' in April 1941 and soon he was UK-bound, to be seconded to the RAF. After arriving in Britain, he was posted to 22 Operational Training Unit (OTU) before moving on to 405 (Royal Canadian Air Force) Squadron at Pocklington, Yorkshire. Despite a preference for flying fighter aircraft, he was allocated to a bomber squadron.

Thiele began his first operational tour on the last day of October 1941. He went on to complete thirty-two sorties in 405 Squadron's Wellingtons and Halifaxes, including participation in the first '1,000-bomber raid' on Cologne in May 1942. He also took part in the '1,000-bomber raid' against Essen two nights later. In an interview with the *New York Times Magazine*, Sergeant A. J. Campbell, an American and fellow crew member, spoke of his admiration for Thiele at this time: 'He is the best little old bomber pilot in the whole Air Force and every one of us looks up to him as a little tin God. I've made fifteen trips with him. More than once he has got us out of the ticklish spots when we've been caught in a cone of German searchlights and had enemy anti-aircraft gunners pumping everything they had all around us. I wouldn't like to go out in any kite now that didn't have Keith at the controls.' Campbell described one attack in particular:

As we stooged around we got caught in a big cone of searchlights. Then things began to get really hot. The Germans kept their searchlights trained on us while on the ground the gunners tried to take our range and let us have it. The skipper gave them a good run for their money by diving, twisting and weaving in and out of the barrage, and finally wriggled out. All the while we could hear Keith singing – at least he calls it singing; we don't. But he had some New Zealand song in his bean that night and he kept singing it over and over, stopping every once in a while, when ack-ack came quite close, to shout 'Look at those so-and-sos trying to get us!'

By then holding the rank of squadron leader, Thiele was awarded the DFC on 11 August 1942 after the recommendation for his decoration stated: 'Squadron Leader Thiele has been attached to this squadron for eight months during which time he has completed 25 successful sorties. On every occasion he has shown great skill and has pressed home his attacks regardless of opposition. His keenness and efficiency have been an inspiration to other members of the Squadron. He has always been a leader and has just proved a thoroughly courageous and skilled Flight Commander.'

Thiele was now rested for just a month or two before volunteering towards the end of 1942 for a second tour. He was posted to 467 (Royal Australian Air Force) Squadron, a Lancaster unit based at RAF Bottesford, Leicestershire. Here, Thiele went on to complete another twenty-four sorties, his tour including no fewer than four trips to Berlin, four to Essen, two trips apiece to Düsseldorf, Hamburg, Nuremberg and Stuttgart, and single visits to other heavily defended targets such as Bremen, Dortmund, Duisburg and La Spezia. It was on a mission to Cherbourg on the night of 6/7 January 1943 that Thiele's Wellington crash-landed on its return to RAF Home-Upon-Spalding-Moor in Yorkshire.

Thiele's DSO was announced on 14 April 1943 after the recommendation for his award stated:

This officer has, at all times, displayed outstanding keenness and determination during operations. The majority of his sorties have been attacks on well defended and distant targets which have all been highly successful. On one occasion, during an attack on Berlin, his Rear-Gunner lost consciousness from lack of oxygen, but Flight Lieutenant Thiele proceeded with the mission although two of the crew were fully occupied with the unconscious man. Later he returned to this country at a very low altitude, in an attempt to succour the Gunner. While on a flight to Nuremberg in March 1943, the port engine caught fire early on the outward journey. The flames were extinguished however, and the whole flight accomplished with success. His outstanding courage and devotion to duty and confidence have earned the admiration of all.

Thiele's Bar to his DFC was announced on 28 May 1943 after the recommendation for his award stated:

Squadron Leader Thiele was Captain of a Lancaster of No. 467 (R.A.A.F.) Squadron detailed to attack Duisburg on the night of 12/13 May 1943. While over enemy territory, and nearly at the target, the Lancaster was badly hit by a shell bursting right underneath the fuselage, severely damaging the aircraft. This did not in any way deter Squadron Leader Thiele from carrying on to bomb his target. While doing his final bombing run-up, the aircraft was caught in a cone of searchlights at about 16,000 feet. Despite this, Squadron Leader Thiele maintained his straight run-up to the target, in order to ensure accurate bombing by his Bomb-Aimer, thereby displaying courage, determination and devotion to duty of the highest order.

Just as the Bomb-Aimer had let the bombs go, the aircraft

was again severely damaged by shell bursts all round, one burst completely destroying the starboard outer engine. Squadron Leader Thiele, however, by expert airmanship, managed to feather this airscrew. Almost immediately afterwards the starboard inner engine was hit and put out of action. Again this officer showed complete coolness and airmanship of the highest order in managing to feather the second engine. The bursting flak had also smashed the entire Perspex on the starboard side of the pilot's cabin and Bomb-Aimer's cabin, a shell splinter hitting Squadron Leader Thiele on the side of the head and dazing him.

Despite being hit himself, with both starboard engines useless and being still in the searchlight cone, Squadron Leader Thiele, in a dazed condition, managed by his coolness and skill to get out of this perilous position and bring his aircraft and crew back safely. He was unable to maintain height once over the British coast, but, in a display of utmost skill, crash-landed his aircraft at an aerodrome, without injury to any of his crew. Squadron Leader Thiele throughout this entire sortie showed determination, exceptional valour, skill and devotion to duty . . .

After this crash-landing at RAF Coltishall, Norfolk, Thiele had plucked, from the right earpiece of his flying helmet, the flak splinter that had given him a 'terrific clout' on impact and left him with an ear 'swollen like a cauliflower'. Such incidents were part and parcel of the job for Thiele: his pilot's logbook revealing another forced landing at RAF Ford, Sussex, on '2 engines. 1 Wheel' after the raid on Stuttgart on the night of 14/15 April 1943. The crisis had been caused because his aircraft had been hit by a 'chance rifle shot' that cut the cooling pipe of the starboard outer engine and also put out of action part of the hydraulic system.

Thiele was again rested, with an appointment at Ferry Command, a posting that included the occasional transatlantic flight. Next, Thiele realised his ambition to join Fighter Command. After a conversion course on Spitfires at 57 Operational Training Unit (OTU), he was posted to 41 Squadron in February 1944. The Squadron's motto, 'Seek and Destroy', suited Thiele's approach down to the ground. Over the next six months, operating out of several airfields, he flew nearly 100 operational sorties. Indeed, he flew a Spitfire during the D-Day landings of 6 June 1944. Soon Thiele was employed in the hazardous and extremely difficult pastime of 'buzz bomb' and 'doodle bug' patrols for unmanned rockets, claiming at least one confirmed V-1.

In October 1944, and following a conversion course to Tempest aircraft, Thiele transferred to 486 (Royal New Zealand Air Force) Squadron. In January 1945, he took command of 3 Squadron. These two roles saw him complete another fifty sorties, mainly over Holland and Germany. His logbook detailed many successes by way of destroyed or damaged enemy transport. He also bagged a brace of Junkers Ju 52 transport aircraft on the ground at Detmold on 14 January 1945. Thiele also had a mounting tally of successful air-to-air combats: Me 109 fighters being claimed over Malmedy, Germany, on Christmas Eve 1944 and over Münster five days later. In his combat report for the 24 December 1944 incident, Thiele stated:

> . . . When I had closed to about 250 yards, the No. 2 stopped turning and climbed again. I fired a short burst from about 50

yards down astern. I saw pieces fly off the starboard wing, the outer half of which crumpled. The enemy aircraft turned over to starboard and spun slowly down, pouring white smoke from the engine. I was unable to follow as the first Hun was getting on my tail. The enemy aircraft I attacked was seen to crash by 274 Squadron, and I claim one Me. 109 destroyed.

Luck played a part in every long-serving pilot's survival but Thiele's eventually ran out during an armed reconnaissance on 10 February 1945. His Tempest was hit by flak and he was forced to bale out east of Dorsten, Germany, where he was captured. In his subsequent official debriefing report, he wrote:

On 10 February 1945, I was flying a Tempest I on an armed reconnaissance. I attacked a train north of Dortmund and as I climbed after the attack I was hit in the engine and main petrol tank. The engine failed immediately and the aircraft caught fire in the cockpit. I baled out at about 2000 feet and was severely burned on the face, eyes and wrists. I landed 200 yards from a small railway station in which was the flak battery which had shot me down. They picked me up immediately I touched down. I was marched across the station where there was considerable demonstration and then [they] shut me up in a locker on a flak truck under guard – my boots were taken off. Green [civilian] police arrived about one hour later and took me to a police station nearby. Here I was kept for nearly two days without food or any form of covering. It was bitterly cold. I was only given two drinks of water. My burns were not treated and my eyes became completely stuck up. I was taken to Dortmund aerodrome where I was locked up in solitary confinement for five days. My wounds were dressed and I had a mattress but no blankets. Left Dortmund by train for Oberursel which we reached in 24 hours. Here I was searched, but not thoroughly owing to my bandages. I was placed in solitary confinement. I went before interrogators and gave my number, rank and name adding that I was under orders not to converse further. I was threatened with the Gestapo and returned to my cell. Interrogated again by a Major, I was told that I could not go to hospital, which he described in glowing terms, until I had given the particulars [he] wanted. I refused to talk and was shown a book with particulars of all other fighter pilots shot down and then a diagram on the wall behind me showing a complete layout of 2nd T.A.F. [Territorial Air Force]. I couldn't study my Wing closely for fear of giving a clue but glancing around I saw the layout and names were pretty accurate. As I still refused to talk I was taken back to my cell. I was taken to hospital with seven other P.O.Ws at Hohemark – half an hour's walk from Oberursel. I stayed there until 6 March 1945. I was then taken with other P.O.Ws to Dulag Luft at Wetzlar. Here I was isolated as I had a sore throat and was suspected of having diphtheria. With the aid of Captain Griffiths, Dental Officer Para. I, I avoided being evacuated to Nuremberg and left with Squadron Leader Spencer on 31 March 1945.

As the Germans started to come to terms with the prospect of defeat, Thiele and a friend escaped from their PoW camp, commandeered a motorbike (using a small compass for directions) and rode to safety – the advancing American forces – on 4 April 1945, more than a month before the Nazis' final surrender.

Back at 3 Squadron, Thiele was declared unfit for further operational duty and grounded. As he was recovering, he learnt that he had been awarded a third DFC, a distinction equalled by only forty-six other aircrew in the entire war. This, announced on 8 May 1945, followed the recommendation for his award that praised his 'skilful leadership and determination'. It also stated: 'His complete disregard for his own safety and his boundless energy have been an inspiration to the whole Squadron.' It meant that with the addition of his earlier DSO, Thiele became one of just fifteen aircrew to receive a similar combination of four gallantry awards in the same conflict. Perhaps the most remarkable aspect of it all was that he was only twenty-four.

Thiele returned to New Zealand after the war and was discharged from the RNZAF in April 1946. However, because of his remarkable wartime career and earlier experience as a journalist, he was given the honour of writing the official history of the RNZAF in the 1939–45 conflict, and returned to England to carry out research. Unsurprisingly, perhaps, such desk work proved too dull for such a man of action as Thiele and he abandoned the project to become a commercial pilot, first in Britain, then in Australia. Thiele joined Qantas in 1948, remaining with the Australian airline until 1964. In the post-war years, Thiele also became a yachtsman of international repute, enjoying his time at sea as much as he had once enjoyed his time in the air.

Thiele's gallantry and service medals were sold at auction along with an array of fascinating documents and memorabilia. These included his logbook covering the period January 1941 to February 1946; his Caterpillar Club membership card (awarded to those who have successfully parachuted from a stricken aircraft); a telegram reporting the recipient 'missing in action' (dated 13 February 1945); and his first letter home from a prisoner-of-war camp (dated 24 February 1945 and in which he succinctly reported: 'I got slightly scorched before I was able to bale out but am being well looked after and am almost healed.').

After he retired, Thiele lived in New Zealand before moving to Australia. Today, a widower, with a daughter (his son died at birth) and two grandchildren, Thiele is ninety-one and lives in Bundaberg, Queensland. Speaking by telephone from Australia, he said: 'I had always wanted to be a fighter pilot but then I got stuck into bombers for a long time. I was very lucky to survive the war', and of his Bomber Command comrades: 'They were very brave men because they did a very dangerous job. I did around fifty bombing trips so I know what they went through.'

Thiele, known for calling a spade a spade, said that he has written a so-far unpublished autobiography that he originally titled *A Fine Line in Bullshit*. However, he has now given the book a more conventional title: *I Was Born Lucky*. I hope he gets his autobiography published because he certainly has a story to tell; they do not make pilots more courageous, tough or versatile than Jimmy Thiele.

FLIGHT SERGEANT (LATER FLIGHT LIEUTENANT) STANLEY DENNIS GUNNELL

RAF
DECORATION: DISTINGUISHED FLYING MEDAL
(DFM)
GAZETTED: 20 OCTOBER 1942

Stanley Gunnell was born on 2 December 1922 and enlisted in the RAF in 1941. After completing his pilot training, he was posted to 61 Squadron flying Lancaster bombers from RAF Syerston, Nottinghamshire.

On the night of 24/25 September 1942, Flight Sergeant Gunnell was the second pilot to Flight Sergeant Campbell on a mission to drop mines in the Baltic. After the crew of the Lancaster completed their task, they turned for home. However, while flying over Denmark at 6,000 feet, they were hit by anti-aircraft fire and a shell exploded in the aircraft's bomb compartment. This explosion, in turn, caused a large fire in the fuselage of the Lancaster and both reconnaissance flares and distress signals started to burn. Then another shell-burst hit the front of the aircraft, blowing in the Perspex nose and the majority of Perspex of the pilot's cupola (domed roof). The second hit caused chaos inside the Lancaster: the air bomber, who had been seated in the nose, was blown back beside the pilot, while Gunnell, who had been standing beside Campbell, was blown back on to the floor beside the navigator. Furthermore, Gunnell, Campbell, the navigator and the wireless operator received facial burns from the explosion.

With the aircraft full of smoke and the pilot unable to see his instruments, the Lancaster was then attacked by two enemy fighters. The accurate cannon and machine-gun fire from the fighters hit the Lancaster, entering both its rear and mid-upper turrets. The Lancaster then stalled and lost 2,000 feet before the smoke cleared from the cockpit and Campbell somehow gained control of the aircraft. Seeing some low clouds just below, the pilot dived into them to give his aircraft cover from both the fighters and anti-aircraft fire. The fire in the fuselage was growing in intensity and, to make matters worse, ammunition began exploding inside the aircraft. By this point, the rear gunner was seriously wounded, his injuries including a broken leg. The navigator, the air bomber and the mid-upper gunner frantically tried to keep the fire under control and prevent the flames spreading to the rear turret. Eventually, they fought their way through the flames and reached their injured comrade. They carried the rear gunner out of the turret and placed him on the rest chair. However, much of the fuselage had now burnt away. Although the navigator, air bomber and mid-upper gunner started to get the fire under control, they were unable to extinguish the flames and, with the Perspex missing from the nose, there was a massive draught blowing through the aircraft.

The pilot's attempts to control the Lancaster were hindered by the fact that all maps, navigation, wireless logs and other documents had been blown out of the aircraft when the nose was hit by the shell. Even though the wireless operator was badly burnt around his face and hands, he remained at his post and succeeded in contacting RAF Syerston from the Danish coast. As the badly damaged aircraft made for home, the wireless operator stayed in contact with his base and the pilot gave him regular bearings which he relayed over the radio. After Gunnell had digested readings from all the instruments, he took over the controls of the aircraft from Campbell and flew the aircraft for the next two hours. Once the Lancaster was back over British soil, Campbell again took over the aircraft and prepared to land it. Despite poor visibility, he made a perfect 'belly-landing' at an unidentified aerodrome and none of the crew received further injuries. It was only when the Lancaster was examined that it was revealed the hydraulic and emergency equipment for the operation of the undercarriage and flaps had been completely destroyed.

Gunnell's DFM was announced on 20 October 1942 after the recommendation for his award stated: 'Throughout, Sergeant Gunnell gave the greatest assistance to the Captain. It is considered that Sergeant Gunnell displayed outstanding gallantry and devotion to duty. His efforts were a very considerable factor in ensuring the safe return of this aircraft and crew.'

Gunnell's Air Officer Commanding (AOC), who examined the damaged aircraft, praised him and the entire crew: 'It is almost inconceivable that any crew would have carried on, had a 400 mile sea crossing, and landed without further incident.' Gunnell's DFM was part of a joint citation with the six other crew. However, there was a sad ending to the crew's bravery: just five days before the seven men were due to receive their decorations from George VI, four of them, including Campbell, were killed when their aircraft crash-landed in Devon after returning from a mine-laying operation in the Bay of Biscay.

Gunnell was promoted to pilot officer in March 1943 and to flying officer in June of that year. After the end of the Second World War, he took a permanent commission and was promoted to flight lieutenant. For the last five years of his service, he was employed on the staff of the Directorate of Intelligence.

Gunnell retired in 1966 and his whereabouts after that are not known.

FLYING OFFICER LESLIE THOMAS MANSER

Royal Air Force Volunteer Reserve (RAFVR)
DECORATION: VICTORIA CROSS (VC)
GAZETTED: 23 OCTOBER 1942

Leslie Manser was born on 11 May 1922 in New Delhi, India, where his father was employed as an engineer with the Post and Telegraph Department. After the family moved to Britain, Manser attended St Faith's School, Cambridge, and Aldenham School, Elstree, Hertfordshire. After completing his schooling, he decided to join the Armed Forces but he was turned down by both the Army and the Royal Navy. In August 1940, however, Manser was accepted as a prospective pilot by the RAFVR. He was commissioned as a pilot officer in May 1941 after completing his training. On 27 August 1941, he was posted to his first operational unit: 50 Squadron (Hampdens) based at RAF Swinderby, Lincolnshire. He also served briefly with 420 Royal Canadian Air Force Squadron (Hampdens) until 2 April 1942, when he rejoined 50 Squadron, by then operating from RAF Skellingthorpe, Lincolnshire. At the time, the squadron was in the process of converting to the new Manchester heavy bomber. On 8 April, Manser piloted one of the new aircraft in a leaflet drop over Paris, then flew five further sorties into May. He was a skilled pilot and on 6 May – still in his teens – he was promoted to flying officer.

In early 1942, Bomber Command had been having a torrid time, with almost 5 per cent of its aircraft lost on major operations and fewer than one bomb in ten falling within five miles of its target. After relatively successful raids against the cities of Rostock and Lübeck in March and April, Air Marshal Sir Arthur Harris, the new head of Bomber Command, had conceived a plan – codenamed Operation Millennium – whereby 1,000 British bombers would attack a German city in a single night. The proposal, which was approved by Winston Churchill, involved a massive mobilisation of aircraft, and by 26 May everything was in place. After three false starts targeting Bremen, Cologne (Germany's third largest city) was chosen to be bombed. Harris sent a personal message to all the air-crews which ended: 'Let him [Jerry] have it – right on the chin.' The force of more than a thousand aircraft took off from fifty-two airfields, mainly in the east of England, on the night of 30 May.

Manser was captain and first pilot of one of the new Manchesters. His eventual citation for this VC takes up the story:

As the aircraft was approaching its objective it was caught by searchlights and subjected to intense and accurate anti-aircraft fire. Flying Officer Manser held on his dangerous course and bombed the target successfully from a height of 7,000 feet. Then he set course for base. The Manchester had been damaged and was still under heavy fire. Flying Officer Manser took violent evasive action, turning and descending to under 1,000 feet. It was of no avail. The searchlights and flak followed him until the outskirts of the city were passed. The aircraft was hit repeatedly and the rear gunner was wounded.

The front cabin filled with smoke; the port engine was over-heating badly. Pilot and crew could all have escaped safely by parachute. Nevertheless, Flying Officer Manser, disregarding the obvious hazards, persisted in his attempt to save aircraft and crew from falling into enemy hands. He took the aircraft up to 2,000 feet. Then the port engine burst into flames. It was ten minutes before the fire was mastered, but then the engine went out of action for good, part of one wing was burnt and the air-speed of the aircraft became dangerously low.

Despite all the efforts of the pilot and crew, the Manchester began to lose height. At this critical moment, Flying Officer Manser once more disdained the alternative of parachuting to safety with his crew. Instead, with grim determination, he set a new course for the nearest base, accepting for himself the prospect of almost certain death in a firm resolve to carry on to the end. Soon, the aircraft became extremely difficult to handle and when a crash was inevitable, Flying Officer Manser ordered the crew to bale out. A sergeant handed him a parachute but he waved it away telling the non commissioned officer to jump at once as he could only hold the aircraft steady for a few more seconds. While the crew were descending to safety they saw the aircraft still carrying their gallant captain plunge to earth and burst into flames. In pressing home his attack in the face of strong opposition, in striving, against heavy odds, to bring back his aircraft and crew and finally, when in extreme peril, thinking only of the safety of his comrades, Flying Officer Manser displayed determination and valour of the highest order.

Manser, aged only twenty, had sacrificed his own life in the knowledge that to do otherwise would have resulted in the almost certain deaths of his crew. His five crew, including the wounded rear gunner, survived but could only watch as the aircraft plunged to the ground and burst into flames east of the Belgian village of Bree. The navigator was injured as he landed, but he and the others, who were relatively unscathed, were hidden by locals who helped them escape back to Britain via Gibraltar. Of the 1,046 aircraft on the mission, 989 claimed to have reached and attacked their targets. In total, 1,455 tons of bombs were dropped and 600 acres of Cologne were destroyed in a little over an hour and a half. This resulted in almost as much devastation as had previously been inflicted on Germany up to that point in the war.

Manser's posthumous VC was announced on 23 October 1942 and the decoration was presented to his family at an investiture on 3 March 1943. Years later, at a modest ceremony on 31 May 1965, attended by most of Manser's crew at RAF Waddington in Lincolnshire, Cyril Manser, Leslie's brother, formally presented the VC on loan to Wing Commander W. J. Stacey of 50 Squadron. It was the first ever occasion on which the RAF was invited to take custody of a VC.

WING COMMANDER HUGH GORDON MALCOLM
RAF
DECORATION: VICTORIA CROSS (VC)
GAZETTED: 27 APRIL 1943

Hugh Malcolm was born in Broughty Ferry, Dundee, Scotland, on 2 May 1917. He was educated at Craigflower Preparatory School, Dunfermline, and Trinity College,

Glenalmond, Perthshire. After completing his schooling, Malcolm entered RAF College Cranwell, Lincolnshire, as a cadet in January 1936, where he graduated as a commissioned pilot in December 1937. The following month Malcolm was posted to 26 Squadron (Lysanders), RAF Catterick, Yorkshire, where he took part in various training exercises. On 20 May 1939, he was piloting a Lysander 4784 in a practice flight for a forthcoming Empire Air Day display when he was involved in a major accident which wrote off the aircraft. Malcolm suffered serious injuries, including a fractured skull, and was told he would never fly again. However, after four months in Princess Mary Hospital at RAF Halton in Buckinghamshire (where he met the nurse who would become his wife), his recovery was so complete that he returned to his squadron in September 1939. As the Second World War intensified, Malcolm was promoted, first to flight lieutenant in 1940 and then to squadron leader in 1941.

Malcolm served as a flight commander with 18 Squadron (Blenheims) based at RAF Wattisham, Suffolk. With this squadron, he flew mainly night sorties, the first being on 6 May 1942. Many of these sorties were in support of main bomber force raids and his role was to attack German night-fighter airfields. Malcolm and his crew participated in Bomber Command's first '1,000-bomber raid', to Cologne on the night of 30/31 May 1942. It involved eighteen Blenheim IVs from 18 Squadron which flew intruder sorties against three Luftwaffe air bases, with Malcolm leading seven of the these aircraft against St Trond airfield. On 1 June 1942, while involved in another major raid, this time on Essen, Malcolm and his crew again returned to attack St Trond. Malcolm and his crew were present during the next '1,000-bomber raid', this time to

Bremen, on the night of 25/26 June. On 1 July, Malcolm and his crew were commended for their bravery in searching for and locating a dinghy (containing British aircrew) some fifty miles off the Dutch coast. This was carried out in daylight and clear weather – which put them at great risk of an enemy attack – and Malcolm remained in the air for four hours to obtain seven 'fixes' on the dinghy so that the crew could be rescued.

In September 1942, Malcolm was promoted to wing commander. Two months later, he moved with his squadron to North Africa, where he was initially based at Blida airfield in Algeria. By then, his squadron, part of 326 Wing, was flying the new Blenheim Vs, which were proving unreliable in these new conditions. The aircraft's failings became apparent on their first operational sortie in North Africa on 17 November 1942. Malcolm and his squadron attacked Bizerte airfield in Tunisia at low level in daylight and without a fighter escort. They bombed and strafed their target, but encountered both bad weather and the Luftwaffe on their return flight: 18 Squadron lost two bombers to the German fighter aircraft and two more in an air collision. Undeterred, the squadron returned to Bizerte eleven days later to bomb and strafe the airfield once again, despite a massive barrage of fire from the German air defences.

By this point, the ground war in North Africa had become intense and, on 4 December, eleven Blenheim Vs from No. 326 Wing were flown to Souk-el-Arba in Tunisia to support the Army units in the battle area. Six Blenheims, led by Malcolm, took off at 9.15 that morning to search for targets in the Chouigui area. When they located a Luftwaffe landing strip some ten miles north of Chouigui, they bombed and strafed it before flying to Canrobert, to refuel, and then returned to Souk-el-Arba. However, less than an hour after landing, Malcolm received a message from the forward Army battle zone, requesting an air operation in the area they had just come from. However, this meant flying in broad daylight over a battle area without fighter aircraft support – this could not be organised in the time available. Malcolm was aware quite how hazardous the mission would be but, knowing the infantry desperately needed support, he did not hesitate. Eleven Blenheims from No. 326 Wing were chosen for the sortie but one burst its tail wheel attempting to take off and was taken out of commission. The ten remaining aircraft kept a tight formation knowing this was their only defence against the Luftwaffe. Within twenty minutes, one of the crew had to make a crash-landing fifteen miles east of Souk-el-Arba. The crew survived but the mission was now down to nine aircraft. After circling their target, the Blenheims started to bomb but they were set upon by a huge number of Me 109 fighters, possibly as many as fifty at any one time. One by one, in a five-minute 'battle' that was little more than a massacre, the Blenheims were shot down until only Malcolm and his crew remained. However, their Blenheim was then hit, too, and the aircraft, with its three crew, crashed and burst into flames some fifteen miles from its target.

Malcolm, who died aged twenty-five, was awarded a post-humous VC on 27 April 1943 for the bravery during his final sortie and his earlier courage in North Africa. His citation praised his 'leadership, skill and daring' and stated: 'Wing Commander Malcolm's last exploit was the finest example of the valour and unswerving devotion to duty which he constantly displayed.'

Yet, it was one of the survivors from Malcolm's final sortie who perhaps best summed up the bravery of Malcolm and his men. He said that everyone on the fateful raid knew there was only a small chance of success and a smaller chance of getting back safely. 'But we would gladly have followed Malcolm anywhere. He was superb, Malcolm radiated a joy of living and fighting which was irresistible.'

Several months after Malcolm's death, Lady Tedder, the wife of the Middle East Air Commander-in-Chief, came to open the first in a series of rest and leisure recreation centres in North Africa. To people's surprise, she named it the 'Malcolm Club' despite the fact that she had barely known him.

SERGEANT RONALD HORACE DAVID WILSON
RAF
DECORATION: DISTINGUISHED FLYING MEDAL (DFM)
GAZETTED: 25 MAY 1943

Ronald Wilson was born in Yeovil, Somerset, in 1920 and enlisted in the RAF in 1939 at the start of the Second World War. He served as an air gunner in Halifaxes with 35 (Madras Presidency) Squadron, which was based at RAF Linton-on-Ouse, Yorkshire.

On 27 April 1942, Wilson was part of one of the eleven Halifax crews from the squadron that were chosen to operate in conjunction with other aircraft from 10 and 76 Squadrons on a specific raid. Their target was the *Tirpitz*, the Bismarck-class German battleship, which was anchored in the Aas Fjord at Trondheim, Norway. The Halifaxes were ordered to make a low-level attack on the *Tirpitz* and did so from a height of around 150 feet. While doing so, they faced heavy fire both from the battleship and the guns placed on either side of the fjord. Wilson's aircraft, flown by Pilot Officer MacIntyre, was fatally damaged by flak. The starboard wing was ablaze and the pilot had to make a forced landing, using superb airmanship to put the aircraft down on a frozen lake near Hocklingen, Norway.

After landing, MacIntyre, Wilson and three more of the crew escaped into the countryside, knowing that German search parties would be sent out from Trondheim to look for them. The final crew member had suffered a broken leg and was unable to escape with the others. For the next eight days, the five remaining crew suffered terrible hardships as they tramped through the snow and mountains in an attempt to reach the safety of Sweden. Eventually, having travelled forty-five miles, they reached the border. The recommendations for their gallantry awards stated: 'By sheer determination and will-power, they crossed safely into Sweden. For this outstanding example of good airmanship on the part of the captain, initiative and devotion to duty on the part of the whole crew, Pilot Officers MacIntyre and Hewitt are strongly recommended for the immediate award of the D.F.C., and Sergeants Blanchet, Perry, and Wilson, the Distinguished Flying Medal.' Wilson's DFM was announced on 25 May 1943.

It is understood that Wilson died in late 2000/early 2001, aged eighty. The Halifax that carried him and the rest of the crew was on its maiden flight. After landing on the frozen lake, it burnt fiercely, the heat of the flames ultimately sending the aircraft through the melting ice. In 1973, the near-complete wreckage was recovered from the lake and put on display at the RAF Museum in Hendon, north London.

FLIGHT LIEUTENANT DAVID SAMUEL ANTHONY LORD
RAF
DECORATIONS: DISTINGUISHED FLYING CROSS (DFC) AND VICTORIA CROSS (VC)
GAZETTED: 16 JULY 1943 AND 13 NOVEMBER 1945

David Lord was the only member of RAF Transport Command to be awarded the VC. Among his comrades he was known as 'Lumme', his favourite expression.

Born in Cork, in the Republic of Ireland, on 18 October 1913, Lord was the son of a serving warrant officer in the Royal Welch Fusiliers. After the Great War, he accompanied his parents to India and was educated at Lucknow Convent School, travelling to and from it each day by bullock cart. Later, he went to St Mary's School, Wrexham, and St Mary's College, Aberystwyth. He considered careers in both the Church and journalism but a fascination with flying led him to enlist in the RAF on 6 August 1936. He was awarded his pilot's 'wings' on 5 April 1937 and promoted to sergeant that August, then posted to 31 Squadron stationed in Lahore, then India.

Lord's subsequent bravery was recognised on 16 July 1943 when his DFC was announced. The recommendation for his award stated:

The very large number of operational hours flown by this officer in Iraq (during the rebellion of 1941), the Western

Desert (where this Squadron had a detachment from October 1941 to January 1942 and where this officer was shot down in a Douglas aircraft by 2 Me. 110s), and in Burma 1942–43 are in themselves eloquent testimony to his sticking power and devotion to duty. His flying during the Burma campaign has included the evacuation of casualties, women and children in the face of enemy opposition and supply dropping to troops in the field. During the past two months he has made a great many S.D. [special duties] sorties deep into enemy territory often without fighter escort. This on slow and virtually unarmed aircraft calls for courage of a high order. In addition this officer's cheerful acceptance of risks and keenness have been a fine example to the younger pilots of the Squadron. I sincerely believe that he is deserving of recognition.

Lord received his DFC at Buckingham Palace in January 1944 but his parents were unable to take a photograph of him with the medal because, being a man who did not enjoy such attention, he leapt into a taxi and fled, saying he would rather have a tooth pulled. In the same month, he was promoted to flight lieutenant and, at the end of January, he reported to 271 Squadron, another Dakota (Douglas DC-3) unit, which was based in Doncaster.

That September, Lord took part in the first phase of the 'Arnhem lift' in Holland, a three-day operation to support ground troops who were fighting a losing battle against superior enemy forces. The first two days of the operation were fraught with difficulty and Lord was handicapped by not having two of his regular crew.

The citation for his VC, announced on 13 November 1945, gives a moving account of the action for which he was decorated:

Flight Lieutenant Lord was Pilot and Captain of a Dakota aircraft detailed to drop supplies at Arnhem on the afternoon of 19 September 1944. Our airborne troops had been surrounded and were being pressed into a small area defended by a large number of anti-aircraft guns. Air crews were warned that intense opposition would be met over the dropping zone. To ensure accuracy they were ordered to fly at 900 feet when dropping their containers.

While flying at 1,500 feet near Arnhem the starboard wing of Flight Lieutenant Lord's aircraft was twice hit by anti-aircraft fire. The starboard engine was set on fire. He would have been justified in leaving the main stream of supply aircraft and continuing at the same height or even abandoning his aircraft. But on learning that his crew were uninjured and that the dropping zone would be reached in three minutes he said he would complete his mission, as the troops were in dire need of supplies.

By now the starboard engine was burning furiously. Flight Lieutenant Lord came down to 900 feet, where he was singled out for the concentrated fire of all the anti-aircraft guns. On reaching the dropping zone he kept his aircraft on a straight and level course while supplies were dropped. At the end of the run, he was told that two containers remained. Although he must have known that the collapse of the starboard wing could not be long delayed, Flight Lieutenant Lord circled, rejoined the stream of aircraft and made a second run to drop the remaining supplies. These manoeuvres took eight minutes in all, the aircraft being continuously under heavy anti-aircraft fire. His task completed, Flight Lieutenant Lord ordered his crew to abandon the Dakota, making no attempt himself to leave the aircraft, which was down to 500 feet. A few seconds later, the starboard wing collapsed and the aircraft fell in flames. There was only one survivor, who was flung out while assisting other members of the crew to put on their parachutes. By continuing his mission in a damaged and burning aircraft, descending to drop the supplies accurately, returning to the dropping zone a second time and, finally, remaining at the controls to give his crew a chance of escape, Flight Lieutenant Lord displayed supreme valour and self-sacrifice.

Flying Officer Harry King, his navigator, was the sole survivor from the aircraft. His parachute opened at the last moment and he survived a heavy fall to become a prisoner of war (PoW). The incident was watched from the ground as soldiers stopped fighting and observed King hurtle out of the Dakota. He made a report on Lord's courage after being repatriated to England on 13 May 1945. As a result, the commander of 271 Squadron recommended Lord for a posthumous VC, and his parents received their son's award on 18 December 1945.

FLIGHT SERGEANT (LATER WARRANT OFFICER) JOHN BETTANY
Royal Air Force Volunteer Reserve (RAFVR)
DECORATION: CONSPICUOUS GALLANTRY
MEDAL (CGM)
GAZETTED: 24 APRIL 1945

John 'Jack' Bettany, who was born in 1920, enlisted in the RAFVR on 16 March 1941, motivated to do so after his sister's house in Coventry was hit by German bombs. Having then flown as a wireless operator in several sorties with 578 Squadron, he joined 625 Squadron in October 1944, in which latter capacity he was to display supreme gallantry during a sortie flown early in the following year.

At 4.29 p.m. on 23 February 1945, Bettany and his comrades took off in a Lancaster from RAF Kelstern, Lincolnshire. The crew was part of a massive operation involving 366 other Lancasters and 13 Mosquitos that targeted the town of Pforzheim in south-west Germany. It was the first and only 'area-bombing' raid of the war on this target. Bettany's Lancaster, piloted by Flight Officer D. R. Paige, had dropped its bombs on the town at 8.02 p.m. Moments later, the Lancaster became the victim of 'friendly fire', or, to be more accurate, 'friendly bombing'. Incendiary bombs dropped by a higher flying aircraft crashed on to the Lancaster and lodged themselves either in or on top of the airframe. There were incendiaries on the wings, too, which set fire to the starboard inner motor. Furthermore, up to twenty bombs entered the fuselage where they knocked out the wireless intercommunications and jammed the doors of the rear turret. Bettany immediately started to throw out the incendiaries with his bare hands through the holes in the fuselage. With the internal comms down, he was ordered by the pilot to contact the gunners to check on their safety. As he performed this task, he threw out more bombs at the same time. Eventually, he threw out a total of fifteen incendiaries.

Just as it seemed that Bettany had averted disaster, an incendiary that had been lodged in number three tank on the starboard side ignited and set fire to the starboard outer engine. The pilot then gave the order to bale out and instructed Bettany to pass on the message to the mid-upper and rear gunners. As he went back deeper in the fuselage, however, his parachute was partially pulled open by some of the wreckage. Disregarding his own safety, he ensured that both the mid-upper and rear gunners jumped safely from the aircraft. Only then did he go back to collect a spare parachute to enable himself to jump from the aircraft. The recommendation for his CGM stated: 'By forming the connecting link between the captain and the two gunners and by his prompt action in throwing the burning incendiaries out of the aircraft, Flight Sergeant Bettany was primarily responsible for saving the lives of his entire crew. His conduct showed a complete disregard for his own safety and devotion to duty of a very high order.'

Interestingly, since it is said that the first victim of war is the truth, when Bettany's CGM was announced on 24 April 1945 the citation failed to mention that the damage to the aircraft had been caused by 'friendly' bombs. The following sentence of the citation implied the damage to the aircraft was from either German fighters or anti-aircraft fire: 'Soon after the target had been bombed the aircraft sustained serious damage.' The citation concluded, more accurately, however, on Bettany: 'His coolness, bravery and resolution in a critical situation set an example of the highest standard.'

Both the recommendation and the citation failed, however, to tell the colourful story of Bettany's landing. He grounded inside enemy territory and then walked in full uniform and in broad daylight across the River Rhine. Bettany was found by some American troops who at first wanted to string him up as a spy: they had just captured six German spies, all wearing RAF uniforms. However, when they realised Bettany spoke English and was clearly a British airman, they got him drunk on schnapps and put him on a train to Paris which, by this time, was back in Allied hands.

The Allied bombing of Pforzheim – when 1,825 tons of bombs were dropped in just twenty-two minutes – had been devastatingly accurate: the raid claimed more than 17,000 civilian lives and an estimated 83 per cent of the town's urban area was destroyed. It is believed that only the bombings of Hamburg and Dresden led to a larger death toll of civilians. British losses amounted to ten Lancasters in the immediate area, and two more crash-landing in France.

Bettany was promoted to warrant officer on 1 October 1945, before being discharged on 15 August 1946. From 1955, he worked as a recruiting officer for the RAF in Manchester. His next job was as an air traffic controller at Warton and Squires Gate airfield, near Blackpool, before he undertook the same role at Salmesbury airfield, Lancashire. He retired in 1979 and died after a long illness at a nursing home in Bamber Bridge, Lancashire, in April 2005, aged eighty-four. Only after his death did his widow, Alice, provide further information about the fateful day that he baled out of his blazing aircraft: 'He was lucky that one of the previous crew who had been using the plane had forgotten to take his parachute out with him and Jack had a spare to pull out and bale out.'

Bettany's gallantry and service medals were auctioned shortly after his death, along with various memorabilia. This included an article on his Caterpillar Club membership, awarded to those who have successfully parachuted from a stricken aircraft. Among his documents was an invitation by the King to his investiture at Buckingham Palace, dated 27 February 1946. Bettany is one of only 107 airmen ever to have been awarded the CGM and I believe that his decoration is among the finest CGMs to have been bestowed.

SERGEANT (LATER WARRANT OFFICER) NORMAN CYRIL JACKSON

Royal Air Force Volunteer Reserve (RAFVR)
DECORATION: VICTORIA CROSS (VC)
GAZETTED: 26 OCTOBER 1945

In 2004, the sale of Norman Jackson's VC set what was then the world record for a medal when it went under the hammer at auction for £200,000. As with all gallantry medals, its value is largely dictated by the story behind the decoration and acts of bravery do not come any more remarkable than Jackson's. In his book *British VCs of World War 2*, John Laffin writes of the action that led to Jackson's VC, 'His exploit may have been the most amazing of the war and certainly it was the most unusual.' Jackson also had the distinction of being the first flight engineer in the RAF to be awarded the VC.

Jackson was born in Ealing, west London, on 8 April 1919. He was adopted by the Gunter family and attended Archdeacon Cambridge Primary School in Twickenham, followed by the local grammar school, where he developed an interest in engineering. After completing his education, he became a fitter and turner. At the outbreak of war in September 1939, Jackson, who was by then married, could have been exempted from service because of his occupation. However, he enlisted in the RAFVR on 20 October 1939. Initially, he worked as a fitter in Freetown, Sierra Leone, where he was attached to 95 Squadron, but in January 1941 he had the opportunity to join an aircrew. Thereafter, he applied for training as a flight engineer and, in September 1942, he returned to England and spent six months at 27 Operational Training Unit (OTU). In July 1943, and by then a sergeant, he joined 106 Squadron at RAF Syerston,

Nottinghamshire, and completed nine sorties before the squadron moved to RAF Metheringham, Lincolnshire, in early November.

By 24 April 1944, Jackson had completed his first tour of thirty operations, mostly against heavily defended German targets. However, before taking some time off with friends, he volunteered for one more sortie 'for luck' on the night of 26/27 April. Earlier in the day he had been told that his wife had given birth to their first son, and the crew decided to celebrate the news on their return from the mission.

It would be an understatement to say that things did not go according to plan. The *London Gazette* announced Jackson's VC on 26 October 1945:

This airman was the flight engineer in a Lancaster detailed to attack Schweinfurt on the night of 26th April, 1944. Bombs were dropped successfully and the aircraft was climbing out of the target area. Suddenly it was attacked by a fighter at about 20,000 feet. The captain took evading action at once, but the enemy secured many hits. A fire started near a petrol tank on the upper surface of the starboard wing, between the fuselage and the inner engine. Sergeant Jackson was thrown to the floor during the engagement. Wounds which he received from shell splinters in the right leg and shoulder were probably sustained at that time. Recovering himself, he remarked that he could deal with the fire on the wing and obtained his captain's permission to try to put out the flames. Pushing a hand fire-extinguisher into the top of his life-saving jacket and clipping on his parachute pack, Sergeant Jackson jettisoned the escape hatch above the pilot's head. He then started to climb out of the cockpit and back along the top of the fuselage to the starboard wing. Before he could leave the fuselage his parachute pack opened and the whole canopy and rigging lines spilled into the cockpit. Undeterred, Sergeant Jackson continued. The pilot, bomb aimer and navigator gathered the parachute together and held on to the rigging lines, paying them out as the airman crawled aft. Eventually he slipped and, falling from the fuselage to the starboard wing, grasped an air intake on the leading edge of the wing. He succeeded in clinging on but lost the extinguisher, which was blown away.

By this time, the fire had spread rapidly and Sergeant Jackson was involved. His face, hands and clothing were severely burnt. Unable to retain his hold, he was swept through the flames and over the trailing edge of the wing, dragging his parachute behind. When last seen it was only partly inflated and was burning in a number of places. Realising that the fire could not be controlled, the captain gave the order to abandon aircraft. Four of the remaining members of the crew landed safely. The captain and rear gunner have not been accounted for. Sergeant Jackson was unable to control his descent and landed heavily. He sustained a broken ankle, his right eye was closed through burns and his hands were useless. These injuries, together with the wounds received earlier, reduced him to a pitiable state. At daybreak he crawled to the nearest village, where he was taken prisoner. He bore the intense pain and discomfort of the journey to Dulag Luft [prisoner-of-war-camp] with magnificent fortitude. After 10 months in hospital he made a good recovery, though his hands require further treatment and are only of limited use. This airman's attempt to extinguish the fire and save the aircraft and crew from falling into enemy hands was an act of outstanding gallantry. To venture outside, when travelling at 200 miles an hour, at a great height and in intense cold, was an almost incredible feat. Had he succeeded in subduing the flames, there was little or no prospect of his regaining the cockpit. The spilling of his parachute and the risk of grave damage to its canopy reduced his chances of survival to a minimum. By his ready willingness to face these dangers he set an example of self-sacrifice which will ever be remembered.

The morning after he landed, Jackson had staggered to a cottage on the edge of a forest and had been roundly abused by its German occupant before two young girls nursed him. He was then paraded through the nearest town, where he was jeered, before being sent to Dulag Luft. While there, he made two escape attempts. In the second, he managed to contact US troops near Munich but was recaptured before he could reach them.

Jackson returned to Britain on VE Day and was reunited with his wife and the son he had not yet seen. However, two of the crew, the captain, Flying Officer Fred Mifflin, and Flight Sergeant Hugh Johnson, Jackson's close friend, had perished. Jackson spent ten months in hospital recovering from his injuries, though he never again had full movement in his badly burnt hands. It was Jackson's fellow crew who told the story of his courage after the war and ensured that he was recommended for the VC. His decoration was announced on 26 October 1945 and he received his VC at Buckingham Palace from George VI on 13 November 1945. Another recipient of the VC that day was Group Captain Leonard Cheshire.

Jackson became a sales executive after the war and died at

Hampton Hill, Middlesex, on 26 March 1994, aged seventy-four.

SERGEANT DENNIS RONALD BOWERS
RAF
DECORATION: CONSPICUOUS GALLANTRY
MEDAL (CGM)
GAZETTED: 18 MAY 1945

Dennis Bowers was training as an optician in South Wales at the outbreak of hostilities in September 1939, where he was also a member of the Auxiliary Fire Service. In due course, he achieved his desire to join the RAF and, by early 1945, he was serving as a flight engineer in the Lancaster aircraft of 156 Squadron, a Path Finder unit.

The story of his subsequent gallantry is best told by the official report submitted by his pilot, Flying Officer G. B. Hampson, following the miraculous return of their aircraft after a raid on Harpenerweg in Germany on the night of 24/25 March 1945:

Evasive action was taken but the Flight Engineer was struck in the thigh with shrapnel which splintered the bone and caused profuse bleeding. He continued windowing [dropping metalled paper strips to confuse enemy searchlight and gun battery radar on the ground]. At approximately 16.27 hours the aircraft received a direct hit in the bomb bay from a heavy anti-aircraft shell and went into a slight dive. A member of my crew reported, 'Fire skipper, she's on fire.' My cabin filled with smoke and I immediately ordered the whole of my crew to abandon aircraft, at the same time selecting bomb doors open and pulling the bomb jettison toggle.

When at a height of 13,000 [feet] I found the aircraft handling fairly satisfactorily and the smoke cleared I indicated to my Set Operator, F/Sgt. Reynolds, that I had cancelled my order. He in turn informed my Flight Engineer, Sgt. Bowers, who had just succeeded in opening the escape hatch. I called the remainder of the crew on the inter-com but only received a reply from my Rear Gunner, F/Sgt. Mann, who I told to remain in his turret. My Set Operator informed me that he had seen the Wireless Operator, F/Sgt. Hart, and Navigator 1, F/Sgt. French, on their way to the rear exit.

I was still taking evasive action from predicted flak and had turned on to the approximate course out of the target when my Flight Engineer was once again hit by flak which all but severed his leg at the knee. He called me on the inter-com telling me that his right leg was trapped under the escape hatch which was then positioned diagonally across the exit and that he could not hold on. My Set Operator immediately went to his assistance and I told the Rear Gunner to vacate his turret and to come forward bringing with him the first aid equipment from its stowage. This he did and on reaching my cabin told me that my Mid Upper Gunner, Sgt McWilliams had left the aircraft but that his parachute was still in its normal position [in the aircraft].

My Set Operator had been unable to help my Flight Engineer very much but my Rear Gunner was able to help him to lie my Flight Engineer on the Flight deck beside me. An ampoule of Morphia was prepared and my Engineer injected himself in the left wrist whilst my Rear Gunner applied a tourniquet to his left thigh. My Flight Engineer took over the tourniquet, adjusting the pressure to his requirement, while the Rear Gunner cut away his battledress and applied two shell dressings to his injured leg. This combination stopped the loss of blood and a further ampoule of Morphia was administered some 25 minutes after the first.

My Set Operator . . . gave me the flight plan courses to steer and I was able to follow the bomber stream to the coast of Holland. I map read to Ostend and my Set Operator, using the Navigator 1's last found wind, gave me a course to steer for Manston [Kent]. The North Foreland was recognised from about 20 miles away and as it had been ascertained by my Set Operator that we were still carrying 9 x 500lb bombs I turned on to a reciprocal course of 135° (T) out to sea and once more endeavoured to jettison the bombs without success. I reached Manston at a height of 11,000 feet and, whilst losing height over the airfield, checked the undercarriage hydraulics which were found to be unserviceable. My Set Operator tied my Flight Engineer's harness to the stanchion of the Navigator's seat as he was considered too weak to brave himself for the landing and whilst circling the airfield my rear Gunner fired off red signal cartridges.

During the final approach my Set Operator operated the emergency undercarriage control, the undercarriage locked down and claps were lowered by emergency air. On becoming stationary we were immediately met by two ambulances and my Flight Engineer was removed to hospital where he underwent a blood transfusion. From the time of his first wound my Flight Engineer showed great fortitude and failed to lose consciousness. He continued windowing operations until he was completely disabled and even whilst lying on the Flight deck advised me of the fuel state and noticed that two booster pump switches were 'OFF'. He reminded me that if the hydraulics were unserviceable and I opened the bomb doors, I would be unable to reclose them. On hearing that I proposed to use the emergency system he impressed upon me that I must ensure that the flaps selector was not already in the down position. My Set Operator and Rear Gunner reacted very well and were of great assistance to my Flight Engineer and myself. On checking the numbers on the remaining parachutes it seems certain that my Mid Upper Gunner left the aircraft without his parachute but I do not know whether he baled out or fell out through the large cavity in the bomb bay. The aircraft suffered a direct hit in the rear bomb bay and other flak damage.

Hampson managed to land the stricken aircraft successfully. His report was used, in an abridged form, as the basis of the recommendation that Bowers should be awarded the CGM, and the decoration was announced on 18 May 1945.

Bowers subsequently acted as best man at his pilot's wedding. It is not known what happened to him after that.

6

SECOND WORLD WAR – SPECIAL BOMBING MISSIONS

As detailed in the introduction to Chapter 5, Britain became renowned for its prolific use of strategic bombing, which it was hoped would have the long-term effect of both reducing the enemy's supplies and demoralising the home population. However, when the need arose, Bomber Command was also highly effective at precision bombing: striking a small target with great accuracy. Major J. F. C. Fuller, the military strategist and historian, regarded 'accuracy of aim' to be one of the five recognisable attributes of weaponry, along with range of action, striking power, volume of fire and portability.

At the beginning of the Second World War, bombers were expected to drop their bombs in daylight to ensure the greatest accuracy and to reduce civilian casualties. However, repeated low-level bombing in the face of anti-aircraft fire and enemy fighters proved to be highly costly. As the war advanced and both bombing technology and air reconnaissance improved, bombers increasingly dropped their loads at night, a move which reduced losses among crew but did little for accuracy.

Some of the bravest actions of the war by the RAF were to attack specific targets – ships, ports, canals, transport links and even a jail – often in broad daylight and at great risk to the pilot and aircrew. Individuals who showed exceptional courage were, quite rightly, recognised with gallantry awards for a specific incident, or incidents, in the same way as the more glamorous fighter pilots were decorated throughout the war.

FLIGHT LIEUTENANT (LATER WING COMMANDER) RODERICK ALASTAIR BROOK LEAROYD
RAF
DECORATION: VICTORIA CROSS (VC)
GAZETTED: 20 AUGUST 1940

SERGEANT WALTER ELLIS
RAF
DECORATION: DISTINGUISHED FLYING MEDAL (DFM)
GAZETTED: 22 NOVEMBER 1940

LEADING AIRCRAFTMAN (LATER SERGEANT) WILLIAM RONALD RICH
RAF
DECORATION: DISTINGUISHED FLYING MEDAL (DFM)
GAZETTED: 22 OCTOBER 1940

It was a warm summer's evening – 12 August 1940 – when the twenty-four aircrew left their briefing room at RAF Scampton, Lincolnshire. Shortly afterwards the men from 49 and 83 Squadrons were clambering into eleven Hampden bombers. Their objective that night was to destroy the Dortmund–Ems Canal and, in doing so, delay Germany's planned invasion of the British mainland. The aircraft which took off at around 8 p.m. included 49 Squadron's Hampden P4403 EA-M bearing a distinctive 'Pinocchio' emblem beneath the cockpit. It was the aircraft of Flight Lieutenant Roderick 'Babe' Learoyd. With the unflappable Learoyd, on his twenty-fifth bombing sortie, was an experienced crew: the navigator and bomb aimer was Pilot Officer John Lewis, the wireless operator and dorsal air gunner was Flight Sergeant Walter Ellis and the ventral air gunner was Leading Aircraftman William Rich.

Roderick 'Babe' Learoyd was born in Folkestone, Kent, on 5 February 1913. He was educated at Hydreye House Preparatory School, Baldstow, Sussex, and Wellington College, Berkshire. After leaving school, Learoyd attended the Chelsea College of Aeronautical and Automobile Engineering in London. After working as a fruit farmer in Argentina and then a motor engineer back in Britain, Learoyd enlisted in the RAF and was given a short-service commission in March 1936. He graduated in December 1936 and was posted to 49 Squadron. Learoyd flew Hawker Hind light bombers from RAF Worthy Down, Hampshire, before 49 Squadron moved to RAF Scampton, Lincolnshire.

On the night of 12 August 1940, the Handley Page Hampden aircraft, the so-called 'flying glass house', that Learoyd and others were flying was already in urgent need of replacement: not only did it lack power but it was highly vulnerable to enemy fire. By 11.05 p.m., Learoyd's aircraft was just ten miles north of its target. Each aircraft had been instructed to strike its target at pre-set intervals while four of the Hampdens had orders to launch a diversionary raid. Unfortunately, two of the Hampdens failed to identify their target and, instead of bombing the canal, they hit the nearby island of Texel. This left just five Hampdens to target the canal and Learoyd's crew knew they would be the last to attack – and therefore the most vulnerable.

Squadron Leader 'Jamie' Pitcairn-Hill and his crew, of 83 Squadron, were the first to attack. They, like those after them, had to fly between two rows of well-placed flak guns. Pitcairn-Hill dropped the aircraft to just 100 feet through a mass of shells and tracer fire before dropping his bombs. The aircraft was hit several times but it banked away and headed for home. The next Hampden, flown by Pilot Officer E. H. Ross, an Australian, was hit shortly after entering the 'flak lane'. The aircraft and its four crew were lost. Flying Officer R. Mulligan, another Australian, was the third pilot to take his Hampden into the target area only for his port engine to be hit by anti-aircraft fire short of the bomb-dropping point. Mulligan acted quickly: he jettisoned his bombs, took his aircraft to 2,000 feet and gave the order to bale out. All four crew survived and were taken as prisoners of war. The fourth aircraft was flown by Pilot Officer Mathews. His crew dropped their bombs successfully but their aircraft was also hit and had to limp home on one engine.

Finally, it was the turn of P4403, flown by Learoyd. Having already dropped to 300 feet three miles north of the target, Learoyd made a shallow dive attack levelling out at 150 feet above the canal that reflected the half-full moon. Like the four pilots before him, Learoyd flew into the blinding glare of searchlights, but by then they were also entering a 'flak lane' where the German gunners had calculated the height of the arriving aircraft. Unable to see ahead of him, Learoyd flew through the gauntlet of flak relying solely on Lewis's instruments for his direction. As they entered the 'flak lane', Ellis and Rich were blasting away at the searchlight positions on

Above: Acting Flying Officer (later Acting Wing Commander) David 'Wilkie' Wilkerson was awarded the DFC in March 1942 and the DSO in May 1944 for his bravery and leadership as a bomber pilot. He and a comrade were killed when their aircraft inexplicably crashed as it returned from a visit to RAF Rednal, Shropshire, in September 1944.

Above left: During and between the First and Second World Wars Air Commodore Arthur 'Father' Wray was decorated five times for gallantry. He was known as 'Father' during the latter conflict because of his age and his protective attitude to his young airmen.

Above centre: Squadron Leader Keith 'Jimmy' Thiele, from the Royal New Zealand Air Force (RNZAF), was one of the few pilots to enjoy a successful career as both a bomber and a fighter pilot during the Second World War. Between August 1942 and May 1945, he was awarded the DSO, along with the DFC and two Bars.

Above right: Flying Officer Leslie Manser was awarded a posthumous VC in October 1942 when he sacrificed his own life to save the crew of his Manchester bomber after it was badly damaged during the first 1,000-bomber raid on a German city – Cologne – in May 1942.

W/O. NORMAN CYRIL JACKSON, V.C.
The Victoria Cross has been awarded to Sergeant (now W/O.) Norman Cyril Jackson, R.A.F.V.R., 106 Squadron, for conspicuous bravery when he was flight engineer in a Lancaster detailed to attack Schweinfurt on the night of April 26, 1944. Though wounded, Sgt. Jackson climbed out and back along the fuselage to the starboard wing where a fire had been started near a petrol tank by an enemy fighter. Though burnt, he made repeated attempts to conquer the flames. Finally, the captain gave the order to abandon aircraft and Sgt. Jackson was taken prisoner.

Above left: Wing Commander Hugh Malcolm wa awarded a posthumous VC in April 1943 after courageously flying in daylight with nine other Blenheim bombers to a battle area without figh support. One by one the aircraft were picked o by Messerschmitt 109 fighters over North Africa. Malcolm and his three crew were the last to be shot down and killed in December 1942.

Above centre: Already the holder of a DFC, Flight Lieutenant David Lord was awarded a posthumous VC in November 1945 after a courageous, but ill-fated, low-level mission to drop supplies to ground troops in Arnhem in September 1944. After his Dakota bomber was he desperately tried to save his crew. All but the navigator, who had been flung from the aircraft as they put on their parachutes, perished when the aircraft fell apart in mid-air.

Above right: Sergeant Dennis Bowers was awarded the CGM in May 1945 for his bravery while serving as a flight engineer with 156 Squadron, a Lancaster bomber unit. During a bombing raid on Germany in March 1945 one of his legs was nearly severed by a flak hit, but despite this he helped his injured pilot land the badly damaged aircraft.

Left: A report of the VC awarded in October 1945 to Sergeant (later Warrant Officer) Norman Jackson for his bravery when, as a flight engine on a Lancaster bomber, he climbed along the to of the fuselage of his burning aircraft at night, at 20,000 feet and 200 mph, to try to extinguish the flames caused by enemy fire. He fell, but hi burning parachute opened and he was taken as prisoner of war.

Top: Flight Lieutenant John Broadley (right) makes adjustments to Wing Commander (later Group Captain) Charles 'Pick' Pickard's life jacket for a promotional film in 1943. Broadley was awarded three gallantry medals during the war, but he and Pickard were killed when their Mosquito was shot down at the end of a daring attack on Amiens Prison in February 1944.

Above: Squadron Leader (later Group Captain) Charles 'Pick' Pickard, in his role as the commanding officer of 51 Squadron, examines a captured German helmet after Operation Biting – the successful Bruneval raid of February 1942. Between July 1940 and March 1943, Pickard was awarded the DSO and two Bars, and the DFC.

Above right: Flight Lieutenant (later Wing Commander) Roderick 'Babe' Learoyd was awarded the VC in August 1940 for his bravery in attacking the Dortmund-Ems Canal. After the successful mission earlier that month,

Learoyd flew his badly damaged Hampden bomber back to RAF Scampton, Lincolnshire.

Right: A newspaper report of the posthumous VC awarded in November 1943 to Flying Officer Lloyd (also know by his second name of Allan) Trigg, the only recipient to receive the decoration solely on evidence from the enemy. Trigg, from the Royal New Zealand Air Force (RNZAF), was shot down and killed in August 1943 after a daring attack on a German U-boat. He had earlier been awarded the DFC.

FLYING OFFICER L. A. TRIGG, V.C.
Flying Officer Alan Trigg, R.N.Z.A.F., is the first airman engaged in operations against U-boats to be awarded the V.C. He is reported missing, believed killed. He attacked a surfaced U-boat with his Liberator in flames. The submarine sank, and the Liberator dived into the sea with her gallant captain and crew.

Above left: Flying Officer (later Wing Commander) Adrian 'Warby' Warburton inspired the film *The Malta Story* with his daring reconnaissance flying from the besieged island. He was awarded the DSO and Bar, and the DFC and two Bars, between February 1941 and August 1943. Warburton disappeared on a mission in April 1944 and his aircraft was only discovered, buried in a Bavarian field, in 2002.

Above right: Squadron Leader Manfred Czernin, a Berlin-born count, was a pilot and, later, a Special Operations Executive (SOE) agent. His bravery in the air and on the ground was recognised with the awards of the DSO, MC and DFC between October 1940 and October 1945.

Below: Flight Sergeant Leslie Hyder shares a joke with a nurse treating him as he recovered from serious facial and leg injuries received during an attack on a large car plant near Turin, Italy, in November 1942. Hyder, who along with his fellow crew flew their damaged Stirling bomber back to the UK, was awarded the DFM in February 1943.

Captain Edward Maslen-Jones was awarded the DFC and the MC in 1945 for bravery in Burma in support of the 14th Army's operations against the Japanese. As an air observer, he preferred to fly his Auster reconnaissance aircraft alone, unarmed and without a parachute. He is pictured both during the war and as he is today, aged ninety-two. Maslen-Jones's gallantry and service medals, along with his Certificate of Gallantry, are also shown.

CERTIFICATE OF GALLANTRY

To:- 134644 Lt (T/Capt) Edward Walter Maslen-Jones
Royal Artillery, 656 Air OP Squadron

Your name has been brought to my notice for GALLANTRY IN ACTION.

...u for the fine example you ...lace on record my high ...ur soldierly qualities.

...ris Mountbatten

Date: 16 Nov 44

SUPREME ALLIED COMMANDER
SOUTH EAST ASIA COMMAND

Left: Leading Aircraftman (later Corporal) Ernest Coxhall was awarded the Military Medal in October 1945 for his bravery while serving with the little-known Royal Air Force Serving Commando. As an instrument repairer, he broke cover, under shellfire, to rescue wounded comrades from their damaged Dakota aircraft during heavy fighting in the Burma Campaign.

THE ASHCROFT COLLECTION

SCOPE FEATURES

MIKE FINN-KELCEY

ILN / MARY EVANS

Above left: Flight Lieutenant Sydney Dowse was shot down in September 1941 while on a reconnaissance mission to photograph German battleships. Nicknamed 'The Laughing Boy' for his cheery demeanour, he was awarded the MC in August 1946 for his courage in repeatedly trying to escape as a prisoner of war. Dowse spent nearly four years in captivity.

Above: Friends reunited: Flight Lieutenant Sydney Dowse (right) and Squadron Leader Jimmy James take part in celebrations in March 2004 to mark the sixtieth anniversary of the 'Great Escape', when some 200 tried to dig their way to freedom from Stalag Luft III. Of the seventy-six prisoners who escaped, all but three were recaptured. Fifty of those caught were shot on Hitler's orders.

Above: Flight Lieutenant (later Squadron Leader) Kenneth Letford was awarded a Bar to his DFC in July 1949 for his part in assisting HMS Amethyst during the 'Yangtse Incident' earlier that year. During the Second World War, while serving with Bomber Command, he had been awarded the DSO and Bar, as well as the DFC.

Above: Captain (later Major) Jeff Niblett was awarded the DFC in October 1982 for bravery during the Falklands War when his own and another helicopter were attacked by Argentine Pucara aircraft. Niblett's helicopter eventually emerged unscathed but the other one was shot down.

Top left: Flight Lieutenant (later Squadron Leader) Peter Middleton, of the Royal Australian Air Force (RAAF), was awarded the DFC in December 1952 for gallantry in the Korean War. Many of his 189 sorties in his Meteor aircraft took place in the face of intense anti-aircraft fire.

Above left: Warrant Officer (later Captain) Bill Scarratt in the cockpit of his helicopter. He was awarded the DFC in March 1975 for courage when his aircraft was attacked as he dropped off a patrol in South Armagh, Northern Ireland. The area was known as 'bandit country' because it was full of armed terrorists.

Left: Flight Lieutenant (later Air Commodore) Vincent Hill's thirty-four year flying career saw him participate in three wars: the Second World War, the Korean War and the Vietnam War. He received the DFC and Bar, along with the AFC, between September 1953 and January 1962.

Above: Acting Sergeant (later Lieutenant-Commander, Royal Naval Reserve) William 'Uncle Bill' O'Brien received the DFM in October 1982 for repeated bravery while flying his Gazelle helicopter during the Falklands War. His military career eventually spanned thirty-eight years and he served, aged fifty-five, in Afghanistan as recently as 2010.

Left: Staff Sergeant (later Warrant Officer) Shaun Wyatt immediately after receiving his DFC at Buckingham Palace. His decoration was announced in April 1994 for his bravery under fire during a massive IRA ambush of three helicopters in South Armagh, Northern Ireland, in September 1993. Wyatt flew calmly out of the ambush zone and then pursued the heavily armed terrorists from the air.

Below: Wyatt's gallantry and service medals: his DFC was one of only three such decorations for the entire period of the 'Troubles' in Northern Ireland.

either side. Two shells smashed into the aircraft in quick succession: one went through the starboard wing and the other passed between the cockpit and the engine. However, at 11.23 p.m., Lewis released the special canister bombs from their racks that fell directly on to the target. At this point, Learoyd quickly pulled his aircraft into a banking turn and climbed away from the worst of the flak. The four crew were uninjured but the aircraft was badly damaged: checks revealed that the flaps were inoperative and the hydraulic system was ruptured, which left the undercarriage indicator useless. The seriousness of the crew's predicament was momentarily lightened, however, when Ellis announced that one of their carrier pigeons had laid an egg during the height of the attack . . . Learoyd was able to nurse his damaged aircraft back to Scampton, where he decided it was unwise to attempt a landing in the dark. After several circuits, he eventually landed his Hampden without mishap at dawn – just a few minutes before 5 a.m.

The mission had been a great success. The canal remained closed for ten days, creating a huge problem for Germany's proposed invasion of mainland Britain. It is widely believed that by delaying the movement of large barges and motor boats from the Rhineland to the invasion ports, the German D-Day was postponed from 15 September to 21 September.

Learoyd's VC was announced just eight days later, on 20 August, when he became the first member of Bomber Command to receive the VC. As well as detailing the mission, his citation stated: 'This officer as first pilot of a Hampden aircraft has repeatedly shown the highest conception of his duty and complete indifference to personal danger in making attacks at the lowest altitudes regardless of opposition . . . The high courage, skill and determination which this officer has

301

invariably displayed, on many occasions in the face of the enemy, sets an example which is unsurpassed.'

Rich's DFM was announced on 22 October 1940 and his citation stated:

Leading Aircraftman Rich is an armourer and member of a ground crew who volunteered for training as a part-time Air Gunner. He has shown exceptional keenness and ability in his work, both in the air and on the ground, and by his enthusiasm, skill and courage very quickly became operationally fit as an Air Gunner. He has carried out a total of 8 operations against the enemy during the course of which he has completed 49 hours flying.

He was the Air Gunner in the aircraft flown by Flt. Lt. R. A. B. Learoyd, V.C., when a low level attack was carried out on the Dortmund–Ems Canal. In this and in all other operations in which he has taken part, L. A. C. Rich has shown outstanding skill and courage in operating his guns against the enemy defences. By his enthusiasm, courage and devotion to duty, he has set an outstanding example to other airmen in this squadron.

Rich is believed to be the first leading aircraftman of the Second World War to be awarded the DFM. Furthermore, the recommendation for his award was endorsed by the legendary 'Bomber' Harris, who wrote: 'Strongly recommended. A keen and efficient volunteer for dangerous duty without the pay and rank of regular crew.'

Ellis's DFM was announced a month later, on 22 November 1940, and his citation stated:

This N.C.O. has carried out a total of 39 operations against the enemy during the course of which he has completed 230 hours flying as a Wireless Operator/Air Gunner. Throughout these operations, Sergeant Ellis has shown outstanding ability, determination and devotion to duty, and has been of the greatest assistance to his Pilot, both as an Air Gunner and as a Wireless Operator.

Amongst other notable and successful operations in which he has taken part, he was Wireless Operator/Air Gunner in Flt. Lt. Learoyd's aircraft which carried out a successful low-level attack on the Dortmund–Ems Canal. His work has always been of the highest order and his efficiency and enthusiasm have been an inspiration to other Wireless Operator/Air Gunners in the squadron.

Learoyd later gave a speech about the action for which he was awarded the VC:

So, coming down to 300 feet at a distance of four to five miles north of the target, I commenced my run in, the aqueduct being clearly silhouetted against the light of the moon. Within a mile of the target I came down to 150 feet. By this time, however, Jerry had got our range to a nicety, and was blazing away with everything he'd got.

The machine was repeatedly hit and large pieces of the main plane torn away. I was completely blinded by the glare of the searchlights and had to ask my navigator to guide me in over the target. This he did with the utmost coolness and praiseworthy precision. Then, suddenly, I heard him shout: 'Bomb gone.' The delayed-action bomb was fitted with a parachute which, provided the altitude was sufficiently low, gave us a chance of seeing just where it fell. This is what happened on this occasion. For I heard a sudden triumphant shout from the wireless officer: 'Got it!' The bomb had fallen on the aqueduct, which, as a result of the combined attack, was destroyed, and our object successfully accomplished. Then for home!

Learoyd's VC was awarded in an investiture at Buckingham Palace on 9 September 1940, by which time he had been taken off operations and had been promoted to squadron leader. He was further honoured in November 1940 when he received the Freedom of the Borough of New Romney, Kent.

Learoyd resumed operational flying on 28 February 1941 when he was appointed commanding officer of 83 Squadron at RAF Scampton. In June that year, however, he took up a new post as Wing Commander Flying at 14 Operational Training Unit (OTU), RAF Cottesmore, Rutland. In December 1941, Learoyd succeeded to the command of 44 Squadron, based at RAF Waddington, Lincolnshire, and in May 1942 he was posted to 25 OTU, RAF Finningley, Yorkshire, where he carried out more instructional duties. From then until the end of hostilities in Europe Learoyd remained non-operational, with postings to the Air Ministry and two further OTUs (109 and 107). However, in May 1945, he returned to flying when he joined 48 (Dakota) Squadron, which was posted to West Africa the following month. It was not until 14 October 1946 that Learoyd was finally demobilised. Little is known about the subsequent careers and lives of the rest of his crew.

Learoyd was one of just seven VCs from the RAF to survive the war. For his first three years as a civilian, he worked for the Malayan civil aviation department, but he then returned to

Britain in 1950 and accepted a job with a tractor and road construction company. In 1953, he became the export sales manager to the Austin Motor Company. Learoyd died in Rustington, Sussex, on 24 January 1996, aged eighty-two.

In recent years, as they became available, I have not only bought the VC and service medals of Learoyd, but also the gallantry and service medals of Rich and Ellis. I have taken great pleasure in reuniting the decorations of three of the four men who flew in the same aircraft on that special night of 12 August 1940.

FLIGHT LIEUTENANT (LATER GROUP CAPTAIN) PERCY CHARLES PICKARD
RAF
DECORATIONS: DISTINGUISHED FLYING CROSS (DFC), DISTINGUISHED SERVICE ORDER (DSO) AND TWO BARS
GAZETTED: 30 JULY 1940, 7 MARCH 1941, 26 MAY 1942 AND 26 MARCH 1943

SERGEANT (LATER FLIGHT LIEUTENANT) JOHN ALAN BROADLEY
RAF
DECORATIONS: DISTINGUISHED FLYING MEDAL (DFM), DISTINGUISHED FLYING CROSS (DFC) AND DISTINGUISHED SERVICE ORDER (DSO)
GAZETTED: 23 SEPTEMBER 1941, 20 APRIL 1943 AND 19 OCTOBER 1943

Charles 'Pick' Pickard was undoubtedly one of the greatest pilots of the Second World War, a unique character who was immortalised in the 1941 film *Target for Tonight*. His long operational career included participation in some of the most daring episodes of the aerial conflict, most notably the epic Amiens Prison raid of February 1944. In the air, he was fearless, determined, skilled, tactically astute and a great leader of men. On the ground, Pickard was unmistakable: 6 feet 4 inches tall, blond, debonair and somewhat shy, except while doing his party piece of being lifted by his feet to the Mess ceiling to drink a pint of beer upside down. Invariably, he had his loyal Old English Sheepdog, Ming, at his feet and his pipe clenched between his teeth. Pickard formed a great friendship and working partnership with his co-pilot, John 'Bill' Broadley, and they flew together on the Amiens Prison raid.

Pickard was born in Handsworth, Sheffield, on 16 May 1915. The youngest of five children born to a stone merchant and his wife, he moved with his family to Hampstead, north London, in 1920. Once in the capital, Percy Pickard, the father of young Pickard and his four siblings, ran a successful catering business. The young Charles was educated at Framlingham College in Suffolk, where he starred on the sports field but not in the classroom. He was a good shot and an able horseman who thrived on an outdoor life. At seventeen, Pickard, like many young public schoolboys of the time, went to farm in Kenya, where he stayed for four years and became an accomplished polo player. In November 1935, he joined the King's African Rifles Reserve as a territorial. In 1936, he returned to Britain set on a career in the military. He failed to qualify as an Army officer but was accepted by the RAF. He was commissioned in 1937 as a pilot officer in the RAF reserve and was posted to Bomber Command. By 1939, Pickard was assistant and personal pilot to Air Marshal Sir John Baldwin, the commandant of the RAF College at Cranwell, Lincolnshire. Against his parents' wishes, in November 1939 Pickard married Dorothy Hodgkin, the daughter of an Army lieutenant colonel. She gave birth to a son in 1943.

John Broadley, meanwhile, was born in Leyburn, near Richmond, Yorkshire, in 1920. Educated at Richmond School, Broadley enlisted in the RAF in 1939. After training as a sergeant observer, he flew many missions over Germany during the first two years of the war. By the time Pickard forged his partnership with Broadley, the former had already survived some formidable scrapes, namely with 7 and 21 Squadrons.

With his wife, Dorothy, and their dog, Charles Pickard moved to quarters at Newmarket, Suffolk, from where he and other Wellington crews from 99 Squadron flew almost non-stop sorties during the Norwegian and French campaigns. On the night of 19 June 1940, Pickard's aircraft was hit by flak as he attacked an industrial complex east of the Ruhr. With his starboard engine failing, Pickard lost height and, although he struck out for the coast, he was eventually forced to ditch his aircraft in the North Sea. It was 3.20 a.m. and, at that very moment, back in England Ming awoke and became restless. Aware of the dog's sixth sense, Pickard's wife rang the operations room and was told that 'O-for-Orange' (his aircraft) had gone missing. By this time Pickard and his crew were using his shoes to bale water from their leaking dinghy – a task they continued to perform for the next fourteen hours, while navigating with the aid of a button compass given to Pickard by his sister, Helena. The crew were blissfully unaware that the sea around them was mined, but somehow they negotiated it and were eventually picked up by an Air Sea Rescue launch the following afternoon.

Following his rescue, Pickard was awarded the DFC and his citation, published on 30 July 1940, detailed his coolness during the North Sea rescue. It also stated: 'This officer has carried out 21 bombing raids over Norway, Belgium, France, Germany and Italy . . . Flight Lieutenant Pickard has displayed persistent determination and outstanding skill, and has at all times set an example of the highest order.'

By late July, Pickard had completed thirty-one operations over Europe and was due a much deserved rest. Instead, he took command of 311 Squadron. Broadley, his navigator since earlier in the year, went with him. 311 was the first Czech bomber squadron in Britain and Pickard put the bomber crews through rigorous training from their base at RAF East Wretham, Norfolk. The Czech airmen spoke little English and one of them in particular exasperated Pickard with his inability to carry out basic piloting skills. It was only after they had landed that the individual, when confronted by Pickard about his failings, said: 'Me no pilot, me air gunner.' Yet by the end of the year, the Czechs were in good shape and were often accompanied on their sorties by Pickard himself, acting only as a passenger.

On 7 March 1941, Pickard was awarded the DSO and his citation stated:

Since joining No. 311 Czech Squadron in July 1940, this officer has invariably taken out new Czech crews on their initial operation, or first long distance mission. On such occasions, he has been the only British member amongst the crews who have been inspired by his splendid leadership and example. On one occasion it was undoubtedly due to his determined efforts that one Czech crew was rescued after being adrift in the North Sea for over 13 hours. On another occasion when a crew was forced down in the North Sea, his persistence, and good airmanship in failing light, and his sound use of recognition signals, enabled surface craft to effect a rescue. His complete disregard for danger was particularly shown on an occasion when a fully loaded bomber crashed and caught fire. He led a rescue party and personally extricated two members of the crew and succeeded in eventually conveying them to safety, although compelled to remain prone in the danger area during the explosion of some of the bombs. He has displayed coolness and courage of a high order and, by his magnificent work, contributed largely to the present efficiency of the Squadron.

March 1941 saw Pickard reluctantly dispatched to the Crown Film Unit to work on *Target for Tonight*. His real-life persona was transformed into 'Squadron Leader Dickson', the skipper of 'F-for-Freddie'. Harry Watt, the film's director, noted sadly – four years later, at the end of the war – that most of those immortalised on celluloid had been killed in action.

In May 1941, Pickard was awarded the Czech Military Cross and on the 14th of the same month he joined 9 Squadron (Wellingtons) as a flight commander. He flew on raids to numerous German cities with Broadley as his navigator. By August 1941, Pickard had flown sixty-five operational sorties and, although he was again due a rest, he took part in two 'special duties' trips to Holland and Occupied France to deliver half a million cigarettes. On 11 November 1941, Pickard was promoted to wing commander and took command of 51 Squadron, based at RAF Dishforth, Yorkshire. Yet again, he flew with Broadley who, by then, had been awarded the DFM and had recently been commissioned. 51 Squadron, operating Whitley aircraft, was responsible for 'special duties' and operated under the auspices of Lord Mountbatten's Combined Operations Headquarters. On 7 January 1942, Pickard flew a reconnaissance sortie over the French port of St Nazaire. However, 51 Squadron became best known, under Pickard's command, for its part in the Bruneval raid of 27/28 February 1942.

By early 1942, the Germans were using Würzburg radar which, unlike its predecessor (Freya radar), was capable of plotting with its 'box' the altitude as well as the course of enemy aircraft. The scientific branch of British Intelligence was keen to examine the radar system and so a plan was hatched to raid the installation near Bruneval, France, and seize its equipment. The raid was codenamed Operation Biting and it was due to be carried out by 119 men, including those from the 2nd Parachute Battalion and the Royal Engineers. Pickard was responsible for the aerial aspects of the raid and twelve of his squadron's Whitleys were adapted for the role, with each due to take ten men. On the night of the raid, Pickard confided his reservations about the operation to Flight Sergeant C. W. H. Cox, who was to dismantle the Würzburg instrument once on the ground. Pickard told him: 'I feel like a bloody murderer.' However, the raid was an overwhelming success, even though Pickard's aircraft was one of two to suffer the worst of the flak.

Several days later the King and Queen visited Dishforth to meet some of the men who had played a prominent role in the daring raid. George VI got into a rather unusual conversation with Pickard when he asked him about the significance of the 'ceiling decoration'. Pickard, who had been unaware that black footprints remained on the walls and ceiling, replied with refreshing honesty: 'I am afraid it's the result of the Mess party to celebrate our return from Bruneval. At the height of the proceedings my shoes were removed, my feet blacked with boot polish, chairs stacked on each other, and I was perched at the top making footprints as you can see. I'm sorry, Sir.' The King, clearly intrigued, then asked: 'But what are those especially large blobs at the centre of the ceiling?' Pickard replied: 'I'm afraid to say, Sir, those are the marks of my bottom.' Meanwhile, it was for his planning and execution of the Bruneval raid that Pickard was awarded a Bar to his DSO on 26 May 1942.

After a short period apart, Pickard and Broadley were reunited again in October 1942 when they were both posted to 161 'Moonbeam' Squadron at RAF Tempsford, Bedfordshire. The mysterious base was home to 161 and 138 Squadrons and was used to fly Special Operations Executive (SOE) agents into enemy territory and to provide supplies to the French Resistance. Pickard, flying Hudsons and Lysanders, thrived on his new 'moonlight' duties as did Broadley, who had flown before with a 'special duties' squadron. Inevitably, there were more near-misses: in November 1942, after a drop and flying a Lysander, Pickard continually had to avoid the attention of three Luftwaffe night fighters that pursued him well beyond the enemy coastline. Early in 1943, Pickard completed another dangerous mission for which the Operations Record Book for 161 Squadron recorded: 'the C.O. Wing Commander Pickard, D.S.O., D.F.C., pulled off a particularly hazardous job in a Lysander.' Pickard flew an agent and 'four suitcases' to the Issoudon area of France on the night of 26/27 January 1943. However, there was confusion over whether he or the Resistance would signal first, which meant he spent too long in the air and only just made it back to the UK at 6.30 a.m. with near-empty fuel tanks.

An injury caused by more antics in the Mess resulted in Pickard flying several sorties with one hand in plaster, but he never considered standing down to allow his injury to heal. Yet another close call occurred on 24/25 February (see the following joint write-up on Flight Lieutenants Henry Figg and Albert Putt, pp. 271–76).

Pickard was awarded a second Bar to his DSO on 26 March 1943 and his citation stated: 'This officer has completed a very large number of operational missions and achieved much success. By his outstanding leadership, exceptional ability and fine fighting qualities, he has contributed in a large measure to the high standard of morale of No. 161 Squadron.' By May, Pickard had flown more than 100 operations while Broadley, who had flown more than seventy, was promoted to flight lieutenant, having been awarded the DFC on 20 April 1943. Meanwhile, Pickard was promoted to group captain and, in July, was appointed as station commander of RAF Sculthorpe, Norfolk. Here he encountered 2 Group's legendary commander, Basil Embry, perhaps one of the few men to have survived more scrapes than Pickard himself. Embry was hugely impressed by Pickard and, in October 1943, appointed him to command No. 140 Wing of the 2nd Tactical Air Force (TAF), which consisted of three Mosquito squadrons. Pickard, like Embry, seized every opportunity to lead his men on operations. The speciality of No. 140 Wing became daylight, low-level precision bombing and, typically, Pickard led the first raid. On 3 October 1943, Pickard and Broadley were part of an operation that targeted the Pont Château power station. As they approached the target, their aircraft was hit by a curtain of flak and Pickard's starboard engine caught fire and seized. However, he made it back to Predannack airfield in Cornwall. On 19 October 1943, Broadley was awarded the DSO and his citation stated: 'Flight Lieutenant Broadley is a navigator of exceptional merit. He has completed a large number of sorties, rendering most valuable service, and his efforts have contributed to the successes achieved.'

There were many more operations in December 1943 and January 1944 but by early February 1944 plans were afoot for Pickard and Broadley's most daring mission to date. Air Marshal Sir Arthur Coningham, the Commander-in-Chief of 2nd TAF, asked Basil Embry if he thought 2 Group's Mosquitos were capable of carrying out an operation to release some 700 inmates, including French Resistance fighters facing trial and death in Amiens Prison (100 of the executions were imminent). Embry concluded that the mission could succeed but that some French prisoners would inevitably die. Since the prisoners had said they would prefer to lose their lives at the hands of the RAF than the Gestapo, Embry and an experienced team of specialists were detailed to plan Operation Jericho. On 8 February Embry met Pickard and asked him to be his number two and to select eighteen crews for the operation. Embry used a specially constructed model of Amiens Prison to outline the plan: three waves of six Mosquitos, under fighter escort, would be involved. The intention was for the first wave to breach the twenty-feet-high by three-feet-thick prison walls and destroy the German guardhouse. Then it was hoped the second wave could drop their bombs on the walls with the ambitious aim of jarring open the cell doors. The third wave was briefed to stand by in the event of the first or second wave being unsuccessful or if they were needed to attack another target. The prisoners had been warned in advance that this was their opportunity to escape and that fellow members of the Resistance would be waiting outside the prison walls to aid their breakout. Knowing that most prisoners assembled in the central hall shortly before noon, this was the time chosen as the ideal hour to launch the attack.

Coningham quickly decided that Embry could not in any circumstances fly in the raid and so Pickard was left in command of the operation in the air. Poor weather prevented the plan being executed for more than a week but British Intelligence then learnt that the Gestapo intended to execute 100 prisoners within a couple of days. So, on 17 February, Embry was briefed that it was now or never: so, too, the nineteen crews (including a photographic unit that was to record the results of the operation from the air). Snow fell the next morning but the raid went ahead regardless. Pickard ended his briefing with the words: 'It's a death or glory job, boys.' After take-off, four aircraft became separated from the main party in the white-out conditions and shortly afterwards, as the Mosquitos linked up with their fighter escort, two of them nearly collided. But as the Operation Jericho team flew over the Channel they were soon in bright sunshine. As they made for their target, they flew at just fifteen feet above the Albert–Amiens road that led to the prison. Brilliant flying skills meant the attack was successful but, as Pickard ordered everyone to head for home, a 464 Mosquito flown by Squadron Leader A. I. McRitchie was hit by flak, instantly killing the navigator, Flight Lieutenant R. W. Sampson. The pilot made a forced landing on French soil and was taken prisoner. Pickard and Broadley were circling over the wreckage, almost certainly to assess if there were any survivors, when 'F-for-Freddie' was suddenly attacked by a Fw 190 fighter. The Mosquito's tail section was shot away by the first burst of fire, causing it to flip on to its back, dive into the ground and explode on impact. The seemingly invincible duo were killed: Pickard was twenty-eight, Broadley twenty-three. Pickard's pilot's 'wings' and medal ribbons were, in fact, taken off his battle dress by a young French girl who found his body and they were returned to his widow after the war. Ming, his dog, was said to be inconsolable.

I purchased Pickard's gallantry and service medals at auction along with various documents and memorabilia, including his pilot's logbooks. The last entry for 18 February 1944 stated: 'Operations, Special Target, Nr Amiens, Missing'. A later stamp recorded: 'Killed in Action'. I subsequently purchased Broadley's gallantry and service medals privately along with his logbook, photographs and various documents. It is thoroughly appropriate that the decorations of these two heroes, who flew together and died together, should be united so long after their deaths.

There have been countless tributes over the years to Pickard and Broadley. However, the contribution of the former was perhaps best summed up in a single sentence by Basil Embry who said: 'It is impossible to measure Charles Pickard's loss to the RAF and Britain, but in courage, devotion to duty, fighting spirit and powers of real leadership, he stood out as one of the great airmen of the war and as a shining example of British manhood.'

LEADING AIRCRAFTMAN (LATER FLIGHT LIEUTENANT) HENRY ROBERT FIGG

RAF
DECORATIONS: DISTINGUISHED FLYING MEDAL (DFM) AND DISTINGUISHED FLYING CROSS (DFC)
GAZETTED: 5 NOVEMBER 1940 AND 26 MARCH 1943

FLIGHT LIEUTENANT ALBERT JAMES PUTT

Royal Air Force Volunteer Reserve (RAFVR)
DECORATIONS: DISTINGUISHED FLYING CROSS (DFC) AND BAR
GAZETTED: 20 SEPTEMBER 1941 AND 26 MARCH 1943

The daring night-time operation had been carefully planned between the RAF and the French Resistance. Yet it was only earlier that day, on 24 February 1943, that Flight Lieutenants Albert Putt and Henry Figg learnt they were to fly that night deep into Occupied France. Putt was the first to learn of his role after being summoned to a morning briefing in the presence of the legendary 'Pick' Pickard at RAF Tempsford, Bedfordshire. RAF Tempsford was home to 138 and 161 Squadrons, the so-called 'cloak and dagger' specialists responsible for Special Operations Executive (SOE) activities in Occupied Europe. The briefing was low key and relaxed and the two men were invited to what might be 'quite a party'. Putt was new to 'special duties' but he was an experienced formation gunnery leader and the veteran of two tours of operations. He was also honoured to have been chosen to be a member of Pickard's crew. It was only as Putt was preparing to leave the briefing that Pickard asked him if he knew how to fire a Sten gun. Putt admitted that he did not, so, after leaving the meeting, he found an aerodrome defence officer to give him the 'gen'. That afternoon Putt and Figg learnt the details of their mission: they were to fly in a Hudson aircraft – one belonging to the King's Flight – to Tournais in full moonlight. Once they had arrived, they would land in a field that the French Resistance had turned into a makeshift runway by laying out hundreds of bricks on the turf. The plan was that, after spending just seven minutes on French soil, the aircraft would take on seven passengers and return to England in the dead of night.

Pickard, Putt and Figg ran through the final details of their mission at 9.45 p.m. and took off forty-five minutes later, setting a course for the south coast. Other than some 'light flak' over the French coast, their journey was so quiet that Putt wondered if the Germans had, for some reason, allowed them to enter unmolested. The trio had been flying for three hours when they spotted the red and white torches of their 'reception committee': the French Resistance members who had been waiting patiently for their arrival. Their night-time landing in a makeshift 'aerodrome' was made even more hazardous by a haze which obscured a large part of the field. After twenty circuits, which the three men feared would alert the Germans to their presence, Pickard managed to land the aircraft. Even after Pickard landed, he found excitable French torch-bearers running all around the field, thereby making the flare path hard to navigate. To add to his troubles, one hand was in plaster thanks to his falling from a beam in the Mess while celebrating his son's birthday. So this meant that Figg had to operate the throttles as well as the wheels and flaps.

Putt, armed with his Sten gun, threw open the door ready

to check on the seven passengers. Instead, a mass of people surged towards him, many shouting, waving and gesticulating wildly. Despite the loud roar from the engines, forward progress was slow and Putt struggled in his 'Franglais' to find out the cause of the problem. Eventually, a Frenchman grabbed him by the arms and pointed directly at the cause of their consternation: the wheels of the aircraft had sunk almost to the axles in the soft mud.

Putt reported the problem to Pickard, who switched off the engines. The airmen then debated their dilemma, concluding they had two options: to 'de-bog' the aircraft (which might take a long time) or to burn it (so it did not fall into enemy hands) and make good their escape overland. Putt, the oldest member of the crew, was allowed to decide the course of action they should take. He opted to try to fly rather than escape on foot, but the men were concerned that, while they were digging the aircraft out, the Germans might arrive. Pickard took control of the situation asking the locals in his poor French: 'Qui est le chef de cette bande de sauvages?' ('Who is in charge of this band of savages?'). When a young Frenchman volunteered that he was in charge, Pickard admonished him: 'Well, you've got nothing to be proud about. Not only have you landed me in the back yard of a brick factory, but in the centre of a bog into the bargain.'

Moments later, the Frenchman and his countrymen were digging away as fast as they could. The first attempt to move the aircraft ended with the port wheel getting stuck in the mud after the Hudson had taxied for only about twenty yards. By then, so many locals were milling around in the darkness that Figg was worried one of them would be struck by a rotating propeller. When a local produced an ancient horse with chains, the airmen burst into laughter at the prospect of it moving the Hudson. However, the animal dragged the aircraft from the mud and a second, successful, attempt was made to taxi. This time the Hudson was able to move on to firmer ground and Pickard, accompanied in the Hudson by Figg, moved to the position selected by the Resistance leader for the take-off. Pickard was still unhappy with the makeshift runway and he told Putt to direct it towards the furthest corner of the field. Putt was saying his final farewells when two cars, which everyone assumed to be full of German soldiers, sped through the gate leading to the field. The aircraft charged down the 'runway' and took off. Moments later, there was a crunching noise as the starboard wing smashed through the tree tops. The next day, Peter Churchill, one of the SOE agents, and who was working with the French Resistance, found a thirty-inch-long strip of wing in the field.

However, the aircraft flew on to the French coast where it was already daylight. As they were flying at only 4,000 feet, Pickard feared they would be easily picked off by a patrolling German fighter or an opportunist anti-aircraft gun crew, so he ordered Figg to request a fighter escort to join them before they reached Le Havre. In the end, however, the Hudson encountered no fighter aircraft. Knowing that the Hudson only had sufficient fuel for seven hours, personnel at RAF Tempsford had given up the aircraft as missing long before they returned. As they flew over Brighton, Putt pointed out the town to his relieved passengers. By the time they landed safely on the morning of 26 February, the three airmen had been gone for nine hours and forty minutes.

This special operation contributed towards Pickard's third Distinguished Service Order (DSO), Putt's second DFC and to Figg's DFC, all of which were announced on 26 March 1943. Writing about the incident later in an article entitled 'A Midnight Rendezvous', Putt told how apprehensive the team had been as they took off: 'One wondered if the Maquis – the French Resistance – had picked a field large enough, were the Germans wise to the trip and waiting for us, would we be followed by German radar? However, we were too busy and keyed up doing a job of work, but a job of an unusual nature, the sort of job one reads about in boys' books.' Putt had been awarded his first DFC on 20 September 1941 after the recommendation for his decoration praised his 'utmost enthusiasm for operation sorties'.

More is known about Figg's career than Putt's. Figg enlisted in the RAF at seventeen, and trained as a wireless operator and air gunner. His first operational posting was to 150 Squadron in France, a unit which operated under the auspices of the Advanced Air Striking Force. He was awarded the DFM on 5 November 1940 after the general recommendation for the decorations stated:

These airmen have been together as an air crew since the outbreak of war. By mutual trust and co-operation in their duties, they have produced a really first-class crew which can be relied upon to complete any air operation allotted them. Since 10th May 1940, this crew has flown in one day and eight night operations against the enemy, sometimes in very difficult weather conditions. On each occasion, the target was located and attacked and valuable reconnaissance information obtained.

After a night sortie on 14 September 1940, Figg was posted to the King's Flight at RAF Benson, Oxfordshire. His role was to convey VIPs to various functions. It meant that between the end of 1940 and January 1942, Figg completed more than 100 trips and his royal passengers included George VI. Figg returned to active service in early 1942 when 161 Squadron was reformed with men from 138 Squadron and the King's Flight. As stated, his new role soon involved secret operations over Occupied Europe, dropping off SOE and supplies. His first sortie took place on 13 February 1943 when Pickard completed the first ever Hudson landing in Occupied France. Just eleven days later, the two men, along with Putt, took part in the memorable adventure detailed above. After this mission, Figg carried out more SOE operations and was later posted to 624 Squadron. Carrying out similar operations for the more renowned 138 and 161 Squadrons, this unit kept Figg busy with eleven clandestine sorties to locations such as Sardinia, Corsica, the South of France and Yugoslavia. He was hospitalised in December 1943 but returned to flying duties in 1944, although he saw no further active service for the remainder of the war.

It is not known what happened to Figg and Putt after the war.

FLIGHT SERGEANT LESLIE ANDERSON HYDER
RAF
DECORATION: DISTINGUISHED FLYING MEDAL (DFM)
GAZETTED: 12 FEBRUARY 1943

Leslie Hyder, a former pupil of Rutherglen Academy, near Glasgow, Scotland, was working in an aircraft factory on the outbreak of hostilities in September 1939. Enlisting in the RAF on his eighteenth birthday, he trained as a pilot in Canada, where he qualified for his pilot's 'wings' in October 1941. Having then gained early operational experience in Wellington aircraft, he converted to the Stirlings of 149 Squadron. Hyder was decorated for his gallantry as second pilot in a daring raid on the occasion in which the first pilot, Flight Sergeant Rawdon 'Ron' Middleton, was awarded one of the finest VCs of the war.

Flight Sergeant Hyder took off from RAF Lakenheath, Suffolk, at 6.14 on the evening of 28 November 1942 as part of a massive night-time raid involving 228 aircraft: Lancasters, Stirlings, Halifaxes and Wellingtons. Hyder's Stirling, which contained a crew of eight, had been tasked with carrying out a special low-level attack on a car-production plant south of Turin. While over the target area, the aircraft was hit by anti-aircraft fire and a large hole was blown in the port mainplane. The damage made the Stirling difficult to fly and Hyder assisted Middleton in keeping control of the aircraft. However, a flak shell then burst in the centre of the cockpit wounding Hyder in the face and legs and rendering Middleton, who was captaining the aircraft, unconscious. When the aircraft was hit a further time, it was flying at 2,000 feet but, owing to the temporary loss of control, it dropped to 800 feet before control was regained by Hyder. With the first pilot still unconscious, Hyder decided it would be impossible to attack the target and, in order to make use of the bomb load, he closed the bomb doors and started to climb. The bombs were then dropped shortly afterwards from 1,500 feet on the outskirts of Turin.

Middleton's injuries were horrific: the flak had destroyed his right eye and exposed the bone over it, while he also had other injuries to much of his body. However, he regained consciousness shortly after the bombs were dropped and sent

Hyder to receive first aid treatment from comrades. After some brief medical aid, Hyder insisted on returning to the second pilot's seat because he feared that the captain might once more lose consciousness. Once the aircraft reached the French coast, it was engaged by enemy fighters at 6,000 feet but the co-pilots were able to take evasive action.

Over France, and by then desperately short of fuel, Middleton and Hyder discussed the best course of action. They considered abandoning their aircraft and landing in Occupied France where they would be taken as prisoners of war, but Middleton was determined to make the English coast so that his crew would be in safe hands if they were forced to bale out. During the return journey of four and a half hours, Hyder remained at Middleton's side, until, when they were over the Channel, their aircraft ran out of fuel.

The crew helped the injured Hyder to bale out from the forward escape hatch and four men followed him out of the stricken Stirling and parachuted to safety. However, the remaining three crew, including Middleton, were unable to get out of the aircraft before it crashed into the sea off Dymchurch, Kent, at around 3 a.m. on 29 November. Their bodies were later washed ashore.

Hyder's DFM was announced on 12 February 1943 after the recommendation for his award stated: 'It is considered that Flight Sergeant Hyder's quick thinking in the face of considerable difficulties and pain when he was wounded over the target area was responsible for the return of the aircraft over this country. His courage and devotion to duty in remaining beside his Captain throughout the return journey are worthy of high praise . . .' Middleton had earlier been awarded a posthumous VC.

It is not known what happened to Hyder after the war.

FLYING OFFICER LLOYD ALLAN TRIGG

Royal New Zealand Air Force (RNZAF)
DECORATIONS: DISTINGUISHED FLYING CROSS
(DFC) AND VICTORIA CROSS (VC)
GAZETTED: 16 JUNE 1943 AND 2 NOVEMBER 1943

Lloyd Trigg has the distinction of being the only recipient of the VC to receive the decoration solely on evidence given by the enemy. It was the fair treatment afforded by the British to their captives that led German naval officers to provide such a detailed eyewitness account of his gallantry that Trigg was awarded a posthumous VC. Furthermore, Trigg was the first airman to be awarded the VC for engaging a U-boat (German submarine).

Trigg was born in Houhora, New Zealand, on 5 June 1914. After university he became a farmer, but prior to the Second World War he joined the North Auckland Rifles, his local Territorial unit. On 15 June 1941, he enlisted in the RNZAF. On 1 October 1942, Trigg was promoted to flying officer and sailed for England, leaving behind his wife and their two young sons. Before leaving, he told his wife that he 'would not go looking for decorations'. At the end of November, he was posted to 200 Squadron, which was based at Yundum airstrip at the mouth of the River Gambia in West Africa.

From the start, Trigg specialised in sea operations. By the end of February 1943, he had completed nearly eighty hours of flying on reconnaissance and escort patrols but had not seen any action. This changed the following month when he attacked a U-boat with depth charges. However, he failed to score a direct hit. Two days later, he attacked another U-boat and this time a depth charge struck the submarine's bow. His determination in hunting out the enemy led to him being awarded the DFC on 16 June 1943, when his citation stated: 'During the course of a fine operational career this Officer has set a conspicuously good example of keenness to fly under all conditions.'

On 11 August 1943, Trigg displayed even greater heroism and the *London Gazette*, of 2 November 1943, takes up the story:

Flying Officer Trigg has rendered outstanding service on Convoy, Escort and Anti-Submarine Duties. He has completed 46 Operational Sorties and has invariably displayed skill and courage of a very high order. One day in August 1943, Flying Officer Trigg undertook, as Captain and Pilot, a patrol in a Liberator Bomber, although he had not previously made any Operational Sorties in that type of aircraft. After searching for eight hours, the Liberator sighted a surfaced U-boat. Flying Officer Trigg immediately prepared to attack. During the approach the aircraft received many hits from the submarine's anti-aircraft guns and burst into flames, which quickly enveloped the tail. The moment was critical. Flying Officer Trigg could have broken off the engagement and made a forced landing in the sea, but if he continued the attack the aircraft would present a no-deflection target to deadly anti-aircraft fire and every second spent in the air would increase the extent and intensity of the flames and diminish the chances of survival.

There could have been no hesitation or doubt in his mind. He maintained his course in spite of the already precarious condition of his aircraft and executed a masterly attack. Skimming over the U-Boat at less than 50 feet, with anti-aircraft fire entering his opened bomb doors, Flying Officer Trigg dropped his bombs in and around the U-Boat, where they exploded with devastating effect. A short distance further on the Liberator dived into the sea with her gallant Captain and crew. The U-Boat sank within 20 minutes and some of her crew were picked up later in a rubber dinghy that had broken loose from the Liberator. The Battle of the Atlantic has yielded many fine stories of air attacks on underwater craft, but Flying Officer Trigg's exploit stands out as an epic of grim determination and high courage. His was the path of duty that leads to glory.

On 12 August a Sunderland from 204 Squadron sighted the dinghy and asked a British ship, HMS *Clarkia*, to pick up the survivors, hoping and expecting them to be Trigg and his seven crew. The dingy, however, contained six Germans – the only survivors from the sunken U-boat – who were worried that they would be badly treated for being responsible for the death of Trigg and his crew. In fact, they were given all the respect demanded for prisoners of war by international conventions. The newly captured Germans therefore later provided a full report to their captors about what had happened.

As stated, this evidence – in particular that of two German officers – gave rise to Trigg's VC. The decoration was presented to his widow in New Zealand on 28 May 1944. At the time, the fact that the VC was awarded on the evidence of U-boat personnel was not stressed, although after the war the honourable behaviour of the German PoWs was acknowledged.

FLIGHT SERGEANT (LATER FLYING OFFICER) CHARLES ERNEST FRANKLIN
Royal Air Force Volunteer Reserve (RAFVR)
DECORATIONS: DISTINGUISHED FLYING MEDAL (DFM) AND BAR
GAZETTED: 18 MAY 1943 AND 28 MAY 1943

Charles Franklin was awarded a Bar to his DFM for his bravery during the legendary 'Dambusters' raid of May 1943. It resulted in him becoming one of just sixty men – and the only one from his 617 Squadron – to receive this combination during the Second World War.

Franklin was born in London on 12 November 1915 and entered the RAFVR in 1940. He attended a number of training establishments between June 1940 and April 1942 before being posted to 44 Squadron. However, on 21 April 1942, he transferred to 49 Squadron and, within two months, he started his first operational tour. Franklin subsequently completed twenty-eight operations, largely against German and Italian targets.

The recommendation for his first DFM stated:

This N.C.O. has completed 26 sorties of 161.30 hours operational flying as an Air Bomber. His work on the ground and in the air has consistently been of the highest standard, and his great skill and determination in searching for and locating the target has resulted in a very high proportion of most successful sorties. Often hampered by bad weather and menaced by fighter aircraft and enemy defences, this N.C.O. has displayed a marked singleness of purpose in his determination only to bomb the correct target, involving as it frequently has done several runs to identify it positively before releasing his bombs. By his quiet efficiency he has gained the complete confidence of his crew and set an example to all . . .

His decoration was announced on 18 May 1943, only hours after Franklin had taken part in the 'Dambusters' raid.

In March 1943, along with other members of 49 Squadron, Franklin was transferred to the newly established 617 Squadron. He and his fellow airmen soon began training for a top-secret assignment: codenamed Operation Chastise, it would involve a spectacular attack on the dams of northern Germany. By the end of April, twenty Lancasters had been gathered at RAF Scampton in Lincolnshire. They were under the command of Wing Commander Guy Gibson and their training was intense, sometimes flying at night as low as sixty feet. The pilots had to cope with the added pressures of flying at a steady speed of 250 mph and the complexities of using a double-spotlight mechanism to ensure that they flew at the exact height that was required. Franklin's role was to fly as the bomb aimer of aircraft O-for-Orange (sometimes abbreviated to O-Orange), the Lancaster flown by Flight Sergeant Bill Townsend.

It was eventually decided to conduct the attack on the night of 16/17 May, shortly after midnight and in three waves of bombers each using the newly invented 'bouncing bomb'. The Möhne and Eder dams were chosen as the primary targets, while the Sorpe and Ennepe dams were chosen as secondary targets for any surviving aircraft still equipped with their ingenious weapons. Townsend was appointed as flight commander of the third and final wave of the attack. His target would depend on the success of the first and second wave, though ultimately his target became the Ennepe Dam on the River Schwelme.

Townsend and his fellow airmen in the third wave knew they would be at a disadvantage because, unlike the earlier two waves, they would not have the benefit of surprise. Furthermore, by the time they arrived over the valleys of northern Germany a mist was gathering that made the Ennepe Dam extremely hard to locate, let alone attack. Eventually, they had to take a fix from hills three-quarters of a mile away. After circling several times, Townsend brought his aircraft down to sixty feet above the water, which remained covered by a swirling mist. Yet, even now, the cool-headed Franklin refused to be rushed and he asked Townsend to make three runs over the dam before he released the aircraft's bomb at 3.37 a.m. The bomb bounced once and then exploded some thirty seconds later, sending up a large column of water and mud. O-Orange then informed Scampton over the radio that it was leaving the scene.

As the last of the squadron's aircraft to head for home, Townsend and his fellow airmen found themselves caught up in the bright rays of the dawn sun. The pilot therefore thought it prudent once again to bring the Lancaster down to an extremely low level and skim over the rooftops at 250 mph. Daylight, however, enabled the aircrew to observe the devastation left by Gibson and his crew as a result of their earlier visit to the Möhne Dam. Indeed, they were later able to report to intelligence officers that they had seen only the roofs of houses sticking up above the waterline in some areas. After a tense journey over Occupied Europe, O-Orange soared out over the Dutch coast through another blanket of flak and touched down at Scampton at 6.15 a.m. The last of the 'Dambusters' crews had arrived home unscathed.

Franklin was soon put forward for a Bar to his DFM in a joint recommendation involving his two fellow airmen: Townsend was put forward for the Conspicuous Gallantry Medal (CGM) and Pilot Officer C. L. Howard for the Distinguished Flying Cross (DFC). Their awards were announced on 28 May 1943: in Franklin's case his Bar was awarded just ten days after his first DFM. Gibson was awarded the VC for his part in the raid, while the Squadron's motto later became: 'Après moi, le Deluge' ('After me, the Flood'). The operation had been an overwhelming success: the skill of the 'Dambusters' crews, totalling 133 men, had left the Ruhr under an estimated 330 million tons of water. Roads, railway bridges and an important military aerodrome were all washed away, leaving the area's infrastructure in ruins. But at great cost: eight of the nineteen Lancasters that had taken off failed to return.

The day before the awards were announced, the King and Queen visited the successful crews at Scampton. In all, thirty-four men were decorated and they attended an investiture at Buckingham Palace on 22 June 1943. Contrary to convention, they were decorated together and they took precedence over all the others waiting to be honoured. After attending the 'Dambusters' investiture, Franklin was promoted to flying officer on 4 November 1944 and transferred to 83 Squadron. He survived the war and afterwards moved to Birmingham. With his parents, he set up a successful catering business. He acquired a certain celebrity in 1955 when he became Birmingham's 'Forgotten Dambuster' after his name was omitted from the guest list for the royal premier of the film *The Dam Busters*. However, the ensuing publicity ensured that he received a belated invitation and, once again, he met up with his former comrades. Franklin died on 25 January 1975, aged fifty-nine. His funeral was attended by more than 200 mourners, including members of O-Orange, and its ground crew and representatives of 617 Squadron. At the funeral, Sir Barnes Wallis, the inventor of the 'bouncing bomb', was represented by his daughter as Franklin's coffin was covered by a Union flag.

FLIGHT SERGEANT (LATER FLIGHT LIEUTENANT) LEONARD JOSEPH SUMPTER

Army/RAF
DECORATIONS: DISTINGUISHED FLYING MEDAL (DFM) AND DISTINGUISHED FLYING CROSS (DFC)
GAZETTED: 28 MAY 1943 AND 9 JUNE 1944

Leonard Sumpter was one of twelve men to be awarded an immediate DFM for the 'Dambusters' raid, one of them as a Bar. However, Sumpter's association with 617 Squadron lasted much longer than the legendary raid, when, under new commanding officer Leonard Cheshire, he participated in a spate of daring precision raids that would add the DFC to his accolades.

Sumpter was born in Kettering, Northamptonshire, on 20 September 1911. He initially embarked on a career in the Army, serving with the Grenadier Guards from 1928 to 1931 and again, after the outbreak of the war, from 1939 to 1941. However, in 1941, Sumpter transferred to the RAF and was posted to 57 Squadron in September 1942. During his six months with the squadron, he flew as bomb aimer on thirteen operations in Lancasters. His enemy targets included Wismar, Genoa, Turin, Stuttgart, Berlin, Nuremberg and St Nazaire.

During the Wismar raid on 12 October 1942, his aircraft sustained major damage and he was wounded in the foot.

Sumpter, described by a comrade as 'tougher than a prize fighter', was selected to join the new 617 Squadron. By March 1943, he was taking part in the special training ahead of the 'Dambuster' raid, codenamed Operation Chastise. On the night of the raid, 16/17 May 1943, he was bomb aimer in Flight Lieutenant Dave Shannon's Lancaster crew. This crew was, in turn, part of Wing Commander Guy Gibson's first wave of nine aircraft. The aircraft took off in three batches of three aircraft ten minutes apart. The intention was that they would attack the Möhne Dam and, once breached, the aircraft that had not bombed would attack the Eder Dam.

At 9.47 p.m., Shannon and his crew took off in Lancaster 'L-for-London' (known to her crew as 'L-for-Leather'). Initially, they were ordered to attack the Möhne Dam but, almost at once, that order was countermanded when Gibson saw the dam had been breached by an earlier bomb. Four aircraft, including Shannon's, were therefore ordered to move on to attack the Eder Dam, a task which proved difficult because of low fog cover in the region. Furthermore, the Eder lay in a fold of hills surrounded by ridges of about 1,000 feet. Shannon made several dives but failed to get into a good enough position for Sumpter to release his 'bouncing bomb'. Eventually, however, he came in on a perfect approach and Sumpter dropped his bomb. It struck the water, bounced twice and smashed against the dam wall, producing a huge column of water nearly 1,000 feet high. Shortly afterwards, a gap was seen to the east of the dam and soon a bomb dropped by Pilot Officer Les Knight completed the successful strike on the Eder Dam. Using the call sign 'dinghy', Gibson signalled back to

Group Headquarters that the dam had been breached at 1.54 a.m. Shannon's crew then headed for home and landed at 4.06 a.m, mission accomplished.

Sumpter's DFM, along with decorations for the rest of the 'Dambusters' team (including a DFC for Shannon), was announced on 28 May 1943. Afterwards, Sumpter continued flying with Shannon as part of 617 Squadron, first from Scampton, and then from RAF Coningsby and RAF Woodhall Spa, the latter also both in Lincolnshire. They were given the job of attacking special targets. Sumpter was commissioned – promoted to pilot officer – on 27 June 1943 and then promoted again, to flying officer, on 27 December 1943. The two men flew together on many more operations. After Mosquitos were introduced to 617 Squadron, the old partnership continued with Sumpter as Shannon's navigator and bomb aimer. By this point, their role was to mark targets accurately, which they did on a series of them in Occupied France.

The recommendation for Sumpter's DFC noted that he had completed twenty-one operational sorties as a bomb aimer in a special duties squadron. It stated:

> He has taken part in many low level attacks of a most hazardous nature which have included such targets as the Dortmund/Ems canal, Clermont Ferrand and Brunswick. During the past few months this officer has operated in a Deputy Leader's aircraft and his principal task has been to aim and release the marker bombs for the Main Force. Flying Officer Sumpter, by his outstanding skill and determination in the face of extreme danger, has played a big part in the remarkable run of successes recently achieved by his squadron.

The development of a technique for marking a target at

night automatically led to the immediate selection of Flying Officer Sumpter as bomb-aimer and navigator for Mosquito aircraft which were employed, the aiming point had to be accurately marked at a precise moment just before the arrival of the Main Force. This demanded very accurate navigation and a low-level dive attack against one of the most strongly defended cities in Germany. In spite of his limited experience on Mosquito aircraft and the very heavy opposition which was encountered both along the route and over the target, this officer directed his captain to the aiming-point exactly at the selected time. The markers were thus accurately and punctually laid and the unqualified success of the operation was therefore in no small measure due to the skill, determination and indomitable courage of this gallant officer. His outstanding operational record has, moreover, always been an example and a potent source of inspiration to his Squadron.

Sumpter's DFC was announced on 9 June 1944.

Towards the end of the war, Sumpter reverted to Lancasters as part of Flight Lieutenant L. M. Marshall's crew. Their targets included the U-boat pens at Hamburg and Hitler's retreat, the Eagle's Nest, at Berchtesgaden.

Sumpter completed two tours before being released from the RAF on 11 March 1946. However, he immediately rejoined and served with the physical fitness branch of the RAF from 1946 to 1950. After retiring from the RAF, Sumpter lived for many years in Canada. However, in later life he returned to Britain and died in Luton, Bedfordshire, in late 1993, aged eighty-two.

7

SECOND WORLD WAR – RECONNAISSANCE OPERATIONS

RAF reconnaissance played a crucial role in the conduct of operations in the Second World War, the pilots of Photographic Reconnaissance Units (PRU) gaining hugely important evidence of enemy activity on land and at sea. Early reconnaissance operations, flown in Blenheims and Lysanders, were somewhat sporadic and haphazard, but following the intervention of Air Marshal Sir Geoffrey Tuttle, KBE, CB, DFC, after the fall of France in 1940, photo-reconnaissance was firmly placed on the map and, over the ensuing years of the conflict, PRU pilots were operating with great success in Mosquitos and stripped-down Spitfires, the latter sometimes unarmed.

Many such reconnaissance pilots were decorated for their gallant work, a case in point being Group Captain John Merrifield who won a DSO and DFC and Bar after completing 160 perilous missions in order to gather intelligence – it was he who captured on film the sinister activities at the enemy's secret rocket installation at Peenemünde, the German Baltic port. This resulted in a successful strike on the installation in August 1943. Another classic reconnaissance 'find' is detailed in this chapter: the one obtained by one of the great heroes to emerge from the defence of Malta, Flying Officer (later Squadron Leader) Adrian Warburton. He found the Italian fleet at Taranto in November 1940: huge damage was subsequently inflicted in a strike on the southern Italian port.

However, not all reconnaissance work was enacted for a glimpse of the bigger picture, certain pilots being called upon to report on more local fronts, and no better example of such activity can be found than the work of the Army's observation flights, whether in the European or Far Eastern theatres of war.

FLYING OFFICER (LATER WING COMMANDER) ADRIAN WARBURTON

RAF
DECORATIONS: DISTINGUISHED FLYING CROSS (DFC) AND TWO BARS, DISTINGUISHED SERVICE ORDER (DSO) AND BAR
GAZETTED: 11 FEBRUARY 1941, 9 SEPTEMBER 1941, 3 NOVEMBER 1942, 20 MARCH 1942 AND 6 AUGUST 1943

Adrian 'Warby' Warburton was described by one senior officer as 'the most valuable pilot in the RAF' and earned legendary status in Malta and beyond. His flying career on the island was the inspiration for the film *The Malta Story*, starring Alec Guinness in the role as the dashing reconnaissance pilot who falls in love with a local girl. After Warburton disappeared during a reconnaissance flight, he never received the funeral he deserved, but this was eventually rectified in 2003, almost sixty years after his death and the year after the remains of his body were found in a German field.

Born in Middlesbrough, Cleveland, on 10 March 1918, Warburton was the son of a Royal Navy officer who chose to have him christened on a submarine in Grand Harbour,

Valetta, Malta – most appropriate given his activities on the island nearly a quarter of a century later. Warburton was educated at St Edward's School, Oxford, where, coincidentally, two other legendary pilots, Douglas Bader and Guy Gibson, were also educated. After school, he became a bank clerk before, in 1937, joining the Territorials as a private in the Royal Tank Regiment. Warburton was commissioned into the RAF in January 1939 and, shortly after the outbreak of the Second World War, he was posted to 22 Squadron based at RAF North Coates, Lincolnshire, flying Bristol Beauforts. It was after his commanding officer was asked to supply crews to form 431 Flight to go to Malta that Warburton, who had already completed a general reconnaissance course, volunteered for the vacant role of observer. The island of Malta was of huge strategic importance in the Mediterranean and its effectiveness from a reconnaissance viewpoint centred on the RAF providing accurate information about the movement of enemy ships.

431 Flight was formed on 19 September 1940 and was equipped with three Maryland reconnaissance aircraft, each with a crew of three. Warburton flew twelve missions in October, the first full month of operations, although only half of them as a pilot. Most of the missions were over Taranto, where the Italian Fleet was based and where Admiral Cunningham, the Commander-in-Chief in the Mediterranean, planned to destroy ships using the Fleet Air Arm. In November 1940, and by then a full-time pilot, Warburton was attacked by four enemy aircraft on the 2nd and, again, on the 7th. On 10 November 1940, while on a reconnaissance mission, he emerged from heavy cloud so low over Taranto harbour that he could read the ships' names. Despite heavy anti-aircraft fire, he again flew low over the harbour on his return to Malta,

by then with the accurate locations of five Italian battleships, fourteen cruisers and twenty-seven destroyers. He was also able to produce an excellent set of aerial photographs, which were immediately forwarded to the aircraft carrier HMS *Illustrious*. Having studied these, Cunningham ordered attacks for the next night and, largely due to Warburton's accurate observations, they were one of the great successes of the war, with half the Italian Fleet being put out of action.

Not only was Warburton's reputation assured, but the success at Taranto proved the value of 431 Flight, which was then strengthened to five Maryland aircraft. Despite the reconnaissance nature of the flights, Warburton attacked enemy aircraft that appeared during the course of his missions. He even strafed an Italian submarine on 15 December 1940, while, nine days later, on Christmas Eve, he shot down an Italian Savoia-Marchetti 79 bomber. In January 1941, 431 Flight was transformed into 69 Squadron. Warburton's DFC was announced on 11 February 1941 and his citation stated: 'This officer has carried out numerous long distance reconnaissance flights and has taken part in night air combats. In October 1940, he destroyed an aircraft and again, in December, he shot down an enemy bomber in flames. Flying Officer Warburton has at all times displayed a fine sense of devotion to duty.'

Warburton was prolific throughout the first six months of 1941, flying numerous missions and invariably returning with important photographs and information. He was involved in several combats during this time but he always managed to get 'home'. On 25 June 1941, while on patrol with his squadron, an enemy convoy was spotted and attacked. Although one aircraft was shot down, Warburton succeeded in hitting a ship with a 500-lb bomb. Air Marshal Hugh Lloyd, the Air Officer

Commanding, Malta, was so impressed that he insisted on Marylands regularly carrying bombs, which further boosted Warburton's reputation. After flying a successful combat with 69 Squadron on 29 September 1941, Warburton was posted to Middle East Command for a period of non-operational duties. The first Bar to his DFC was announced on 9 September 1941 and his citation stated: 'This officer is a most determined and skilful pilot and has carried out 125 operational missions. Flying Officer Warburton has never failed to complete the missions he has undertaken and, in the actions fought, he has destroyed at least three hostile aircraft in combat and another three on the ground.'

On 20 March 1942, Warburton was awarded the DSO, in particular for his part in the Taranto harbour raid. His citation stated: 'This officer has never failed to obtain photographs from a very low altitude, regardless of enemy opposition. His work has been most valuable and he has displayed great skill and tenacity.'

Warburton flew a variety of aircraft during his rest period in Egypt and, in August 1942, he returned to Malta in a new Spitfire. The squadron now consisted of three flights, including B Wing, which was led by Warburton. He flew his first sortie in his Spitfire on 12 August 1942, the day after his return – another reconnaissance mission over Taranto. Having been promoted to squadron leader, he was one of the most senior pilots on Malta. For the next six months, Warburton was involved in operational sorties over much of the Mediterranean, including Italy and North Africa. Malta's air force was increasingly successful in its targeting of enemy convoys and Warburton often flew to observe the attacks that resulted from the information he had gathered. The second Bar to his DFC was awarded on 3 November 1942 and his citation stated: 'In October, 1942, his gallantry was well illustrated when he directed an enemy destroyer to a dinghy in which were the crew of one of our aircraft which had been shot down. Although he was fired upon by the destroyer and engaged by Italian aircraft he remained over the area until he observed the drifting crew were picked up by the destroyer.'

683 Squadron was formed early in 1943 from B Wing and 69 Squadron, and Warburton was given command. Initially, the new squadron carried out reconnaissance sorties, although now operating at a higher altitude than 69 Squadron. However, in May 1943, Warburton, whose rebellious nature meant he often sported hair that was longer than the standard of the day and dressed scruffily, began a series of 'special' low-level missions. This provided information that was invaluable for the invasion of Sicily on 10 July. For the remainder of the summer, following the invasion, he flew numerous missions often in the face of fierce opposition. A Bar to Warburton's DSO was awarded on 6 August 1943 and his citation stated:

This officer has undertaken a very large number of reconnaissance flights over a wide range of targets in the Middle East theatre. His work throughout has been of the highest order and the information he has obtained has proved of incalculable value. On one occasion in December, 1942, he made a low-level flight over Naples and achieved success in the face of heavy anti-aircraft fire and fighter opposition. Wing Commander Warburton's great courage and devotion to duty were well illustrated during a reconnaissance of Pantellaria [Italy] in May, 1943. Although his aircraft was continuously subjected to fire from the coastal batteries, he skilfully accomplished his task securing information of the highest importance. Wing Commander Warburton's record of operational flying is outstanding.

Warburton was ordered to rest: his last mission with 683 Squadron took place on 6 September 1943. However, having made friends among the US pilots based at La Marsa in Tunis, he flew photographic missions for the Americans. Despite his fine record in the air, Warburton was less fortunate on the ground: on 26 November 1943, he was seriously injured in a car crash outside Tunis. Warburton was eventually sent back to the UK where he became frustrated at being unable to fly. His spirits must have been lifted when, on 18 January 1944, he was awarded the American DFC. As preparations were under way for the D-Day landings, Warburton, who was still grounded, found himself posted on 1 April 1944 to the US air base at Mount Farm, Oxfordshire. Eventually, he persuaded his commanding officer to allow him to fly again.

On 12 April, Warburton, now aged twenty-six, took off in a Lockheed F-5B for a mission that was expected to see him fly across Europe and land at San Severo in Italy. However, having flown over Lake Constance, Germany, he disappeared and was never seen again. His disappearance baffled air historians until the end of 2002 when his remains were found in the wreck of his aircraft, which was discovered buried in a field near a Bavarian village, west of Munich. One of the propellers had bullet holes in it, which suggests that Warburton had been shot down. Parts of this wreckage can be seen today in the Malta Aviation Museum. Warburton was buried in May 2003 in a brief ceremony conducted in driving rain in the shadow of the Alps. Betty Westcott, the barmaid he had married before his departure for Malta even though he barely knew her, was present, aged ninety-one. 'It was a wartime thing,' she said. 'He was incredibly young and I was simply bowled over by him. In a way, we were never really married.' Warburton was also the subject of the 'Mystery of the Missing Ace' episode of *Timewatch*, the BBC investigative documentary series first broadcast in November 2003.

SERGEANT (LATER FLIGHT LIEUTENANT] LESLIE ROBERT COLQUHOUN
Royal Air Force Volunteer Reserve (RAFVR)
DECORATIONS: DISTINGUISHED FLYING MEDAL (DFM), DISTINGUISHED FLYING CROSS (DFC) AND GEORGE MEDAL (GM)
GAZETTED: 17 JULY 1942, 10 OCTOBER 1944 AND 1 AUGUST 1950

Les Colquhoun was born in Hanwell, Middlesex, on 15 March 1921. Educated in Ealing, west London, he enlisted in the RAF as a sergeant pilot in August 1940. After pilot's training, he was posted to 603 (City of Edinburgh), an Auxiliary Air Force fighter squadron operating in Spitfires. The primary role of the squadron was to carry out fighter sweeps over France and convoy protection patrols.

It was, however, in southern Europe, particularly Malta, that Colquhoun left his mark. His association with Malta began when he was sent to deliver a photo-reconnaissance Spitfire to Cairo in 1941. He landed on Malta en route and was ordered to stay there, flying operational sorties from Luqa aerodrome. Once settled in Malta, he was attached to 'Warby Warburton's unit', 69 Squadron. For nine months, spanning

1941 and 1942, Colquhoun carried out countless reconnaissance flights often at great risk.

In an unarmed Spitfire, Colquhoun acted as the 'eyes' of the beleaguered island, which came under relentless attack because of its strategic importance in the Mediterranean. The high-speed, high-altitude sorties were flown to destinations such as Sicily, southern Italy, North Africa and the east coast of Greece. Colquhoun's task was to photograph airfields, naval dockyards and German convoys carrying reinforcements to Libya. He was also able to report on the number of enemy bombers taking off from Italian airfields and to monitor possible Axis invasion plans. During this momentous period of the battle for Malta, Colquhoun flew 154 operational sorties and was awarded the DFM on 17 July 1942. His citation stated: 'Much valuable information was secured as a result of his determined and skilful efforts.'

Colquhoun's war continued with a posting as an instructor at a reconnaissance unit in Dyce, Scotland. Having been commissioned, he was posted to 682 Photographic Reconnaissance Unit (PRU) Squadron in North Africa in October 1943. From a temporary airfield in Corsica, he flew over southern France to gather information useful to the Allies as they prepared for the Operation Dragoon landings on the Mediterranean coast in August 1944. For these activities, he was awarded the DFC on 10 October 1944.

Colquhoun subsequently returned to work as an instructor and, in February 1945, he was appointed as a test pilot to Vickers Supermarine. He was involved in testing the later marks of the Spitfire and its successors, the Spiteful and Seafang, along with Vickers' first jet, the Attacker. An outstanding test pilot, he was asked to stay on in a civilian capacity after the war. In May 1950, while flying an Attacker at 450 mph, the tip of his starboard wing suddenly folded to the vertical position. Colquhoun lost control of the aircraft and would have been fully justified in ejecting to safety, but he knew that if he did this the Attacker would crash and the cause of the fault would not be discovered. Instead, he opted for a highly dangerous alternative and, having regained control, managed to land the aircraft at 200 mph – twice the normal landing speed – on the 1,800-yard runway at Chilbolton, Hampshire. Colquhoun eventually brought the aircraft to a halt twenty yards from the end of the runway and with just a single burst tyre. On 1 August 1950 he was awarded the GM and his citation stated: 'Colquhoun showed exceptional courage and coolness in circumstances of great danger and deliberately risked his life to bring the aircraft down intact.'

Colquhoun continued his career as a test pilot after the incident and flew jet fighters, as well as trying out early hovercrafts. Indeed, he was in charge of the first hovercraft service between Wallasey and Rhyl, North Wales, in 1962 and, four years later, he was appointed operations manager of Hoverlloyd. Later he became managing director of the company and oversaw operations of its car ferries between Ramsgate, Kent, and Calais. When Hoverlloyd was taken over by Seaspeed, Colquhoun ran the jetfoil service between Brighton, Sussex, and Dieppe. He retired to Broadstairs, Kent, where he died on 27 April 2001, aged eighty. Colquhoun was survived by his wife, Katie, and their four daughters.

CAPTAIN EDWARD WALTER MASLEN-JONES

Army

DECORATIONS: DISTINGUISHED FLYING CROSS (DFC) AND MILITARY CROSS (MC)

GAZETTED: 8 MARCH 1945 AND 19 APRIL 1945

Ted Maslen-Jones was born in Balham, south London, on 11 October 1919. The eldest of three sons, his parents met in Cairo towards the end of the First World War, when his father, an obstetrician, was serving with the Royal Army Medical Corps (RAMC) and his mother was an Army nurse. Following their marriage in Cairo, Maslen-Jones was conceived on the voyage home. Later he was educated at Oundle School, Northamptonshire, and Brasenose College, Oxford. However, his university education was interrupted by the Second World War and he enlisted in the Royal Artillery on 18 October 1939, a week after his twentieth birthday. Commissioned as a 2nd lieutenant on 17 July 1940, Maslen-Jones served with 119 Field Regiment but a chance meeting on a train with a brigadier from the Royal Artillery Flying Club (RAFC) led to him being seconded to the RAF. Early in the war, the RAFC had persuaded the military command of the benefits of using light, manoeuvrable aircraft to observe and control artillery fire in battle. At RAF Old Sarum, Wiltshire, Maslen-Jones received operational flying training, the emphasis being on low-flying, cross-country navigations and short landings, often in difficult situations. He was presented with his pilot's 'wings' in early February 1943 and was posted to 656 Squadron, which was an Air Observation Post unit based at Bury St Edmunds, Suffolk. The squadron, including Maslen-Jones, embarked for India in

August 1943 at a time when the journey by ship from Liverpool to Bombay took more than a month. Their aircraft arrived shortly before Christmas, just as the squadron learnt it was bound for Burma to join the 14th Army's operations.

Once in Burma, 656 Squadron had its baptism of fire early in 1944 when the Japanese 55th Division launched a massive offensive. The tension felt by the British servicemen as they were surrounded by the Japanese is described by Maslen-Jones in his book *Fire by Order:* the first week of February 1944 was noted in squadron records as 'never to be forgotten'. Initially, Maslen-Jones, and his colleagues (who knew him as 'Mas') flew Austers to evacuate casualties and transfer documents and supplies. However, as the heavy fighting continued, he was soon carrying out observation flights and helping to range guns. While examining an enemy-occupied tunnel from tree-top level, Maslen-Jones's aircraft was hit by small-arms fire. On another occasion, his unarmed aircraft was chased by a Japanese Zero fighter but Maslen-Jones flew low and managed to avoid being shot down.

On 6 August 1944, Maslen-Jones was recommended for a MC for his courage as an air observer between 26 March 1944 and 11 May 1944. The recommendation for his award, from a senior Artillery officer, stated:

> During this period he has ever been the first to suggest some cunning ruse to outwit the Jap and has ever been eager to go into the air to carry these schemes into effect. For several weeks I gave him a pretty free hand to control the open country South of Maungdaw and between the hills and the sea, putting certain guns at his disposal for the purpose. Day after day this officer flew long hours to accomplish his task. In

addition he was used to search for Jap guns and observe in the hill country. Frequently shot at, his courage was unfailing. He was ever ready to take extra risks in low flying to report some minute detail of a target or observe the results of fire.

However, after various internal military discussions, it was the DFC that Maslen-Jones was awarded on 8 March 1945.

In his book, Maslen-Jones wrote of his wartime role: 'I had at my disposal a troop of 25 pounders from 5th Indian Field Regiment, and a troop of 8th Belfast HAA [Heavy Anti-Aircraft] Regiment. I could therefore conduct shoots as far as twelve miles into the area. For other targets I would rely upon air strikes or the mortars belonging to the patrols.'

In fact, 656 Squadron, whose motto was 'Flying and Seeing', was quick to adapt to the 14th Army's needs. Maslen-Jones wrote:

Although in general playing no direct part in operations, it [656 Squadron] rapidly developed expertise in specialized functions which were to become valuable services in the terrain which it was to pass. One such service was cable-laying. This was made possible by an ingenious adaption, invented by the CO, which enabled the pilot to pay out signal cable while flying over the top of dense jungle. In providing a quick way of setting up communication between formations in such difficult terrain the facility was soon in great demand. Another was photography. Using a hand-held camera specially selected for the purpose, there were unique opportunities to provide factual evidence of ground positions and reconnaissance information from relatively low levels of flight.

Maslen-Jones remained heavily involved in the Burma campaign throughout 1944 and into 1945. He was recommended for the MC for his courage in aiding the capture of Monywa. The recommendation, from a senior Infantry officer, stated:

The enemy was well dug in perfectly camouflaged positions which proved most difficult and expensive in casualties for infantry ground patrols to locate. Capt Maslen-Jones, in addition to his normal duties, and at great personal and continuous risk from enemy small arms fire, made many tree top reconnaissances over enemy positions in compiling sketches on which were based the final plans for artillery and air strikes for the assault on Monywa.

It was only after the capture of Monwya that the full value of the daring work done by this officer and the risks he must have taken in doing it could be appreciated after examination of the enemy positions. It is no exaggeration to say that the success of the assault on Monywa and the comparatively small casualties incurred by our infantry are due in no small measure to the initiative, personal continuous gallantry and devotion to duty with which this intrepid young officer carried out his reconnaissances.

In his book, Maslen-Jones describes how a senior officer, Brigadier Steevens, visited the squadron.

We all thought that we were about to be inspected, but the Brigadier started to tell us how proud he was of Air OP Flight and congratulated us all on the contribution we had made. He particularly singled out those who had kept the aircraft and transport operational in such adverse conditions and wished us well in the forthcoming battles for Mandalay and the river crossings. He then said, 'Captain Maslen-Jones will you please come forward.' He pinned the medal ribbon of the Military Cross on my chest and said he has been instructed to do so by the 14th Army Commander and the Commander of 20 Indian Division. He simply added, 'Well done, Maslen-Jones.' I was completely taken aback. I had absolutely no idea that this was about to happen and such a thing was furthest from my mind.

Maslen-Jones's MC was announced on 19 April 1945 and his citation stated: 'In recognition of gallant and distinguished services in Burma and on the Eastern Frontier of India.' Meanwhile, 656 Squadron continued its activities until the end of hostilities in 1945 and played a key role in the advance to, and the crossing of, the Irrawaddy, and the march on Rangoon which defeated the Japanese and brought a close to the war. The squadron ended the Burma campaign with the award of two MBEs, two MCs, nine DFCs, a Certificate of Gallantry and numerous Mentions in Despatches. In his foreword to Maslen-Jones's book, General Sir Martin Farndale wrote:

The story of 656th Air Observation Post Squadron RAF/RA is remarkable by any standards. Ted Maslen-Jones, a pilot in the Squadron, recounts how one single squadron composed of three Flights each of five tiny Auster aircraft provided air observation for the whole of the famous 14th Army in Burma from 1943 until the end of World War 2 in 1945 . . . The part played by the gallant few of this splendid squadron is out of all proportion to their size. Their flying hours broke all records, their feats of endurance and airmanship in appalling weather conditions set standards seldom equalled, and they never once failed to answer a call for help from comrades on the ground. Between October, 1944, and May, 1945, alone, they flew 6,712 sorties in 5,170 flying hours! Some of the artillery attacks they directed had decisive impact on the great battles raging below them. The Japanese dreaded them and stopped all firing when they saw them above. To the British they gave confidence, help of all kinds and above all information.

Maslen-Jones also received two Mentions in Despatches and a Certificate of Gallantry for his courage in Burma. In his book, he gives an insightful view on the bond of comradeship:

> Comradeship is an amazing thing which is not always fully understood. Being something deeper than friendship, it withstands long periods without any sort of contact and yet the coming together again is instant. Although some of the detail will have been forgotten the experiences shared in action will have been unforgettable and there are, I believe, no adequate words to describe the bond that had been created, not only between those who became friends but between all those who served in the same unit.

In an interview at his home in Liss, Hampshire, Maslen-Jones fondly recalled his wartime role in a two-seater Auster that had no weapons and no parachute: it would have been impossible to get out of his aircraft with a parachute on. 'I am a bit of a lone wolf and so I always preferred flying alone whereas other pilots preferred flying with an observer. I flew four, five, six sorties a day. I didn't think of the dangers and even now I only remember the enjoyable bits, not the nasty bits. I was a bit of a Biggles: an old-fashioned flyer.'

After the war, Maslen-Jones returned to Oxford in 1946 to complete his degree. For the next thirty-six years, he worked in the agricultural supply industry. When *Fire by Order* was first published in 1997, more than half a century after the events described, he was seventy-seven. Maslen-Jones, who said his story had been 'bursting to come out', then went back to his old school, Oundle, as the guest of honour on speech day where he autographed copies of his book. The following year his book won the Alfred Burne Medal, a literary prize awarded by the Royal Artillery Historical Trust. In 2005, by then having served as President of 656 Squadron Association for five years, he was introduced to the Prince of Wales at the sixtieth anniversary of VJ (Victory over Japan) Day celebrations in London. Maslen-Jones, who is now ninety-two, is due to celebrate his golden wedding anniversary with his second wife, Jill, next year. He has a grown-up son by his first marriage and three step-daughters from his second. He still drives and enjoys gardening, fly-fishing and singing in his local church choir. 'I have had an absolutely wonderful life. I am very fortunate. Every day at 6 p.m. my wife and I raise a glass [of whisky],' he told me. 'And even now the occasional exciting thing still happens to me – like being in this book.'

8

SECOND WORLD WAR – ESCAPE AND ACTION ON THE GROUND

The ingenuity displayed by many prisoners of war (PoWs) in courageously attempting to gain freedom from captivity needs little introduction. High on the list of such heroes are those of the British and Commonwealth air forces. Famously, seventy-six such officers broke out from Stalag Luft III in the 'Great Escape' in March 1944, but only three of them evaded recapture – and fifty of them were murdered in cold blood on Hitler's orders. However, hundreds of men of all ranks were prolific in escape activity – they considered it their duty to try to escape whenever the opportunity arose, either through a carefully planned initiative or, if a chance arose, on the spur of the moment. Many of those who tried to escape, both successfully and unsuccessfully, were honoured for their bravery during and after the war.

Once on the run, many escapees were assisted by brave men and women who ran a highly successful network of evasion lines across Occupied Europe – indeed, hundreds of aircrew returned to operations as a result of such gallant deeds, the majority being evaders, namely those who were picked up shortly after baling out of their downed aircraft and before the enemy could intervene.

The work of such clandestine evasion lines leads neatly to another episode of the war in which a handful of RAF officers were employed on the ground – those that volunteered to serve as agents for the Special Operations Executive (SOE). One such story is related in this chapter, so, too, that of a gallant member of the little-known RAF (Serving) Commando, an elite force established under the auspices of the commanding officer of Combined Operations, Lord Mountbatten: and that of a gallant member of the Glider Pilot Regiment.

Some, if not all, of those men featured here might well have been included in one of the earlier chapters for their courage in the air but, on balance, I feel they belong here.

SERGEANT (LATER WARRANT OFFICER) NORMAN JACK PAWLEY

RAF
DECORATION: DISTINGUISHED FLYING MEDAL (DFM)
GAZETTED: 20 JULY 1943

Norman Pawley was born in Battersea, south London, in 1922 but was brought up in Fowey, Cornwall. He enlisted in the RAF in July 1939 and flew Stirlings with 15 Squadron based at RAF Mildenhall, Suffolk. Pawley, who was the air gunner/wireless officer, had a busy year in 1943, when his operational sorties included bombing raids to Düsseldorf, Krefeld, Aachen, Hamburg and Essen.

The recommendation for Pawley's DFM provided a detailed account of his bravery after being shot down:

On the night of 24th/25th June 1943, Sergeant Pawley was a Wireless Operator on Stirling aircraft in Sergeant Towse's crew which was detailed to attack Wuppertal. When proceeding to the target just after crossing the Dutch coast this aircraft was attacked by a [Junkers] Ju. 88, the enemy being successfully destroyed. After bombing the target the aircraft was hit five times by flak, eventually catching fire. The captain made a series of dives which eventually put the fire out but left a starboard engine u/s [unserviceable] and damaged four petrol tanks from which petrol was lost. This left the aircraft with only 70 minutes endurance to reach England. Sergeant Pawley, the Wireless Operator/Air Gunner of the crew, was called upon to give the maximum wireless assistance to the Navigator to provide accurate navigation in order that, if the possibility existed, the aircraft could be flown to England on what petrol remained. This he did in such a commendable manner that the aim was almost achieved. Owing to the loss of a large quantity of petrol it became apparent to the crew over the North Sea that the aircraft would have to be force-landed in the sea. Sergeant Pawley was then ordered to carry out distress procedure with the object of obtaining assistance from the Air/Sea Rescue Service. In doing this, his procedure was faultless and his coolness highly commendable. Having previously made contact with the D/F [direction finding] organisation, he realised there was no necessity for unduly high priority for his signals, and no greater priority than 'Important' was ever used . . .

When the crew was ordered to take up ditching stations, Sergeant Pawley remained on watch, transmitting signals in order that the D/F service could get the latest possible fix on his aircraft. Only when the trailing aerial struck the water, thereby rendering further transmissions impossible, did he leave his post. When the aircraft was ditched, he was responsible for rescuing the injured Navigator and Captain of the aircraft and transferring them to the dinghy. Confident in the reception of his signals and the co-operation of the Air/ Sea Rescue Service and despite loss in the sea of all the ancillary equipment from the dinghy, he assumed command of the dinghy until an aircraft of the Air/Sea Rescue Service located them and was responsible for the crew being picked up by the Air/Sea Rescue Service. During the whole flight, the manner of the execution of his duty was an example for the whole of his crew, and during distress conditions, his courage, coolness and devotion to duty, together with the realisation of the possibility of other aircraft being in distress, enabled the D/F Service and Air/Sea Rescue Service to be put into action smoothly and promptly. He was responsible for the successful rescue of this crew from the sea. His coolness and courage were further revealed in the fact that, during the whole of the ditching and rescue, he retained possession of and brought ashore his confidential documents.

His DFM was announced on 20 July 1943.

However, on the night of 25/26 July 1943, Pawley's aircraft was shot down by an enemy night fighter, crashing at Osterwick, eight miles south-east of Ahaus, Germany. Of the crew of seven, one was killed and the other six were taken as prisoners of war (PoWs). Pawley's eventual debrief revealed how determined he had been to escape:

I landed in a forest on the outskirts of Essen and after burying my Mae West [life jacket], parachute and harness, I set off walking. I walked for about half a mile to the edge of the forest and decided to hide until daylight when I could see the lie of the land and get my bearings.

At dawn on 27th July I started walking in a westerly

direction with the intention of getting to Eindhoven. After I had walked 20 kms [12.5 miles], I saw an isolated cottage so I knocked on the door. The owner of the cottage asked me in and whilst he was giving me a meal – quite unknown to me – sent one of his children to fetch the police. A short while later I was arrested by a German policeman and marched down to the local police station (name unknown).

Whilst the police were telephoning the Luftwaffe authorities I asked if I could go to the lavatory, I was escorted there by a guard and once inside I climbed through the window and down the drain pipe. I then ran out through the courtyard of the police station, over a wire fence and into an orchard. I could hear voices so I ran into a toolshed and hid in a big box which looked like a coffin. After I had been there ten minutes a German civilian (name unknown) came and told me to get out. He then took me across to his kitchen and pointed upstairs indicating that I was to go up there. I climbed up until I came to an attic and hid myself behind a large wardrobe in the corner. After half an hour I heard sounds of the house being searched and shortly afterwards the attic was entered and a search carried out. I was not discovered and remained standing behind the wardrobe for eight hours. At the end of that time the same German came to the attic and I managed to understand by the constant repetition of the word 'nacht' that he meant me to make my getaway that night.

At midnight I therefore walked downstairs. Luckily the front door had been left unlocked and I was able to walk out into the road. I walked all that night in a north westerly direction until 0800 hours when I hid in a field and went to sleep. At dusk on 28th July I set off walking and after two hours I was arrested by a German soldier who was patrolling the area. I was taken to the frontier post near Bocholt where I was searched. I was then taken by car to Bocholt where I was put in a cell at the Police Station. I was kept there until the following morning when I was taken to Abwehr Headquarters and placed in solitary confinement. On the afternoon of 29th July I was taken to a local aerodrome and placed in a Luftwaffe cell. That evening I was taken by train to Dulag Luft.

Pawley was held in at least three different camps, ending up at Stalag IVB, Mühlberg, from August 1943 to April 1945. He again takes up the story:

At Stalag IVB in January, 1944, I changed identity with 1761110 Pte. F.A.S.C. Watter R.A.O.C. [Royal Army Ordnance Corps] for the purpose of escape. I was sent on a working party in a wood factory making prefabricated houses at Chemnitz. I planned to escape with another member of the R.A.F. (P/O [Pilot Officer] Davidson) who had changed identities with a South African army private.

On the night of 10th January, 1944, P/O Davidson and I took the bars out of our hut in the lager [parking place for armoured vehicles]. At midnight we climbed out of the window and after crossing a river got on to the main road. Our intention was to get to a railway marshalling yard in that area and jump a train going to Switzerland. We were equipped with food, maps and compasses but had no civilian clothes or money.

We set off walking north east to get to the marshalling yard (name forgotten) but after two and half hours we were arrested by two German policemen and marched down to the local police station. We were then taken by car to the police station at Chemnitz where we were put in cells. The following morning we were collected by the military police and taken to the Divisional Headquarters in the Chemnitz area. Here we were briefly interrogated and sentenced to seven days, solitary confinement.

Later, Pawley made another attempt at freedom:

In July, 1944 whilst on the working party at the Josef Wicks Spinnery near Chemnitz, I made another attempt to escape. This time I planned to escape with Sgt. G. Brown, R.A.F., who had changed identity with an army private. We had previously told Pte. Jones A.A. (Tank Corps) who was Man of Confidence at the working party of our plan to escape. On the evening of 23rd July Sgt. Brown and I hid behind some bags of cement until dark.

We then just walked out on the road with the intention of getting to Prague. We were not equipped with any escape aids or civilian clothes but had been given the address of a contact in Prague who would help us. We walked all night and hid during the day. We continued like this without incident for six days living on what we were able to find in the fields. On 29th July we skirted the town of Ave (in the Sudetenland) and were seen by about a dozen of the German Home Guard. Sgt. Brown and I immediately ran off in the opposite direction. But Brown unfortunately stumbled and fell and was captured. He was carrying the haversack containing our few rations and personal kit. I managed to get away and after running for ten minutes hid under the trunk of a fallen tree. I lay there for half an hour till it was practically dark and then set off walking again. I walked all night and at 0800 hours on 30th July I slept for a couple of hours and then set off walking again. Owing to the fact that I had lost all my rations I decided that my only way was to jump a train and get to my destination as quickly as possible.

That evening at 2000 hours I came to a goods yard 10 kms north of Karlsbad. I remained hiding watching the trains shunting backwards and forwards for some time. I eventually saw one train that appeared to be heading south so I decided to board it. Whilst I was trying to climb onto the train I was seen by a couple of railway officials who accosted me and took me to the Station Master's office.

I was then taken by car to Ave where I was put in a cell for one day. On 31st July I was taken by lorry back to the working party at Chemnitz. I was interrogated there and my true identity was discovered. I was then moved to Stalag IVB and put into the Punishment Compound where I was kept for two months. At the end of that period I served 17 days in cells.

Pawley was liberated by Russian forces from Stalag IVB on 23 April 1945. He then cycled to Torgau in north-west Saxony, Germany, where he made contact with the American forces. On 31 May 1945, he was flown from Halle in Saxony to Britain via Brussels.

It is not known what happened to Pawley after the war other than that he retired to Porthleven, Cornwall.

SERGEANT ERNEST BRUCE LASCELLES
RAF
DECORATION: DISTINGUISHED FLYING MEDAL
(DFM)
GAZETTED: 11 DECEMBER 1945

Ernest 'Leatherneck' Lascelles was born in Sydney, Australia, in 1912. After moving to Britain, he enlisted in the RAF in 1936 and served with 269 Squadron stationed at RAF Montrose, Forfarshire, Scotland. In 1940, the squadron converted to Hudsons and moved to RAF Wick, Caithness, Scotland.

Sergeant Lascelles commenced operational flying on anti-submarine patrols and, on 15 September 1939, he is believed to have located and sunk a U-boat (German submarine) in the North Sea. Lascelles was also involved in reconnaissance flights for the squadron before being chosen to take part in a daring raid on Trondheim harbour, central Norway, on 11 June 1940. Twelve Hudsons, led by Wing Commander Pearce, took off from RAF Sumburgh, Shetland Islands, Scotland, and made good ground so that they were over the harbour by 2.37 p.m. Their targets were the German battleships *Scharnhorst* and *Gneisenau*, the heavy cruiser *Admiral Hipper*, three destroyers and two supply ships. With the sun behind them, they carried out the attack from 15,000 feet in four flights of three aircraft. The bombs fell accurately among the enemy vessels and the *Admiral Hipper* was hit, setting it on fire. Smoke could also be seen rising from one of the supply ships. The Hudsons faced heavy anti-aircraft fire before at least five Messerschmitt fighters confronted them in the air. Skilful piloting from Lascelles and accurate fire from his gunners saw both a Me 109 and a Me 110 shot down. However, Lascelles' Hudson was also eventually shot down and he was taken as a prisoner of war (PoW).

Lascelles was flown from Oslo to Germany, where he was repeatedly moved from one prison camp to another. Wherever he was held, he made it his priority to try to escape. Lascelles was imprisoned in Stalag Luft I (Barth) from July 1940 to June 1941 and, while there, was an active member of the camp's escape group, which decided it needed more information about what lay on the other side of the wire. Lascelles, who was codenamed 'Leatherneck', volunteered to go out on working parties to note down information of a military nature, including the nearby flak school, the aerodrome at Barth and the gun emplacements near Zingst. This was high-risk: technically he was now spying and might have faced the death penalty if caught. However, he passed on all the useful information he could gather to a fellow PoW called Fanshawe. When Lascelles was confined to sick quarters with impetigo in the spring of 1941, he continued his intelligence-gathering role. On one occasion, he discovered from wounded prisoners being repatriated via Barth that large numbers of German troops were moving eastwards.

Lascelles was still in the sick quarters when he found out from Fanshawe (codename 'Murgatroyd') that his written message regarding troop movements had been found by the Germans during a search. This message, along with several more, had been concealed behind a panel in the officers' canteen. At the end of June 1941, Lascelles was arrested and formally charged with espionage after being handed over to the Gestapo. Despite being moved between several prisons over the coming months, Lascelles was never tried. However, his impetigo was not treated and soon it had moved to his chest. Lascelles found himself transferred from Barth to the Gestapo headquarters at Stettin in August 1941 where, after four months of tough interrogation, he admitted to acquiring plans for escape purposes only – not for espionage purposes. On 18 March 1942, Lascelles and Fanshawe, who had also been arrested, were informed that the spying charge against them had been dropped.

Lascelles' subsequent report of his time in captivity also gave details of an escape bid:

> While I was at Stalag Luft VI, Heyderkrug [from July 1943 to June 1944], we ran a theatre show, the properties of which were kept in a barn outside the camp. W/O [Warrant Officer] Snowden planned that boxes of new stuff which were brought into the camp should be sent out as unwanted and that a prisoner should go out in the box. W/O Snowden got out but was later caught. Sgt Standford and I were taken out the next day in two separate boxes that were put in the barn. The box went out by lorry and I was put in the barn by prisoners. A German guard sat on the box and put his fingers in it. Feeling the warmth, he opened the box and I was discovered. A search of all the boxes was made and Stanford was found. I got 21 days [solitary] confinement for this.

As the end of the war neared, and having spent almost five years in captivity, Lascelles finally made a successful escape attempt. On 8 April 1945, he and Warrant Officer Brodie escaped from a column of prisoners marching from Fallingbostel. They hid for ten days and eventually obtained food from some Russian troops, who informed them that the British had taken Fallingbostel. Lascelles was eventually liberated by the British at Fallingbostel on 18 April 1945.

After the end of the war, Lascelles was recommended for the DFM, partly for his bravery in the air but also for his courage as a PoW. Of the Trondheim raid, in which two aircraft were lost, the recommendation for his award stated:

> It was probably due to the excellent combat carried out by the aircraft of which Sergeant Lascelles was the pilot that no more of the formation was shot down. It is reported that this N.C.O. on one occasion during the sortie attacked and destroyed an Me. 110, which was preparing to attack another aircraft in the formation. Sergeant Lascelles so skilfully manoeuvred his aircraft that his gunner was able to shoot down an Me. 109 and an Me. 110, thus greatly assisting his comrades in the formation . . . Sergeant Lascelles displayed great bravery and determination to aid his comrades and his country, both in action and later when in captivity. His conduct was in every manner exemplary . . .

Sadly, Lascelles never learnt of his award, which was announced on 11 December 1945. For on 13 November 1945, aged thirty-three and by then serving with 6 Operational Training Unit (OTU), he was flying a Warwick aircraft which disappeared without trace. He is commemorated on the Runnymede Memorial, near Windsor, Berkshire.

FLIGHT LIEUTENANT SYDNEY HASTINGS DOWSE

Royal Air Force Volunteer Reserve (RAFVR)
DECORATION: MILITARY CROSS (MC)
GAZETTED: 16 AUGUST 1946

Flight Lieutenant Sydney Dowse was an able pilot but he became better known for his bravery on the ground, most notably as one of the principal constructors of the tunnel used in the 'Great Escape'. Furthermore, Dowse was among those who got away from the notorious Stalag Luft III prison camp, and was at large for fourteen days before being recaptured and sent to the German 'death camp' at Sachsenhausen, where he proceeded to dig another escape tunnel.

Dowse was born in Hammersmith, west London, on 21 November 1918, and was educated at Hurstpierpoint College, Sussex. He enlisted in the RAFVR in July 1937 and learnt to fly at weekends. At the outbreak of the Second World War in 1939, Dowse was called up for regular service and completed his pilot training. He was commissioned as a pilot officer on 21 October 1940. Dowse initially flew Coastal Command Ansons on anti-submarine and convoy escort operations with 608 Squadron. However, at the end of 1940, he volunteered to join the expanding reconnaissance force and, after converting to the Spitfire, joined 1 Photographic Reconnaissance Unit (PRU).

During this period, much of Dowse's time was spent monitoring the movements of Germany's capital ships. On 20 September 1941, he set off for the Brest Peninsula to photograph the German battleships *Scharnhorst* and *Gneisenau*, but his aircraft was shot down over the French coast and he was forced to bale out. Once he landed, suffering from a leg wound, he was swiftly captured. Dowse's first escape bid came on 1 December 1941, when he fled from his hospital bed at Stadtroda. He was on the run for three days but was captured while trying to cross the German/Dutch border.

His next escape attempt came less than two months later from Stalag IX-C at Bad Sulza on 21 January 1942. After exchanging identity with a Canadian prisoner of war (PoW), he managed to slip away from a working party. He travelled by train to Werwitz, then continued on foot towards the German/ Belgian border. However, it was the height of winter and he had to trek through heavy snow. After five days on the run, and by then suffering from extreme exhaustion and exposure, Dowse was recaptured. After hospital treatment he was imprisoned at Oflag VI-B, where he helped to build four tunnels, through one of which six officers escaped in April 1942. A month later Dowse was transferred to Stalag Luft III at Sagan, a PoW camp built specifically for Allied aircrew. Here he made two unsuccessful attempts to escape from the camp.

However, the next escape attempt was to be on a different scale. Indeed, it was put on to a more formal footing by the formation of an escape committee under the chairmanship of Roger Bushell, known as 'Big X'. The committee decided to attempt a mass breakout through three tunnels – known as 'Tom, Dick and Harry' – each one dug from the north compound to the nearby woods. Dowse, who had dug tunnels at his previous camps, was enthusiastic about the renewed prospect of freedom and he worked on 'Harry'. A twenty-five-foot shaft was dug into the sandy soil beneath the block before the tunnel headed for the camp perimeter.

As well as being a committed tunnel digger, Dowse was

wily, too: he befriended a German corporal who worked at the camp headquarters. His new contact provided him with numerous documents, which were passed to the escape committee for copying, and a great deal of military intelligence. Dowse even managed to persuade the corporal to provide him with a suit, which he subsequently wore for his escape. By mid-March 1944, 'Harry', 336 feet in length and the only surviving tunnel of the original three, was completed. On 24 March, 'Big X' gave the green light for up to 200 PoWs to attempt the 'Great Escape'. Dowse had used his German contact to obtain three weeks' supply of genuine food vouchers and his original plan was to head alone to Poland, where he intended to meet up with the Polish Resistance.

On the night of 24 March, the tunnellers broke through to the surface, but they were a few yards short of the covering woods. This caused delays and Dowse, who was the twenty-first man to exit, found himself in the woods with a Polish friend, fellow escaper Flying Officer Stanislav 'Danny' Krol, and they were unable to catch their intended train. Instead, the two men set off on foot and followed the main railway line eastwards: they were among seventy-six officers who escaped that night. Having walked for thirteen days, Dowse and Krol were close to the Polish border when a member of the Hitler Youth spotted them. They were arrested on 6 April 1941, among the last to be recaptured. While Dowse was taken to Berlin for interrogation, Krol was handed over to the Gestapo. Hitler was incensed by the 'Great Escape' and, once all but three of the seventy-six escapers were recaptured, he insisted that fifty of them should be shot. Krol was the last of the prisoners to be executed, while Dowse was one of those spared. He was descended from a distinguished German family and, it was assumed, once the Gestapo realised this, his family connections saved his life.

Dowse, nicknamed 'The Laughing Boy', and three other escapers spared the death penalty were taken to Sachsenhausen concentration camp. The others were Wing Commander Harry 'Wings' Day, Major Johnny 'The Dodger' Dodge and Flight Lieutenant Bertram 'Jimmy' James. There, the four men witnessed the full horrors of the Nazi regime, including the crematoria where countless men, women and children were sent to their deaths. Dowse and James found themselves sharing a cell and the former said: 'We're not staying in this bloody place, are we?' The two men tossed a coin to decide under whose bed they should start digging their tunnel, and soon they were hard at work yet again. On or around 23 July, the PoWs learnt for the first time that fifty of their fellow officers from the 'Great Escape' had been executed, along with the German claim – it was a lie – that the men had been killed while resisting capture, or attempting to re-escape. By then, Day and Dodge were also aware of the new tunnel and the news of the 'massacre' increased the resolve of the four men to escape once again. Later, Lieutenant Colonel 'Mad' Jack Churchill, of 2 Commando, was also made aware of the tunnel and he leapt at the chance of joining the escape party. By September the tunnel was complete and the 23rd was chosen as the night for the escape. The five men tunnelled through to the surface at 4 a.m., with Dowse and Day having already decided to stick together, but they were soon arrested hiding out in a house. They were taken back to Sachsenhausen by the Gestapo, but this time to Zellenbau (the 'death block') where they were eventually joined by Churchill, James and Dodge. Heinrich Himmler, the Gestapo chief-turned-Minister of the

Interior, ordered interrogation under torture before the men were to be executed. However, with an Allied victory increasingly likely, other German military commanders were becoming more cautious lest they face war crimes after a military defeat. The Kriminalpolizei, better known as the Kripo, and under the command of the SS, accepted the five men's assurance that there had been no contact with subversive Germans and that they were only carrying out their sworn duty to escape. In January 1945, the five officers were released from Zellenbau and taken back to Sonderlager A, from where they had most recently escaped. On 3 April, they realised their lives were once again in danger when they were taken to Flossenbürg concentration camp, where executions were routine. After several days, they were moved to Dachau, from where they journeyed to the Austrian mountain village of Niederndorf. The SS's desire for the men to be executed was again blocked and they were eventually 'liberated' by a column of US jeeps arriving in Niederndorf at the end of the war. After four years in captivity, Dowse was a free man at last. He was awarded the MC on 16 August 1946 and his citation detailed his various escape attempts and pointed out that, after the 'Great Escape', he had been kept in solitary confinement for four months.

Dowse served as an equerry at Buckingham Palace and had a long and successful career as a civil servant after leaving the RAF in 1946. For a number of years in the 1950s, at the time of the communist insurgency, he served in Malaya as assistant secretary to the Penang Settlement. In 1966 Dowse and his colleagues sought compensation from the Foreign Office for those who had suffered in concentration camps during the Second World War. Airey Neave, the Conservative MP, who had himself escaped from Colditz, championed the cause of the former PoWs. After an acrimonious debate in Parliament, a lengthy inquiry was held. Later the Ombudsman found in favour of twelve British servicemen who had been imprisoned in Sachsenhausen, including the RAF men.

In March 1994, to commemorate the fiftieth anniversary of the escape from Stalag Luft III, Dowse organised, and financed, a memorial service at the RAF church of St Clement Danes, central London, followed by a champagne reception at the RAF Club. Seventeen of the survivors were among those who attended and, exactly a decade later, some of them were reunited at the Imperial War Museum in London.

After retiring, Dowse, who was married three times, divided his time between his homes in Chelsea, London, and Monte Carlo, and continued his lifelong passion for rugby and luxury cars. A regular diner at the Savoy Hotel in London, he often said: 'Once one escapes from [Sachsenhausen], life holds no difficulties.' Dowse died on 10 April 2008, aged eighty-nine.

SQUADRON LEADER MANFRED BECKETT CZERNIN

RAF
DECORATIONS: DISTINGUISHED FLYING CROSS (DFC), MILITARY CROSS (MC) AND DISTINGUISHED SERVICE ORDER (DSO)
GAZETTED: 1 OCTOBER 1940, 1 DECEMBER 1944 AND 30 OCTOBER 1945

Manfred Czernin had a remarkable and varied career during the Second World War: he was both a fifteen-victory fighter ace, who flew during the Battle of Britain and, later, a Special

Operations Executive (SOE) agent who was decorated twice for his bravery behind enemy lines when still, strictly speaking, a commissioned officer in the RAF. When his biography, written by Norman Franks, was published long after his death, it was titled *Double Mission: R.A.F. Fighter Ace and SOE Agent Manfred Czernin*. The book claimed his two distinct roles provided a 'unique combination' and Czernin's colourful origins and strong character all added to his charisma. Franks wrote: 'His life and personality set him apart both as a man and a fighter.'

Czernin was born from aristocratic stock in Berlin, Germany, on 18 January 1913. He was the fourth son of Count Otto Czernin, an Austrian diplomat, and his English wife, who was the daughter of the 2nd Baron Grimthorpe. After his parents divorced several years later, the young Czernin moved to Italy with his mother. However, he was educated in the UK, at Oundle School in Northamptonshire. After completing his education, Czernin travelled to Rhodesia (now Zimbabwe) to work on a tobacco plantation. In April 1935, he returned to Britain to take up an appointment as an acting pilot officer on a short-service commission. After qualifying as a pilot, he was posted to 57 Squadron at RAF Upper Heyford, Oxfordshire, and he enjoyed several more squadron postings until placed on the Class A Reserve of Officers.

Following the outbreak of hostilities in 1939, Czernin was recalled and, after various short-term postings, served in May 1940 with 85 Squadron, a Hurricane unit based in France. On 16 May, he had to carry out a forced landing after being hit by enemy aircraft fire and he returned on foot to his unit at Lille Seclin. On 19 May, Czernin shot down a He 111 bomber and two Do 17 bombers, and the next day he shot down a Henschel

Hs 126 reconnaissance aircraft. On 21 May, he travelled by sea from Boulogne to Dover. On 8 June, he was posted to 17 Squadron at RAF Martlesham Heath, Suffolk, from where he flew a Hurricane out to France to join the forward elements at Le Mans. More victories followed – another He 111 fell to Czernin's guns on 12 June – before he again returned to Britain.

Still with 17 Squadron, Czernin flew with distinction throughout the Battle of Britain, raising his tally with a share in the destruction of a Do 17 on 12 July – after a series of head-on and quarter-stern attacks – his victim crashing into the sea off Orford Ness, Suffolk. In August, Czernin shared in the destruction of a Ju 88 bomber on the 21st and destroyed two Me 110 fighters and shared another on the 25th, his victims succumbing to a neat combination of head-on and rear attacks. In September, his tally increased: two more Me 110s on the 3rd, a Me 109 and two shared He 111s on the 5th, a Me 110 on the 11th, a Ju 88 shared on the 19th, and yet another Me 110 on the 27th. September also saw him sit for his portrait by Cuthbert Orde, the distinguished war artist.

Czernin was awarded the DFC on 1 October 1940 and his citation stated: 'This officer has displayed great keenness in his desire to engage the enemy and has destroyed nine of their aircraft. In August 1940, he led his section in a head-on attack on large formations of enemy aircraft, destroying three of them.' More combat success followed in October and Czernin shared in the destruction of a Do 17 on the 24th. However, on 17 November, in a combat over RAF Wattisham, Suffolk, he was shot down by Adolf Galland, the renowned German ace. Czernin baled out, slightly wounded, and his Hurricane crashed just west of Bradfield church.

In May 1941, he was rested but he was promoted to acting

squadron leader in mid-December. In February 1942, he was posted to India, where he took command of 146 Squadron at Dinjan, a unit he built up to a good operational standard before being appointed to HQ 224 Group as a Staff Officer (Operations). Returning to the UK to take up a similar appointment at 28 Group, Uxbridge, Middlesex, in April 1943, Czernin was officially transferred to an Air Ministry posting that September. In fact, he had just joined the SOE and a new life beckoned.

Trained over the next eight months in his new role as an SOE agent, Czernin was parachuted into German-occupied northern Italy in mid-June. For this courage, he was awarded the MC on 1 December 1944 and his highly confidential recommendation stated:

On the night of 12th–13th June 1944, Squadron Leader Czernin and his W/T [Wireless] Operator were to be dropped into enemy-occupied territory, but the reception signals were not satisfactory and they returned to base. On the following night, the reception was again incorrect. Entirely regardless of his own safety, Squadron Leader Czernin decided to jump with a view to making a personal reconnaissance of the situation. This he did without arms of any description and with the full knowledge that the Germans are constantly arranging bogus receptions for the receipt of Allied personnel and stores. On landing, he found the reception committee to be friendly. Thereupon he flashed a signal to the aircraft which dropped the Wireless Operator and equipment. But for this courageous action, a most vital operation would have had to be postponed at a stage when the time [timing] was of the utmost importance to the success of the major plan.

Afterwards, showing similar courage and stamina, and operating out of a farmhouse in the Tramonti region, Czernin set up a successful network of partisans before being picked up by a Lysander aircraft and flown back to the UK at the end of the year. Then, as outlined in the confidential recommendation for his DSO, Czernin returned to Italy in March 1945, this time parachuting into a location just south of the Swiss border. Here, he led the operations that culminated in the surrender of Bergamo. His DSO was announced on 30 October 1945 and the recommendation for his award stated:

Squadron Leader Czernin was parachuted behind the enemy lines in N.W. Italy on 21 March 1945. His task was to co-ordinate the various scattered Partisan units into a unified command and with these forces to carry out the directions of 15 Army Group. In order to reach his area of operation in the Bergamasco district he had to cross the 9,000 ft. Passo del Diaviolo which was completely covered with snow six feet deep. He made two attempts to cross the pass but without success. At 4 a.m. on 4 April he made a further effort and after marching continuously for 24 hours, suffering severely from cold, frostbite and lack of food, he succeeded in crossing the pass. Squadron Leader Czernin immediately commenced to organise the various Partisan forces and by his energy and personality quickly built up a large aggressive Partisan Command. This force, under his direction, went into action on 28th April 1945. He secured the unconditional surrender of three enemy garrisons whilst other forces under his command eliminated or captured the garrisons of three other places. Later the same day, after the whole area had been cleared of the enemy, he, with the Partisan Leader, drove into

Bergamo in a car draped with the Union Jack to demand the unconditional surrender of the German Forces. The Germans opened fire and Squadron Leader Czernin was forced to withdraw. He then ordered the Partisans to attack the city and arranged for the underground elements in Bergamo to rise simultaneously. At 7 a.m. on the 28th April 1945, Squadron Leader Czernin obtained an unconditional surrender from the German General. Throughout this period in the field Squadron Leader Czernin displayed the highest qualities of leadership and by his courage and daring made a notable contribution to the Allied success in North Italy.

Released from the RAF in October 1945, Czernin found it difficult settling back into civilian life after the war. He tried a variety of jobs before becoming sales manager for Fiat in England. However, he lost control of his financial affairs and became reliant on alcohol. Norman Franks, Czernin's biographer, ends his book thus:

Manfred Czernin, full of life and adventure, brave and fearless warrior, man of action, died peacefully in his sleep [aged forty-nine] following a heart attack during the early hours of Saturday, October 6, 1962. His poor body had finally succumbed to the alcohol that he used to fight his pain. Manfred's mortal ashes were buried at Ravello by courtesy of a friend ... who had purchased the beautiful Villa Cimbrone. Here he rests from his earthly labours in the warm Italian sun, in the land of his childhood, the country he loved.

LEADING AIRCRAFTMAN (LATER CORPORAL) ERNEST COXSHALL

Royal Air Force Volunteer Reserve (RAFVR)
DECORATION: MILITARY MEDAL (MM)
GAZETTED: 2 OCTOBER 1945

Ernest 'Nobby' Coxshall was born in Waltham Abbey, Essex, on 5 November 1914. He enlisted in the RAFVR on 13 May 1941, after which he was an instrument repairer. Coxshall was a member of the little known Royal Air Force Serving Commando. Their wartime work is less well known than that of their counterparts in the Army, Royal Marines and Royal Navy. The RAF unit was created because military planners, including Lord Mountbatten, the head of Combined Operations, saw a need to provide forward aircraft servicing support as the Allies advanced in the latter stages of the Second World War. It was deemed that it would take too long for squadron ground crew to reach forward positions and that, instead, self-contained mobile units were required. It was dangerous work: they had to be able to set up operations under fire and they also had to assist in assault landings. The recommendation for the unit's formation came in a memo signed by Lord Mountbatten on 27 January 1942. All ranks had to undergo military training supervised by Army officers and, since they were involved in amphibious landings, they were trained to swim well. Men were recruited from the RAF squadrons and notices were posted at RAF stations saying: 'Volunteers wanted in all trades for units to be formed to service aircraft under hazardous conditions.'

The Battle of Meiktila was a crucial offensive against the Japanese at the end of the Burma campaign. Along with the

Battle of Mandalay, it is sometimes known as the Battle of Central Burma. At one point during the heat of battle at Meiktila in March 1945, Dakota aircraft arrived to evacuate casualties and one was badly damaged in the fighting.

The recommendation for Coxshall's MM stated: 'Leading Aircraftman Coxshall broke cover under shell fire to rescue wounded from a Dakota which had received a direct hit. On every occasion when casualties arose, due to enemy shelling and mortar fire in the vicinity of "D" Box, he was on the spot to remove wounded, to cover and to assist in any possible way. His complete disregard for danger was an undoubtable inspiration to all airmen.'

This recommendation was further supported by the Air Chief Marshal commanding South East Asia, who wrote: 'In view of the fact that it was largely due to this airman's bravery and devotion to duty under shell fire that all the wounded were successfully rescued, I most strongly recommend that he be awarded an immediate Military Medal.' His award was announced on 2 October 1945.

This was not the only occasion, however, on which Coxshall showed great bravery. At about the same time, there was another incident which is recounted in *A History of the RAF Servicing Commandos* by J. Davies and J. P. Kellett. The authors wrote:

[The Gurkhas] frequently took off on forays and harassed the Japs when and wherever they could. It was amazing how quietly they could move, even when loaded with packs and weapons. 'Nobby' Coxshall went out on a patrol with them and they were ambushed on a railway line, which was most unusual for the Gurkhas. He tried to carry out a wounded

Gurkha back to our positions, but he died in spite of Nobby's efforts ... The dead Gurkha had a brother in the same regiment and he persuaded his father that instead of accepting the dead boy's kukri [a Gurkha's traditional, curved fighting knife], which was the custom, he should present it to Nobby, who was very proud.

Coxshall was discharged from the RAF on 5 July 1946.

Coxshall then enlisted in the South African Air Force on 22 December 1948 and served in it for four years. He served in the Royal New Zealand Air Force for fifteen years from 10 April 1953. It is not known what happened to him after he ended his military service in 1968.

STAFF SERGEANT EDGAR ENGLAND
Army
DECORATION: DISTINGUISHED FLYING MEDAL (DFM)
GAZETTED: 19 OCTOBER 1944

The motto of the Glider Pilot Regiment was 'Nothing Is Impossible'. Given the extremely hazardous nature of some of its assignments during the Second World War, they were appropriate words. The Glider Pilot Regiment was part of the Airborne Force, formed on the orders of Winston Churchill, the Prime Minister. It was officially inaugurated on 24 February 1942 as part of the Army Air Corps, which then consisted of the Glider Pilot Regiment, the Parachute Regiment and elements of the Special Air Service (SAS). Volunteers were called from Army units and – after military and RAF aircrew selection tests – they were subjected to a rigorous training regime designed to make them 'total soldiers'. They were instructed in the use of all the weapons and equipment of the combat soldiers that they carried into battle so that they could, if necessary, fight alongside them.

As part of the D-Day operations, the 6th Airborne Division was charged with landing on the left flank of the invasion area on the night of 5/6 June 1944, where it was to capture and hold the bridges of the River Orne, and destroy the Merville battery in order to assist in the landings on Sword Beach. High on the list of those responsible for the success of Operation Tonga – as it was codenamed – were the men of the Glider Pilot Regiment, their task being to ensure their Horsa and Hamilcar gliders reached the correct Landing Zone (LZ), on being parted from their 'tugs', this being crucial to the effectiveness of subsequent operations on the ground.

Even in the best of conditions, the gliders were hard to fly because of their heavy loads. However, England, originally from Burnley, Lancashire, successfully landed his Hamilcar on 'N' LZ on the Ranville ridge with his 17-pounder anti-tank gun and crew, the whole vital to the needs of the 3rd and 5th Parachute Brigades. In common with all members of the Glider Pilot Regiment, England was a fully trained infantryman so, although he had successfully completed the airborne element of his task, he was now required to support combat operations on the ground, operations that were quickly reinforced by elements of Operation Mallard the following day.

The recommendation for his decoration stated:

On the night of 5th/6th June, 1944, Staff Sergeant England flew a Hamilcar glider to France and in spite of the most difficult weather conditions and bad visibility, he succeeded in landing his glider safely in the correct area regardless of flak and ground opposition from the enemy. It was a very hazardous undertaking as the landing area was obstructed by poles and small pits and were it not for Staff Sergeant England's skill and coolness, his load, a vital 17 pounder, could not have been delivered intact at the right time and place.

The DFM, announced on 19 October 1944, was unique to a Hamilcar pilot for the D-Day offensive.

It is not known what happened to England after the war.

9

Post-Second World War Gallantry

For many, conflicts after 1945 failed to recapture the death or glory days for pilots and aircrew of the Second World War. This did not mean that aerial combat in conflicts such as the Korean War or the Vietnam War were safe – they were anything but. However, as aircraft and aerial equipment became more sophisticated, the nature of flying gradually changed and the opportunity for traditional dogfights – a life or death test of one pilot's ability against another's – became far less commonplace. Modern-day military flying has undoubtedly lost some of the romance of the era of the two world wars, but, clearly, not the gallantry.

Helicopters began to appear at the end of the Second World War and eventually matured into an indispensable part of military aviation. Improved designs of helicopters were tested in both the Korean and Vietnam wars. In conflicts, such as Northern Ireland, where there was a terrorist enemy, and the Falklands War, when the terrain made the presence of helicopters highly desirable, they repeatedly proved their worth. In recent times, attack helicopters such as the Apache have proved a lethal weapon in theatres such as Iraq and Afghanistan.

I have awards for gallantry in my collection relating to six different conflicts between the Second World War and the present day: the 'Yangtse incident', the Korean War, the Vietnam War, *the 'Troubles' in Northern Ireland, the Falklands War and Afghanistan.*

Although Flight Sergeant Kenneth Letford was decorated three times during the Second World War, it is for the 'Yangtse incident' of 1949 that he received his most acclaimed award and I have therefore included him in this chapter rather than Chapter 5.

FLIGHT LIEUTENANT (LATER SQUADRON LEADER) KENNETH HENRY FRANCIS LETFORD

Royal Air Force Volunteer Reserve (RAFVR)/RAF

DECORATIONS: DISTINGUISHED FLYING CROSS (DFC) AND BAR, DISTINGUISHED SERVICE ORDER (DSO) AND BAR

GAZETTED: 7 SEPTEMBER 1943, 5 JULY 1949, 23 NOVEMBER 1943 AND 21 SEPTEMBER 1945

Kenneth Letford served with the RAFVR and RAF for almost thirty years from 1939 to 1968. During the Second World War, he served as a pilot with Bomber Command and, as a result of his wartime exploits, he was awarded three gallantry decorations. However, it was some years after the end of the war that Letford received his fourth decoration: a rare DFC (a Bar to his wartime award) for the famous 'Yangstse incident' in the Far East in 1949.

Little is known about Letford's early life. In 1942, he flew as a flight sergeant but he was commissioned on 10 September 1942. He was awarded the DFC on 7 September 1943 and his citation for his service with 207 Squadron stated: 'This officer, now on his second tour of operational duty, has attacked most of the enemy's heavily defended targets. A first rate captain of aircraft, he has consistently shown the great determination to press home his attacks regardless of difficulties or enemy opposition. He has obtained some excellent photographs.'

Letford was awarded the DSO less than three months later when his citation, announced on 23 November 1943, stated:

One night in October, 1943, this officer was captain and pilot of an aircraft detailed to attack Leipzig. During the sorties, the bomber was engaged by a fighter and was hit by a hail of bullets. The mid-upper gunner was wounded and his gun turret rendered useless; the wireless operator was also wounded and some of his wireless equipment was destroyed. The inter-communication gear was put out of action and other damage was sustained. The situation became alarming when some incendiary bombs and accumulators caught fire. Nevertheless, Flight Lieutenant Letford coolly organised his crew to fight the flames and under his able directions they succeeded in quelling the fire. When base was reached, Flight Lieutenant Letford affected a perfect landing without the aid of flaps. In circumstances fraught with danger, this officer displayed inspiring leadership, great courage and determination.

His final wartime gallantry award was announced on 21 September 1945 for his courage in the Lancaster bombers of 156 Squadron, a Path Finder unit. The citation to the Bar to his DSO, announced on 21 September 1945, stated: 'Squadron Leader Letford is now on his fourth tour of operational duties. His skilled airmanship and fine fighting spirit have earned him the confidence of his crew and of the squadron. He is a fearless captain who has shown complete disregard for any opposition when pressing home his attacks. His courage and devotion to duty have been a splendid example to those who have served with him.'

After the end of hostilities, Letford gained a permanent commission in the RAF and was serving 88 Squadron at Kai Tek, Hong Kong, at the time of the 'Yangste incident' in April 1949, an inspiring chapter in post-war conflict famously portrayed in the 1957 film, *Yangtse Incident*, starring Richard Todd.

HMS *Amethyst* first came under fire from Chinese communists on 20 April 1949, while making her way from Shanghai to Nanking to relieve HMS *Consort* of her duties as guard ship to the British Embassy, thus setting in motion many striking acts of gallantry on the part of her crew. In fact, the crew were to remain stranded on the Yangtse River for more than three months, an ordeal made all the more perilous for the loss of some twenty men in the opening action, as well as numerous wounded. It was the suffering of the latter that quickly prompted a daring attempt to fly in a doctor, Flight Lieutenant M. E. Fearnley, and medical supplies – for the ship's surgeon and attendant were among the fatalities. Responsibility for undertaking this vital mission fell to Letford at the helm of one of 88 Squadron's Sunderland flying boats.

He arrived over the stranded *Amethyst* in the afternoon of the 21st, among his passengers being Group Captain C. Jefferson and a naval doctor, in addition to Fearnley. Landing immaculately on the river, Letford cut engines and dropped anchor at 1630 hours, and a sampan (flat-bottomed Chinese boat) was quickly under way from the *Amethyst*, but moments after Fearnley had boarded it with his morphia supply, the communists opened a heavy fire. Quickly straddled by about ten shells, the Sunderland's immediate prospects looked bleak, but, displaying the utmost calm and skill, Letford managed a record-breaking downwind departure, thereby saving his passengers from certain death and with, to all intents and purposes, his mission complete. He did, however, return the following day in the hope of transferring further medical equipment, but such was the ferocity of the communists' fire that he had to abandon any such intention.

A replacement skipper, Lieutenant Commander J. S. Kerans, was put in place, having reached the *Amethyst* after a eventful journey overland. However, costly attempts to relieve the ship by fellow naval consorts having failed, it was decided to make a bolt for it downriver for the open sea, under cover of darkness, on 30 July. The rest, as they say, is history, not least Kerans' wonderful signal sent on the following day: 'Have rejoined the Fleet. Am south of Woo Sung. No damage or casualties. God save the King.'

Fifteen of the *Amethyst*'s crew were decorated or Mentioned in Despatches, including a DSO for Kerans, while Fearnley, the RAF medic, was awarded a DFC; so, too, Letford, by way of a Bar to his earlier award, thereby creating a unique set of gallantry awards – only twenty-five airmen had equalled his earlier combination of a DSO and Bar and DFC in the Second World War.

Letford, who retired from the RAF in 1969, died in British Columbia, Canada, in October 1985, aged sixty-three.

FLIGHT LIEUTENANT (LATER SQUADRON LEADER) PETER MONTAGUE MIDDLETON

Royal Australian Air Force (RAAF)
DECORATION: DISTINGUISHED FLYING CROSS (DFC)
GAZETTED: 30 DECEMBER 1952

Peter Middleton was born in Sandringham, Victoria, Australia, on 16 November 1924. He enlisted in the RAAF in Melbourne on 30 March 1943.

Aged twenty-eight and by then a flight lieutenant, Middleton served in the Korean War, a conflict that lasted from June 1950 to July 1953 and was fought between the Republic of Korea (supported largely by the US) and the Democratic People's Republic of Korea (supported by China and, to a lesser extent, the Soviet Union).

Middleton was awarded his DFC on 30 December 1952 and the citation stated:

> Flight Lieutenant Middleton has since his posting to 77 Squadron in January 1952 flown a total of one hundred and eighty nine sorties on all types of operational missions in Meteor aircraft in support of the United Nations Forces in Korea. Ground attack missions have constituted a large proportion of those he has carried out and on all of these he has pressed home his attacks with vigour and determination, often in the face of intense and accurate enemy anti-aircraft fire. Flight Lieutenant Middleton's leadership of his Squadron has been exemplary and his fearlessness, personal behaviour and devotion to duty have been an inspiration to all those with whom he served and in keeping with the highest

traditions of the Royal Australian Air Force.

Middleton enjoyed writing and, long after the Korean War, he produced an account of some of his experiences in the conflict. In one article entitled 'The Chongdan Raid', Middleton gives a vivid description of the intensity of a raid on a targeted village.

The sun rolls to the horizon when the CO calls 'Attack positions' and swings to the south to allow us to fall into loose line astern more readily. He skirts the village and will dive out of the west taking what little advantage the sinking sun offers. I see the village now. The main road from Haiju dissects a jumble of houses, perhaps two hundred, all clustered around the intersection of the main road and a secondary track from the north. The surrounding countryside is fairly flat and smudged with paddy fields. An overlay of mist and smoke hangs heavy in the ominously still air.

'One diving,' calls the CO brusquely. Down he plummets into that mist-filled bowl. I'm last to dive. I wait like a spectator in the high bleachers, watching a play of life and death. The CO's rockets explode blackly in the jumbled cluster of buildings. That really stirs them up. Someone in the village pulls the flak switch and it suddenly showers upward like rain in reverse. In the gathering gloom, every bullet streaks red. The effect of all this lead inspires so much awe that I forget to be frightened.

Down the aircraft dive, one after another. Calls come with hard regularity combining with the black and red bruises of the rockets crashing into the village. Still the sheets of small arms fire shower blindly upwards even through the rocket bursts . . .

In addition to his DFC, Middleton was awarded the Air Medal by the United States. Post-Second World War DFCs seldom appear on the market. During the Korean War, Australians received a total of forty-one DFCs and six Bars were also issued.

In October 1966, while serving in Vietnam, Middleton was co-piloting an Iroquois helicopter when it crashed in Phouc Tuy Province. The aircraft came to rest in a position that left Middleton wedged in his seat by a tree with 200 lb of TNT and numerous detonators on board. However, his passenger, a sergeant, was able to extricate Middleton from the crushed seat shortly before the helicopter's fuel tanks exploded. Flight Lieutenant Middleton was discharged from the services in July 1967, retiring with the honorary rank of squadron leader.

After retiring from the RAAF, Middleton moved to America. He died in Elfrida, Arizona, on 19 September 2007, aged eighty-two.

FLIGHT LIEUTENANT (LATER AIR COMMODORE) VINCENT JEROME HILL

Royal Australian Air Force (RAAF)
DECORATIONS: DISTINGUISHED FLYING CROSS (DFC) AND BAR, AND AIR FORCE CROSS (AFC)
GAZETTED: 29 SEPTEMBER 1953, 10 DECEMBER 1968
AND
1 JANUARY 1962

Vincent Hill's distinguished flying career, which spanned thirty-four years, involved participation in no fewer than three wars: the Second World War, the Korean War and the Vietnam War. During this time, he was decorated three times and earned a reputation as a skilful, courageous and determined combat pilot, as well as a talented test pilot in 'hazardous experimental flying'.

Hill enlisted as an aircrew trainee in the Empire Air Training Scheme on 10 October 1942 and, on 8 June 1943, he graduated as a pilot with the rank of sergeant. Hill served with various flying units within Australia and in the South West Pacific area during the Second World War. On 1 March 1945, he was appointed to a commission in the General Duties Branch of the RAAF with the rank of pilot officer. This appointment was terminated upon demobilisation on 19 March 1948. However, on 30 September of the same year, Hill was appointed to a commission in the Active Citizen Air Force. He served with 25 (City of Perth) Squadron until he was transferred to the General Reserve on 26 March 1952. He was transferred to the permanent RAAF on 2 June 1952.

On 29 September 1952, Hill learnt he was to be posted to 77 Squadron for service in the Korean War. His DFC was announced on 29 September 1953 after the recommendation for his award stated:

Flight Lieutenant V.J. Hill has been a member of No. 77 (interceptor/Fighter) Squadron since 22 October, 1952 and as at 14th March, 1953 has completed one hundred and twenty combat missions. For the greater part of his tour his appointment has been that of Flight Commander.

This officer has planned and led many successful attacks against the enemy. The thorough manner in which he has assessed every detail of an impending raid has enabled his formations to hit heavily defended targets with the minimum of loss. During these flights Flight Lieutenant Hill has displayed outstanding skill, determination and personal courage.

On 30th January, 1953 this officer planned and led a sixteen-aircraft armed reconnaissance mission covering the major lines of communication in North Korea. During this flight, he located in the semi-darkness a Communist vehicle park situated near four anti-aircraft batteries. Immediately summing up the dangers involved, he continued his flight in a way that would indicate to the enemy that the target had not been sighted. Having withdrawn from the area he carried out an aerial briefing and led an attack which saturated the enemy's anti-aircraft defences and enabled the vehicle concentration to be smashed. Flight Lieutenant Hill on this occasion personally accounted for 21 tanker-type vehicles. In this and many other attacks Flight Lieutenant Hill by his fine example has been an inspiration to his fellow pilots and has reflected great credit on himself and the Royal Australian Air Force.

From February 1954, Hill worked from Overseas Headquarters, based in London. Here, he successfully completed the No. 13 Empire Test Pilot course and received the coveted McKenna Trophy. In January 1955, he returned to Australia to take up flying duties with the Aircraft Research and Development Unit. This was followed by a two-year exchange posting with the Royal Canadian Air Force, during which time he was posted to the Central Experimental and Proving Establishment in Rockcliffe, Ottawa, Canada. Hill returned to the Australian Aircraft Research and Development Unit in January 1959. On New Year's Day 1962, he was awarded the AFC in recognition of his important and highly dangerous testing work. The recommendation for his award stated:

> Squadron Leader Hill joined R.A.A.F. in June, 1952 and has been Officer Commanding, Flight Test Squadron Aircraft Research and Development Units since January, 1960. He was responsible for flight testing the Sabre Canopy Breaker incorporated in the Sabre ejection seat modification. In December, 1960 he carried out tests on the effect of Sidewinder firing on engine surge in Sabre aircraft at extreme altitudes. He is quite fearless in his approach to test flying and the methodical and thorough manner in which he has carried out his responsibilities clearly shows him to be a test pilot of exceptional capabilities.

In 1962 he undertook the RAAF Staff College course and, after completing it, the newly promoted Air Commodore Hill was posted for staff duties in the Directorate of Personnel (Officers) at the Department of Air. In 1966, Hill returned to flying duties, first with No. 82 Wing and then with 2 Squadron in Vietnam where he was responsible for flying operations. The Vietnam War was fought across Vietnam, Laos and Cambodia from November 1955 until the fall of Saigon on 30 April 1975. Hill was appointed Director of Joint Plans at the Department of Defence on 13 June 1968. On 10 December 1968, he was awarded a Bar to his DFC for his outstanding efforts and devotion to duty during the war.

Hill was made commanding officer of No. 82 Wing on 4 December 1970 and, in 1972, he was posted to America to attend the United States Air Warfare College course. In June 1973, Hill returned to Australia to take up the appointment of

Senior Administrative Staff Officer at Headquarters Support Command. He was appointed Director-General Joint Plans and Operations at the Department of Defence on 7 January 1974 and he retired from the RAAF on 4 February 1976.

It is not known what happened to Hill after his retirement.

WARRANT OFFICER (LATER CAPTAIN) WILLIAM THOMAS SCARRATT
Army
DECORATION: DISTINGUISHED FLYING CROSS (DFC)
GAZETTED: 25 MARCH 1975

Bill Scarratt has the distinction of being awarded the first DFC during the 'Troubles' in Northern Ireland. Indeed, only three were awarded during the entire campaign, making it the rarest gallantry award for that theatre of operations. Scarratt was born in Stoke-on-Trent, Staffordshire, on 4 October 1939. An only child, his father was a pick and shovel coal miner and his mother worked in the local brick factory. After attending the local Wolstanton Grammar School, Scarratt enlisted in the Parachute Regiment as a private in 1957, aged seventeen. He served with that unit for more than twelve years until 1970. In 1963, Scarratt took part in an exchange with American troops that saw him train with the US 82nd Airborne Division at Fort Bragg, North Carolina. While in the US serving as a platoon sergeant, Scarratt also learnt to freefall at high altitude with the American Special Forces, twice jumping, with oxygen and full equipment, from the staggering height of 20,000 feet. On his return to Britain, he was a member of the Red Devils Parachute Regiment Free Fall team from 1964 to 1968. However, in 1970

Scarratt transferred to the Army Air Corps (AAC) and trained to become a helicopter pilot. In total, he flew 8,700 hours in military helicopters and served in the UK, Cyprus, Jordan, Bahrain, Aden, Oman, Malaya, the USA, (West) Germany and Northern Ireland.

It was while serving on his second tour (of five) in Northern Ireland with 655 Squadron on the afternoon of 3 September 1974 that Scarratt, then a warrant officer class 2, took part in the action for which he was awarded the DFC. For security reasons at the time, his citation of 25 March 1975 stated only that his award was 'in recognition of gallant and distinguished service in Northern Ireland during the period 1st August 1974 to 31st October 1974'.

However, in an interview at his home in the North of England, Scarratt recalled that fateful day in vivid detail for the first time: he described how he was flying solo to drop off a four-man patrol from 45 Commando, Royal Marines, in South Armagh, so-called 'bandit country', close to the border with the Republic.

Before taking off, I confirmed the intended location with the corporal and marked it on a map. The place was called Balls Mill. I had never been there before but I knew the area well, having completed a four-month tour in 1973. I took off, with the patrol on board, approaching the village from the north. I was following a small stream, flying low level, and as the village came into sight I had this strange feeling that things didn't look right. Having previously spent twelve years with the Parachute Regiment, you are taught, as an infantryman, to look for abnormal everyday activities. There were no animals in the fields and no people moving about: a sure sign

393

of trouble. Balls Mill consisted of a small main road running east to west, not more than 100 yards in length, with terraced houses facing each other on both sides of the road. Each house had a small back garden with washing lines, various vegetable patches and small sheds. To the north of the village, running parallel to the main road, were four open fields, one of which the patrol commander wanted me to land in to drop off the patrol.

But, as a former infantryman, I knew you did not, in daylight, remain stationary in open ground unless you were dug in and had covering fire. I had neither so, through the headphones to the corporal, I vetoed the plan and proceeded to look for a better place. I found a dip in the ground concealed by some small trees and bushes, just to the west of the four fields. The other reason I chose to stay away from the front of the village was that it appeared to be washing day. All the clothes lines were full, except for two houses together in the middle, facing two of the four fields. Also the large windows were open but there were no curtains at the back, indicating that the houses had either been derelict or had been vacated. The windows open, however, were a give-away. I smelt a rat.

I landed in the recess in the ground behind the small bushes and trees. I could just about see the back of one of the two houses. The four-man patrol disembarked and deployed, two on each side of the helicopter. They then went to ground, covering the houses with their weapons. As I started to take off and return to Forkhill [the Army base], my helicopter was hit by small arms' fire, coming from one of the two houses. I could hear the effects of the hits on the air-frame. I was out of there like a scalded cat. I immediately applied full power, spun around, gained height and started to fly back towards Forkhill. The aircraft didn't appear be affected, according to the instruments which I monitored as I flew. I did, however, notice that I could not transmit on the radio and I had lost sound through the headphones in my flying helmet. I landed back at Forkhill to pick up the second patrol in order to reinforce the first one. Apparently, they had heard the first patrol and were eager to go. I had landed down-wind for speed [normally a helicopter lands into the wind].

It was only then that Scarratt smelt turbine fuel and suspected that his aircraft had been hit. He jumped out of the helicopter to examine the fuel tanks and they were spurting fuel. He immediately cancelled the flight, realising it would be too dangerous to fly. Furthermore, Scarratt realised just how close he had come to being killed: a bullet had shot away the intercom lead that had been hanging down from his helmet, thereby explaining why his radio was useless. Later, the once confidential recommendation for his DFC revealed that the terrorist gunmen had fired a total of eighty-eight shots at the helicopter and the patrol, six of which hit the aircraft, including two in the main fuel tanks. It stated:

Although the aircraft was badly holed through the main rotor blade, which adversely affected the handling characteristics, WO2 Scarratt landed the helicopter safely. The alternative to this action, and probably less dangerous from a personal point of view, would have been to land and abandon the aircraft immediately. In this event the helicopter would undoubtedly have been destroyed by hostile ground fire, a noticeable success of the terrorists. This would have led to re-examination of helicopter tactics in border areas . . . WO2 Scarratt's gallant action was a blow to the terrorists' avowed aim to destroy a helicopter. It enabled a balanced appreciation of the situation to be taken, as a result of which normal helicopter operations have been allowed to continue. Throughout this incident WO2 Scarratt's professionalism and coolness both under fire and afterwards were of the highest order.

Scarratt only heard he had been awarded the DFC when he visited the officers' mess at Aldergrove airport, on the outskirts of Belfast, for a drink during another tour of Northern Ireland – and everyone started applauding. 'Someone said: "You have been awarded the DFC," and I replied: "But what for?" He said: "For when you were nearly shot down last year!" I was stunned.' He received his DFC from the Queen in an investiture at Buckingham Palace attended by his wife, Molly, and their eldest child, James. Scarratt left the AAC in 1980 after twenty-three years' military service, and with the rank of captain, having been commissioned from the ranks five years earlier. From 1980, he served for six years with the Territorial Army (AAC).

At the end of his military career, Scarratt became a commercial helicopter pilot, doing everything from pleasure and private rides (he flew both Margaret Thatcher and Tony Blair when they were prime ministers) to low-level, highly dangerous crop spraying. More recently, he taught helicopter flying, only finally retiring at sixty-seven with more than 10,000 hours of military and civilian flying. While still flying commercially, and alone, Scarratt almost died when he ditched his helicopter in foggy conditions into Lake Windermere,

Cumbria, in January 2001. The helicopter sank to the bottom of the lake nearly ninety feet below, but Scarratt, a strong swimmer, swam half a mile to safety in chilly waters. 'I have had a few scrapes in my time, but luckily I have come through,' he said cheerfully. 'I have never injured myself parachuting and I have never injured myself flying. You have to keep your wits about you.'

Now seventy-two, and a widower with three grown-up children and three grandchildren, Scarratt is proud that his two sons have served in the British military and his daughter has served with the UN police force. 'We have more than a hundred and ten years' [military and police] service between us,' he said.

CAPTAIN (LATER MAJOR) JEFFREY PETER NIBLETT

Royal Marines
DECORATION: DISTINGUISHED FLYING CROSS (DFC)
GAZETTED: 8 OCTOBER 1982

Jeff Niblett was born in Aldershot, Hampshire, on 26 September 1949. The younger son of a businessman and his wife, he completed his education at Farnborough Grammar School, Hampshire, aged eighteen. In the same year, he gained his private pilot's licence through a Royal Naval Flying Scholarship while serving in the Combined Cadet Force. After leaving school and failing RAF aircrew selection, Niblett worked locally in a variety of manual jobs which allowed him to continue flying, attended the Eskdale Outbound Course and travelled widely in Europe. During this time he met the son of a family friend who was serving as a Royal Marines officer. It was this chance meeting that led to Niblett's application for a commission to the Royal Marines which was successful in September 1970, just days before his twenty-first birthday. A year later, Niblett completed training and was appointed as a troop commander with 45 Commando, with whom he did two tours of duty in Northern Ireland. In June 1975, Niblett was awarded his Army pilot's 'wings' which led to a Royal Naval Gazelle conversion course and deployment to the Mediterranean for a NATO exercise. In October 1975, he converted to the Royal Naval Wessex V helicopter and the following year he was awarded the Hallam Trophy as the top pilot completing Commando operational training. A further flying tour followed in August 1979 with a conversion course on to the Scout helicopter and appointment to 3 Commando Brigade Air Squadron, based at Plymouth, as commanding officer of the Brunei Flight. After completing his final winter deployment in Norway in March 1982, Niblett was selected to attend the Qualified Helicopter Instructor course at RAF Shawbury, Shropshire. However, the day before he was due to leave the squadron, Argentina invaded the Falkland Islands and instead he began preparing for deployment with the Task Force.

Niblett, by now a captain, kept a diary throughout the whole of his deployment detailing events as they unfolded and highlighting the challenges and demands placed on aircrew flying in support of the Task Force units, particularly following the landings on 21 May. The extreme dangers faced by all crews became apparent within the first hour when two Gazelle reconnaissance helicopters from the squadron were shot down by enemy ground fire, with the loss of three crew. Once deployed ashore, Niblett's flight provided support wherever it was required throughout the beach head as tasked by the Commando Brigade. At the end of the first week, Niblett flew in support of the breakout by the 2nd Battalion, the Parachute Regiment (2 Para) and their subsequent assault on Darwin and Goose Green. It was during this operation that he repeatedly showed great courage for which he was awarded the DFC. His decoration is exceptional for two reasons: it was, until 2006, the only DFC ever awarded to a Royal Marine and it is one of just nine DFCs awarded during the Falklands War.

The citation for his DFC, announced on 8 October 1982, stated:

> During the attack on Darwin and Goose Green, Captain Niblett led a section of two Scout helicopters, supplying ammunition and evacuating casualties for two days, often in the thick of battle and under enemy fire. During one mission both Scouts were attacked by Argentine Pucara aircraft. The helicopters evaded the first attack but one was subsequently shot down. However, with quite exceptional flying skill and superb teamwork with his aircrewman, Captain Niblett evaded three further cannon and rocket attacks, safely completing the mission. He then resolutely continued support and casualty evacuation operations until well after dark.
>
> His courage, leadership and flying skills were also demonstrated in an incident when he evacuated a seriously wounded Marine from Mount Challenger, flying in dark and misty conditions over most hazardous terrain. Captain Niblett proved himself an outstanding Flight Commander and pilot. The superb support that his flight as a whole gave to the landing force reflects his exemplary and dedicated service.

However, what the citation failed to reveal was the identity of the casualty whom the two lightly built and unarmed Scouts had been going to collect on 28 May 1982: Lieutenant Colonel Herbert 'H' Jones, the commanding officer of 2 Para, who was famously awarded a posthumous VC for bravery. In an interview at his home in Norfolk, Niblett told me:

I was commanding a section of two Scouts, flown by myself and Lieutenant Richard Nunn, attached in direct support of 2 Para during the battle for Darwin and Goose Green. Throughout the morning [of 28 May 1982] we had flown over three and a half hours ferrying ammunition forward to the battalion mortar lines and front-line troops and returning to our Forward Operating Base at Camilla Creek House with casualties, both our own forces and enemy troops. Enemy action included artillery fire on and close to our landing points throughout the morning.

While at Camilla and partway through loading further ammunition for the front line with rotors running, I heard the radio call on the battalion command 'net' saying that H [Jones] had been shot: 'Sunray [the radio call sign for the commanding officer] is down.' At this stage additional casualties were mentioned but no exact details. On hearing the call, I immediately radioed Lieutenant Nunn and ordered that the ammo was offloaded and replaced with stretchers, which was done. Less than a minute from the original call we were airborne and heading south toward the Darwin area where 'H' had been shot. I led the pair and, within a minute or so of lifting, a pair of Pucaras appeared directly ahead of us descending from the very low cloud base and crossing ahead of us at approx 500 metres' range. The weather had remained overcast all day with low cloud at about 150–200 feet but with good visibility underneath and no precipitation.

On seeing the enemy aircraft, I ordered a break which we achieved – one aircraft to the right and the other to the left. The Pucaras had seen us and turned toward us and when they saw our break they took one of us each. At very low level and high speed, we manoeuvred hard and fast to escape their attack. Quite early on Lieutenant Nunn and I crossed paths flying in opposite directions and that was the last time I saw his aircraft before he was shot down. The Pucara attacking me engaged us with cannon, machine-gun and rocket salvos trying unsuccessfully to down us with successive passes. The Pucara flew at relatively low speed and was extremely agile, which is not something we had previously encountered . . .

After two or three attacks on my aircraft, my attacker was joined by the second Pucara which had obviously broken away from attacking Lieutenant Nunn. At this stage, we were unaware that he had been shot down. Both Pucaras then continued to attack me in successive passes and, after perhaps two or three more attacks when I was flying at extremely low level, I found myself close to Camilla Creek House where ground troops were able to engage the enemy aircraft with small arms and drive them off. Throughout all the engagements my air gunner, Sergeant John Glaze, was positioned in the back of the Scout and was giving me a running commentary on the Pucaras' attacks which I was able to respond to. The ground we were flying over was very exposed with no cover whatsoever and the low cloud base had kept the enemy aircraft close to our operating height.

The closest to being hit was a salvo of rocket fire which passed ahead and behind my aircraft simultaneously throwing large amounts of dirt and soil in the air as a result of the explosions. It was during this attack that I recall instinctively reaching down to the control panel and operating the windscreen wipers to clear the windscreen and offer better vision. Other attacks by cannon and machine gun were equally close but luckily the aircraft suffered no material damage. Following the breaking off of the enemy aircraft, I immediately found a safe area to land near the Camilla Creek defences, made my fastest ever shutdown and dived into the nearest trench with Sergeant Glaze. I had been lucky during my two or three minutes under attack: I was so at one with the aircraft, after nearly three years, that it was like a second skin. I could fly it to its limits and at times we had been literally inches off the ground.

On hearing of the loss of the second Scout, Niblett and another helicopter flew to the scene of where Nunn's helicopter had crashed, killing him. His air gunner, Sergeant Belcher, was seriously injured and had lost part of a leg, but Niblett flew him for urgent medical treatment. The next day he returned to recover Nunn's body from the crash scene.

It later emerged that one of the Argentinian Pucaras which had attacked the two Scouts flew into a mountain on its return trip, killing the pilot, Teniente Giménez, whose remains were not discovered for another four years.

Niblett also recalled how, on 3 June 1982, he had been involved in another rescue:

The weather that day was particularly bad and had stopped all helo [helicopter] support to the front line. A call was received in Brigade requesting an urgent casevac [casualty evacuation] for a Marine who had lost a foot in a minefield explosion during an overnight reconnaissance patrol. The injury was such that they could not move the casualty themselves and a helo casevac was the only safe option in the circumstances as speed was important. I elected to accept the mission and, with Sergeant Glaze, departed Teal Inlet in a slow hover taxi, once again following the only set of telephone wires which the map showed led toward the area we needed to reach which was over fifteen kilometres away. On the first attempt, the weather closed in completely and we were unable to climb on to the higher ground and instead diverted to pick up another casualty from a nearer unit who we returned to the Field Dressing Station at Teal. We immediately made a second attempt with similar results and, on the third attempt, we finally succeeded in reaching the mountainous area where 42 Commando was operating. After a quick brief on the ground, we continued to move forward, still in very poor visibility, and eventually we located the casualty, loaded him on board and returned him to Teal Inlet for treatment. All in all a very testing but satisfying sortie carried out in almost impossible weather conditions. Luckily the Marine concerned recovered well.

Niblett only learnt of his gallantry award when back in Britain – on the morning that it was later announced in the *London Gazette*. He was called to see his squadron CO, Major Peter Cameron, and was 'dumbfounded', but proud, to discover the news.

Between 1983 and 1995, Niblett completed further staff and flying tours in the Royal Marines. However, in 1987 he realised that he was suffering from the effects of post-traumatic stress disorder (PTSD) as a result of his experiences in the Falklands. Niblett has spoken honestly and movingly about his battle with PTSD – which eventually cost him his first marriage from which he has a son – in *The Scars of War*. He told the book's author, Hugh McManners, how life had been difficult in the five years after the Falklands War and he was burdened by the loss of comrades, particularly Nunn. 'When you lose someone close to you, someone you like very much, you feel anger at the safeness of the normal world, turning against people and the environment in which you once felt comfortable. You come to distrust and resent authority,' he said. It was not until Niblett read a newspaper article about a survey on post-Falklands trauma, conducted by Royal Navy psychiatrist Surgeon Commander Morgan O'Connell, that he realised he had all the symptoms of someone with PTSD. For the first time, he addressed the issue and had psychiatric sessions with O'Connell, which eventually involved him returning to the Falklands to relive incidents that had troubled him and to visit Nunn's grave to pay his final respects. However, a recurrence of his health problems associated with PTSD resulted in Niblett retiring early from the Royal Marines in 1995, aged forty-five.

After ending his military service, Niblett worked initially as a Ministry of Defence civil servant and then with his local health authority. After finally retiring in early 2002, aged fifty-two, he moved to France with his second wife, Mary, and they lived in Brittany for eight years. Two years ago, Niblett and his wife returned to Britain and they now live happily on a smallholding near King's Lynn, Norfolk, with their three horses, five chickens, four cats and a dog.

ACTING SERGEANT (LATER LIEUTENANT COMMANDER, ROYAL NAVAL RESERVE) WILLIAM CHRISTOPHER O'BRIEN

Royal Marines/Army/Royal Naval Reserve
DECORATION: DISTINGUISHED FLYING MEDAL (DFM)
GAZETTED: 8 OCTOBER 1982

William 'Uncle Bill' O'Brien, whose military career spanned thirty-eight remarkable years, is the only Royal Marine ever to have been awarded the DFM. No other Marine will in future receive the decoration because it is no longer awarded. Furthermore, O'Brien has the distinction of being awarded the only DFM of the Falklands War. He has enjoyed a long and varied military career that included serving on the streets of Belfast, the battlefields of the Falkland Islands, the mountains of northern Iraq and the most recent conflict in Afghanistan. During a tour of duty in Afghanistan from 2009 to 2010, O'Brien became both the only reservist pilot to fly front-line combat missions and the oldest Apache pilot to fly on operations, celebrating his fifty-fifth birthday in Helmand Province.

O'Brien was born in Romford, Essex, on 16 November 1954. He was the son of two Irish car factory workers living in Coventry, where he attended Caludon Castle School, Wyken. He left school at sixteen and, after a brief period working in the same factory as his parents, enlisted in the Royal Marines in 1972, aged seventeen. On completion of basic training he was awarded the 'King's Badge' as the best all-round member of his recruit troop, 29 King's Squad. He was initially posted to 41 Commando, based in Malta, and then volunteered to join 42 Commando on a tour of Northern Ireland. He was promoted to corporal and, after completing an Arctic survival instructors' course, became part of the cadre set up to train 42 Commando in Arctic warfare techniques for the first time. Between 1974 and 1978, and at the height of the 'Troubles', O'Brien completed three tours of Northern Ireland. In 1978 he qualified as an air gunner with 3 Commando Brigade Air Squadron and he then completed his fourth tour of Northern Ireland. His career changed direction after he successfully applied for aircrew training before raising his aspirations and applying for training as a pilot. O'Brien gained his pilot 'wings' in 1981 and was awarded the Bob Bowles Trophy for best student on his course. After being posted to Montfortabeek Flight 45 Commando Group, Royal Marines, he completed his fifth, and final, tour of Northern Ireland. After the outbreak of the Falklands War in 1982, it was with this unit that O'Brien found himself deployed to the South Atlantic to play his part in helping to regain the British territory as part of Operation Corporate. In the war zone, O'Brien flew one of Montfortabeek Flight's three Gazelle helicopters in direct support of the 2nd Battalion, the Parachute Regiment, at Goose Green and then, at one time or another, most of the other units involved in the conflict.

His DFM for courage during the Falklands War was announced on 8 October 1982 when his citation stated:

During the attack on Darwin and Goose Green Sergeant O'Brien piloted a Gazelle helicopter of M Flight, 3rd Commando Brigade Air Squadron. For two days his helicopter conducted supply and casualty evacuation operations, often under enemy fire. With his Flight Commander, he also took part in 17 night flying sorties to evacuate wounded personnel and resupply vital ammunition. At times these sorties necessitated flying forward to company lines in the heat of battle and in appalling weather. The conspicuous gallantry and cool professionalism displayed on all these occasions was superb and Sergeant O'Brien made an outstanding contribution. His expertise and competence as a pilot has been widely admired and recognised.

In an interview at his home in Somerset, O'Brien told me how he and his fellow helicopter pilots had, on the voyage down to the Falklands, trained themselves to use the then new and fairly rudimentary night-vision goggles (known at the time as passive night goggles). He also said he felt a strong sense of responsibility for the troops on the ground, regardless of the threats posed by Argentinian air and land forces: a number of Royal Marine and Army helicopters were shot down. 'I felt a huge obligation to the infantry because I knew what it was like to be running short of ammunition, to be wet, dirty, bone-tired, hungry and thoroughly frightened. These were the same men with whom, up until just a few years earlier, I would have been sharing the trenches. So I felt a huge affinity towards them and felt I had to go the extra mile to discharge my responsibility.' O'Brien added: 'I landed one time at Goose Green during a mortar barrage. I could see the plumes of smoke and explosions and could feel a slight concussion through the airframe, but I felt detached in my own space – because the helicopter was so noisy, you couldn't hear the battle unfolding. I really thrived on the intensity of it, the test if you like, and frankly missed it when I returned to Britain after the war.'

O'Brien heard the news of his gallantry medal while back in Britain undergoing a senior command course, required for promotion from corporal to substantive sergeant (he had been an acting sergeant during the Falklands campaign). He was 'very pleased' to discover he was being awarded the DFM and soon afterwards, along with his wife, Helen, and their two daughters, found himself at an investiture at Buckingham Palace. O'Brien received his medal from the Queen, who mentioned during their brief chat that her son Prince Andrew had also flown helicopters during the war. As O'Brien was leaving Buckingham Palace, Lieutenant General Sir Steuart Pringle, then Commandant General of Royal Marines, stopped his staff car at the gates in order to shake him by the hand. Next, O'Brien qualified on Lynx helicopters and in 1984 he became a qualified helicopter instructor, being awarded the Westland Trophy as the best student on his course. O'Brien was commissioned into the Royal Marines in 1985. Serving with 3 Commando Brigade Air Squadron, he took part in Operation Haven in southern Turkey and northern Iraq at the time of the First Gulf War – his first experience of working with and observing the US Apache attack helicopters in action. He became the Lynx flight commander of 3 Commando Brigade Air Squadron and then served as the first Royal Marines officer on Army Flying Standards, the group responsible for maintaining the highest standards of flying in the Army. In 1999, he had another change of career direction, transferring with the rank of major to the Army Air Corps (AAC) in order to fly Apaches. 'I had wanted to fly attack helicopters for as long as I could remember and so I took the opportunity when it was offered,' he said. O'Brien was posted to America where he became a qualified Apache pilot at Fort Rucker, Alabama, in 1999. On his return to the UK, he was posted to the Attack Helicopter Training Unit (which later became 673 Squadron Army School of Aviation). In 2005, at the age of fifty, O'Brien retired from the military but was then employed by a private company as its first civilian qualified helicopter instructor flying with 673 Squadron.

In 2008, O'Brien was commissioned into the Royal Naval Reserve and volunteered for service in Afghanistan. Although his wife suggested it might have been a 'mid-life crisis', O'Brien insists his reasons for wanting to serve in the war zone were straightforward: 'I had never been on operations in an Apache. I was training Apache pilots to fly but I was also a gunnery instructor and so, in order better to understand their requirements, I thought I should experience operations in Afghanistan for myself. Once I was there, I again felt a huge, almost parental, responsibility, to the troops on the ground.'

O'Brien was deployed with 663 Squadron, based at Camp Bastion, on 4 September 2009 – a week before the eighth anniversary of 9/11. Christened 'Uncle Bill' by his more youthful comrades, O'Brien found himself alongside many of the pilots he had trained, none of whom had even been born when he was awarded his Green Beret (presented to those who complete the tough qualifying course to become a Royal Marine). O'Brien's operational duties ended in January 2010, when he was fifty-five, and he then briefly returned to his duties as a flying instructor with 673 Squadron.

O'Brien, a married man with three children and four grandchildren, finally retired in 2010 and now lives near Yeovil, Somerset.

STAFF SERGEANT (LATER WARRANT OFFICER) SHAUN ANTHONY WYATT

Army
DECORATION: DISTINGUISHED FLYING CROSS (DFC)
GAZETTED: 26 APRIL 1994

Staff Sergeant Shaun Wyatt was awarded one of only three DFCs for the entire period of the 'Troubles' in Northern Ireland. However, at the time of his bravery and the announcement of his gallantry award in the early 1990s, details of what happened were kept secret for security reasons. Only now can Wyatt's repeated bravery during a massive ambush by IRA terrorists on Army helicopters be told for the first time.

Wyatt, the son of an engineer in the Merchant Navy, was born in Liverpool on 3 April 1962 and established his military links when he joined the Army Cadets at Hele's School (now St Peter's), Exeter, Devon. He joined the Junior Leaders' Regiment of the Royal Artillery in September 1978, aged sixteen. Two years' later, he joined 21 (Gibraltar) Air Defence Battery, 27 Field Regiment Royal Artillery, based at Lippstadt, Germany. In 1982, he was mobilised with his unit for the Falklands War. Wyatt saw active service, aged twenty, commanding a Blowpipe detachment, which provided air defence for commandeered merchant ships. During the conflict, he served on motor vessels *Contender Bezant* and *St Edmund*. Wyatt returned to duties in Germany after the end of the Falklands War. He was promoted to sergeant in 1988 and served with the UN peacekeeping forces in Cyprus in 1990. Later in the same year, Wyatt completed his pilot selection training. In December 1990, he was posted to the

Middle East, and deployed on air defence duties, in preparation for the First Gulf War. However, he was recalled to the UK at the end of the war to finish his helicopter pilot training, which he completed in December 1991. Wyatt's talents as a pilot were recognised when he won the best fixed-wing and best student awards on his course. Once his training was over, he converted to flying Lynx helicopters and was posted with 655 Squadron to Northern Ireland. In early 1993, Wyatt became an aircraft commander.

During late morning one day in September 1993, two Lynx helicopters, Lynx 1 and 2, the latter commanded by Wyatt, were escorting a Puma helicopter that was picking up troops at Crossmaglen, South Armagh, in the heart of 'bandit country'. Suddenly the two Lynx helicopters – each manned by two pilots and an air gunner – were ambushed by the IRA, with the aircraft initially coming under fire from two heavy and three light machine guns. It was later established that there were up to thirty terrorists who had been based at at least five firing points in the area. In an interview at his home, Wyatt took up the story:

The terrorists were clearly after a helicopter – they wanted to shoot down the Puma, which can carry up to sixteen troops. It seems they thought we had seen them so they opened fire before the Puma had even taken off. But, in fact, we hadn't seen them. I heard a tap, tap, tap, tap, tap: the thought ran through my head that surely this was not the sound of a gun. They had opened up on us with a heavy machine gun when we were at about 1,200 feet. I told my co-pilot to get us out of there. I put out a contact report: 'Contact Crossmaglen. We are taking hits from the [town] square.' I told the Puma to

411

stay on the ground but it lifted anyway and was hit by a round before climbing away above us. I told Lynx 1 to stay high and we descended to low level when we were again engaged by a further firing point with a GPMG [general-purpose machine gun] mounted on the back of a 4x4. There were another two Lynx in the area – Lynx 5 and 7 – and they came to join us. We had escaped the ambush at low level to the north: it was now quiet [no gunfire] and so I climbed to position ourselves behind Lynx 5 and 7 which had joined us at high level. We were now trying to find the terrorists and our door gunner reported that he could see two lorries travelling east out of Crossmaglen, and they looked like they had weapons on the back. I then took control of our aircraft and put it into a dive to get back to low level so we were below the threat band [the height at which the aircraft became an easier target]. I flew to the south of the vehicles – by now there was a red car with the two lorries. I got ahead of them and hovered the aircraft on the A-road with our gun – another GPMG – facing towards them. When they were 500 or 600 metres away, I told the door gunner to open fire. But the gun fired just two rounds and jammed. We were gutted.

We moved off again and the convoy of three vehicles now turned north. We had a hill between us and them, and every time we were able to shoot, we were broadside to them and so they were firing back at us. But our gun kept on jamming and so I accelerated to get ahead of them. Again I put the aircraft over the middle of the road. When they came into sight, I told the door gunner to fire but the gun yet again fired two or three rounds and jammed. We then moved off and went south. The gun was now working but, because of all the banking, we couldn't fire. I then tried to get directly above the convoy so we could shoot down on them but they couldn't fire on us. I did a rapid climb up to 800 to 1,000 feet over the convoy but one of the lorries turned off into a farm and into a barn. We went back to concentrate on the other lorry – we had lost the car by this stage. At this point, just as we were about to open fire on the second lorry, one of the other Lynx flew through our line of fire and so we obviously had to stop firing.

The [second] lorry went into the middle of a village near Crossmaglen and stopped next to a white transit van. We couldn't open fire with a machine gun because the terrorists were in a main street. But we watched as they transferred weapons from the lorry into the back of the white van. The van came out of the village and headed south. The Lynx that had originally been with me when we were shot at had meanwhile gone back [to the base] and collected around eight troops. It landed in a field next to the road, the troops got out and they engaged [opened fire on] the van. But the terrorists got out of the van and ran into a bungalow. I saw three guys come out of the other side of the bungalow and get into a car. I followed the car but we didn't open fire because I couldn't say, hand on heart, that the three men who ran out of the bungalow were definitely the men who had run into it moments earlier. The rules of engagement meant we couldn't shoot at them. The car headed off towards where the Puma and two Lynx were so I went back to base to pick up troops so we could go back to the farmyard where the first lorry had disappeared into the barn. But everyone had gone by the time we arrived.

Despite a massive firefight lasting almost twenty minutes, after one of the biggest IRA ambushes of the entire 'Troubles' no terrorists or servicemen were left dead or wounded. However, the Army captured a large number of weapons, including a heavy machine gun (12.7mm Dushka), two GPMGs and a substantial quantity of ammunition. Shortly after the ambush, Wyatt was promoted to Warrant Officer Class 2, rebadged (formally transferred from the Royal Artillery to the Army Air Corps) and posted to Gütersloh, Germany. He learnt of his DFC in a phone call while still serving in Germany: the rules had changed in April 2004 enabling someone of his rank, a staff sergeant, to be awarded the DFC (rather than the Distinguished Flying Medal: DFM). His decoration was announced on 26 April 1994 when, publicly, it was simply recorded as in 'recognition of gallantry and distinguished services in Northern Ireland'. He received his DFC from the Queen at Buckingham Palace in July 1994 in the presence of his first wife and their two children.

In 1995, he flew with 661 Squadron in Bosnia. Initially, he was tasked with carrying out peacekeeping patrols but this soon developed into armed reconnaissance patrols. Once his tour was completed, he returned to Gütersloh, where he successfully applied for a flying instructors' course in 1997. In 1998, Wyatt was chosen to fly with the Blue Eagles helicopter display team, being promoted to team leader in 1999. Furthermore, on completion of the first display season, Wyatt was promoted to Warrant Officer Class 1 and was selected to convert to the Apache attack helicopter, which involved training in the US at Fort Rucker, Alabama. Later, he was chosen to introduce the Westland aircraft company's version of the Apache to the Army Air Corps. Wyatt joined 673 Squadron and was appointed a flight commander. In 2007, he left the Army, after a twenty-nine-year career, to become a civilian flying instructor on the Apache at Middle Wallop, Hampshire. Now aged fifty, Wyatt lives in nearby Amesbury, Wiltshire, with his second wife, Caraline.

WARRANT OFFICER ED MACY
Army
DECORATION: MILITARY CROSS (MC)
GAZETTED: 2007 *

Ed Macy, an Apache helicopter pilot, was awarded the MC for one of the most dramatic and dangerous incidents of the current conflict in Afghanistan. Macy, whose name has been changed for security reasons, wrote a dramatic account of his career in his book, *Apache*.

Macy was born in the North East (again, for security reasons, the precise date and location are not being disclosed). One of five brothers, he worked as an apprentice engineer before enlisting in the Army in 1984. He trained as a paratrooper before joining the 2nd Battalion, the Parachute Regiment. During a distinguished career with 2 Para, he served in Belgium, Belize, Kenya, Germany, Morocco, the Netherlands, Northern Ireland and Oman. In the Paras, he rose from private to sergeant, before successfully applying to transfer to the Army Air Corps (AAC). He was awarded the trophy for best student on his pilots' course, before being posted as a reconnaissance pilot to 9 Regiment AAC in 1992. He went on to serve with 3 Regiment AAC, 4 Regiment AAC, 5 Regiment AAC and 25 Flight AAC, flying both Gazelle and Apache helicopters. As well as Afghanistan, he flew in Belgium, Belize, Bosnia, Canada, Croatia, France, Germany, Greece, Kosovo,

Macedonia, the Netherlands, Northern Ireland, Oman and the USA.

Macy's last tour of duty was to Afghanistan as a pilot in an Apache attack helicopter from 2006 to 2007. It was during a time when the British were trying to crush fierce Taliban resistance in Helmand Province. With the Taliban on the defensive after the successful Koshtay raid of 11 January 2007 (in which 150 insurgents were believed to have been killed), Britain's military commanders wanted to seize the initiative from the enemy. However, the intended night-time attack on Jugroom Fort, a major Taliban stronghold, had been delayed until first light by which point the enemy, also far more numerous than had been anticipated, was ready and waiting. Eight Vikings, tracked armoured fighting vehicles, had made their way across the Helmand River, but as soon as they reached the other side they came under a hail of fire from guns and rocket-propelled grenades (RPGs). Eventually, having taken casualties, the order was given to withdraw but in the chaos one Royal Marine, Lance Corporal Mathew Ford, was left behind, lying apparently wounded, outside the fort. The British military has a rule that it never leaves a casualty (even a dead one) behind because of the horrendous treatment he or she is likely to receive at the hands of the Taliban. Initially, the plan had been for four Vikings, supported by two Apaches, A10 aircraft and artillery fire, to go back across the river to retrieve Ford. However, much to the relief of the troops on the ground, two Apache pilots volunteered to mount a rescue operation after spotting Ford lying on the outside wall of the fort. The intention was that each pilot should fly in and land with one man on the two rails on each of their helicopters. As soon as the helicopters landed, the men would rush to Ford, carry him back to one of the helicopters and, all being well, they would fly him to safety. One of those helicopter pilots was Warrant Officer Class 1 Ed Macy.

Macy had asked the commanding officer [Lieutenant Colonel Robert Magowan] for permission to rescue Ford after being told the troops on the ground needed ninety minutes to prepare for their rescue mission back over the Helmand River. 'Give me four volunteers and we'll be in and out with Ford in two minutes,' he said. After a long pause, his plan was approved and the volunteers were chosen at the command post more than three miles west of the fort. The first volunteer was Captain Dave Rigg of the Royal Engineers, who had been watching the whole incident unfold on the aerial 'feed' to the command post. He and the other three volunteers were soon in position and the two helicopters, by then desperately low on fuel, took off, at just after 10.30 a.m. A 2,000-lb bomb was dropped on the fort from a B-1 bomber just before the two helicopters went in and there was other covering fire from the air (notably from two Apaches) and the ground (from troops on the other side of the Helmand River).

In the end, one of the Apaches had to land inside the fort, opening fire as it landed, while Macy's helicopter landed outside the fort close to where Ford had been lying. The two men on the rails of his helicopter leapt off, knowing they had just two minutes to get Ford and be back on the Apache. '[Marine Chris] Fraser-Perry whipped past my left window and rounded the aircraft's nose. Rigg shot off to the right, just ahead of him,' Macy later wrote. 'They ducked under the thumping rotor blades and disappeared into the dust cloud which had begun to merge with the fallout from the 2,000 pounder and now completely blotted out the sun . . . Every second felt like an hour. Then, incredibly slowly, the brown mass began to recede. We could see five metres . . . then eight . . . then twelve . . .'

Eventually, Macy and his co-pilot could see Rigg and Fraser-Perry slowly coming towards the Apache dragging Ford. At this stage, Macy leapt out of the cab to give the two men a hand, with all of them under a heavy fire. In his body armour and other kit, Ford weighed fully twenty stone and it took a huge effort to drag him through the soft ground. Macy could tell that his body was still warm but his pulse had stopped. Yet another RPG whooshed over the rescuers' heads and some Taliban were seen advancing through nearby trees. By this point, the two other men from the other helicopter had arrived on the scene and everyone helped tie Ford to Macy's Apache using two straps. 'Go, go, go,' yelled Macy to his co-pilot. They had been on the ground for five minutes and ten seconds; tragically, Ford was dead but the efforts to save him were hugely appreciated by the Royal Marines. One Regimental Sergeant Major told Macy: 'What you boys did there was outstanding. Thank you for bringing him back. We always tell them this, but you showed all my young lads for real that we never leave anyone behind.'

Two of the four Apache pilots on the rescue mission were awarded the MC and the other two the DFC. When Macy's MC was announced his citation stated: 'Macy [name changed] demonstrated selfless gallantry and leadership as he helped inspire a hastily drawn together team to recover the casualty in the face of an emboldened enemy. Macy's courage, quick thinking and determination to find and recover the casualty, with complete disregard for his own safety, were an outstanding act of valour and leadership.'

Macy received his MC from the Queen at Buckingham Palace in December 2007.* He told her: 'This is my last day in uniform ever, ma'am. It's the greatest day of my life.' Macy officially left the Army in January 2008 after twenty-three years' service: 645 of his 3,930 flying hours had been in an Apache. Today, for security reasons, Macy seeks to be 'invisible' but he says he will not spend the rest of his life looking over his shoulder. He ended his book, *Apache,* with the words: 'The one thing my service taught me is that life's too short to worry.'

* Full date omitted for security reasons

SELECT BIBLIOGRAPHY

Abbott, P. E., and Tamplin, J. M. A., *British Gallantry Awards*, Nimrod Dix & Co., London, 1981

Anderson, Lars, *The All Americans*, St Martin's Press, New York, 2005

Arthur, Max, *Last of the Few*, Virgin Books, London, 2011

Ashcroft, Michael, *Victoria Cross Heroes*, Headline Review, London, 2006

Bader, Douglas, *Fight for the Sky*, Pen & Sword Aviation, Barnsley (South Yorkshire), 2003

Bekker, Cajus, *The Luftwaffe War Diaries*, Da Capo Press Inc., Cambridge, MA, 1994

Bennett, Tom, *617 Squadron: The Dambusters at War*, Patrick Stephens, 1986

Beurling, George, and Roberts, Leslie, *Malta Spitfire*, Grub Street, London, 2011

Bishop, Edward, *Book of Airmen's Obituaries*, Grub Street, London, 2002

Boiten, Theo, *The Bristol Blenheim*, The Crowded Press, Marlborough (Wiltshire), 1998

Bolitho, Hector, *Finest of the Few*, Amberley Publishing Plc, Stroud (Gloucestershire), undated

Bowyer, Chaz, *The Air VCs*, William Kimber, London, 1978

Boyne, Walter J., *Gabreski*, *Air Force Magazine*, Vol. 88 No. 11, Air Force Association, Arlington, VA, November 2005

Brickhill, Paul, *Reach for the Sky*, Cassell, London, 2004

Brickhill, Paul, and Norton, Conrad, *Escape to Danger*, Faber and Faber, London, undated

Cawdron, Hugh, *Based at Burn MkII*, The David Wilkerson Prize for Citizenship, Bristol, 2001

Chisholm, Roderick, *Cover of Darkness*, Chatto & Windus, London, 1953

Churchill, Peter, *Duel of Wits*, Hodder & Stoughton, London, 1953

Cooksley, Peter G., *The Air VCs: VCs of the First World War*, Sutton Publishing, Stroud (Gloucestershire), 1996

Cooper, Alan, *Bravery Awards for Aerial Combat*, Pen & Sword Aviation, Barnsley (South Yorkshire), 2007

Cooper, Alan W., *The Men Who Breached the Dams*, William Kimber, London, 1982

Cull, Brian, *Spitfires Over Malta,* Grub Street, London, 2005

Cull, Brian; Lander, Bruce, and Weiss, Heinrich, *Twelve Days in May*, Grub Street, London, 1995

Embry, Basil, *Mission Completed*, The Quality Book Club, London, 1956

Frayn Turner, John, *Douglas Bader*, Pen & Sword Aviation, Barnsley (South Yorkshire), 2009

Frayn Turner, John, *VCs of the Air,* Airlife Publishing, Shrewsbury (Shropshire), 1993

Gabreski, Francis, *Gabby: A Fighter Pilot's Life*, Dell Publishing, New York, 1992

Golley, John, *Hurricanes Over Murmansk*, Patrick Stephens, Wellingborough (Northamptonshire), 1987

Gribble, Leonard R., *Heroes of the Fighting R.A.F.*, George G. Harrap, London, 1941

Hamlin, Paul, and Davies, Ann, *Coolham Airfield Remembered: Memories and Anecdotes of a Sussex D-Day Fighter Station and Village*, Paul Hamlin, Horsham (Sussex), 1996

Holland, James, *The Battle of Britain*, Bantam Press, London, 2010

Holyoak, Vincent, *On the Wings of the Mornings: RAF Bottesford 1941–1945*, Vincent Holyoak, Leicester, 1992

Iliff, Jay (ed.), *Airmen's Obituaries: Book Two*, Grub Street, London, 2007

Johnson, 'Johnnie', *Wing Leader*, Crécy Publishing Limited, Manchester, 2000

Kellett J. P., and Davies J. A., *History of the R.A.F Servicing Commandos*, Airlife Publishing, Shrewsbury (Shropshire), 1989

Laffin, John, *British VCs of World War 2*, Sutton Publishing, Stroud (Gloucestershire), 1997

Lucas, Laddie, *Thanks for the Memory*, Grub Street, London, 1998

Maslen-Jones, E.W., *Fire by Order*, Leo Cooper, Barnsley (South Yorkshire), 1997

McManners, Hugh, *The Scars of War*, HarperCollins, London, 1994

Monks, Noel, *Squadrons Up! A First Hand Story of the R.A.F.*, The World Publishing Company, Cleveland, OH, 1942

Nolan, Brian, *Hero: The Falcon of Malta*, William Blackwood, Edinburgh, 1982

O'Connor, Bernard, *RAF Tempsford: Churchill's Most Secret Airfield*, Amberley Publishing Plc, Stroud (Gloucestershire), 2010

Olds, Robin, *Fighter Pilot*, St Martin's Griffin, New York, 2010

Overy, R.J., *The Air War 1939–45*, Stein and Day, New York, 1981

Oxspring, Bobby, *Spitfire Command*, William Kimber, London, 1984

Price, Alfred, *Late Mark Spitfires Aces 1942–45*, Osprey Publishing, Botley (Oxfordshire), 1995

Price, Alfred, *Spitfire Mark 1/11 Aces 1939–41*, Osprey Publishing, Botley (Oxfordshire), 1996

Ralph, Wayne, *Aces, Warriors & Wingmen*, Wiley, Ontario, 2005

Richardson, Anthony, *Wingless Victory*, The Companion Book Club, London, 1953

Rivaz, R. C., *Tail Gunner*, The History Press, Stroud (Gloucestershire), 2011

Rolls, W. T., *Spitfire Attack*, William Kimber, London, 1987

Ross, David, *Richard Hillary*, Grub Street, London, 2000

Shacklock, Pauline, *Eric Genders: Legendary Fighter Ace and Test Pilot*, Henry Matthews, Beirut, 1998

Shores, Christopher, and Williams, Clive, *Aces High*, Grub Street, London, 1994

Shores, Christopher, *Aces High Volume 2*, Grub Street, London, 1999.

Spooner, Tony, *Warburton's War*, Crécy Publishing Limited, Manchester, 2003

The Register of the Victoria Cross, This England, Cheltenham, 1981

Townshend Bickers, Richard, *Ginger Lacey: Fighter Pilot*, Pan Books, London, 1969

Verity, Hugh, *We Landed by Moonlight*, Crécy Publishing Limited, Manchester, 2000

Yeoman, Christopher, and Freeborn, John, *Tiger Cub: The Story of John Freeborn DFC*, Pen & Sword Aviation, Barnsley (South Yorkshire), 2009

INDEX

Note: Main entries for the medal recipients featured in the book are in **bold**.

Adams, C.W. 247–8
Adnams, A.S. 132
AFC *see* Air Force Cross (AFC)
Afghanistan 382, 405, 409, 415–19
AFM (Air Force Medal) 9, 11–12
Air Force Cross (AFC) 9, 11
    Harry Broadhurst 142–50
    Basil Embry 229–35
    Eric 'Jumbo' Genders 186–92
    Vincent Hill 388–92
    Robert Oxspring 105–9
    Gartrell 'Sailor' Parker 160–5
    John Thompson 151–4
    Arthur 'Father' Wray 249–55
Air Force Medal (AFM) 9, 11–12
Air Medal (US) 179, 388
Alexander of Teck, Prince 25
Apache helicopters 381, 408
Appleton, H. 138
Army
    First World War medal
        recipients 22–30, 35–43
    Second World War medal
        recipients 142–50, 249–55,
        331–4, 345–51, 378–80
    post-Second World War medal
        recipients 392–7, 405–19
'Arnhem lift' 282–3
Ashcroft, Eric 5
Atkinson, George 134–7
Australian airmen 83–9, 386–92

Bader, Douglas Robert Steuart
    123–5, 145–6, 154–60, 171,
    172, 337
Baldwin, Sir John 306–7
Balthasar, Wilhelm 145
Bars 10–11
Battle of Barking Creek 53–4
Battle of Britain 45–6, 144,
    166–7, 180–1
    medal recipients 47–139, 157,
    372
Beamish, F.V. 131
Beaverbrook, Lord 75

Bekker, Cajus 223–5
Belcher, Sergeant 402
Bettany, John 'Jack' 284–7
Beurling, George Frederick 'Screwball' 194–200
Bishop, 'Billy' 38
Blake, Maurice 20
Blanchet, Sergeant 280
Blenheims 335
Blériot-Experimental (BE) 18
the Blitz 46, 138–9
Bolitho, Hector 47, 49
bomber aircrew 221–95
  special bombing missions 297–334
Bomber Command 7–8, 46, 221–2, 382
Bomber Command Memorial xi, xii, 7, 8–9
Bonin, Hubertus von 82, 83
Bowers, Dennis Ronald 292–5
Brickhill, Paul 133, 159
Bristol Blenheims 46
Broadhurst, Harry 'Broady' 46, 142–50
Broadley, John Alan 'Bill' 305–15
Brodie, Warrant Officer 363
Bronze Star (US) 79
Brookes, G.E. 243
Brown, G. 359
Burma campaign 121, 282, 346–9, 376–7
Burnside, D.H. 243

Bushell, Roger ('Big X') 366, 367

Caister, James Russell 'Bill' 80–3
Cameron, Peter 403
Campbell, A.J. 260–1
Campbell, Flight Sergeant 269–71
Canadian airmen 176, 194–200
Caterpillar Club 109, 165, 257, 267, 287
Caudwell, John 8
Cawdron, Hugh 248–9
CB (Companion of the Order of the Bath) 179, 234
CBE (Commander of the British Empire) 153, 159, 179
Certificate of Gallantry 349, 350
CGM see Conspicuous Gallantry Medal (CGM)
Cheshire, Leonard 245, 291, 331
Chisholm, Roderick 'Rory' 138–9
Churchill, 'Mad' Jack 368–9
Churchill, Peter 319
Churchill, Winston 45, 46, 51
Clarkson, Rodney 252
Coastal Command 46, 221
Cohen, Leonard 199
collection, of Lord Ashcroft 5–7
Colquhoun, Leslie Robert 342–4
Commander of the British Empire (CBE) 153, 159, 179
Commander's Cross of the Order of Polonia Restituta 194

Companion of the Order of the Bath (CB) 179, 234

Coningham, Sir Arthur 313, 314

Conspicuous Gallantry Medal (CGM) 12, 330
John 'Jack' Bettany 284–7
Dennis Bowers 292–5
Geoffrey 'Chuffo' Keen 240–4

Constance, D.S.N. 'Tinny' 257

Coonts, Stephen 210

Copeland, Gordon 165

Cox, C.W.H. 310

Cox, 'Pan' 66

Coxshall, Ernest 'Nobby' 376–8

Croix de Guerre (Belgian) 100, 179

Croix de Guerre (French) 64–5, 213

Cross of Valour (Polish) 131, 184, 193, 202

Cunningham, Admiral 337

Cunningham, John 'Cats Eyes' 139

Currant, Christopher Frederick 'Bunny' 93–101

Czernin, Manfred Beckett 46, 370–5

D-Day (Normandy landings) 149–50, 177, 379–80

da Vinci, Leonardo xv

Dalton-Morgan, John 79

Dalton-Morgan, Thomas Frederick 76–80

'Dambusters' raid (Operation Chastise) 5, 327–34

David, Dennis 'Hurricane' 127

Davidson, Pilot Officer 358–9

Davies, J. 377

Day, Harry 'Wings' 368–9

DCM see Distinguished Conduct Medal (DCM)

de Havilland, Geoffrey 191

Deere, Al 52, 57, 60

Desert Air Force 147–9

Desmond, Richard 8

DFC see Distinguished Flying Cross (DFC)

DFM see Distinguished Flying Medal (DFM)

Distinguished Conduct Medal (DCM), Thomas Mottershead 30–4

Distinguished Flying Cross (DFC) 9, 10, 330, 385
Douglas Bader 154–60
George 'Screwball' Beurling 194–200
Harry Broadhurst 142–50
John Broadley 305–15
Les Colquhoun 342–4
Christopher 'Bunny' Currant 93–101
Manfred Czernin 370–5
Tom Dalton-Morgan 76–80
Kenneth Doran 223–8
Bryan 'Ben' Draper 116–21
Alan 'Shag' Eckford 122–9

Basil Embry 229–35
Henry Figg 316–21
Athol Forbes 101–5
John Freeborn 53–6
Francis 'Gabby' Gabreski 216–20
George Gribble 56–62
John Hancock 200–1
Charlton 'Wag' Haw 180–3
Vincent Hill 388–92
'Johnnie' Johnson 169–80
Kenneth Letford 382–5
David Lord 281–4
Michal Maciejowski 130–4
Jim 'Zulu' Malley 237–9
Ted Maslen-Jones 345–51
Howard Mayers 83–9
Peter Middleton 386–8
Jeff Niblett 397–404
Robin Olds 210–16
Robert Oxspring 105–9
Gartrell 'Sailor' Parker 160–5
Charles 'Pick' Pickard 305–15
Albert Putt 316–21
Bill Rolls 109–16
Bill Scarratt 392–7
John Simpson 47–9
Edward 'Bulls Eye' Smith 206–9
Harbourne Stephen 72–6
Leonard Sumpter 331–4
Keith 'Jimmy' Thiele 259–68
John Thompson 151–4
Lloyd Trigg 324–6
Ralph Van den Bok 255–9

Adrian 'Warby' Warburton 336–42
Edward Wells 166–9
David 'Wilkie' Wilkerson 244–9
Stefan 'Steve' Witorzenc 192–4
Arthur 'Father' Wray 249–55
Kazimierz Wünsche 202–3
Shaun Wyatt 410–15
Distinguished Flying Cross (DFC) (US) 4, 179, 220, 341
Distinguished Flying Medal (DFM) 9, 10–11
George Atkinson 134–7
George 'Screwball' Beurling 194–200
John Broadley 305–15
James 'Bill' Caister 80–3
Les Colquhoun 342–4
Walter Ellis 298–305
Edgar England 378–80
Henry Figg 316–21
Charles Franklin 327–31
Sidney Fuller 235–7
Eric 'Jumbo' Genders 186–92
Stanley Gunnell 269–72
Charlton 'Wag' Haw 180–3
Leslie Hyder 321–3
Józef Jeka 183–6
Geoffrey 'Chuffo' Keen 240–4
Pavel Dmitrievich Klimov 204–5
James 'Ginger' Lacey 62–72
Ernest 'Leatherneck' Lascelles 361–4

Michal Maciejowski 130–4
Percy 'Ronnie' Morfill 90–3
William 'Uncle Bill' O'Brien
    405–9
Norman Pawley 354–60
Lionel Pilkington 50–2
William Rich 298–305
Bill Ripley 137–9
Bill Rolls 109–16
Edward 'Bulls Eye' Smith 206–9
Leonard Sumpter 331–4
Ronald Wilson 279–81
Kazimierz Wünsche 202–3
Distinguished Service Cross (US)
    220
Distinguished Service Medal
    (DSM), Gartrell 'Sailor' Parker
    160–5
Distinguished Service Medal (US)
    220
Distinguished Service Order
    (DSO) 385
    Douglas Bader 154–60
    George 'Screwball' Beurling
        194–200
    Harry Broadhurst 142–0
    John Broadley 305–15
    Christopher 'Bunny' Currant
        93–101
    Manfred Czernin 370–5
    Tom Dalton-Morgan 76–80
    Basil Embry 229–35
    'Johnnie' Johnson 169–80
    Kenneth Letford 382–5

Jim 'Zulu' Malley 237–9
Edward 'Mick' Mannock 35–9
Howard Mayers 83–9
Charles 'Pick' Pickard 305–15
Harbourne Stephen 72–6
Keith 'Jimmy' Thiele 259–68
John Thompson 151–4
Adrian 'Warby' Warburton
    336–42
Edward Wells 166–9
David 'Wilkie' Wilkerson
    244–9
Arthur 'Father' Wray 249–55
Dodge, Johnny 'The Dodger'
    368–9
Dolan, Lieutenant 37
Doran, Kenneth Christopher
    223–8
Dornier (Do) bombers 46
Douglas, Sholto 20
Douglas-Hamilton, Lord 80
**Dowse, Sydney Hastings ('The
    Laughing Boy')** 7, 365
Draper, Bryan Vincent 'Ben'
    116–21
DSM see Distinguished Service
    Medal (DSM)
DSO *see* Distinguished Service
    Order (DSO)
Dundas, Hugh 'Cocky' 170
Dunkirk 54, 232

Eaker, Ira 146
Earhart, Amelia 4

Eckford, Alan Francis 'Shag'
122–9
Eeles, H. 78
Ellis, Walter 7, 298–305
Embry, Basil Edward 229–35,
312, 315
England, Edgar 378–80

Falklands War 381, 382, 398–404,
406–7
Farndale, Sir Martin 349–50
Fearnley, M.E. 384, 385
Figg, Henry Robert 312,
316–21
Fighter Command 45, 46, 221
fighter pilots 141–220
Battle of Britain 45–139
First World War 16, 28–9,
32–3, 40
Finucane, 'Paddy' 128
First World War 2–3, 9, 10, 11,
13, 15–16
medal recipients 249–51
VCs 16–43
Fisher, G.C. 257
Focke-Wulf (Fw) fighters 45
Forbes, Athol Stanhope 101–5
Ford, Mathew 416–17
431 Flight (later 69 Squadron)
337–8, 339, 342
Franklin, Charles Ernest 327–31
Franks, Norman 371, 375
František, Josef 101–2
Fraser-Perry, Chris 417–18

Freeborn, John Connell 53–6
French, Flight Sergeant 293
French, Sir John 20
Fuller, J.F.C. 297
Fuller, Sidney Ben 235–7

**Gabreski, Francis Stanley
'Gabby'** 216–20
Galland, Adolf 372
Gardner, Charles 51
GCB (Knight Grand Cross of the
Order of the Bath) 235
**Genders, George Eric Clifford
'Jumbo'** 186–92
George Medal (GM), Les
Colquhoun 342–4
George V 9
George VI 12
Gibson, Guy 8, 328, 330, 332–3,
337
Giménez, Teniente 402
Glaze, John 401–2, 403
Glider Pilot Regiment 378–9
GM *see* George Medal (GM)
Gold, Pilot Officer 189
Goldfish Club 161
Goodman, Michelle 10
Gower, W.E. 33
Gray, Colin 57, 58, 60
'Great Escape' 133, 353, 365–70
Great War *see* First World War
Gribble, Dorian George 56–62
Griers, Thomas 85
Griffiths, Captain 266

Griffiths, Charles 64
Gunnell, Stanley Dennis 269–72

Hafner, Anton 107
Hampson, G.B. 292–5
Hancock, Allan John 200–1
Harris, Sir Arthur ('Bomber') 273,
  302
Hart, Flight Sergeant 293
Haw, Charlton 'Wag' 46,
  180–3
Hayhurst, R.J. 243
Heather, R.J. 242
Heinkel (He) bombers 46
helicopters 381, 408, 411–15
Herget, Wilhelm 257
Hewitt, Pilot Officer 280
Hill, Vincent Jerome 388–92
Hillary, Richard 81–2
Hope, Sir Archibald 84, 85
Howard, C.L. 330
Hugo, P.H. 'Dutch' 129
Hull, Caesar 77
Hulton-Harrap, Montague 54,
  56
Hunt, Lieutenant 27
Hurricane fighters 45
Hyder, Leslie Anderson 321–3

Imperial War Museum 6
Inglis, Donald 38

Jackson, Norman Cyril 288–92
James, Bertram 'Jimmy' 368–9

Jefferson, C. 384
Jeka, Józef 46, 183–6
Jerrard, Alan 40–3
Johnson, Amy 4
Johnson, Hugh 291
Johnson, James Edgar 'Johnnie'
  46, 168, 169–80
Jones, Herbert 'H' 400
Jones, Ira 38
Jones, Private 359
Junkers (Ju) bombers 46

Kain, E.J. 'Cobber' 50, 65
Keen, Geoffrey Frank 'Chuffo'
  240–4
Kellet, J.P. 377
Kellett, Ronald 102
Kelsey, Howard 206–8
Kenley Wing 167–8, 175–6
Kennington, Eric 49
Kerans, J.S. 385
King, Harry 284
Kingaby, Donald 11
King's Commendation for
  Valuable Service in the Air
  165
Klimov, Pavel Dmitrievich
  204–5
Knight Grand Cross of the Order
  of the Bath (GCB) 235
Knight, Les 332
knighthoods 150, 160, 234
Korean War 179, 219–20, 381,
  386–7, 389–90

Krol, Stanislav 'Danny' 367
Kum Sok 185

Lacey, James Harry 'Ginger' 7,
62–72, 91, 195
Laffin, John 288
Lange, Franz 187–8
Lapkowski, Flying Officer 102
**Lascelles, Ernest Bruce
'Leatherneck'** 361–4
**Learoyd, Roderick Alastair
Brook 'Babe'** 6, 298–305
Leefe Robinson, William 6,
26–30
Legion of Merit (US) 149, 179, 213
Leigh, Joe 182
Leonardo da Vinci xvii
Letford, Kenneth Henry Francis
382–5
Lewis, John 299, 301
Liddell, John Aidan 22–5
Lindbergh, Charles 3–4
Lloyd, Hugh 338–9
London Gazette xviii
Lord Ashcroft Gallery 6
**Lord, David Samuel Anthony
'Lumme'** 281–4
Luftwaffe 45
Lysanders 335

Mabbett, Sergeant 171
McElroy, George 37
Maciejowski, Michal Karol
130–4

MacIntyre, Pilot Officer 280
Mackay, Lieutenant 27
McManners, Hugh 404
McRitchie, A.I. 314
McWilliams, Sergeant 293
Macy, Ed 415–19
Magowan, Robert 417
Mahoney-Jones, G.J. 33
Maitland, I. 257
Malan, 'Sailor' 177–8
Malcolm, Hugh Gordon 275–9
Malley, James Young 'Zulu'
237–9
Malta 114–15, 152–3, 196–7,
198, 336–9, 342–3
Mann, Flight Sergeant 293
Mannock, Edward 'Mick' 35–9
Manser, Cyril 275
Manser, Leslie Thomas 272–5
**Maslen-Jones, Edward Walter
'Mas'** 345–51
Mathews, Pilot Officer 300
Mayers, Howard Clive 83–9
MBE (Member of the Most
Excellent Order of the British
Empire) 349
MC *see* Military Cross (MC)
Medal of Honor (US) 4
Mentions in Despatches 65, 234,
349, 350, 385
Merrifield, John 335
Messerschmitt (Me) fighters 45
Middleton, Peter Montague
386–8

Middleton, Rawdon 'Ron' 322–3
Mifflin, Fred 291
Military Cross (MC)
  Manfred Czernin 370–5
  Sydney Dowse 365–70
  Aidan Liddell 22–5
  Ed Macy 415–19
  Edward 'Mick' Mannock 35–9
  Ted Maslen-Jones 345–51
  Arthur 'Father' Wray 249–55
Military Cross (1st Class) (Belgian) 153
Military Cross (Czech) 309
Military Medal (MM), Ernest 'Nobby' Coxshall 376–8
Mollison, Jim 4
Moore, Frank 31
Morfill, Percy Frederick 'Ronnie' 90–3
Mottershead, Thomas 30–4
Mountbatten, Lord 354, 376
Mulligan, R. 300

Neave, Airey 369–70
New Zealand airmen 166–9, 259–68, 324–6
Niblett, Jeffrey Peter 397–404
Normandy landings (D-Day) 149–50, 177, 379–80
Northern Ireland 381, 382, 392–7, 406, 410–15
Norton, Conrad 133
Nunn, Richard 400–2, 404

OBE (Officer of the Most Excellent Order of the British Empire) 79, 104
O'Brien, William Christopher 'Uncle Bill' 405–9
O'Connell, Morgan 404
Olds, Robin 210–16
Operation Chastise ('Dambusters' raid) 5, 327–34
Operation Dragoon 343
Operation Jericho 313–15
Operation Jubilee 128, 173
Operation Millennium 273
Orde, Cuthbert 49, 55, 106, 157, 372
Order of Lenin (Russia) 181–2, 205
Order of Leopold (Belgium) 179
Overy, R.J. 141
Oxspring, Robert Wardlow 105–9

Paige, D.R. 285
Parker, Gartrell Richard Ian 'Sailor' 160–5
Pawley, Norman Jack 354–60
Pearce, Wing Commander 361
Peck, Richhard 23–4, 25
Perry, Sergeant 280
Photographic Reconnaissance Units (PRU) 335, 365
Pickard, Percy Charles 'Pick' 7, 241, 305–15, 316–19

Pilkingon, Lionel Sanderson 50–2
Pitcairn-Hill, 'Jaimie' 300
Polish Air Force 130–4, 183–6, 192–4, 202–3
post-Second World War Gallantry 381–2
  medal recipients 342–4, 382–419
Price, Alfred 124
Pringle, Sir Steuart 408
prisoners of war (PoWs), escape attempts 133, 158, 159, 227–8, 233, 266, 353, 354–61, 361–4, 365–70
Putt, Albert James 312, 316–21

RAAF (Royal Australian Air Force) 386–92
Radley, James 17
RAF *see* Royal Air Force (RAF)
RAF (Serving) Commando 354, 376
RAFVR *see* Royal Air Force Volunteer Reserve (RAFVR)
Raleigh, Sir Walter xvii
Rawnsley, Sergeant 139
RCAF (Royal Canadian Air Force) 194–200
Reynolds, Flight Sergeant 293, 294, 295
Reynolds, G.W.H. 189
RFC *see* Royal Flying Corps (RFC)

Rhodes-Moorhouse, William Barnard 6, 16–21
Rhodes-Moorhouse, Willie (son of William Barnard) 21
'Rhubarb' operations 127–8, 171
Rich, William Ronald 7, 298–305
Richardson, Anthony 233
Richthofen, Manfred von (the 'Red Baron') 3, 29
Rigg, Dave 417–18
Ripley, William George 137–9
Rivaz, R.C. 245–6
RNZAF (Royal New Zealand Air Force) 166–9, 259–68, 324–6
Robinson, Wing Commander 245
Rolls, William Thomas Edward 109–16
Rosier, Sir Fred 79
Ross, David 80
Ross, D.B. 243
Ross, E.H. 300
Royal Air Force (RAF) 10, 16, 221–2
  First World War 35–43
  fighter pilots 142–92, 200–3
    Battle of Britain 47–9, 53–72, 76–83, 90–109, 122–39, 130–9
  bomber aircrew 223–37, 240–4, 249–55, 269–72, 275–84, 292–5
    special bombing missions 298–323, 331–4

reconnaissance operations
336–42
escape and action on the ground
354–64, 370–5
post-Second World War
gallantry 382–8
Royal Air Force Serving
Commando 354, 376
Royal Air Force Volunteer Reserve
(RAFVR)
fighter pilots 62–83, 169–83,
206–9
Battle of Britain 50–2, 62–76,
83–9, 109–21
bomber aircrew 237–9, 244–9,
255–9, 272–5, 284–92
special bombing missions
327–31
reconnaissance operations
342–4
escape and action on the ground
365–70, 376–8
post-Second World War
gallantry 382–8
Royal Australian Air Force (RAAF)
386–92
Royal Canadian Air Force (RCAF)
194–200
Royal Flying Corps (RFC)
xvii–xviii, 15, 249–51
VC recipients 16–43
Royal Marines 397–404
Royal Naval Reserve 405–9
Royal New Zealand Air Force

(RNZAF) 166–9, 259–68,
324–6
Runnymede Memorial 8

Sampson, R.W. 314
Sanders, G. 248
Scarratt, William Thomas 392–7
Second World War 5, 10, 11, 12,
13
Battle of Britain 45–6, 144,
166–7, 180–1, 372
medal recipients 47–139, 157
fighter pilots 141
medal recipients 142–220
bomber aircrew 221
medal recipients 223–95
escape and action on the ground
353–4
medal recipients 354–80
reconnaissance operations 335–6
medal recipients 336–51
special bombing missions 297–8
medal recipients 298–334
Shacklock (*née* Genders), Pauline
191–2
Shannon, Dave 332, 333
Silver Star (US) 213, 220, 248
Simpson, John William Charles
47–9
Smith, Edward Miles 'Bulls Eye'
206–9
Snowden, Warrant Officer 363
Sopwith Camel 16
Soviet Air Force 204–5

Sowerby, Fred 27
Spaatz, Carl 146
Special Operations Executive
    (SOE) 311, 316, 319, 320–1,
    370–1, 373–5
Spencer, Squadron Leader 266
Spitfire fighters 45
squadrons
    1 Squadron 144, 213
    2 Squadron 18, 391
    3 Commando Brigade Air
        Squadron 398–9, 406, 406–7
    3 Squadron 264, 267
    7 Squadron 23
    9 Squadron 309
    11 Squadron 142
    15 (B) Squadron 252
    15 Squadron 354
    17 Squadron 71, 372
    18 Squadron 276
    19 Squadron 41, 142
    20 Squadron 32, 70
    23 Squadron 155
    25 Squadron 31
    26 Squadron 276
    28 Squadron 252
    29 Squadron 249–50
    30 Squadron 229
    31 Squadron 281
    32 Squadron 122, 124
    33 Squadron 186–8
    35 (Madras Presidency)
        Squadron 245–7, 279
    40 Squadron 36–7

41 Squadron 142, 166–7, 196,
    264
43 Squadron 47, 73, 77–9,
    252
44 Squadron 304
45 Squadron 121, 229
49 Squadron 299–300, 328
50 Squadron 272, 275
51 Squadron 240, 247, 309–10
54 Squadron 57, 58–61, 62
57 Squadron 331
61 Squadron 269
64 Squadron 201
66 Squadron 41, 103–4, 105–6
69 Squadron (formerly 431
    Flight) 338, 339, 342
72 Squadron 107–8, 110
73 Squadron 50–2
74 (Tiger) Squadron 37, 53,
    73–4, 116–20
77 Squadron 386, 389
80 Squadron 200–1
83 Squadron 300, 304
85 Squadron 38, 371
88 Squadron 384
94 Squadron 87–8
99 Squadron 307
106 Squadron 288–9
107 Squadron 223–5, 230–2
110 Squadron 223–5, 232
111 Squadron 143, 151
122 (Bombay) Squadron 112
126 Squadron 113
129 Squadron 201

131 Squadron 152
139 Squadron 238–9
141 Squadron (Beaufighters)
    139, 206–8
144 Squadron 235
146 Squadron 373
149 Squadron 237–8, 322
150 Squadron 320
151 Squadron 135–7
154 Squadron 127–9
156 Squadron 292, 383
161 'Moonbeam' Squadron 311,
    312, 321
178 Squadron 238
200 Squadron 324
207 Squadron 382
214 Squadron 258
219 Squadron 162–3
222 Squadron 156
228 Squadron 183
242 Squadron 122–3, 129,
    156–7
245 Squadron 48
249 Squadron 130–1, 196
253 (Hyderabad) Squadron
    125–7
269 Squadron 361
271 Squadron 282
302 (Polish) Squadron 193
303 (Polish) Squadron 102–3,
    183–4, 202–3
306 (Polish) Squadron 193
308 Squadron 184
311 Squadron 308–9

315 Squadron 203, 217–18
317 (Polish) Squadron 131
350 Squadron 152
403 Squadron 196
405 Squadron 260–1
408 Squadron 256–7
427 (Royal Canadian Air Force)
    Squadron 242–3
467 (Royal Australian Air Force)
    Squadron 261, 262
485 Squadron 167
486 (Royal New Zealand Air
    Force) Squadron 264–5
501 (County of Gloucester)
    Squadron 63, 65, 69, 90–2,
    97, 193
504 Squadron 180–1
515 Squadron 209
578 Squadron 247, 248
601 (County of London)
    Squadron 83–7
602 Squadron 70
603 (City of Edinburgh)
    Squadron 80–3
604 Squadron 138–9
605 (County of Warwick)
    Squadron 93–4
610 (County of Chester)
    Squadron 173–4
611 Squadron 144
616 (South Yorkshire) Squadron
    170–2
617 Squadron 328, 331, 332,
    333

624 Squadron 321
625 Squadron 285
655 Squadron 393, 411
656 Squadron 345–6, 347–8
661 Squadron 414
663 Squadron 411
682 Photographic
  Reconnaissance Unit (PRU)
  Squadron 343
683 Squadron 340, 341
830 Squadron 161
Stacey, W.J. 275
Standford, Sergeant 363
Steevens, Brigadier 348–9
Stephen, Harbourne Mackay
  72–6
Sumpter, Leonard Joseph
  331–4
Sutton, Douglas 254–5

Taranto 335–6, 337–8, 339
Tedder, Lady 279
Thiele, Keith Frederick 'Jimmy'
  259–68
Thomas, Flight Lieutenant 113
Thompson, John Marlow
  'Tommy' 46, 151–4
Thompson, Sub Lieutenant 161
Tietzen, Horst 'Jacob' 193
Townsend, Bill 328–9, 330
Townsend, Peter 47
Trigg, Lloyd Allan 324–6
Trondheim raid 361–2, 364
'Troubles' (Northern Ireland) 381,

382, 392–7, 406, 410–15
Tuck, Bon Stanford 90
Tuttle, Sir Geoffrey 335
Twain, Mark xvii, 2
Twigg, J.D. 257

US Air Force 210–20

Van den Bok, Ralph 255–9
Victoria, Queen 12
Victoria Cross (VC) 6, 8, 9, 13,
  222, 322
  Norman Jackson 288–92
  Alan Jerrard 40–3
  Roderick 'Babe' Learoyd
    298–305
  Billy Leefe Robinson 26–30
  Aidan Liddell 22–5
  David Lord 281–4
  Hugh Malcolm 275–9
  Edward 'Mick' Mannock 35–9
  Leslie Manser 272–5
  Thomas Mottershead 30–4
  William Rhodes-Moorhouse
    16–21
  Lloyd Trigg 324–6
Vietnam War 210, 213–14, 381,
  388, 391
Virtuti Militari (5th class) (Polish)
  104, 131–2, 184, 193, 202,
  253
Vliegerkruis (Dutch Flying Cross)
  108–9
von Bonin, Hubertus 82, 83

Wallis, Sir Barnes 331
Warburton, Adrian 'Warby'
  336–42
Watt, Harry 309
Watter, F.A.S.C. 358
Waziristan campaigns 230, 252
Wells, Edward Preston
  'Hawkeye' 46, 166–9
Westcott, Betty 341–2
Wilkerson, David Scott
  Shearman 'Wilkie' 244–9
Williams, Sergeant 245
Wilson, H.J. 11
Wilson, Ronald Horace David
  279–81

Witorzenc, Stefan 'Steve' 192–4
Wittering Wing 144
Wooley, Sergeant 85
World War I see First World War
World War II see Second World
  War
Wray, Arthur Mostyn 'Father'
  249–55
Wright brothers 1–2
Wünsche, Kazimierz 202–3
Wyatt, Shaun Anthony 410–15

'Yangtse incident' 383–5

Zemke, Hubert 'Hub' 217